MAGIC PRAGUE

A WAKE FOREST STUDIUM BOOK

Pro Humanitate

Magic Prague

ANGELO MARIA RIPELLINO

Translated by
David Newton Marinelli

Edited by
Michael Henry Heim

UNIVERSITY OF CALIFORNIA PRESS
Berkeley   Los Angeles

English translation © The Macmillan Press Ltd 1994
First published in Italian as 'Praga Magica'
© 1973 Giulio Einaudi editore s.p.a., Torino

University of California Press 1994
Berkeley and Los Angeles, California

Published by arrangement with The Macmillan Press Ltd, London

Library of Congress Cataloging-in-Publication Data
Ripellino, Angelo Maria, 1923–
[Praga Magica. English]
Magic Prague / Angelo Maria Ripellino: translated by David Newton
Marinelli: edited by Michael Heim.
p.   cm.
Includes index.
ISBN 0–520–07352–5
1. Prague (Czechoslovakia)   I. Heim, Michael Henry.   II. Title.
DB2610.R5613   1994
943.7'12—dc20   92–11065
                                                                        CIP

Printed in Hong Kong

Contents

Acknowledgements

We would like to thank Anita Lucia Grahame for her assistance in overseeing the editorial changes to the text.

The assistance of Dr Miloslav Hirsch and Dr Vladimír Just in pinpointing the exact location of various inns, cabarets, dives etc. on the map is gratefully acknowledged.

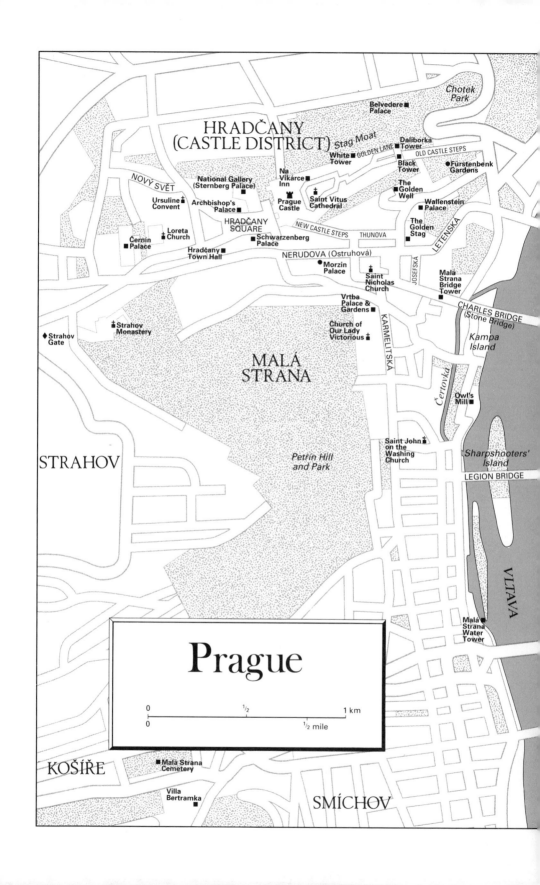

Prague

CHOTEK PARK

Belvedere Palace

HRADČANY
(CASTLE DISTRICT) Stag Moat

Daliborka Tower

GOLDEN LANE
OLD CASTLE STEPS

White Tower

Black Tower

Fürstenbenk Gardens

NOVÝ SVĚT

National Gallery
(Sternberg Palace)

Na Vikárce Inn

The Golden Well

Ursuline Convent

Archbishop's Palace

Prague Castle

Saint Vitus Cathedral

Wallenstein Palace

Loreta Church

HRADČANY SQUARE

NEW CASTLE STEPS

THUNOVA

The Golden Stag

Černín Palace

Schwarzenberg Palace

LETENSKÁ

Hradčany Town Hall

NERUDOVA (Ostruhová)

Morzin Palace

JOSEFSKÁ

Malá Strana Bridge Tower

Saint Nicholas Church

Vrtba Palace & Gardens

CHARLES BRIDGE
(Stone Bridge)

Strahov Monastery

Church of Our Lady Victorious

KARMELITSKÁ

Kampa Island

Strahov Gate

MALÁ STRANA

Čertovka

Owl's Mill

STRAHOV

Saint John on the Washing Church

Sharpshooters' Island

Petřín Hill and Park

LEGION BRIDGE

VLTAVA

Malá Strana Water Tower

0   ½   1 km
0   ½ mile

KOŠÍŘE

Malá Strana Cemetery

Villa Bertramka

SMÍCHOV

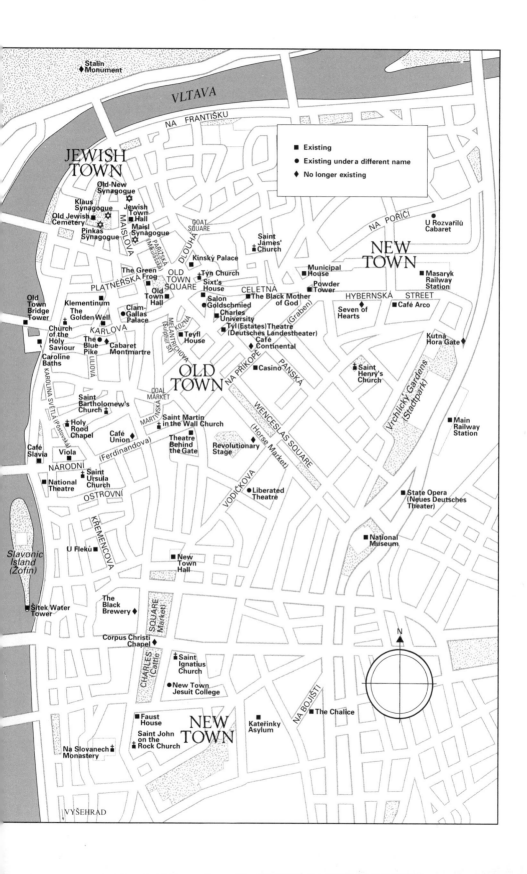

Part One

Part One

1

To this day, every evening at five, Franz Kafka returns home to Celetná Street (Zeltnergasse) wearing a bowler hat and black suit. To this day, every evening, Jaroslav Hašek proclaims to his drinking companions in one or another dive that radicalism is harmful and wholesome progress can be achieved only through obedience to authority. To this day Prague lives under the sign of these two writers who better than all others expressed its irrevocable condemnation and therefore its malaise, its ill-humour, the ins and outs of its wiles, its duplicity, its grim irony.

To this day, every evening at five, Vítězslav Nezval returns from the oppressive heat of the bars and pubs to his garret in the Troja district, crossing the River Vltava on a raft.[1] To this day, every evening at five, the stout brewery draft horses leave their coach houses in Smíchov. Every evening at five the Gothic busts of the gallery of sovereigns, architects and archbishops awaken in the triforium of Saint Vitus' Cathedral. To this day, every morning, two limping soldiers with fixed bayonets escort Josef Švejk down from the Castle across the Charles Bridge towards the Old Town, and every evening, to this day, two pallid, plump, third-rate actors, two waxwork dummies, two automatons in frock coats and top hats accompany Josef K. across the same bridge in the opposite direction by moonlight to Strahov and his execution.

To this day Arcimboldo's *Fire* plummets from the Castle with flowing hair aflame, the humpbacked wooden hovels of the ghetto flare up, Königsmarck's Swedes roll cannon through the streets of Malá Strana, Stalin winks malevolently from his enormous monument and bands of soldiers crisscross the countryside in endless marches as they did after the defeat at White Mountain. Prague "was always a city of adventurers", Miloš Marten writes,

> and for centuries it was a cove for pitiless adventurers. They came in droves from the four corners of the earth to plunder, make merry and lord it over the natives. And each of them tore a piece of living flesh from this wretched land, which gave all it had and received nothing in return.[2]

It was too often subjugated and afflicted by theft and acts of tyranny, too often the scene of contumely on the part of haughty foreigners, brutal

swarms of mercenaries and blusterers who tore it apart, making off
with whatever they could. How many villains and knaves interfered in
Prague's affairs and set up camp here over the decades and centuries:
rodomonts, all gilt armour and puffed-up chests jingling with trinkets;
plump friars of every order; prelates from the gates of hell; *Obergauner* in
sidecars spreading ruin; Machiavellians and treacherous "brethren"; sinister Meyrinkesque Mongolians; Caucasian headmasters appointed to gag
thought; motley crews of rule-makers and thugs who blather ideological
inanities behind a submachine gun; and whole conclaves of dim-witted
generals, of whom I will mention Epishev, the ever zealous crimson
nincompoop, because of his innumerable medals and decorations.

On the eve of the Second World War, Josef Čapek, who was later to
die in a Nazi concentration camp, told the story of two arrogant boots,
two shiny, slimy black boots, multiplying like newts and spreading lies,
decay and death throughout the universe.[3] To this day heavy boots tread
Prague underfoot, snuffing out creativity, intelligence and the very breath
of life. And although none of us should give up hoping that, as in Čapek's
story, the iniquitous old boots will end up on the trash heap of Chronos,
the Great Junkdealer, many of us wonder whether, given the brevity of
life, it will not happen all too late.

2

Detlev von Liliencron was convinced he had lived in the Bohemian capital
during a previous life not as a poet but as a captain of Wallenstein's
Landsknechte.[1] I too am certain I once lived there. Perhaps I arrived in the
retinue of the Sicilian princess Perdita, who marries Prince Florizel, the
son of Polixenes, King of Bohemia, in Shakespeare's *The Winter's Tale*. Or
as a student of the "ingegnosissimo pittor fantastico" Arcimboldo, who
lived for many years at the court of His Imperial Majesty Rudolf II.[2] I
helped him to paint his composite portraits, those grotesque, disturbing
faces bloated with warts and scrofula, which he contrived by heaping
together fruits, flowers, ears of grain, straw and animals, as the Incas
placed pieces of squash in the cheeks and gold eyes of their dead.[3]

Or I was a charlatan in a booth in the Old Town Square who at about
the same period in history fobbed off lectuaries and concoctions on the
gullible and, once the cops uncovered my cozenage, made a quick exit,
leaving Prague like a dock-tailed magpie. Or I arrived with a Caratti, an
Alliprandi or a Lurago, that is, with one of the many Italian architects
who brought the Baroque to the city on the Vltava. And when I look
at the painting in which Karel Škréta portrayed the engraver Dionysius
Miseroni (1653) with an onyx goblet in his hand, I, who so love to polish

words like semi-precious stones, I am certain I worked in his studio and helped him to curate the Imperial collections.

Or perhaps there is no need to go back so far: I was simply one of the many Italian stucco decorators and statuette makers who flocked to Prague during the last century to sell their plaster of Paris figurines.[4] Though it is more likely I belonged to the large group of those who walked the narrow streets and courts of the Bohemian capital at every hour of the day with a barrel organ containing a shiny glass-covered puppet theatre in the front: I would set the barrel organ down on a stool, remove the hemp cloth, turn the crank, and tiny couples of young gallants in white frock coats and breeches and petite white crinolinned ladies with upswept Rococo coiffures and slender fans would begin to dance inside the glass case depicting small rooms with a background of mirrors.[5]

For some time now people have identified me with Titorelli, the dauber, the purveyor of kitsch who, in addition to doing portraits, painted identical unnatural landscapes that many do not care for because they are "too depressing".[6] Then there are those who think I am the bank client to whom K., who knew a little Italian and a lot about art, was supposed to show the Prague sights in *The Trial*. The client's Southern origins, his perfumed "large blue-grey moustache", his "tight and short jacket" and the many gestures he makes with his nimble hands lead me to believe that there is an element of truth in this odd comparison. If such is the case then I am sorry I did not go to the appointment in the cathedral built during the fourteenth century by Mathieu d'Arras and Peter Parler of Gmünd on that cold, damp, rainy day; I am sorry I made the assessor wait for no reason.[7] If I recall that Titorelli is said to be "in the confidence of the Court"[8] and that the Italian client is undoubtedly a secret tool of the Court, its messenger, I then realize that my futile incarnation game has enmired me in the morbid muddle of accusations, secret information, mysterious messages and suffering that makes up the mystery and cross of Prague.

One thing, however, is certain: I have been walking about the city on the Vltava for centuries; I mingle with the crowd, I trudge, I wander, I smell its beer, train smoke and river mud; you can see me where, as Kolář puts it, "invisible hands knead the dough of pedestrians on the pavement's pastry boards";[9] where, to quote Holan, "the croûtons of streets spread/with the garlic of the crowd reek a bit".[10]

3

"Prague doesn't let go. Either of us. This old crone has claws. One has to yield, or else. We would have to set fire to it on two sides, at Vyšehrad

and the Castle; only then would it be possible for us to get away. Perhaps
you'll give it some consideration before Carnival," Kafka wrote in a letter
to Oskar Pollack on 20 December 1902.[1]

Ancient folio of stone parchments, city-book[2] in whose pages there is
"still so much to be read, to dream, to understand",[3] city of three peoples
(Czechs, Germans and Jews) and, according to Breton, the magic capital
of Europe.[4] Most of all Prague is a breeding ground for phantoms, an
arena of sorcery, a source of *Zauberei*, or *kouzelnictví* (in Czech), or *kishef*
(in Yiddish). It is a trap which – once it takes hold with its mists, its black
arts, its poisoned honey – does not let go, does not forgive. "She never
ceases to enchant with her magic spells," wrote Arnošt Procházka, "the
old she-devil Prague."[5]

Do not go there if you are seeking unclouded happiness. She grabs
and burns with her sly glances; she bewitches and transforms the unwary
who enter her walls. After going bankrupt, the occultist banker Meyer
became the charlatan mystic Meyrink, a writer of spiritualistic stories.
I too writhe bewitched inside her opaque crystal ball like the Pierrot
who pines in a bottle in a Meyrink story.[6] I have sold her my shadow,
as Peter Schlemihl sold his to the devil. In exchange, however, she
rewards me with the highest interest: she is the Klondyke of my spirit,
an extraordinary pretext for my verbal whims, for my *Nachtstücke*. I often
recite these verses by Nezval to her:

> I bend over forgotten corners Prague
> woven by your gloomy splendour
> smoke of inns in which the chirping of birds is lost
> evening like a harmonica player makes the weeping doors creak
> long fat keys lock up indecipherable things
> and footsteps scatter like a broken rosary.[7]

This is one of those harmonica players painted by Josef Čapek: I often
ran into him in Dejvice and other outlying districts. "Prag, die Stadt
der Sonderlinge und Phantasten, dies ruhelose Herz von Mitteleuropa."[8]
City in which strange commandos of alchemists, astrologers, rabbis,
poets, headless Templars, Baroque angels and saints, Arcimboldesque
figures, puppetmasters, tinkers and chimneysweeps wander about. City
made grotesque by eccentric humours, city auspicious for horoscopes,
metaphysical clowning, outbursts of irrationality, chance encounters,
combinations of circumstance, improbable complicity between opposites,
that is, for those "petrifying coincidences" Breton speaks of.[9] And where,
as in Kafka, the executioners have double chins and look like smooth-
skinned tenors,[10] and you might run into Nezval's "talking dolls" (*mluvící
panny*), rather like Bellmer's, with bald heads and porcelain ears,[11] or like

Kafka's Leni, a water nymph, a *rusalka*, with the middle fingers of her right hand connected by a web.[12]

Your destiny, Tycho Brahe is said to have foretold to Rudolf II, is tied to that of your favourite lion; and, indeed, Rudolf died (in January 1612) only a few days after the death of the beast.[13] Bulgakov was right to include Rudolf, principal character of the city on the Vltava, devotee of the stars and cultivator of the spagyric art, among the famous corpses invited to Satan's terrifying ball.[14]

At times the mystery of the *Golemstadt* spreads to the whole of Bohemia, a borderland, a crossroads exposed to all winds, "in the centre of Europe", according to Musil, "at the focal point of the world's old axes".[15] In a story by Apollinaire an old Gipsy woman in a Bosnian village claims to come from Bohemia, "le pays merveilleux où l'on doit passer mais pas séjourner, sous peine d'y demeurer envoûté, ensorcelé, incanté".[16] A dream: to cross the Bohemian countryside on foot one summer, from Dobříš to Protovín, from Vodňany to Hluboká, from tavern to tavern with their filthy tablecloths and flat beer, scare the geese on the threshing floors, sleep on the grass like rascals, like tousle-headed pícaros, "lilies of the field,/with the naive soul of an apostle", like Karel Toman's vagabonds,[17] like the intemperate Baroque painter Petr Brandl, like Jaroslav Hašek.

"When I seek another word for music, I always and only find the word Venice,"[18] Nietzsche declares in *Ecce Homo*. And I say: when I seek another word for mystery, the only word I can find is Prague. She is dark and melancholy as a comet; her beauty is like the sensation of fire, winding and slanted as in the anamorphoses of the Mannerists, with a lugubrious aura of decay, a smirk of eternal disillusionment.

Watching her at night from atop Hradčany Castle, Nezval wrote:

> If you look at Prague from up here, as her lights flicker on one by one, you feel you would gladly plunge headlong into an unreal lake in which you had seen an enchanted castle with a hundred towers. This sensation, which I feel almost every time I am surprised by the evening chimes on that black lake of starry roofs, has long since merged in my mind with the image of an absolute defenestration.[19]

Sparkling words that capture the bond between the sadness of a landscape permeated by a cosmic mourning, a mourning magnified by reflections from the river and the brittle substance, the mesh of cataclysms, the prohibitions, the turmoil of the history of Prague.

Nezval was not, however, the first to suggest the "Prague = mystery" ontology. Miloš Marten wrote in a similar vein about contemplating the city from the Castle Hill at sunset:

Soon the lights will flare up in the black crystal of night, hundreds of unsteady eyes gazing upwards . . . I know them all! The fiery keepers of the embankments duplicated in the mirror of the glimmering Vltava, a glowing avenue rising to the hill as if to infinity, and, here, the thicket of candles burning on the catafalque of a corpse changed every day. The phosphorescent pupils of a bird of prey down near the bridge and the oblique glance of a house that resembles the face of a smiling Chinaman.[20]

or Moldau

The cryptic city on the Vltava does not show her hand. The antiquary coquetry with which she pretends to be nothing more than a still life, a silent succession of glories long since past, a dead landscape in a glass ball, only increases her sorcery. She slyly works her way into the soul with spells and enigmas to which she alone holds the key. Prague does not release anyone she has taken hold of. So make up your mind before Carnival.

4

It is no accident that a number of writers belonging to the early twentieth-century *secese* (*Secession* or Art Nouveau) movement portrayed the city on the Vltava as a tempting and treacherous woman, a capricious harlot. Oskar Wiener, comparing her to a "dark Salome" who dances with the heads of her paramours, writes, "Anyone who has looked once into her deep, trembling and mysterious eyes remains a slave of the temptress for the rest of his life . . . If your passion for Prague does not spell your downfall, you fall victim to a permanent yearning."[1] And Miloš Marten: "She is fair, fascinating like a woman, elusive like a woman when she huddles in the blue veils of twilight beneath the blossoming slopes girt by the steel belt of her river, covered by the emeralds of her verdigris domes . . . "[2] And Miloš Jiránek: "There are evenings when Prague, our filthy, gloomy, tragic Prague, is transformed by the golden light of sunset into a blonde fairy-like beauty, a miracle of light and brilliance."[3]

Yet as early as his 1893 novel *Santa Lucia* Vilém Mrštík depicts the city as a "black beauty", a "black temptress . . . hidden in the négligé of the white mists of the Vltava".[4] For young men from the Moravian countryside at the beginning of the nineteenth century, Prague with its noble palaces, its river and legends was like Moscow for Chekhov's three sisters, a source of sleepless nights, a mirage, a kindler of desires. Without plans, work or funds they fled from the remote countryside to the capital, that is, the unknown, and many of them, entangled in her spell, did not return.

The protagonist of Mrštík's novel, Jiří Jordán, son of a poor Brno worker, goes to the city on the Vltava to study law, but becomes fascinated by her: she becomes his promised land, his temptress, and he comes to love her with an unhealthy lust.[5] But Prague is peevish with her lovers: "Her stone embrace smothers the innocent enthusiast, the fiery dreamer from Brno, who is attracted to her with every fibre of his being and all his senses."[6] Winter comes, no one looks after him, and once he has used up his meager savings he suffers cold, hunger and the thousand disappointments known to all students who leave the provinces for the capital. As a result, he "is consumed in the intoxicating flame of Prague like a fluttering butterfly".[7] Yet disappointment does not lessen his ardour:

> The temptress continued to lure him; she attracted him even when, viewed from a distance, she seemed to rest in the darkness, asleep in the arms of those who paid her most . . . She rustled behind his back, accompanying the suffocating sighs of her insatiable lips with a dark rumbling, and, if incapable of anything else, she reminded him with shrill cries that trains were approaching her body and ever new crowds, ever new victims disappearing into her infinite womb.[8]

A marvellous image. The woman whose womb the trains approach is no "mother" (*matička*), she is an enticer, an inconstant paramour who makes herself up with an ever-changing eye shadow of lights and wraps herself in billowing gowns of mists as though they were bizarre brothel négligés. One may presume that instead of requiting the affections of a sad, confused student she would much prefer to be the wanton of a rich dolt from the provinces, of an infatuated *baalboth* like the one Werfel includes among the clients of the luxurious house of ill repute in one of his stories.[9]

Ill, hungry, emaciated, in his shirtsleeves and tattered shoes, Jordán wanders clumsily about Prague like an automaton, consumed by her severity, wounded by her luring glances, feverish and delirious, the rejected one, the outcast, the stranger; he wanders about constantly talking to the stone flirt who, though indifferent to his sufferings, both fancies and eludes him. He collapses on the street and dies in hospital, yet to the very end the icon of Prague, the most vain of women, shines in his eyes, so disturbing and provocative as to bring to mind the female figures of *secese* paintings. And, indeed, something in Mrštík's sexualized, meretricious personification of the city on the Vltava looks ahead to the languid women, the "white camellias" Max Švabinský will paint at the beginning of the century.[10]

The novel also contains Impressionistic elements in the musical succession of watercolours and gouaches that pervades it. Mrštík renders with extraordinary visual sensibility the most subtle, impalpable nuances of atmosphere, the changes of weather and hue of the Bohemian capital, an illusory Santa Lucia, during various hours of the day and night: the gentle glimmer of the moon and the grey-blue shadows, the whiteness of the snow-covered roofs, the gleaming of the string pearls of the Vltava, the pale yellow of the sad gas streetlamps. With its flickering, blurred contours softened by the river dampness, Mrštík's mother-of-pearl Prague seems, like a painting by Loie Fuller, to dissolve in the fluttering of the iridescent veils of fog, in the whirl of the layers of multicoloured light enveloping her.

5

Now that I am far from her, perhaps forever, I catch myself wondering whether Prague really exists or whether she is not an imaginary land like the Poland of King Ubu. Yet every night in my dreams I feel the pavement of the Old Town Square underfoot, stone by stone. I often go to Germany and gaze from afar, like the student Anselmus from Dresden, on the serrated mountain ranges of Bohemia.[1] "Mein Herr, das alte Prag ist verschwunden."

Members of the host of diaspora phantoms, like Věra Linhartová and me, carry the longing for this lost land from one end of the earth to the other. The Baroque portraitist Jan Kupecký, a Protestant refugee, never ceased to call himself *pictor bohemus* whether he lived in Italy, Vienna or Nuremberg, and remained loyal to the Czech language and the faith of the Bohemian Brethren to his last breath.[2] The Baroque engraver Václav Hollar, though long exiled in Frankfurt am Main, Strasbourg, Antwerp and London, likewise considered himself Czech, as demonstrated by a number of etchings signed "Wenceslaus Hollar Bohemus", the caption (1646) "Dobrá kočka, která nemlsá" (A good cat does not nibble) and the Czech words (*les* [forest], *pole* [field]) he inserted into his drawings and many *vedute* of Prague.[3]

After only a few years of exile the Bohemian capital, its tedious day-to-day routine, seems faded and wrinkled in the chill of our memory, faded yet more fabled, as in your stories, Věra Linhartová. Linhartová's prose, especially the six *capricci* of *Meziprůzkum nejblíž uplynulého* (Interanalysis of the Immediate Past, 1964), attempts to transfer the processes of descriptive geometry to the dimension of language, its plot a succession of solos for lines and points, a series of projections, trajectories, rotations and ellipses of geometric bodies.[4]

Yet this geometrically precise world is wrapped in dense patches of fog (which correspond to gaps in memory). The contours of all things, nature, even stones, evaporate into a milky-white, cotton-fluff air, as in Šíma's paintings,[5] and shapes, ever-changing and blurred, barely penetrate the thick mists of her own particular landscape.

Figures of complicated mental schemes, they are the author's blood-less extensions and alter ego and, like her, dreamy and somnambulist. Pale, with cheeks that seem smeared with ceruse, Linhartová resembles the wax dolls one sees in a hairdresser's window, "talking dolls", those enigmatic silhouettes so dear to the Prague Surrealists, and like her shining creatures she is able to create an arcane aura, a zone of the inexplicable, wherever she goes.

If Bohumil Hrabal makes use of Prague pop art, the advertisements and kitsch of old albums in his prose, Linhartová underpins her brain teasers and puzzles with constant references to Czech painters like Josef Šíma and the surrealists Jindřich Štyrský and František Muzika. Yet the dreamlike staggering, the dripping gauze screen ("dripping" is her equivalent for "humorous"), the talismanic transpositions, the constant demonically logical ruminations, the phantoms like Dr Altmann, a Carnival-like Venice dissolving into the precarious Prague of the sixties – it all brings us back to the works of E. T. A. Hoffmann.

On the other hand, the intricacies and agonies of the dialectic, the rarified abstractness of Linhartová's discourse spur her on to rummage helter-skelter through history and bring together people from different lands and periods in her parables. Thus Prague, shrouded in mist and drenched in an alcoholic light similar to the one permeating Nezval's *Edison*, becomes the adoptive city of Charlie Parker (who plays the saxophone at the Orlík), Billie Holiday, Dylan Thomas (who lives in the industrial outskirts of town), Verlaine and Rimbaud (who lodge together in a furnished room in the Old Town), Nijinsky and Linhartová herself (actually Mr Linhart, as she uses a masculine *persona*) in an eighteenth-century satin coat. Linhartová's Prague is a kind of metaphysical insane asylum in which the characters, patients and perhaps inventions of the shady psychiatrist Dr Altmann (of the ilk of Coppelius and Lindhorst) become pawns of the occult element we may call "Praguesque". It is both insane asylum and world-stage, with its observatories, vertiginous staircases, bizarre machines and jazz and with the camels Rimbaud drags up to his Prago-Kafkaesque lodgings.

The subtleties, the axioms, the incongruous comings and goings of sorry figures, the relentless motives for deviating from the straight and narrow, the dizziness, turmoil and ultimate fall lend Linhartová's discourse a tone of cold delirium, an analytical madness all the more exacting the more lifeless it becomes. With their tension constantly broken as if by logopathy, on again off again like certain performances by Charlie Parker, with their imbalances, sophisms, ups and downs, their mouse-like scramblings through the labyrinth, her verbal *capricci* create a spiritualistic zone, a disconsolate region of spectres in whose foggy skeins she hides like Else Lasker-Schüler's Prince Jussuf in her imaginary Thebes and Baghdad.[6]

A number of years ago – I don't quite remember when, but it was before the forges of destiny created new thunder and lightning for the city on the Vltava – we spent a damp, rainy Christmas Eve together in Rome at the home of Achille Perilli. The painter, whose long Chagallian mane was even then tinged with grey, sported a demonic fiery red tie. Věra had on the same silver-grey trench coat she had worn the first time I saw her, at the entrance to the Café Slavia one August morning: silver becomes sleepwalkers. Another painter, Gastone Novelli, who has preceded us to Hades, had taken off his huge boots and was left in rough red wool socks. Věra quietly withdrew to a corner and drank: Beaujolais, whisky, cognac. "How I loved you, bottles full of wine,"[7] writes the poet.

By the time I offered to take her home, she could no longer remember the address of the family she was staying with. We began driving desperately through the already empty centre of town. Rome, flickering behind the wet windscreen, seemed filled with patches of Prague fog. Věra chatted incoherently, paying not the least attention to my nerves, which were caught up in the zigzag of the streets. Her speech imitated the ductus of her *capricci*, which sprang into being before one's eyes like obsessive snarls of a sinuous, schizoid dialectic, full of hesitations, repetitions, doublings, oxymorons, gaps, forgettings, dissonances, insertions of jarring levels, illogical grammatical games – and all with amazing timidity and an idle, backward gait, a kind of "crab canon". That drunken night, caught up in the relentless, confused chatter further complicated by our meanderings, I understood that dialectics, like every futile search, is, to quote Richard Weiner, Věra Linhartová's favourite writer, "a devil who pursues us in circles like dogs chasing their own tails".[8]

Sixty-five, sixty-five, she kept repeating. It was probably a street number. Like masks in a Hoffmannesque carnival we drove up and down the Corso, from Piazza Venezia to Piazza del Popolo, from Piazza del Popolo to Piazza Venezia, past San Carlo, where, during the day, the charlatan Celionati sells miracle-working roots and infallible remedies for unrequited love, toothache and the gout.[9] "Near via Condotti, near . . . " she repeated angrily, but by now via Condotti had become Na Příkopě in Prague. She stubbornly rummaged in her purse for the slip of paper with the address, emptying hairpins, compacts, amulets and combs onto the seat. By now I drove on slowly like a taxi-driver, using my left hand as a pillow against my cheek.

Finally, after hours and hours of driving, she let out a cry: via di Monte Brianzo! With the green light, off we flew. The long-awaited words had aroused me from my torpor. I pressed down on the accelerator and turned into the long-sought street. Knock, knock, knock on a rotten front door. Then, *dobrá kočka, která nemlsá* (a good cat does not nibble), she vanished into the dark entrance hall without so much as a good-bye. At that moment I realized she too was a character in my magic, picaresque Prague, one of the company of alchemists, astrologers, eccentrics, puppets and *odradeks* who perform there.

Paris or Rome, what difference does it make? You yourself wrote that we each carry our landscape with us, that it is not binding for those who temporarily move within it and that we leave behind "the best-loved landscape with less regret than if it had been an uncomfortable snakeskin".[10]

6

Like the city on the Vltava, this book will be dominated by the silhouette of the Hradčany, the Castle, the dominant fortress of the Prague basin. In contrast to the Baroque structures in Malá Strana below, the Cathedral of Saint Vitus in the Hradčany boasts rampant arches, notched, flame-tongued spires, ogee windows and gargoyles with sneering grimaces.[1]

Like an enchanted snail I would return to muse on the host of busts decorating the triforium. My thirst for colours delighted in the precious stones of Bohemia, the amethysts, chalcedonies, jaspers, agates and chrysopases fitting together in gold mortar to adorn the walls of delicate Saint Wenceslas' Chapel, aglow in the faint candlelight. That intimate, meditative, magical place and the three-arched Golden Portal with its Venetian mosaics satisfied my hunger for the miraculous. The array of insignias, relics, jewels, patens and monstrances amassed in the Cathedral indulged both my mania for names and my passion for accumulations of objects. And since I identify the Gothic with youthful daring, I was pleased that following the death of the first builder, Mathieu d'Arras, in 1352, Charles IV entrusted the construction of Saint Vitus' to an unknown young man of twenty-three, Peter Parler of Schwäbisch Gmünd, who proved an architect of genius.

Yet even that vertical sonata, that druse of crystalline stone, that triumph of the ogee arch always breathes a certain mystery, an ambiguity, that is, something Praguesque, as if swarms of hairy-vetch demons had merged with generations of saints. In my imagination the gargoyles always mingle with the grotesque; they are disturbing spectres of Prague literature. There are a number of pointed objects in league throughout the skies of the Bohemian capital: the Cathedral pierces the thorax of the heavens with its spires, as does the magnificent belfry of the Old Town Hall, the Powder Tower, the towers of the Týn Church, the Water Towers, the towers of the Charles Bridge and a hundred others. It is no accident that Nezval compares the towers in the clear night air to a "gathering of magicians".[2] The Prague sky recovers from these pinnacle pricks by resting its cheeks on the soft cupolas of the Baroque age, though their marshy emerald conceals an admixture of witchcraft: according to Seifert you can hear the croaking of frogs in the verdigris when the moon rises.[3]

At the vesper hour we would listen to the clamour of all Prague's churches from up there. We would look down on the enchanting confusion of glossy tile roofs, galleries, turrets, chimneys and dormers.[4] Do you remember the holiday evenings when the spotlights set the verdigris of Saint Nicholas, the statues on the Charles Bridge and the façade of the Holy Saviour Church ablaze? From high atop the Hradčany the city seemed submerged in a cloud of glittering yellowish dust. The buildings reflected in the river and rocked by the waves turned into shimmering underwater castles, retreats for *vodníci*, water goblins. On those evenings the gulls, blinded by the white glare, shrieked more shrilly, like Janáček's music, outdoing each other in buffoonery, diving in impulsive jousts. Of the purest white, with black beaks, they circled restlessly over the Legion Bridge, finally settling exhausted on the water like paper boats. Meanwhile, at the nearby National Theatre, the superb Ladislav Pešek, with cunning face and outlandish artiface, hopped about with equal agility in the role of the trickster Vocilka.[5]

Do you remember the frosty evenings when we walked up snow-covered Petřín, the Laurenziberg, slowly, like water vendors? "All right," Kafka writes, "if you really want to I'll come along, but I still say it's ridiculous to go now, in the winter and at night, to go to the Laurenziberg."[6] The honey-coloured filaments inside the streetlamps oozed a yellowish light. You wore black felt ankle-boots and drew incoherent alphabets on the snow-covered paths with the tip of your umbrella. The moon peeked out from behind the curtain of clouds like a chubby actress on the day of her benefit performance; the menacing red eye of the observatory winked down at us. Fragments of shining memories teem like broken handbag mirrors piled haphazardly in a large pannier. I will take them out, one by one, and attempt to evoke the elusive image of the city on the Vltava with the many barely matching pieces:

The Romanesque rotunda of the Holy Rood Chapel in Karolina Světlá Street opposite our dwelling decorated with graffiti from the nineteenth century. Saint Matthew's Fair in Dejvice, 24 February, where your shoes sank into the thick mud, a pandemonium of carousels, waxworks and booths packed full of combs and papier-mâché trumpets, wrought-iron lanterns and tin hearts and fruit cake, pictures and statues of saints and portraits of Stalin. And the carriages on the sidings at Masaryk Station. And Villa Bertramka, where as a guest of the singer Josefina Dušková, Mozart is said to have composed the overture to *Don Giovanni* a few hours before the première in October 1787 while copyists waited impatiently.[7] And the statues on the Charles Bridge decked in hoods of snow. And the crossed eyes of the gas streetlamps along the crooked lanes of the Hradčany district. And the mills on Kampa Island, especially the Owl's Mill (Sovovský mlýn, Eulenmühle) next to the damp house that had once been a tannery, the "house of the tragic poet",[8] the house in which the gloomy poet Holan lived and held running arguments with the tenant from the floor above him, Jan Werich, Bohemia's greatest clown. Legend has it that the mill took its name from the owls (*sovy*) that made their nests in the hollow of an ancient poplar, part of the original forest of the area, whereas the real, and more modest, reason was that its owner was named pan Sova, or Mr Owl.[9] And the stagnant waters of the Čertovka (Devil's Arm of the Vltava). And the labyrinth of mirrors on Petřín Hill. And the posters for Bat'a Shoes, sturdy old tubs of indestructible leather. And the windswept sky, open-air cinemas of "blowing blue",[10] on Vyšehrad Hill, from which the passers-by below look like tiny figures in a child's drawing.

And in Wenceslas Square the huge neon sign of the "House of Lyon Silk", the *automaty*, the snack bars with their assortment of cakes, canapes, sausages in mustard and darkish heads of beer. And the Turkish puppets in turbans and light-blue overcoats nodding from the Meinl display windows. And the old red trams ready for the scrap heap lumbering towards Olšany Cemetery with lifesaver-like wreaths hanging from the second car. And the girls who went to their first ball at the Lucerna chaperoned by their mothers, wearing long gowns, their cheeks covered with a thin layer of rouge, figures from the undying Prague Biedermeier like Štyrský's "coffee dolls" (*kávové panenky*).[11] And the meagre hovels in Nový Svět (New World Street), piled haphazardly on one another.[12] And the joyless tenements in Libeň and Žižkov with Baroque secrets to tell despite their threadbare squalour, changing, as Kolář claims, into "church naves with an endless choir of dishware/and dishwater incense raised matches illuming the numbers/of the confessionals (complete with sofa clothes-trees and wash-basin)".[13]

And the tower of the Old Town Hall with the calendar painted by Josef Mánes, the "cycle of twelve idylls from the life of the Bohemian peasant",[14] and the astronomical clock of Master Hanuš, with its allegorical puppet theatre springing to life at every chiming of the hour: a group of small statues moving between two windows, the apostles with the Saviour, Death tempting the miser and the miser rejecting him, the Turk and other figures, until the cock crows and they all vanish.[15] And the blinding gold monstrance studded with over six thousand diamonds in the rapt oratory of Loreta Church, where one feels the silence of the centuries against one's temples, and the faded pomp of the tabernacles, statues, chalices and votive gifts still reveals the sadness of recatholicized Prague.[16] But enough for now: my head is awhirl with memories.

And yet do you remember? In the course of our endless *flânerie* through the streets of the city we sought out the cafés of the Poetists, the *Kaffeehäuser*, as Kafka remarked, "in our time . . . the catacombs of the Jews",[17] the hundred taverns patronized by Jaroslav Hašek, the cabarets of days gone by, at Na Poříčí, the traces of the old *šantány* and *Tingeltangel*.[18] We entered, attracted by the "deep laughter of the pubs",[19] and took part in the war of succession of mugs and glasses, the animated squabbles of the patrons who, bathed in a never ending flow of Pilsner, converse according to the principle of "Já o koze, on o voze" ("I talk about the she-goat; he talks about the wagon", that is, at cross purposes), which also reflects the inconsistency of the Bohemian capital. We entered the *kavárny*, large rooms heady with the aroma of mocha, where we were welcomed by waiters wearing black alpaca jackets and carrying bulging wallets, by the unrelenting prattle of the old women who meet there to gossip after sticking their noses in at all the churches, by the bawdy glances of plump prostitutes, who pester mature dandies pretending to hide behind newspapers in wooden holders, by the feeble minds of fools who stare vacantly for hours on end at the god in a glass of beer and, now and again, by orchestras of fat ladies with heavily made-up eyes and pearl necklaces over their low-cut dresses.

It all comes back at night to compound my insomnia. The arabesqued door-knockers in Malá Strana pound mysteriously at night as their owners and tenants return late.[20] The houses and palaces in this quarter have odd names that stimulate the imagination:[21] The Green Crayfish, The Golden Crayfish, The Golden Angel, The White Turnip, The Golden Pike, The Red Lion, The Three Little Stars, The White Eagle, The Red Stag, The Black Eagle, The Golden Swan, The Golden Wheel, The Golden Grape, The Golden Horseshoe. Although the Castle faces Malá Strana, which lies directly in its lap, Malá Strana does not seem to face the Castle; nor does it face the river.[22] Its buildings, embellished with covered roof terraces, studio flats, towers, mansards and chimney pots are enveloped in sleep, closed within themselves, as antisocial as safes, its lanes resembling hiding places, redoubts, mysterious corridors, all of which increases its aloofness from life in ferment, its cyclothemia, its solitude.

We left a part of ourselves in the *průchody*, the passageways that enable one to cross the centre of Prague without coming out into the open, a dense network of small concealed streets hidden inside blocks of centuries-old houses.[23] In the Old Town we stumbled through this web of surreptitious passages and infernal alleys extending on all sides, infiltrating it completely: small rag-doll lanes intersected by entrance halls; circular paths hard to penerate; narrow underground passageways still smelling of the Middle Ages; neglected, incredibly awkward bottlenecks that made me feel I was inside the neck of a bottle.

There are constricted points in the Old Town where the visitor loses his way in a hostility of walls. Oh, the walls of Prague, that obsessive motif in Holan's works. The inconstant plexus of narrow medieval mews that suddenly expand or contract, withdraw or jut out in a broken line drives a pedestrian mad, obstructing free passage and making the whole mass of the medieval city seem to be coming down on one's head, almost adhering to one's body.[24] I escaped the sinister narrowness of those lanes, the stranglehold of those baleful alleys, those prehensile, misshapen walls, and fled to the green islands, the efflorescent districts, the parks, belvederes and gardens that surround Prague on all sides.

Rave

7

Ladies and gentlemen, this is not a Baedeker, although many *vedute* of the city on the Vltava appear within it, clicking into place like the colour slides of a ViewMaster or a *Guckkasten*. I will not play the know-all companion who disgorges half-baked words like the pedant *dottore* in the *commedia dell'arte*.

This compendium of Prague-related *obiter dicta* is incoherent and confused, written in uncertainty and poor health, with despair and constant second thoughts, with the infinite regret of not knowing everything, of not embracing everything, because a city, even if only the setting for a fond flânerie, is a terrible, elusive, highly complex entity. This is why my narrative will lurch along like the old films they used to show at the Bio Ponrepo, Prague's first cinema, located in The Blue Pike *šantán*. It will be flawed with breaks and jolts and gaps and attacks of heartache, like the music of Charlie Parker's alto sax. On the other hand, as Holan states, "Have you no contradictions? You have no possibilities."[1]

Something irreparable befell the Bohemian capital during an August now long past, something that has deeply affected our lives. This book looks out at me with the moist eyes of my old age, and I lug it around with me out of breath, exhausted. I have a hard time putting together the innumerable notes, collecting the pages from many happy seasons now blown away like ashes in the wind. My sergeant-pen labours to make the sly soldier-words fall in. Meanwhile, Jirka and Zuzanka have had a child. His name is Adam. Does this mean that after all the adversities everything is to begin anew? Yet how many are in prison? How many have died of broken hearts? How many are scattered in the darkness of exile? How many have donned the despicable cloak of servitude?

How then can I write an exhaustive, well-ordered treatise like a detached and haughty scholar, suppressing my uneasiness, my restlessness with the rigor mortis of methodology and the fruitless discussions of disheartened formalists? No, I will weave a capricious book, an agglomeration of wonders, anecdotes, eccentric acts, brief intermezzos and mad encores, and I will be gratified if, in contrast to so much of the printed flotsam and jetsam surrounding us, it is not dominated by boredom. Like Jiří Kolář in his collages and "evident poetry"[2] I will fill these pages with scraps of pictures and daguerreotypes, old etchings, prints purloined from the bottoms of chests, *réclames*, illustrations out of old periodicals, horoscopes, passages from books on alchemy and travel books printed in Gothic script, undated ghost stories, album leaves and keys to dreams: curios of a vanished culture.

The Bohemian capital is by no means only a display window for precious stones, gleaming relics and monstrances that put the sun to shame for its dead light. Prague has another face, its dilapidated, disorderly *tandlmark* (or *tarmark*) side, that is, the tags-and-patches market of junk-shop rejects, in whose midst there are magnificent finds to be made. The original *tandlmark* of the Old Town has spread like a weed throughout every district to the furthest bleary-eyed outskirts.

By throwing together obsolete objects and rummaging through the deep mire of nomenclature I may succeed in rendering the lacerations of the Bohemian capital, all the flea-bitten, worm-ridden curios lurking there, her wounds and her propensity for odds and ends. For I see a double key to Prague: it is not only a repository of splendours and treasures, dainties nibbled at often enough by foreign boars over the centuries; it is also a heap of singed and stained rubbish, showcases exuding resignation like a large family of chipped utensils, broken-down gadgets and spoiled trinkets. For, unfortunately, "every object has its dark side, every object its poison. Thimble, hemlock and blue monkshood dance by night on golden buttercups in the grassy darkness".[3]

8

Like the court physician Thaddäus Flugbeil – nicknamed Penguin, in Meyrink's novel *Walpurgisnacht* (1917), for his wing stumps – I scanned Prague from high atop the Hradčany with a spyglass that enormously magnified the teeming figures below, so much so that they seemed up against my eyes. Down below life wandered about as in a *laterna magica*. I observed the main street, the public walk, the *Bummel* of the city centre: the Germans along the Graben (Na Příkopě) and the Czechs along Ferdinandova.[1] Elegant ladies wearing broad hats decorated with ribbons, aigrettes and other frills and long dresses – underneath which one could surmise a rigid whalebone corset – with trains as in *secese* paintings; dandies wearing bowler hats and moustaches twirled upwards like scorpion tails; gay dogs, eccentrics, beer bellies, ramrod stiff junior officers, German students wearing caps of various colours, Czech students wearing the *poděbradka*, a round cap with a grey Astrakhan fur trim. On the edge of the Graben I saw the ex-banker and oarsman for the Regatta Sport Club Gustav Meyrink: svelte, well-dressed, limping slightly, a magnet for gossip. Rumour had it that he was the illegitimate son of a Wittelsbach, that he had used spiritism to cheat his clients and that he had cured a mysterious disease with a prescription he found in a book by Paracelsus.[2]

The beginning of the twentieth century. The last years of the Monarchy. The reign of His Apostolic Imperial and Royal Majesty Franz Joseph. Derided and reviled by the resentful Czechs though he was, the figure of this old man with the white beard divided down the middle looms large in the fortunes of the city on the Vltava, because, as Werfel noted, "the entire evening of the Habsburg Empire was dominated by the man".[3]

The magic of Prague arose in large part from its being a city of three peoples (*Dreivölkerstadt*): Czechs, Germans and Jews. The commingling and friction amongst three cultures lent the Bohemian capital a special character, an extraordinary abundance of resources and motivations. At the beginning of the twentieth century the population consisted of 414 899 Czechs (92.3 percent) and 33 776 Germans (7.5 percent), 25 000 of whom were of Jewish extraction.[4] The German-language minority had two sumptuous theatres, a large concert hall, a University and a Polytechnic Institute, five *Gymnasia*, four *Oberrealschulen*, two daily newspapers and an endless number of social organizations and institutions.[5]

None of us is naive enough to think this coexistence idyllic (though later events have inclined many to long for such an association of peoples as an Arabia Felix, a *Traumwelt*). Mutual accusations, spite, bad blood and ill will constantly threatened to destroy the delicate balance. Egon Erwin Kisch maintains that no German would have dreamed of setting foot in a Czech middle-class club, and no Czech was ever seen in the German "casino". The two nationalities had their own parks, gaming rooms, swimming pools, botanic gardens, clinics, laboratories and mortuaries. Even cafés and restaurants were often divided according to the language spoken by their clientele. There were neither ties nor interaction of any kind between the German and Czech universities. When the Národní

divadlo (National Theatre), which opened in 1881, hosted the Comédie
Française, the Moscow Art Theatre or a famous singer, German critics
did not mention the fact, and Czechs critics were quiet as mice when the
Vienna Burgtheater, Enrico Caruso or Adolf von Sonnenthal performed
at the Deutsches Landestheater (inaugurated in 1885) or the Neues
Deutsches Theater (opened in 1888).[6]

Add to all this the frequent outbursts of intolerance between Czech
students and German *Burschenschaftler*, the arrogance of the venomously
chauvinist Germans, who regarded the Czechs as upstarts and louts in
need of a lesson in manners[7] and the rancor of the Czech proletariat
against them (and the Jews) for holding the overwhelming share of capital
in the Kingdom of Bohemia. In Kisch's words:

> German Prague! They were almost exclusively the rich bourgeois,
> owners of brown-coal mines, members of the governing boards of
> the Škoda arms factory, hops merchants who travelled back and
> forth between Žatec and North America, manufacturers of sugar,
> cloth and paper, bank directors who hobnobbed exclusively with
> professors, high-ranking officers and government officials.[8]

Yet for all the conflicts and rigidities of both groups, interpenetration
did take place. Czech teemed with German expressions, and despite the
frowns of tedious purists the poet František Gellner's maxim holds true:
"A good Germanism is often more Czech than an old Czech locution."[9]
Prager Deutsch, moreover, "papierenes Buchdeutsch",[10] abounded in
Bohemisms. There was also a Kleinseitner Deutsch (German of the
Kleinseite, that is, Malá Strana, that is, the Small Side or Little
Quarter) about which Kisch wrote several amusing articles,[11] and a
very clumsy Czech-German *pavlač*-and-kitchen gibberish, and so-called
Mauscheldeutsch, a Prague variation of Yiddish.[12] This linguistic Babel,
this proximity of clashing elements within the huge melting pot of the
Habsburg Empire sharpened wits and acted as a tremendous stimulus to
imagination and creativity. The Munch exhibition,[13] the tours of the Art
Theatre – the *Moskevští*, as the actress Hana Kvapilová called the actors[14]
– Max Reinhardt with his *Midsummer Night's Dream*,[15] the Italian opera
seasons at the Deutsches Landestheater directed by the *Theaterzauberer*
Angelo Neumann ("eine mystische Gestalt")[16] and many other similar
events enriched the spiritual landscape of the city and encouraged a
remarkable flourishing of Prague poets, artists and thinkers during the
waning of the Monarchy.

Despite its opulent social life the German minority, a community of
wealthy people with no linguistic hinterland or working class, was an
island in a Slav sea, but in this tottering boarding house of nationalities

Jews were always the most isolated. During the last century, while the Czech nation was undergoing a spiritual rebirth and Prague was re-Slavicized through an influx of the rural population, the vast majority of Bohemian and Moravian Jews opted for German language and culture. Even as they left the ghettos, urban Germanized Jews lived in a kind of vacuum.[17] They were no less alien to the Germans than to the Czechs, who in their nationalistic fervour failed to make much of a distinction between the two German-speaking communities. In addition, the Jews were usually loyal to the House of Habsburg: they not only had the burning desire to wear a white collar, they had ambitions of becoming Herr Kommerzienrat or Kaiserlicher Rat, and the Habsburgs promoted their aspirations.[18] Hence Czechs saw Jews as standard-bearers of the Monarchy they opposed. Not only the plump industrialists but every bank employee, every commercial traveller, every Gregor Samsa, every shopowner or Jewish merchant came to be regarded as a *pán*, a master or gentleman, an unwanted intruder.

An incident reported by Franz Kafka in a boarding house in Merano sheds light on the involved, hopeless situation of the Jews in the city on the Vltava:

> As soon as I uttered my first words they knew I was from Prague; both of them, the general (seated opposite me) and the colonel, knew Prague. Czech? No. Now try and explain to those true-blue German soldier's eyes who you are! One of them says, "Bohemian German", the other, "Kleinseite". Then we stop talking and eat, but the general with his sharp ear trained in philology by the Austrian Army is not satisfied; he begins to doubt the timbre of my German; perhaps he doubts his eye more than his ear. I can attempt to explain this with the fact that I am Jewish.[19]

Hence the insecurity, the alterity, the indefinable guilt that permeates Prague's Jewish literature in German. The authorities of the Castle shun the Land Surveyor, who longs in vain to be accepted as a first-class citizen. Oddly enough, the distress of isolation, the inability to adapt, the uprootedness also torment a number of Jews writing in Czech – the novelist and poet Richard Weiner (1884–1937), for example. Weiner, who was born in Písek and lived most of his life in Paris, was unable to escape the atrabilious outlook so characteristic of the Prague mentality. In certain works – like "Prázdná židle" (The Empty Chair, 1919) – he is tormented by a Kafka-like obsession with a guilt of which he is innocent, a horrible guilt he blows up grotesquely: "I drown in Guilt, it suffocates me; I wallow in sin – and know not what it is, nor ever shall I know."[20]

The German Jews of Prague were always close to or eager to come closer to the Slavs. Many of them spoke Czech, albeit imperfectly. These words by Max Brod in a letter to Janáček are indicative: "Píšu německy, poněvadž v Češtině [sic] dělávám mnoho chyb" (I am writing in German because I make many mistakes in Czech).[21] Willy Haas recalls:

> The highest officials in the bureaucracy spoke an utterly denatured, sterile and grotesque Imperial-Royal Czech-German. The nobles in their huge, mysterious palaces in Malá Strana spoke French and belonged rather to the Holy Roman Empire, which had ceased to exist almost a century before. My wet nurse, my nursemaid, the cook and the maid spoke Czech, and I spoke Czech to them.[22]

The children of well-to-do Prague Jewish families learned more than the language from their wet nurses and nursemaids from the country; they learned Slav fairy tales, songs and even Czech Catholic religious customs.[23] Franz Werfel paid homage to his "Babi" – his wet nurse Barbora, whom he considered the incarnation of purity and shelter from the wickedness of the world – in a number of poems and in a novel.[24] Under her watchful eyes little Franz, dressed in a sailor suit, played beneath the trees of the Stadtpark (Vrchlický Gardens, in front of the main railway station), whose leafy tops reached up to the windows of his parents' house. Over the years *die treue Alte*, the devoted old woman,[25] became for Werfel the symbol of childhood's lost security (*Geborgenheit*), of a mythical age.

The German-Jewish (and non-Jewish) writers and artists idolized, as Paul Leppin (who was not Jewish) claims, "die wiegende und schwärmerische Anmut der slawischen Frauen" (the lulling, passionate grace of Slav women).[26] They had their first amorous experiences with simple Czech girls. Egon Erwin Kisch met a fourteen-year-old girl among the visitors to the Jubilee Exposition (Jubilejní výstava) in 1908. The girl, who came from a proletarian family, worked in a perfume factory and was soon to make a name for herself as ballerina under the name Emča Revoluce, accompanied the "raging reporter" ("der rasende Reporter") on his wanderings through the slums, night spots and inns of ill repute.[27] Willi Haas remembers learning folk songs from his Czech girlfriends.[28] The whole of Prague German literature is pervaded by this erotic symbiosis,[29] as the title of a novel by Max Brod, *Ein tschechisches Dienstmädchen* (1909), would seem to demonstrate. Yet it was perhaps Kafka who best bears witness to these relationships in the person of K.'s mistresses in *The Trial* and *The Castle*, maids like Frida and nurses like Leni, the accomplices of the assistants, watchmen and pettifoggers, but also mediatresses between the protagonists and the impenetrable despotic authorities. These women are false advocates, deceptive and more than a bit witchlike.[30]

In spite of prejudice and social barriers, then, ties between Czech culture and the culture of the German-speaking Jews began to develop. The group "Osma" (The Eight), which held an exhibition in the spring of 1907, brought together Czech, Czech-Jewish and German-Jewish painters such as Emil Filla, Friedrich Feigl, Max Horb, Otakar Kubín, Bohumil Kubišta, Willi Nowak, Emil Artur Pitterman Longen (who later became a playwright and cabaret writer) and Antonín Procházka.[31] The Czech Jewish painter Georg Kars (Karpeles) introduced Bohumil Kubišta to the Fauves in Paris.[32] The intellectually open-minded Jewish-German writers of Prague became ardent champions of Czech letters in the German-speaking countries, translating the hymns of Otokar Březina, the poems of Fráňa Šrámek and the *Slezské písně* (Silesian Songs) of Petr Bezruč. Rudolf Fuchs, Otto Pick and, later, Pavel Eisner did yeoman service in the valuable work of grafting and exchange.[33]

The greatest contribution to the dissemination of Czech talent, however, was made by the generous and indefatigable Max Brod. Brod wrote a number of essays on Czech music[34] and translated the librettos of several operas by Josef Bohuslav Foerster, Jaroslav Křička, Jaromír Weinberger and Vítězslav Novák. He also translated nearly all Leoš Janáček's librettos, thus opening the doors of the world to the art of the Moravian composer. His monograph devoted to Janáček appeared in both Czech (1924) and German (1925).[35] He later regretted not having performed a similar service for the composer Ladislav Vycpálek.[36] He immediately sensed the importance of Hašek's *Osudy dobrého vojáka Švejka* (The Good Soldier Švejk, 1920–3), praising it highly in the German papers and preparing, together with Hans Reimann, a stage adaptation that was directed (with many changes) by Erwin Piscator in Berlin in 1928.[37] The friendship and correspondence between Brod and Janáček (1916–28) takes on special significance considering the latter's strong Slav leanings, Orthodox liturgical roots and affection for Russia.[38]

One could go on at length about bilingual Jewish writers such as Pavel Eisner who wrote a fervent, almost enraptured treatise entitled *Chrám a trvz* (Temple and Fortress, 1946) on the beauties of the Czech language, or Camill Hoffmann, who later represented the First Czechoslovak Republic as a diplomat. Reciprocal influences, the fascination Březina's *Tajemné dálky* (Mysterious Distances, 1895) exerted on Werfel in *Der Weltfreund* (Friend to the World, 1911) which, in turn, seems to anticipate Jiří Wolker's *Host do domu* (A Guest to the House, 1921)[39] are manifold. Whoever reads in Wolker, "I love objects, silent companions,/because everyone treats them/as if they were not alive"[40] must recall an analogous passage in Werfel: "Silent objects/that in a full hour/I caressed like well-behaved animals."[41] A perfect example of this unique synthesis was <u>Egon Erwin Kisch</u>, who not only enjoyed the debauchery of the Czech taverns but also worked with Longen's Revoluční scéna (Revolutionary Stage), for which he wrote a number of plays including *Galgentoni* (Toni the Gallows Bird) starring Longen's wife Xena, and, together with Jaroslav Hašek, the comedy *Z Prahy do Bratislavy za 365 dní* (From Prague to Bratislava in 365 Days), which describes his rambling journey on the tugboat "Lanna 8" along the Vltava, Elbe, North Sea, Rhine, Main and Danube.[42]

Yet the fertility and peculiarity of the encounter between Czech and Jewish cultures is perhaps best symbolized by the Jewish brothers Langer: František, physician, legionnaire in Russia, general of the Czechoslovak Army, writer of plays and narrative fiction in the Čapek circle, whose witty comedy *Periférie* (The Outskirts, 1925) was also staged by Reinhardt;[43] and Jiří, friend of Kafka, student of the Cabala and psychoanalysis and author of poems in Hebrew. Jiří Langer was so possessed by the Chassidic idea that he left Prague for the swamp-infested, backward East Galicia of cheerful, eccentric rabbis, and wrote a Chagallesque collection of anecdotes about the Chassidim called *Devět bran* (Nine Gates, 1937).[44] Jiří Langer, who wandered the stunned streets of Prague bundled up in a black caftan and sporting *peyes* and a round black fur hat.

In the end, however, these reciprocal ties did not mitigate the *Inseldasein*, the inability of the Prague German Jews to adapt. Jiří Langer's pilgrimage to the medieval villages of the *tsadikim*, Brod's support for Zionism (Prague was one of its first centres early in the century[45]), Werfel's love for Verdi as against the Wagner supported by the German minority,[46] Kisch's wanderings around the globe, Kafka's enthusiasm for Jizchak Löwy's company of amateur Yiddish actors – it all comes down to a tormenting desire to escape the "claws" of Prague through a change of location. But flight is not liberation. However far they moved from the city on the Vltava, they felt an uprootedness, a sense of not belonging. Yet it was just this paradoxical jumble of contrasts and convergences, this uneasy life in the vacuum of a border town, that created the large group of great Prague German writers at the end of the Monarchy.[47]

9

Der Weltfreund was first published in 1911. An overly sentimental, self-indulgent collection of verse, it represented Werfel's desire to become one with the homeless and the humble, to perform deeds that would overcome his pangs of loneliness, shore up his faith in the original goodness of man.[1] It initiated a line of Franciscan gentleness in Czech letters that makes itself felt all the way to Orten and resembles, according to Haas, "a stroll with a cheerful boy or the jingling of sleigh bells through a quiet snow-covered town in 1900 or so",[2] that is, not long before a fearful conflict ravaged the artificial domains of an illusory innocence.

Recalling that year and the enchanted season inaugurating the century, as auspicious to the Prague *Dichterkreis* as the twenties were to the Czech Poetists, Otto Pick exclaimed:

> The hours of that winter: memory makes the painful sunset dreams of the ageing glow with a silvery sheen. Oh, the evenings, nights of that blessed winter! How *unified* we were, how harmonious. We sat in the cafés, we rampaged through the nocturnal city, we scaled the defiant Hradčany, we walked along the broad river and, making merry in the company of loose girls, we failed to notice the sun rise through a crack in the window.[3]

Haas recalls the endless, heated debates in their haunts and during their walks around the Belvedere and the narrow streets and parks of Malá Strana.[4]

The Prague German writers used a number of cafés as *Treffpunkte*: Café Central, Café Arco, Café Louvre, Café Edison, Café Geisinger and Café Continental.[5] In the latter, in a room lined with leather tapestries of red and gold lines on a black background, Gustav Meyrink[6] pontificated much like the Czech Jakub Arbes, a fellow author of spine-tingling novels, in U zlatého litru (The Golden Litre).[7] Meyrink discussed topics of the occult with his circle of acolytes, played chess and "drank innumerable glasses of Swedish punch through a thin straw".[8]

"Nights of that blessed winter!" To this day, every evening at five, Franz Kafka returns home to Celetná Street (Zeltnergasse) wearing a bowler hat and black suit. He returns from the Café Montmartre where, as thirsty as the Jews in the desert, Jaroslav Hašek drinks and plays the fool. To this day, every evening at five, Egon Erwin Kisch returns to U dvou zlatých medvědů (Zu den zwei goldenen Bären) at the corner of Melantrichova and Kožná Streets, whose basement was said to be the entrance to a network of passageways running beneath the Old Town and even the river.[9] In the words of Karel Konrád:

Find this

> By the time the night-walker had returned to his home at The Two Golden Bears, the streetlamps wore a fine cataract. One would obtain an amusing sum of thousands upon thousands were one to add up the matches Kisch had to light to penetrate the black crater of the entrance hall and the pitch-black stairs to the second floor.[10]

The Montmartre was opened on 16 August 1911 by the actor and variety singer Josef Waltner in a rundown house known as U tří divých mužů (Zu den drei wilden Männern) because in the distant past three bogus cannibals from Vodňany with rings in their ears, tattoos on their faces and rooster feathers stuck in their hair had been exhibited there.[11] It consisted of two large rooms, one decorated by František Kysela, the other with a dance floor, a piano on a platform and small booths adorned with grotesque parodies of Cubism by V. H. Brunner. This *Künstlerkneipe*, analogous to the "Brodyachaya sobaka" (The Stray Dog) in Petersburg[12] and the "Zielony Balonik" (The Little Green Balloon) in Cracow,[13] was a meeting place for Czech anarchist poets, German-Jewish writers, gipsy painters and actors of the Lucerna Cabaret, where Karel Hašler sang his tearful dirges about old Prague.

It was where the soloists of the National Theatre warbled during their off hours. There was no cabaret performer from Julius Poláček or Eduard Bass to those of Jiří Červený's Červená sedma (The Seven of Hearts) who did not show up there to banter. Emil Artur Longen and Xena Longenová sang their street songs and Artur Poprovský chanted Jewish melodies there. Emča Revoluce, accompanied on the piano by Trumm Slapák (Soft-Shoe Trumm), also known as *der dicke Trumm* (Fat Trumm), danced the tango with Hamlet, the head waiter, or with Kisch, who wore a rakish cap like a young tough from the Podskalí district, a foppish handkerchief around his neck and a cigarette dangling from the corner of his mouth. Hamlet (František Jirák), an ex-actor with the head of a hidalgo covered by a huge mass of curly hair, was one of a trio of waiters, along with Počta of the Národní dům in Prague-Vinohrady and the legendary Patera of Café Union,[14] who took the side of the profligates and helped them out with his modest patronage.

It was where Hašek set up residence, sleeping in a corner on a plush sofa. He would appear late in the evening, drunk, having made the rounds of the taverns and blathering like a fishwife, splashing beer over a wide radius, raising a rumpus. If Waltner threw him out, he found shelter at Na Balkáně (or Kopmanka) Inn in Templová Street, another haven for German and Czech writers and artists, where he would join various cabaret players on stage, or else like a petty pilferer or vagrant Charlie he simply paced back and forth, rain or shine, in front of the Montmartre until Hamlet, a customer or even a policeman put in a good word for him.[15]

Prague at the beginning of the century: a city of poets, habitat of "Oh-Mensch-Lyrik".[16] Karl Kraus, who was extremely hostile to the Werfel group, often harshly excoriated the Prague school,[17] writing, "In Prague, which is bursting with special talents and where everyone who has grown up with someone who writes poetry also writes poetry, the virtuoso-of-childhood Werfel fecundates everyone and poets multiply like muskrats . . ."[18] A verse attributed to Kraus derides the Prague writers as follows: "Es werfelt und brodelt, es kafkat und kischt."[19] Yet many other illustrious names belong to their *Dichterkreis*.

Let me quote a few of them at random, though a bare list is nothing but a sterile cabinet of phantom phonemes: Rainer Maria Rilke, Gustav Meyrink, Hugo Salus, Emil Faktor, Johannes Urzidil, Rudolf Fuchs, Oskar Wiener, Leo Perutz, Paul Kornfeld, Leo Heller, Paul Paquita, Viktor Hadwiger, Oskar Baum, Karl Brand, Otto Pick, Ludwig Winder, Ernst Weiß, Willy Haas and Franz Janowitz.[20] It would take a separate volume to do justice to them all. Two of them especially whet my imagination, however, two "dilettanti in miracles": Paul Adler (1878–1946), with his haunted, discontinuous and dyspnoeic stories, maelstroms of madness, *Elohim* (1914), *Nämlich* (In Fact, 1915) – which is reminiscent of Carl Einstein's *Bebuquin* (1912) – and *Die Zauberflöte* (The Magic Flute, 1916);[21] and Paul Leppin (1878–1945), "der ungekrönte König der Prager Boheme" (the uncrowned king of Prague's Bohème), with his verse collections *Die Türen des Lebens* (The Doors of Life, 1901) and *Glocken, die im Dunkeln rufen* (Bells That Call in the Dark, 1903) and his novels *Daniel Jesus* (1905) and *Severins Gang in die Finsternis* (Severin Walks into Darkness, 1914). Dispirited singer of a declining Prague down on its last, of "sinister lanes, drunken nights, tramps and empty faith in pompous Baroque statues of saints",[22] Else Lasker-Schüler dallied with Leppin in two affectionate poems: "Dem König von Böhmen" and "Dem Daniel Jesus Paul".[23] Of course, Leppin's languid singsong, his fragile, frightened writing imbued with northern *Zwielicht* and occasionally flaring into a burst of satanism seems outdated today, but his love for the city on the Vltava, the crossroads of spirits, is no less ardent than that of Nezval in *Praha s prsty deště* (Rain-Fingered Prague) or Seifert in *Světlem oděná* (Arrayed in Light).

The physical appearance of these figures made the city all the more picturesque. Paul Leppin, tall, thin, with the wax face of a Kabuki actor, wide-brimmed hat, dark tight-waisted suit, is walking along the Graben (I was watching from above with Flugbeil's spyglass) and, like the poets who surround him in the same Biedermeier livery, carrying a red rose with a long stem: "All those floral tongues of flame made one think of candles in a procession."[24] Franz Werfel croons Verdi arias in nocturnal haunts: "The girls were thrilled. They cried 'Caruso, Caruso!' the moment he entered the premises and the more educated even pronounced the name in French: 'Carousseau!' The pianist or the salon orchestra immediately struck up 'La donna è mobile' or 'Questa o quella', and Werfel bellowed away."[25] "The werfel-bird can sing like a Caruso," Franz Blei wrote sarcastically in his *Bestiarium*, "and it does so often and gladly, especially when it is noisy. If there is a war-like uproar, the werfel sings so loud that it could easily fill 308 pages in *ottavo*. The werfel is greatly envied – for its tenor voice and exquisite arias and trills – by all beasts who try to imitate it."[26]

Outstanding among picturesque Prague figures is Leppin's mysterious character Nikolaus, alias Meyrink, who also belongs in the league of Bohemian apparitions. His out-of-the-way house near the gasworks contained "many strange, unusual things: bronze Buddhas with crossed legs, medium-inspired drawings in metal frames, scarabs and magic mirrors, a portrait of Madame Blavatsky and a genuine confessional".[27] Brod writes in his memoirs that Meyrink numbered among his friends a collector of dead flies and a second-hand bookseller who resold rare books only with the consent of a tame raven with clipped wings.[28] I am not saying that the Meyrink I have in my imagination is an ancestor of the dignified gravedigger Kopfringl, though if I think of his morbid eccentricity I find it easier to understand the mellifluous, lugubrious quality of Ladislav Fuks's novel *Spalovač mrtvol* (The Cremator).[29]

The German poets of Prague drew life from the myths, legends and topography of the city on the Vltava. One could almost say that many of their works are mere pretexts for depicting the *corpus mysticum*, the dark pomp and the sinister mood of this entity of stone. It is not modern Prague with its straight streets and box-shaped tenements but rotting Old Prague that kindles all-consuming flames and fits of melancholy in their hearts. Terrified at the thought of dying a thief's death, a traitor's death – much like Indians terrified at the thought of a lunar eclipse – they regard Prague as a phantom (*mátoha*), a chimera. They set their works in Baroque churches, the Golden Lane, Saint Vitus', the hovels and passageways of the Old Town, the crumbling shanties of New World Street, the Jewish Cemetery, the black synagogues, the shacks and narrow, crooked alleys of the *Judenstadt*, the sinister palaces and shadowy byways of Malá Strana.

They turn Prague into an occult, unreal metropolis enveloped in the weak, dripping gauze screen of the *Gaslaternen*, a spent, decrepit city, a tangle of vulgar inns, leprous nyctalopic nooks, diabolic *uličky*, garrulous *pavlače*, dark courtyards, junk shops and *tandlmark* booths, a city in which all phenomena undergo agonizing deformations, assume grotesque and spectral faces, a city benumbed by the torpor (*Verschlafenheit*) of a provincial town, a torpor concealing something wary and menacing, as if, paradoxically, the melancholy and indecision of the days following the White Mountain catastrophe, when the city was at the mercy of pitiless invaders, had been instilled into the temperament of the German and, especially, Jewish writers; in short, dear reader, a city transformed into a *Mittelpunkt* of Expressionism, not so much because a number of her poets belonged to that movement as because she contained the principal motifs of Expressionism in her nature, in the parameters of her scenery, in her mists.

The Prague German writers of the early twentieth century often depict the dives, the nocturnal rendezvous, the last "joy houses" of the Habsburg Empire, whose rooms were decorated with tapestries, mirrors and red velvet curtains, with blind girl harpists and tone-deaf pianists and bawds from all the lands of the Monarchy. Although the most famous of these establishments, the luxurious Salón Goldschmied in Kamzíková Street (Gemsengäßchen), similar perhaps to the Viennese house of ill repute in which Mizzi Schinagl works in Joseph Roth's *Thousand and Two Nights*, is evoked by Werfel in the horrifying story "Das Trauerhaus" (The House of Mourning), the taverns and inns in Kafka's *Castle* with their oppressive store rooms and that throng of ambiguous maids also exude the smell of a Prague bordello.

No one, however, surpasses Egon Erwin Kisch in describing the night life and slums of the city on the Vltava. Kisch was a regular patron of every kind of *abštajg, pajzl, putyka, špeluňka, zapadák* and *knajpa*:[30] Klamovka, Omnibus, Gogo, Jedovna (Poison Inn), Stará paní (The Old Lady), Stará krčma (The Old Tavern), Mimóza (a floral name from the Biedermeier period corrupted to "Phimose"), Brazílie, Apollo, U tří hvězdíček (The Three Little Stars), Eldorado, Maxim, Trocadero, U zeleného orla (The Green Eagle), U města Slaného (The City of Slaný), U dvou beránků (The Two Lambs), V tunelu (In the Tunnel), Artista, Na seníku (In the Barn), U knížete Břetislava (The Prince Břetislav).[31] Beside these, a long list of filthy hovels, cheap dance halls, sleazy brothels, gambling dens, flophouses, homes for wayward girls, reform schools, soup kitchens and prisons runs through his works.

Kisch, who was keen on crime news, interested in lowlife and inclined towards *krváky* (thrillers) and *pitavaly* (criminal sketches), wrote many volumes of Prague features[32] filled with pimps and prostitutes, ruffians and rogues and every sort of king of the pack and queen of the street, thereby renewing a tradition begun during the nineteenth century by Jan Neruda's "police scenes" (*obrázky policejní*) and Karel Kukla's reports on the sewers and the dens of criminals and beggars. In other words, Kisch elucidates the murky and harsh side of Prague, the reverse side of Baroque angelity.

> Kisch had a feeling for the human vulnerability beneath a prostitute's make-up, the real beneath the tinsel. The other side of injustice and poverty. The nocturnal life in the outskirts and slums. The butcher's knife that changed carmine make-up into chilling blood. His understanding of these cause-and-effect relations was

tantamount to a discovery. He listened to bared hearts like a patient physician.[33]

One need think only of his portrait of Tonka, the beautiful prostitute at the sumptuous Salón Koucký in Platnéřská Street. "Blaue Toni", so called for her blue eyes and blue dress, tells her pathetic tale before a heavenly tribunal: because she agreed to console the last night of a murderer condemned to hang for the horrible killing of three girls – *Pfui Teufel!* – she had been given the nickname "Galgentoni", Toni the Gallows Bird. Forced to flee to another *Puff* and from there to walk the streets, she continues to dream of her Empire-style blue dress and the enormous Salón Koucký gramophone until she dies and goes to heaven.[34]

It would be a simple matter to find a connection between the heroes of Kisch's "tramp" ballads, his brief *Dreigroschenoper*-like sketches and the figures of Karel Čapek's crime stories (*Stories from One Pocket and the Other*, 1929) or the "cherubim", that is, rascals and petty thieves in cahoots with the hunchback master thief Ferdinand Stavinoha, a small man of little wit, in the novel *Bidýlko* (1927) by Emil Vachek, or Franci, a waiter and dancer proud of his splendid suit (like Hamlet) in František Langer's play *Periférie*, an unlucky rogue who bumps off the john of a harlot friend – a heart-of-gold harlot like "Galgentoni" – and then torments himself with remorse. From the lost property office to the pawn shop, from the auctions and lottery drawings to the Christmas *tandlmark*, there was no spark of Prague life too small to ignite the pen of the "raging reporter". Like a Stanislavskian actor, he became one with the people he studied to the point of assuming their way of life: frequenting soup kitchens, sleeping in flophouses, breaking ice on the river with the unemployed, flirting with whores and acting on the stage as an extra.[35]

Like Russian Symbolist poets at the beginning of the century, German writers of the Bohemian capital sensed the imminent catastrophe with painful foresight. This Prague seismography corresponded, of course, to the general premonition of the collapse of the Habsburg Monarchy vouchsafed to clear-sighted minds throughout Central Europe. Referring to the final years of the reign of Franz Joseph, Werfel liked to talk in terms of winter: winter's chill, twilight and the proximity of death.[36] The wan, lugubrious, malevolent ambience of Prague (in contrast to the *gaudeamus*, the operetta gaiety of Vienna) broadened the perspective of decline. For her German writers Prague – a *Haßliebe* trap, the heart of a people who did not share their longing for fellowship – became an emblem of death throes and decay. Her courtyards, galleries and passageways assailed them with recriminatory mutterings of *Urteil*, *ortel*, condemnation.[37]

The feverish atmosphere of those years, the anguish of the premonitions makes itself felt in a highly embellished, Baroque style – all adjectives, tubercular red and trembling horror. In the agitated, spiritistic prose of a Meyrink, Leppin or Perutz a decayed Prague rolls her eyes and twists her mouth into grimaces. She is a centre of mystagogy, a repository of cruel sorcerers, bugaboos, monsters of rabbinic clay, *meshugoim*, eccentrics and fierce oriental ghosts much like – during the same period – Bely's Saint Petersburg. She is a city sketched with the banal purple ink of Meyrink-Nikolaus,[38] who, tempering the degradation of her mephitic streets and peeling houses with an aesthete's vanity studs the anguish of her delapidation with festive adornment. Yet Czech Prague flourishes in this apocalyptic marasma; with the collapse of the Habsburg Empire she is reborn and, guided by the sage hand of the philosopher Masaryk, moves onward – to use the title of a march by Josef Suk – "towards a new life" that will in turn be cut short by new suppression.

The German decadents, then, imbibed the city on the Vltava like a curse, clinging to everything ambiguous, dreamy, *unheimlich* and morbid in its nature. The Austro-Prague literature from the age of the decline of the Monarchy (and its continuations) leaves behind a pestilential stench, a depressing *Dämmerung*, a flickering of altar candles on their way out, a surge of sad music, a theatrical grimace, the bleeding wound of an affected farewell and a cloying sweetness. Else Lasker-Schüler wrote of Werfel: "On his mouth / a nightingale is painted".[39]

10

In a story entitled "Kafkárna" (Kafkaria), Bohumil Hrabal imagines walking through Prague one night and stopping to talk to a toothless crone turning sizzling sausages over a fire by the glow of an acetylene lamp:

> I say to the old woman, "Tell me, ma'am, did you know Franz Kafka?"
> "Good heavens," she says. "My name is Františka Kafková. My father was a horse butcher, and his name was František Kafka."

Hrabal identifies with the author of *The Metamorphosis*. In Old Town Square he alludes to Stalinist oppression when he yells at a policeman,

> "No one can live without a crack in his skull or delouse freedom from a man."
> "Don't yell like that!" the policeman responds sternly. "Why

do you yell like that, Mr Kafka? I'll have to fine you for disturbing the peace."[1]

Both in our minds and in reality Prague and Kafka are inseparable. In *America*, Roßmann confesses with a touch of homesickness to the Manageress (a Viennese and therefore a "countrywoman" of his) that he was born in the city on the Vltava.[2] The network of scratches and gashes on Prague walls corresponds to the wounds mentioned so frequently in Kafka's diaries.[3] I cannot refrain from stressing the points the author of the fortunes of Švejk and the creator of K. have in common. If, as Adorno maintains, Kafka "searches for salvation by absorbing his opponents' strength",[4] Hašek does likewise in his fight against the Austro-Habsburg authorities. Similarly, the structure of Hašek's *Švejk* resembles the structure of Kafka's novels in that "the stages of the narrative events become the stations of the Cross".[5]

Kafka's effigy, the "long, noble, olive-coloured face of an Arab prince",[6] is superimposed upon the image of the Bohemian capital. Kafka rarely spoke, and when he did he spoke softly. He wore dark suits.[7] "The kafka," Franz Blei writes, "is a very rare, magnificent moon-blue mouse. It does not eat meat, feeding instead on bitter herbs. It has a fascinating gaze because it has human eyes."[8]

Unlike Rilke, whose bond with the Czech capital remained super-ficial – a kind of literary flirt, the friendly condescension of an aesthete towards an unhappy, underprivileged race – Kafka absorbed all Prague's humours and poisons and descended into its demonic nature. Rather than soil himself in soot along the Vltava, the young Rilke, in his *Larenopfer* collection (1895), remains on the brilliant surface, a highly cultivated tourist keeping a safe distance from what he observes. Allusions to folklore, towers, churches, cupolas, people in the streets, figures like Hus, Tyl, Zeyer or Vrchlický, even Czech words are nothing more than trappings.[9] True Prague lovers can only be irritated by "keepsake verses" such as "bierfrohe Musikanten spielen/ein Lied aus der *Verkauften Braut*" (beery musicians play/a song from *The Bartered Bride*) or the smugness of a poem like the one in which, after singing the Czech national anthem *Kde domov můj* (Where Is My Homeland), a country girl accepts alms from the much moved poet, whose hand she kisses in gratitude. I would give all the picture postcards and elegance of Rilke's Baedeker for a short poem by Kafka in which the soul of Prague, though not explicitly named, shines through a fine mist:

> People who cross dark bridges,
> passing saints
> with faint candles.

Clouds that parade across grey skies,
    passing churches
    with darkening towers.
One who leans on the squared stone railing,
    looking into the evening waters,
    hands resting upon ancient stone.[10]

Young Rilke's ambivalent attitude towards the Slav world around him has its roots in two conflicting influences: his mother, Phia, who was obsessed with class pride and inclined to arrogant anti-Czech chauvinism, and his first love, Valerie David-Rhonfeld (niece of the Czech poet Julius Zeyer), who was Jewish on her mother's side. His love for Valerie and his friendship with Zeyer – the model for his aestheticism, his taste for stylization, his passion for travel and his aristocratic disdain – brought him closer to the Czechs, whom the snobbish Phia had taught him to despise.[11]

As for Kafka, his father Herrmann (or Heřman) was born in the Czech village of Osek near Strakonice (southern Bohemia) to the family of a Jewish butcher. Heřman moved to Prague in 1881 and married Julie Löwy in the following year. She too came from a Czech area, the town of Poděbrady.[12] It is also of some interest that while a schoolboy Franz wrote a play about the Hussite king, George of Poděbrady. Although he attended German schools, he learned Czech at an early age. He spoke Czech with the cook, the maids, the shop assistants in his father's emporium in Celetná Street (later in the Kinský Palace in Old Town Square) as well as with his colleagues at the office.

He was always well informed about Czech affairs.[13] He went to meetings held by the leading Czech political leaders Kramář, Klofáč and Soukup.[14] He hobnobbed with the anarchistic poets and writers of the Klub mladých (Young People's Club), men like Karel Toman, František Gellner, Fráňa Šrámek, Stanislav Kostka Neumann and Jaroslav Hašek.[15] He was in touch with Arnošt Procházka and the littérateurs of the *Moderní revue*.[16] And what is especially noteworthy when one considers that "no Czech bourgeois ever attended the German theatre and vice versa",[17] he regularly went to the Czech National Theatre and the Pištěk Theatre,[18] though these companies inspired him less than Jizchak Löwy's small Yiddish troupe that played at the Café Savoy during May 1910 and October of the following year.[19] Yearning to break out of his isolation, he ruminated in his diaries over the tremendous advantage of being a "Christian Czech among Christian Czechs"[20] and amused himself by describing Czech noses.[21]

The name-plate on his father's shop displayed a black bird, a *kavka*, or jackdaw, *eine Dohle*. He made up a Czech name, *odradek*, for a thread spool that climbs up and down the stairs on two rods, a coiled phantom recalling the absent-minded, imperfect angels in late Klee.[22] Kafka's relationship to the Czech language is not that of a touring lecturer, a traveller, a Liliencron who keeps his ears open for unusual phonemes; the author of *The Metamorphosis* investigates Czech with philological rigour. He bemoaned his imperfect knowledge of the language and read, in addition to the Czech dailies, the purist journal *Naše řeč* (Our Language).[23] More astonishing still, he subscribed to the Boy Scout newspaper *Náš skautík* (Our Scout).[24]

Kafka's interest in Czech is best attested in the letters he wrote to Milena Jesenská:

> Of course I understand Czech. I've meant to ask you several times why you never write in Czech. Not to imply that your command of German leaves anything to be desired. Most of the time it is amazing and on those occasions when it does falter, the German language becomes pliant just for you, of its own accord, and then it is particularly beautiful, something a German doesn't even dare hope for; a German wouldn't dare write so personally. But I wanted to read you in Czech . . . [25]

Czech phrases and expressions recur in those letters as frequently as Dutch words do in the diaries Max Beckmann kept during his exile in the Low Countries.[26] Here Kafka reveals a certain satisfaction at being bilingual: "I have never lived among Germans; German is my mother tongue and as such more natural to me, but I consider Czech much more affectionate . . . "[27] The friendship, love and correspondence (1920–2) between the German-Jewish writer and Milena Jesenská, scion of an old Czech patrician family (counting among her ancestors Dr Jan Jessenius, who was executed after the defeat at White Mountain in 1621),[28] takes on symbolic significance. The same can be said for the opposition between their characters: Kafka's illness, longing for death, timidity, horrible fears and renunciation contrast with the fearless resoluteness, ardent love of life, hatred of prejudice, spirit of sacrifice of this *typically Czech woman* who, after a highly eccentric life (chaotic marriages, morphine addiction, poverty, mania for cats, political disappointments, life in the underground, persecution by her comrades) died on 17 May 1944 in the concentration camp at Ravensbrück.[29]

Kafka took a lively interest in Czech culture. As he wrote to Felix Weltsch from Zürau on 22 September 1917: "I limit my reading here to Czech and French, and nothing but autobiography or correspondence, naturally in fairly good print. Could you lend me one book of each sort?"[30] At the beginning of October he inquires again: "You've misunderstood about the books. I most want to read books that are originally Czech or French, not translations."[31] In his diaries he dwells (25 December 1911) on the literature of small nations, using Yiddish and Czech as examples.[32] In his correspondence he mentions Janáček's *Jenůfa*,[33] Vrchlický,[34] the painter Aleš,[35] and Božena Němcová, whose letters he calls "unsurpassed for psychological acumen".[36] Kafka admired the gentle "musical prose" of this nineteenth-century woman writer.[37] Max Brod was convinced that the episode in Němcová's novel *Babička* (Granny, 1855) in which an insolent Italian in the entourage of the lady of the manor tries to seduce Kristla, the innkeeper's daughter (Chapter 9), influenced the story of Amalia and the high official Sortini in Kafka's *Castle* (Chapter 15).[38] True or not, the host of liveried butlers and conceited servants in Božena Němcová's castle most certainly brings to mind the crew of helpers and go-betweens in Kafka's novel. Kafka was also enthusiastic about the sculptures of František Bílek[39] and asked Brod to write a monograph on Bílek's bare, beseeching art full of visions, mystical longings and pangs of guilt to reveal it to the world as he had revealed Janáček's music.[40] One could indeed point to parallels between Bílek's works, which resemble those of the Symbolist poets Březina and Zeyer, and Kafka's creations "under the common banner of Prague".[41]

Although Kafka's family, like Hašek's, often changed lodgings, it never left the centre of the city, the limits of the former Ghetto.[42] Except for the brief periods in which he lived in Wenceslas Square and the Golden Lane, Franz Kafka, "founding father of the twentieth century",[43] remained within the magic circle of the Old Town. Several streets – Maislova Street (where he was born on 3 July 1883), Celetná Street, Bílkova Street, Dlouhá Avenue, Dušní Street, Pařížská (or Mikulášská) Street, with a view of the river, and the Old Town Square – will always be associated with him, much as Kampa Island will always be linked with Holan. Also in the centre of town were the elementary school and German *Gymnasium* he attended and the Law Faculty where he later studied; indeed, the *Gymnasium* was part of the Kinský Palace into which Herrmann Kafka later moved his shop. Kafka's Na Poříčí office in the Arbeiter-Unfall-Versicherungs-Anstalt für das Königreich Böhmen (Dělnická úrazová pojišt'ovna) was only a few minutes' walk from the Old Town.

The story "Description of a Struggle" is Kafka's only work with references to the topography of Prague. A nocturnal tracking shot along the frozen snow in the moonlight frames Ferdinandova Street, Poštovská Street, Petřín Hill (Laurenziberg), the Vltava, the iron railing along the river bank, "the town on the further shore" in which "a number of lights burning teased the eye",[44] Střelecký ostrov (Sharpshooters' Island), the Mill Tower with its clock, the Charles Bridge, Karlova Street and the

Seminary Church. It has been said that in the scene with a policeman who glides out of a distant black-paned coffeehouse like a skater and the scene with a fat woman carrying a lantern who comes out of a wine tavern where a piano is playing, in Karlova Street, Kafka approaches the local colour of Kisch's sketches.[45]

In *The Trial*, the most Prague-like of all Czech and German novels, Prague is never named. Yet the reserve that prohibits him from naming it cannot keep the city from shining through in filigree. The presence of Prague, reduced to its essential features, is far stronger here than in Rilke's versified *Larenopfer* topography, where the Hradčany, Saint Vitus, Loreta, Vyšehrad, Malvazinky, Smíchov, Zlíchov, the Vltava and the cupola of Saint Nicholas Church appear as in gaudy barrel-organ paintings.[46] It is Kafka's sober and precise, monodic, crystal-clear writing – devoid of ornamentation, grey, objective, Talmudically reasoned – that makes the city more mysterious and dream-like in *The Trial*. His transcendental legal German contrasts with the bloated, impassioned language of the Prague Neoromantics and Expressionists, though, as Adorno has pointed out, it too belongs to Expressionism and reveals the influence of Expressionist painting.[47]

But even if the Bohemian capital remains concealed and anonymous in *The Trial* – anonymous and faceless as the protagonist, a tissue of abstract, archetypal places – many points can be identified. We may assume that the building where Josef K. works is based on the Assicurazioni Generali building in Wenceslas Square where Kafka was employed before he became an insurance official at the Arbeiter-Unfall-Versicherungs-Anstalt für das Königreich Böhmen; or rather, the crumbling, dark, labyrinthine building of the Böhmische Unionbank (Česká Banka Union) facing Na Příkopě, if one takes into account the small dark room filled with old waste paper and empty ink bottles where two guards receive a whipping.[48] The huge building in which Josef K. undergoes his first interrogation – with its amorphous hovels, windows full of mattresses and small shops below street level – makes one think of the dilapidated Jewish Quarter, although it is described as far from the centre of town. The even dirtier, greyer outlying district of Titorelli's depressing abode, which Josef K. must walk up a particularly long, narrow stairway to reach, could well be the working-class district of Žižkov Kafka so loved.

His desire to leave the spell of the centre for the outskirts and his well-to-do family for society's outcasts often drove him to that uncouth district, hardly suited at the time for "gentlemen". It is, however, also possible that in his description of the filthy courthouse Kafka had in mind Prague offices in general: offices hidden in bizarre *barabizny*, in crumbling slum-like hovels with dark corridors crammed full of yellowing files and musty smells. The cathedral is Saint Vitus' and, in the cathedral, the "silver statue of a saint" is the tomb of Saint John of Nepomuk. Josef K. goes to his execution by walking across a "bridge" that is the Charles Bridge, over a small island that is Kampa. The "uphill streets" are those of Malá Strana, the place of his execution – Strahov.

The "Pragueness" of *The Trial* comes out in many other minor details including, for example, the relationship between landlord and tenant, which often occupied Kafka's imagination.[49] Kafka infused *The Trial* – as he did *The Castle* – with the indolence of the city on the Vltava, an indolence that matches her contrariness, her melancholy mistrust, her apathy. The constant recurrence of beds and pallets, the smell of unmade beds Adorno speaks of,[50] the soft world of mattresses into which the perpetually weary characters sink is the reflex not only of the disease spreading throughout Kafka's body but also of the abulia, the forced lethargy of a metropolis whose vital impulses have perennially been crushed. It is therefore not surprising that Haas wrote about the two novels: "I read them as one reads a completely familiar panorama of one's own youth in which one immediately recognizes every hidden cranny, every dusty corner, every lascivious hint, every distant allusion, no matter now delicate."[51]

Unlike *The Trial*, the diaries contain minute references to streets, cafés, theatres, synagogues. Kafka often took walks in Chotek Park,[52] and his strolls to the poor, gloomy outlying districts, particularly Žižkov, recall Blok's excursions to the muddy, foggy outskirts of Petersburg.[53] And what a hunger Kafka has for capturing the moments of clowning, the flashes of delight, the waxwork oddities corresponding to the innocence of childhood: "The old tricks at the Christmas Fair. Two cockatoos on a crossbar pull fortunes. Mistakes: a girl has a lady-love predicted. A man offers artificial flowers for sale in rhyme: *To je růže udělaná z kůže* (This is a rose made of leather)"[54] or, referring to puss-in-the-middle, which is called "Boxes, boxes, make a move": "We're playing *škatule, škatule hejbejte se*; I'm creeping in the shade from one tree to the next . . . "[55]

Kafka's love for Prague is accompanied by a *basso continuo* of impatience and imprecations. In a letter to Hedwig W. written in September 1907 he calls the Bohemian capital an "accursed city".[56] He writes to Max Brod on 22 July 1912: "How do I live in Prague, after all? This craving for people, which I have and which is transformed into anxiety once it is fulfilled, finds an outlet only during vacations."[57] He often dreams of fleeing, of faraway places. To Kurt Wolff: "[I] will marry and move away from Prague, possibly to Berlin."[58] After starting work at Assicurazioni Generali in October of 1907, he informed Hedwig W. that he still had "hopes of someday sitting in chairs in faraway countries, looking out of the office windows at fields of sugar cane or Mohammedan cemeteries".[59] This longing for distant lands – the theme of works such as *America* or

"The Wish To Be a Red Indian" – can perhaps be traced to the example of his two maternal uncles: Alfred Löwy, director of the Spanish railways, and Josef Löwy, who founded a colonial company in the Congo and outfitted caravans.[60]

His notes about Prague often reflect the mystery and gloom the city aroused in him: "Sad, nervous, physically unwell, fear of Prague, in bed"[61] or *"Prague. Religions vanish like people."*[62] Janouch draws a comparison, which makes me shudder, between Kafka seated at his office desk, his head leaning back, his legs outstretched, and the deathly pale painting *A Reader of Dostoevsky* by Emil Filla.[63] "Among the gestures to be found in Kafka's stories," Walter Benjamin writes, "none is more frequent than that of a man with his head bent deep into his chest. This is the exhaustion of the lords of the manor, the noise the doormen make in the hotel, the low roof of the visitors to the gallery."[64] There are frequent allusions in the diaries to a relationship that feeds on the humus of Prague, the relationship between the innocent condemned man and the executioner who kills him.[65] Holan passes judgment: "The hangman makes the poets' bed. Quiet, earth, you shall have a bone!"[66]

11

The protagonist of Prague's magic dimension is the pilgrim, the way-farer who reappears constantly in Czech letters under different names: *poutník* (pilgrim), *chodec* (pedestrian), *tulák* (vagabond), *kráčivec* (walker), *kolemjdoucí* (passerby) and *svědek* (witness). The archetype of this large family is the *poutník*, the pilgrim, of the allegorical novel *Labyrint světa a ráj srdce* (The Labyrinth of the World and the Paradise of the Heart), which Jan Amos Komenský, better known to the world at large as Comenius, wrote at Brandýs nad Orlicí in 1623 after the defeat at White Mountain.

Overrun by military units and bands of rogues, the Czech and Moravian lands were a fierce battleground, a lake of livid blood, a burial ground for bones of the wretched, an arena of conflagration and plundering. Dačický z Heslova writes of the year 1620 in his memoirs:

> When there was no further resistance in Bohemia, the Imperial troops set to sacking, pillaging and stealing through the whole of the Czech lands, searching every corner, capturing the poor and putting ropes around their necks or tormenting them with fire and slaughtering them to find where they had hidden money – and many such matters terrible and pitiful in the telling. And so all one heard was, "Alas and alack!" and "Hand it over and

be quick about it!" Nor were Roman Catholics granted pardon and forbearance: "Give us everything thou ownest and keep thy faith!" each was told. Many who fled to the woods together with their children found nought there but death![1]

Comenius, a young preacher of the Bohemian Brethren, was forced to flee Fulnek when cut-throats set fire to his library and the plague took his wife and two children. His "labyrinth" was born out of disgust at brutality and suffering. Comenius' Pilgrim goes forth into the world to become acquainted with the various social classes and professions. He is met by two guides: Mr Ubiquitous, who places the reins of Curiosity on his neck and the iron bit of Obstinacy in his mouth, and Mr Delusion, oddly disguised and surrounded by mist, who makes him put on the spectacles of Doubt with the horn frames of Habit, because the queen of the world, *Moudrost* (Wisdom) or *Marnost* (Vanity), does not want men to see with the naked eye. Extraordinary spectacles these: "For they had the power . . . of making distant objects appear near and the near distant, the small large and the large small, ugly things beautiful and the beautiful ugly, black white and white black . . . "[2] Thus equipped, the Pilgrim becomes a sort of allegorical puppet, a hybrid, a man-horse similar to Arcimboldo's masked faces. But the spectacles (the nose saddle that becomes the mark of royalty in the folk theatre of the Czech Baroque) do not fit him well, and if he looks up he can still see normally, obliquely, out of the corner of his eye. "Even though you stop my mouth and cover my eyes, yet I trust God that you will not be able to restrain my reason and my mind."[3]

The world is a circular city surrounded by a high wall that can be entered through the Gate of Life, a plexus of streets and squares, each of which is allotted to a different class. Beyond the walls gapes a gloomy abyss. The centre of the city is a *ryňk*, a market teeming with craftsmen and busybodies, a grand stage, a Babylon in which men compete to be known as wise and each wears a mask to look different from the others. Here they toil over a thousand wrong-headed chores, come to blows for no reason, push, caper and fall, and, because their souls are filled with folly, play with toads, bellows, bells and toys. They walk on high buskins or stilts and constantly change costume. They begin a task and leave it, aimlessly dig and move piles of earth, erect buildings they immediately tear down, destroy their own things and others', gaze upon themselves contentedly in the mirror. In this transitory world everything is a flash in the pan and all men are knaves who *transeunt tamquam umbrae*. Death hurls her swift, pointed arrows haphazardly into the crowd of the *ryňk*. The dead are cast into the dark pit encircling the world, and the mob, back from the funeral, immediately resumes its madness.

The Pilgrim witnesses a series of comic episodes demonstrating the frivolity and madness of the world. It is no accident that the Dada-ist clowns Voskovec and Werich dreamed of staging *Labyrinth*.[4] We witness the bizarre practices and fixations of craftsmen, philosophers, musicians, alchemists, geometricians and astronomers. Physicians cut off limbs and poke around in entrails, historians observe past ages through "perspicils", that is, crooked tubes pointed backwards. Nor is there any lack of Grand-Guignol horror such as soldiers' games (an echo of the pillaging in Bohemia after White Mountain) or the scratchings of those plagued with the "French disease".

The choreography of the Comenian city consists of distinct compart-ments, illustrative "stations" similar to the drawings in his *Orbis pictus*, pointing out that all things are false, transient and distorted and, like babbling and human anger, lead to nothing. Some may find an analogy between the course of this Baroque pilgrim and the tortuous journey of the pilgrim Švejk from hospital to prison, barracks to police station, for Hašek's hero also traverses a "labyrinth" full of distractions, fools and madmen whose absurd behaviour often makes one's blood run cold. It makes little difference that Hašek leaves his Švejk without the hope of salvation.

Comenius the pilgrim teaches us to stand to one side of the *theatrum mundi*, theatre of the world, and comment on its actions like a stranger, almost cataloguing them as Tommaso Garzoni does in his *Piazza universale* or Francesco Fulvio Frugoni in *Il cane di Diogene*. Nonetheless, he agonizes the while and at times is swept away as on a sea voyage in which powerful gusts of wind whip the waves to the stars and all but sink his vessel. He finds neither consolation nor joy, nor is there aught in this miserable world he can cling to. In vain does Delusion exhort him to act fondly. After an endless series of promises, about-faces and adventures he asks himself, "Which of these do I possess? None. What have I learned? Nothing. Where am I? I myself know not."[5]

Even Queen Wisdom alias Vanity, all mist and pomp, is a disappoint-ment. When Solomon, accompanied by a retinue of sages, approaches the throne and removes the veil from her face (which had shone with wealth up to then), it turns out to be a spider web. Moreover, the Queen is pale and bloated; she has cracked red rouge on her cheeks, a heavy odour of asafoetida, scabby hands and a deformed body like a phantom in a Meyrink story. Still, Solomon gives in to temptation, deceived as he is by Affability, Suavity and Voluptuousness, counsellors to the Queen, who also sends Power with an army to rout the troop of wise men.

Instead of pursuing his investigation of the false and insolent, the Pilgrim resolves (though Delusion attempts to prevent him and, failing to do so, vanishes into thin air) to contemplate the supreme ceremony:

the hurling of the dead into the darkness beyond the wall. The spectacle overwhelms him; he faints and falls to the ground. Was this his goal? "Oh, that I had never been born! That I had never passed through the gate of life, if after all the futilities of the world I am to become prey to this darkness and horror. O God, God, my God! If Thou existest, O God, have pity on me, a wretched man!"[6]

Having freed himself of his guides, the Pilgrim returns to his inner self, to the deserted house of his heart, whose tiny glass window is so covered by smoke that no light can penetrate it. The magic of the spectacles with frames of the Divine Word and lenses of the Holy Spirit now allows him to see the truth. Illuminated by faith and peace of mind, purged of the dross of terrestrial cares, devoted to Christ and protected by the angels, the Pilgrim finds the meaning of his journey in communion with God.

12

To return to the point, however. Why do I say that the Comenian Pilgrim contains the essence of Prague? Most of all because his large, nearsighted spectacles force him to view the world obliquely. He uses them to see the unfalsified truth and retain his judgment despite the two good-for-nothings Ubiquitous and Delusion. When Delusion and the mob revolt against him in the *ryňk* for his criticisms of them, the Pilgrim, like every good denizen of Prague, withdraws into silence, thus avoiding merciless questioning by those who would confiscate his thoughts.

> I realized that it was useless to argue. Therefore I remained silent, thinking to myself: if they wish to regard themselves as human, so be it. But I see what I see. Moreover, I was afraid lest my companion should readjust the glasses and thus delude me. I decided, therefore, to be quiet and rather to concentrate on those fine things of which I had seen the beginning.[1]

An awareness of the vanity of all things, of the frailty of the world (an awareness deeply rooted in Czech culture) prevents the Pilgrim from taking part, as Delusion would have liked, in the frenzied dance of ghosts, phantoms, ravens made to look like swans. Like every creature of Prague provenance, he remains on the periphery of history, a witness and "occupant", a guest who is never able to alter the lot of the "labyrinth" or mitigate its folly though he is in the midst of its ruin. This explains his meditative quietism, his search for shelter within himself.

But Comenius' Pilgrim is also the archetype of the unjustly accused innocent, who will be legion in Prague. "'You yourself are to blame for your condition,' Delusion tells him, 'because you demand something great and extraordinary, such as is granted to no one.'" To which the Pilgrim replies, "'Not only I myself but the whole human race is so miserable and so blind that it is not conscious of its own miseries.'"[2] Ubiquitous complains about him to the Queen of Worldly Wisdom: "'Despite all our sincere and faithful endeavours we have been unable to induce him to take a liking to any occupation in which he might settle peacefully and become one of the faithful, obedient and permanent citizens of this our common land; for he has shown himself forever displeased and has found fault with everything and has a longing for some other extraordinary thing.'"[3]

Suddenly the Pilgrim's inseparable guides foreshadow the pair of assistants in *The Castle* and the two actors in frock coats in *The Trial* who accompany Josef K. to his execution. And in fact, the Pilgrim in *Labyrinth* is led to the Queen's throne as if he were appearing before a court of law. He is not so much afraid of her as he is of the beast sprawled out in front of the throne – examining him with shining eyes, waiting to pounce on him – and of the two frightening retainers dressed in women's clothes next to the Queen: one in iron armour with quills like a porcupine, the other in fox fur with a fox tail as halberd. Thus, as early as Comenius spitefully zealous keepers devise slanders that turn the Pilgrim into an *obžalovaný*, a defendant.

13

A close relative of the Comenian wanderer is the protagonist of the short philosophical treatise *Kulhavý poutník* (The Limping Pilgrim, 1936) by Josef Čapek, who made wide use of allegory as both writer and painter. The limping pilgrim has a game leg – the result perhaps of a boyhood fall or the malice of others or a congenital defect – which makes him stumble, pause in a ditch because "the ditch always has something of the limits of the world and of life"[1] or loll in the shade of a luxuriant tree.

His is a journey between birth and death, "from an undefined place to a place vaguer still". "In truth," he says, "I go from nothing to nothing, I merely wander within *something*. My path does not pass through places; it is a period of time, a tension in time or rather simply a state",[2] that is, apparent motion, which is actually absolute immobility, because, as Věra Linhartová says in "Crab Canon", "constant speed is the same as motionless rigidity". The pilgrim motif reappears in her works as well when she states, "I am at heart a hermit (*poustevník*), but have added to this the vocation of pilgrim (*poutník*), that is, I have removed three letters from the former word and become the latter. A hermit constantly on a pilgrimage."[3]

But let us return to Čapek. Making haste slowly, moving step by step, stopping everywhere enables the pilgrim to observe minutely what others miss and to reflect on questions of life and death without losing his way. Čapek's treatise has many elements in common with Comenius': the protagonist's contemplative passivity, the way he plods along the periphery of the world at large, the essence of his journey seen less as a plot of actions than as a series of encounters, statements such as "the greatest adventures are those of the inner world",[4] details like the Gate of Eternity (Brána Věčnosti), the glorification of the soul, "harmony between feeling and thought, docile reconciliation between the pains and joys of life, gratitude for being and especially – especially rebellion against nothingness".

Čapek, however, completely forgoes the grotesque and ludicrous metaphors with which Comenius derides the madness of man; he is indebted instead to the second part of that diptych novel, that is, the exit from the "labyrinth" into the "paradise of the heart", where, like Comenius, he sets up virtue as the antidote to the poison of vice and even repeats his model's sermonizing. Here the negative, corrupt aspects of Comenius' "city" are concentrated in Person (Osoba), "a demon of vanity", an aggressive and vain alter ego interested only in success and honours, a veritable lady-in-waiting to Comenius' Queen.

The influence of the "paradise of the heart" on Josef Čapek is also reflected in his pilgrim's strong religiosity. Here too Vanity (Marnost) struts about, yet Čapek's pilgrim, unlike Comenius', does not flee her: "I cling firmly to her with all my vital roots . . . [5] I do not wish to mortify my flesh; I love the world too much."[6] The limping pilgrim's search for spirituality does not, then, exclude the joy of living. His spiritualism, intensified by the constant conflict of Person and Soul, does not negate the pleasures and beauty of the world.

Faith here does not come *ex abrupto* like an apocalyptic thunderbolt or drops to uncloud eyes obscured by a thousand absurdities and lunacies; it is from the very beginning part of the pilgrim's slow, lame gait. Although Čapek wrote his work on the eve of Nazi barbarism, to which he himself fell victim in a concentration camp, *The Limping Pilgrim* does not dwell on the scurrilous or gruesome aspects of the earthly "city". His hero does not roll his eyes like one possessed at the sight; instead – though an outsider, crippled and excluded from the game (like every Prague inhabitant) – he declares himself "indubitably happy"[7] and his life a "great and unexpected gift" whose content he does not know. For this reason the book is "written to the clouds", to use the title of the aphorisms that Čapek wrote while in the concentration camp and that in a sense represent a continuation of the pilgrim's reflections.[8]

14

Čapek's pilgrim made his first appearance under the name of Tulák (Vagabond) in the drama *Ze života hmyzu* (The Insect Play) that Josef Čapek wrote with his brother Karel in 1921. Given its representation of vices, this diorama or, rather, allegorical music hall of human folly performed by insects may be considered in the Comenian context as the "labyrinth" or first part of a diptych of which *Kulhavý poutník*, the "paradise of the heart", is the second. The fact that the Čapek brothers, inclined as they were to see a great mystery in every green plant, substitute nature for the city makes no substantial difference.

Indeed, the drunken Tulák's fall in a forest clearing at the beginning of the play recalls the Pilgrim's lameness. Speaking to a moneywort in the Prologue, he defines his role as a wandering philosopher in the following terms: "If I had roots like you, I would not roam the world as a tramp. That's the way it is. And if I didn't roam the world I would not get to know so many things . . . I do not want to make anyone better. Neither insects nor men. I simply look."[1]

This character is not merely a variant of the pilgrim; it belongs to a type of wanderer and "evil loner" patterned after the *bosyak* of Jack London and Maxim Gorky, a type figuring prominently in the works of the many Czech poets and novelists of the early twentieth century grouped together as "anarchists": Fráňa Šrámek, Ivan Olbracht, František Gellner, Jaroslav Hašek and, especially, Karel Toman. In Toman's verse collection *Sluneční hodiny* (Sundials, 1913), *tuláci* "wander through the world, lilies of the field/with innocent apostle souls" fleeing narrow-minded, conformist society. Hašek was, incidentally, a real-life vagabond as well, incapable of staying in one place or job for very long.

But let us return to the Čapeks. The frivolity and erotic escapades of the butterfly dandies; the greed of the cockroaches, who roll dung balls along in front of them; the gluttony and cruel egotism of the crickets, shrikes and mongeese, who gobble one another up; the relentless efficiency of the worker ants and the bloody war between their two factions, each led by a dictator who thinks himself the chosen one – this Brueghelesque teeming of "Flemish proverbs", these Buffonesque illustrations of moral rectitude call forth biting commentary on the part of the Tulák, who watches and judges from a corner of the stage, that is, from the sidelines, with a string of impassive pronouncements, incapable, like every Prague inhabitant, of changing anything in the wretched muddle, which is all the more monstrous for the tiny animals involved.

Two scenes are particularly striking: the description of an ant hill, a red tenement in which the ants bustle about panting while a blind ant beats time in front of the entrance; and the war, in which soldier ants fight for a worthless piece of land, a "span of land from blade of grass to blade of grass", a "piece of world from the birch tree to the pine tree", for "the road between two blades of grass". "Fifty thousand dead to take twenty paces of latrine",[2] while the dictators cloak the slaughter under the guise of national honour, prestige, law and similar nonsense to dupe the credulous fools. The stupidity, the lunacy, the blindness of it all!

"World rule?" the Vagabond asks the first dictator. "Poor ant, you call this tiny bit of clay and grass you know the world? This miserable, filthy span of earth? If I were to crush your antheap and you along with it, the tree-top above you would not so much as rustle!"[3] Death himself is the general in this battle scene, which, painted as it is with the distorting hyperboles of Expressionism, vividly evokes the horrors in the terrifying episode in *Labyrinth* in which Comenius depicts the soldiers' excesses. Moreover, what a dreadful prediction of the Nazi period the Čapeks' myrmecology offers when after routing the enemy army one of the dictators declares a colonel "Great God of the Ants".

Despite the baseness of human actions, despite moral dereliction and the concomitant suffering, the epilogue expresses faith in the human condition: we are shown a dizzying dance of mayflies who praise life as they die. Yet we are confused by the Tulák's cry "I still have so much to say!" when Death takes hold of him;[4] we think of the futility of a life prevented from intervening in the world. Thus, the "epilogue for the Director", in which the Tulák comes back to life as a Poutník (Wanderer) and finds work as a lumberjack, seems forced.

A thinking man in the heart of Europe who does not go along with the crowd is more often than not compelled to live the life of a wanderer, often confined to a limited area, a narrow valley, for the walls of insuperable national borders are high indeed. This is why it would be desirable at times for the Tuláks and Poutníks to turn from passive observers and philosophers into sorcerers with pointed hats capable of making the evils of their country vanish into thin air. It is frightening to think of a surly foreign vizier enlarging the Pilgrim's spectacles into the enormous sign of a demonic optician and placing them over the dead eye sockets of Prague.

On the other hand, it may also be that today even the vocation of the Tulák is, as Věra Linhartová writes, subject to official control:

> If anyone doubts the possibility of leading the life of a vagabond in our times, let me simply point out that a special department of

the Ministry of the Interior in Prague, on Letná Plain, issues a small book for wanderers on certain days, and all one has to do is present oneself at the proper department at the proper moment.[5]

15

Although primarily a variation on the wayfarer figure so dear to the Romantics, the pilgrim wandering through the nocturnal landscapes of the poet Karel Hynek Mácha also manifests a Prague-like ambivalence and imperfection. Enticed by wanderlust, driven by the desire to move ever onwards, he wanders aimlessly down labyrinthine paths, up steep mountains, yet never reaches his destination. He therefore embodies on the one hand youth's yearning for ideals and, on the other, the failure of the daydream, the futility of desire, of flight from dismal life.

The "feeble wayfarer" (*mdlý chodec*), who longs for truth and beauty, approaches his "country" (the enchanted realm of the imagination) in a moonlight that shimmers elusive before his eyes.[1] Yet he also turns away disillusioned and disappears at sunset behind a boulder, symbol and seal of our fleeting existence.[2] That is why Mácha likened a dying man to a pilgrim who turns to look at his "country" before leaving it forever.[3]

Life as a journey ending in exile is the theme of the short prose work "Pout' krkonošská" (A Pilgrimage to the Krkonoše, 1833), in whose loose narrative structure all Mácha's main motifs appear: suffering here below, the enigma of the hereafter, eternal nothingness, hopeless pessimism, regret at the passing of youth and the bitterness of disillusionment.[4] Early in the work the young pilgrim, dressed completely in black, is trodding a narrow path beneath Sněžka, a steep peak in the Krkonoše Range, as night approaches. "His blue eyes revealed an inutterable melancholy."[5] His breast heaves with passionate sighs: he is distressed by the ephemerality of earthly endeavour, the fading of youthful utopias, of lost love. The poet projects his grief upon the mountains between Bohemia and Silesia, where he had travelled in August of that year. "I will return a solitary pilgrim, crossing the endless night, whose empty silence will be quickened by my lamentation."[6] Once more the limping pilgrim constantly stopping to meditate, with the added element of nocturnal sorcery.

The youth dreams he has reached the peak of Sněžka at dawn in a crumbling Gothic cloister on the one day in the year when the dead monks, frozen in their last poses, come to life and decide whether to return to another year of hibernation or let themselves be buried for all eternity. The entire episode, including the funeral and mournful round of the living monks with the reawakened brethren, reproduces a horrible dream recorded by Mácha in his diary on 14 January 1833.[7] The final scene, the Baroque emblem of an aged Pilgrim who comes down from the mountain with a feeble gait (*mdlým krokem*), grey hair falling over hollow cheeks and a white beard down to the waist,[8] stems from another diary entry entitled "Poutník" (The Pilgrim):

> The night was cold. A deep darkness veiled the narrow path between the rocks, along which the pilgrim advanced with feeble steps, often stumbling over skulls and human skeletons. The fissure in the rock was long and wide. Black darkness reigned on all sides; only the yellowed skulls glowed faintly. Far off, atop the highest cliff, whose peak was covered with eternal snow, a cross arose in the blinding light of the pale Moon. "Good night, good night," he whispered faintly. Like a lost moonbeam a pale shape seemed to rise before him and point to the cross with a gaunt arm, yet the menacingly screeching and moaning storm spoke to him with other, mysterious words. The light of dawn glowed behind him. He wished to turn occasionally and gaze upon the rose-coloured glow guilding the path he had traversed, but the storm forced him onwards, and an ineffable desire drew him into an unknown land along an unknown path.[9]

Bohemia: a Brueghelesque parable of blind men. Swarms of shabbily-dressed pilgrim-philosophers advance groping in the storm, holding one and other like the blind all the way from Sněžka to Prague. "Let them alone: they be blind leaders of the blind. And if the blind lead the blind, both shall fall into the ditch" (Matthew 15:14).

This Gospel text gives us an ideal opportunity to linger for a moment on the words "good night, good night" in the Mácha text above. The obsessively recurring idea of farewell, a final leave-taking of all earthly things, the ultimate good-bye figures as the leitmotif of many of Mácha's characters.[10] That "good night" (which we shall find once more in Nezval's poem *Edison*) appears again and again in his works; it is a magic formula bathed in tears. The entire story "Křivoklád" is woven from the threads of its heart-rending threnody. In "Cikáni" the old Gipsy Giacomo bids farewell to his native Venice before being executed with a "good night";[11] Bohdana leaves the world in "Karlův Tejn" with a "good night".[12] The youth in "Pout' krkonošská" greets the mountains in the crystal-clear darkness with a "good night", and "good night" echoes back across the slopes.[13] Later, when he descends as "weary pilgrim" (*umdlelý poutník*), he again whispers, "Good night, good night."[14]

The "good night" death knell also resounds in a number of Mácha's poems and diary entries. "Good night, O love! thou golden chalice/full of delight portending death!/Thy fair realm of deceit/shall no longer be my country."[15] The dying man addresses his final "good night" to the sun, just as the sun, having completed its daily pilgrimage, says "good night" to the fields.[16] The forest bids "good night" to the lover, the lover to his beloved.[17] Reading Mácha, hearing the pilgrim's constant nocturnal salutation and the mountains' reply makes one wonder whether nature herself is not about to fade away.[18] Yet the source of all this fearful leave-taking is thick, gloomy Prague blood, its Baroque humour, its *memento* that *vox es, praetereaque nihil* ("thou art breath, nothing more"), an announcement of funereal eloquence at nightfall.

16

Kafka's isolation in the land of his birth. The German-speaking Prague Jew living in a form of quarantine amidst a world of Slavs, suffering tragically from being different, equally alien to Germans, with whom he, after all, shares a language, and Czechs, who consider him a German, a foreigner. The malaise of the Jew, tolerated but not admitted, a soul oppressed by an inexplicable sense of guilt and perpetually forced to wait for a decree of acceptance. I have written of this elsewhere.

But the situation is further complicated by the witchcraft of Prague, which works as a kind of bellows to loneliness, fear and loss. Seen in this light, the situation of the Prague Jew becomes analogous to that of the Homo Bohemicus, whose home at this crucial point in Europe is often a ghetto and prison. Kafka's two main novels are mirrors of the Prague dimension irrespective of whether the Land Surveyor is rejected by the Castle or Josef K. is summoned by the court.

Kafka's works enable us to experience the physical malaise of being an outsider experienced by every Prague inhabitant, of being a foreigner in one's own country and the victim of abuse by unapproachable authorities, the swift yet evasive inquisition that hunts, scrutinizes and manipulates. Caught in administrative machinations, the pilgrim loses all power to determine his fate. A mysterious bureaucracy makes decisions for him, and whether his name is Josef Švejk or Josef K. he has no choice but to devise wily expedients to thread his way through the stifling ritual of rules and orders.

It is but a small step from the condition of pilgrim to that of the falsely accused. Moreover, the accused has no choice: he must bend to the arbitrary will of mysterious judges and officials, on whom legal practices and rational arguments have no effect. But by suffering the abuse and absurd logic of their sophism, he ends up *believing* his soul to be sullied with inscrutable crimes. He thus accepts his guilt and even turns accomplice to his executioners.

Do you remember what the landlady says to the Land Surveyor? "You are not from the Castle, you are not from the village, you aren't anything. Or, rather, unfortunately, you are something, a stranger, a man who isn't wanted and is in everybody's way . . . "[1] Elusive Klamm, similar in many ways to Patera, the ruler of Perle in Kubin's *Die andere Seite*, belongs to the very essence of Prague. Kafka's pilgrim does his best to make contact with him, but in vain: Klamm (in Czech *klam* means "deception, deceit", and Deception, Mámení, is one of Comenius' characters) "will never speak to anybody he doesn't want to speak to, no matter how much trouble this anybody may take, and no matter how insufferably forward he may be . . . "[2] After all, not even Barnabas, the messenger who spends days on end in the Castle, is certain who Klamm is or whether the Klamm he sees is the real one. Besides, the messages "change in value perpetually, the reflections they give rise to are endless, and chance determines where one stops reflecting".[3]

Almost as if he wished to find tranquillity within an embalming bureaucracy, the Land Surveyor strives to reach the Castle, a base substitute for the "paradise of the heart". Yet he loafs about and loses himself in vulgar consolations, in the *Tingeltangel* of that watchful power, the "labyrinth" of the Herrenhof and the Bridge Inn, places of metaphysical crudity. Admission to the Castle seems denied to him. But "paradise" and "labyrinth" are not at complete variance with each other: the Castle extends into the village with its false solemnity, its dead, oppressive ritual, its extensive network of agents and secretaries who go there to settle incongruous office matters or continue their sleep or mate with the indentured servant girls. Indeed, only at the Inn does the Land Surveyor manage to catch a glimpse of Klamm – fat, heavy, with a long moustache and pince-nez – through a peep hole.

To reach the paradise destroyed called the Castle, which, incidentally, consists of a mass of crumbling hovels, K. will, unlike Comenius' pilgrim, have to set down roots in the evil, servitude and horrors of the "labyrinth of the world", and this despite the fact that its twisted inhabitants receive him with dread and superstition. For "paradise" has by now become hell, and instead of angels it boasts a bug-infested host of sorcerer copyists and assistants. Besides, K. himself is to blame for failing to push through the web of absurdities and win the favour of the mighty: he is the mouse who turns the cats into tyrants.

The journey of the bank assessor Josef K., arrested the morning of his thirtieth birthday, is the journey of a pilgrim hunted by the mysterious bloodhounds of an invisible court, a journey through the carps and cavils of a pettifogging Prague. No one will ever find out what he did wrong.

Just before Josef K. is executed at Strahov, the author asks, "Where was the Judge whom he had never seen? Where was the High Court to which he had never penetrated?"[4] In *The Trial*, as Marthe Robert notes, the search is for the crime not the criminal.[5] All defence is futile when investigation is carried out in secret by unapproachable investigators and when the bedridden attorney has no access to the files of the case and is content to draw up a petition. That is why Leni urges Josef K., "Don't be so unyielding in future, you can't put up a resistance against this Court, you must admit your fault. Make your confession at the first chance you get. Until you do that, there's no possibility of getting out of their clutches."[6]

Yet inventing guilt is just as futile. The trial spreads like a disease, incited by a brood of shrewd, evil swindlers and masters of simulation, by a gigantic organization "which not only employs corrupt warders, stupid Inspectors and Examining Magistrates of whom the best that can be said is that they recognize their own limitations, but also has at its disposal a judicial hierarchy of high, indeed of the highest rank, with an indispensable and numerous retinue of servants, clerks, police and other assistants, perhaps even hangmen . . . "[7]

A plain, monodic style of relentless rigour, a metaphysical legalese with the glaze of rigor mortis (so different from the feverish outpourings of other Prague Jewish writers) lends allegorical weight to *The Trial*, as does the absence of life stories to define the main characters, who remain personified abstractions. The protagonist's pilgrim identity is revealed by the fact that like Comenius' pilgrim he passes through several exemplary "stations" on his journey to execution (exempla reduced to transparent absurdities of the world), symbolic episodes unrelated except for the fact that they appear in the protagonist's field of action. As Marthe Robert puts it, the world of Josef K. is made up of "petits cercles fermés entre lesquels il est la seule communication possible."[8]

Hence the accused pilgrim's isolation. Yet the waxwork abstractness of the lesser characters does not detract from their distinctly Prague-like features. Titorelli, the presumptuous painter who daubs pompous portraits of judges, perhaps even assembling them from sheafs of waste paper and law codes à la Arcimboldo; the attorney or attorney-as-bed, the back-street lawyer who turns into a piece of furniture; the lecherous washerwoman of the tenement that houses the court; the flabby merchant Bloch who is always waiting for a sign from the advocate; the witch-like Leni who gives herself to all her boss's clients; Frau Grubach the landlady; the uncouth guards and timid court registrars – they all have thick Prague air in their lungs, thick Prague blood in their veins.

17

The Castle is immersed in snow like a winter landscape by Brueghel. The Land Surveyor asks Pepi:

> "How much longer is it till spring?"
>
> "Till spring?" Pepi repeated. "Winter is long here, a very long winter, and monotonous. But we don't complain about that down here, we are safe from the winter. Well yes, some day spring comes too, and summer, and there's a time for that too, I suppose; but in memory, now, spring and summer seem as short as though they didn't last much longer than two days, and even on those days, even during the most beautiful day, even then sometimes snow falls."[1]

Snow recurs constantly, obsessively in the poems and notebooks of Jiří Orten, a Jewish poet writing in Czech, who was run over and killed by a German military ambulance on a Prague embankment on 30 August 1941, the day of his (how Kafkaesque) twenty-second birthday. A snow drift "lies over the numb city like a cold compress".[2] "If the snow listened to me,/the way it listens to children."[3] "I touched the snow, it was cold and warmed the palm of my hand, the fair, fair snow, my dearest."[4] "Always snow! It falls silently,/it is like a hand writing,/how much it must cover!"[5] "Paws of snow scratched me/my face, my eyes, my chest . . . "[6] "Patient snowfall/melts in us quietly."[7] The painting "which falls on the canvas" . . . "is like white snow which does not know, does not even know/ why it must fall."[8] We ourselves "are snow: if we fall silently we melt in our misery".[9] Snow and grape come together to kindle magic "reveries".[10]

Prague and snow: a frequent theme of Prague writers, especially those of Jewish descent. Paul Leppin, describing the beginning of winter, says of his Severin: "For the first time in years he was again aware of the peculiar scent snow has, like apples left for a long time between double windows."[11] Hugo Salus sings of the Hradčany and Saint Vitus covered by a blanket of shimmering snow: "Alchemistengäßchen, you too/are buried in a bed of snow."[12] Grape and snow, apple between double windows, bed of snow: what image brokers!

If Halas's season is autumn, Orten is the poet of winter, "hostile to fruits".[13] Halas claims that winter "worms its way again and again between the nooks of [Orten's] verses."[14] It is no accident that one of his collections of poems has the title *Cesta k mrazu* (A Journey to the Frost). In an age of annihilation, when human beings became more precious than the golden wedge of Ophir (Isaiah 13:12), Orten shared with his generation the concept of "naked man" without social glitter or presumption, crushed by the weight of iniquity. Despite its origins in Francis Jammes the most striking aspect of Orten's writing is its unadulterated sense of decency, the desire for truth, the lingering purity of adolescence. Perhaps this is why there is so much snow in Orten's works, why it is so often winter.

It is the source of the longing for the warmth and happiness of childhood in contrast to the cold of the Protectorate, the theme of *regressus ad uterum*, the return to maternal and even prenatal serenity.[15] It is the source of his love for animals and the humble things around him, especially things without edges – soft, ovular objects that bring warmth into his solitude, though they too are defenceless and in need of comfort. "You will be most forlorn when objects leave you. Objects do not ask questions; they say yes to everything. Objects would be wonderful lovers."[16]

Orten too is a Prague pilgrim. Halas says as much: "Love, purity and compassion were his bag and baggage as he journeyed, pilgrim and poet, to the frost. He would come to rest with them at the gate of fear and alongside the abysses of night . . . "[17] He was a pilgrim who left youth during calamitous times. "So young, so cruelly young and barely mature/that in my youth I resemble/the king of a vanished kingdom."[18] Orten spent the last three years of his life in Prague – he was originally from Kutná Hora – in unmitigated hardship and privation, in the squalour of sublet rooms, in hiding and without regular income (he occasionally shovelled snow).[19] He was aware of his role as a stymied pilgrim;[20] like the poets of Group 42 he knew he was only a passively recording "witness" (*svědek*): "I was born for nothing on earth but to bear witness."[21] Yet he rejects the epithet "limping": other people limp – evil people.

> You ask what I use to help me walk. I've heard something about word crutches. I don't identify with that expression. Crutches, yes, since we get to our feet with difficulty, we're weak and stumble. But what I have in mind are legs, word legs, legs with heels, soles, toes, calves, knees, too, strong legs, delicate and slim legs, small hurried and shuffling legs, drunk and daring, skipping legs and legs that tread on their tips, on the tips of hard vowels! Legs, the little legs of my Czech! If (to put the right word to it), if they let me! Who? The mutes, the people with crutches of clubs, with guns and cruelty, with crutches of stupidity, hatred and arrogance, with crutches of cold, nothingness and calculation, with crutches of many nondescript streets. If only they'd let me live! I'd run. I'd reach my goal. I'd compete with the wind![22]

The pilgrim writes incessantly. As the end approaches, he shines more and more brightly, like an oil lamp about to go out. Abundance in the midst of misery can be explained by a forced maturation, by the fever of a life hanging by a thread, by the torment of the presentiment of death. Besides, during those years of suspicion and stymied human relationships he had little choice but to entrust the exuberance of his thoughts to paper. They were a dialogue with himself, the words of a man finding his way in the dark. He left behind three well-ordered notebooks which he called, according to their covers: *Modrá kniha* (Blue Book, 1938–9), *Žíhaná kniha* (Striped Book, 1939–40) and *Červená kniha* (Red Book, 1940–1). Unlike Kafka's *Tagebücher* or the notebooks of the Romantic poet Karel Hynek Mácha, they contain more than notes on readings, quotations from other writers, dreams, letters and autobiographical passages, for Orten inserts his own poems among the fragments as reflections of his everyday sufferings. The diary is therefore neither a repository of documents and sketches nor a springboard to or hinterland of creation; it is creation itself, a complete literary work, a genre *sui generis*, in short, a work of poetry in both prose and verse. Orten converses with his notebooks as though they were living persons, women he loved (*kniha* is feminine), and in his solitude he pours out his depression to them.[23]

Setting down the impulses of his soul, the capers of his mind, his disillusionments and fears, Orten modulates every sentence to a tonality of lyrical wonder that clothes pain in a veil of myth. In this light even the chilling list of the restrictions imposed on the Jews takes on a poetic quality.[24] Yet rust does not leave iron, as Holan says in *Lemuria*,[25] and the lyrical tone does not alleviate the sting of the despair he tries so hard to keep at bay. "I long for a big, juicy apple. I long for a short walk, biting and full of frost. I long for freedom."[26]

Orten takes up one of the dominant motifs of Prague's demonic nature: obsession with nothingness, eternal error ("to err eternally, until attaining purity"),[27] the nightmare of an insurmountable wall, the feeling of vanity ("I am like you," he says to a canary. "From Canaryland. Born into vanity"),[28] the awareness of guilt. Orten, like Josef K., lives between the narrow walls of a rented room as a condemned innocent. "Poslední báseň" (Last Poem, 24 September 1940) is a litany of self-accusation:

> I am guilty of the smell that smells,
> of the vain longing for a father,
> of verses, I know, for lost love,
> of shame and silence and an earth full of grief,
> of the sky and the Lord who has severely shortened my days
> in a paradise seemingly dead.[29]

If I suffer it is because I cannot be without guilt. I am guilty because I am condemned. And I accept a punishment whose reason I do not know. I accept my neighbours' guilt by declaring myself guilty.[30] In his "First Elegy" Orten writes that the condemned, when asked to state their last wish, never ask for mercy for fear of inconveniencing the judge, who will not be able to grant their request; instead they ask for tobacco, a meal and a sip "that wets the throat,/the throat that will be strangled". "Understanding, quick", they pretend to have tasted that wine "by leave of the hangman".[31] "Take pity on the hangmen, walk straight to the gallows/and sing, sing to the end!"[32]

In so hopeless a situation writing poetry was like breathing. Poetry alone, written day after day, kept him from collapsing under his depression. Poetry, which came to him in a melodic flow (though it did not shun artifice), was the only possible defence for his threatened existence and cure for his lost freedom. As he had written to Halas in 1938: "I want to be a poet with all my heart and more; I want to die for it."[33] His three years of persecution in the twofold estrangement as Prague pilgrim and Jew without a country made Orten's attachment to the "thing called poetry" even more tenacious: it was a fearful mass consuming his entire organism, bleeding him white, poetry as obstinacy, a barrier repelling death even as it was devoured by worms, searching for the essence of man in the impenetrable nothingness around him, yet retaining a ray of hope even as the candle burned quickly at both ends, because "after infinity the Ninth still remains".[34]

Orten overcomes the void of those wicked years with a kind of poetic madness. "This alone is my world, my hope, my faith: writing, writing to the very end."[35] The greater the horror around him grows, the greater his efforts to transform enervating tension into a creative act, as though everything threatening him were only a spur to writing. The pilgrim was well aware he would not change anything, because poetry is not hellebore to heal the unbridled mind and everything is predestined and immutable: "The stone was given,/the stone was given!"[36] And yet one must follow one's destiny, writhe in inextricable absurdity, seek salvation in oneself and give meaning to what is most desperate; one must make the most of one's possibilities before they come and take one away.

18

Foreign visitors to the Bohemian capital have often played the role of pilgrim as well. The protagonist of the mediocre novel *The Witch of Prague. A Fantastic Tale* (1891) by F. Marion Crawford (1854–1909) is a pilgrim.[1] The book is a hotchpotch of tediously minute descriptions, though its detailed topographical references incline one to believe that Crawford, who was born and spent a good deal of his life in Italy, knew Prague quite well.

The gloomy figure of the Wanderer, the scenes in the Jewish Cemetery, the character of the hot-headed Jew Israel Kafka (who resembles Karásek's Ganymedes and whose consumption he shares), the *secese* milieu of the sorceress Unorna (*únor* is Czech for February), the motif of life prolonged (Unorna keeps an old man in suspended animation), the horrific, humpbacked figure of the Oriental Keyork Arabian and his mummy cabinet, the portrayal of the Old Town with its labyrinth of filthy, narrow streets and decrepit houses, the repeated evocation of the sadness weighing upon the capital since the Battle of White Mountain – all this consciously places the novel within the framework of Prague myths.

As the novel begins, the Wanderer appears among the throng praying in the Týn Church by the faint glimmer of the candles for the dead. He then enters U zlaté studny (The Golden Well) in Karlova Street in search of the woman he loves. The porter, who has a fair beard reaching almost to his waist and wears a dark green uniform with gold lacings, leads him into a winter garden teeming with a host of luxuriant plants and tropical trees, a veritable subterranean Eden, a "royaume de la féerie" filled with lianas, Oriental roses and birds of paradise, in which Hadaly, a manikin constructed by Edison, lives in Villiers de l'Isle-Adam's *L'Ève future*. Here he is welcomed by the enchanting Unorna, who is dressed in white, has a diadem of red-gold hair and is enthroned on a high, carved chair beneath a lush palm tree, an ambiguous *secese* figure worthy of Švabinský.

The Wanderer has come to Prague in search of the girl he loves, a journey that has taken him around the world. Although Unorna does everything in her power to make him forget the girl – she has fallen in love with the Wanderer – and to win him with necromancy and the help of the sinister Keyork, he will find his Beatrice in the Bohemian capital. And all this nonsense, all these thrown-together bits of horror stories are mere pretexts for the Wanderer to roam through misty, dark, mournful Prague, for his ravings on the city's tormented nature.

19

In his proclivity for walks and fondness for sophistry, the *chodec*, the pedestrian, in Czech letters is virtually identical to the "pilgrim", the only difference being that instead of moving against the allegorical background of an abstract walled-in city, the pedestrian proceeds through a pedantically exact Baedeker-true Prague landscape.

In the *Pražské obrázky* (Prague Pictures) cycle of his verse collection

Má vlast (My Country, 1903) the poet Jaroslav Vrchlický defines himself a number of times as *chodec, chodec samotář* (solitary pedestrian) and *zpožděný chodec* (belated pedestrian).[1]

The student Jordán, protagonist of Vilém Mrštík's novel *Santa Lucia*, is an indefatigable pedestrian, a melancholy walker, who, as we have seen, loves his adoptive city as if it were a woman. Jordán's perambulations at every hour of the day and night, in every season, especially in the mist, provide Mrštík with an opportunity for composing a musical series of *vedute* with reflections, flashes of light and Impressionistic brush strokes. But Prague's indifferent, fickle beauty stands in tragic contrast to the loneliness and despair of the young man from the provinces, who will find his death there. Jordán's feverish last walk is an uncommonly cheerless spectacle: Mrštík wishes to show that the Prague pedestrian can be at odds with the city and a victim of her inconstancy and demonic nature.

Apollinaire also contributes to the myth of the Prague pilgrim in the story "Le passant de Prague" (1902), in which he strolls through the Bohemian capital with Isaac Laquedem, a reincarnation of the Wandering Jew. Apollinaire's Ahasuerus is every bit a match for the wayfarer-philosopher of the Bohemian tradition. His even-paced steps ("like those of someone who, having a long walk ahead of him, does not wish to arrive at his destination exhausted") and calm acceptance of life ("I am not travelling the Way of the Cross; my roads are happy")[2] make Isaac Laquedem a close relative of Čapek's limping pilgrim.

Apollinaire's suggestive story and Aragon's *Le paysan de Paris* come together in Vítěslav Nezval's *Pražský chodec* (The Prague Pedestrian, 1938). Nezval's *chodec*-clochard (Nezval himself) wanders with the leaping rhythm of his poetry, a caper unto exhaustion, a conjurer's cartwheel, a geyser of metaphors – fluttering through churches, dives, bridges, cafés, pubs, churches and theatres, searching through the winding labyrinth of the streets for the city's hidden miracles and mystery on the eve of difficult times.

Nezval uses the filter of Paris to rediscover his menaced city, soon to be a target of lightning bolts, a nest of ominous birds of the night. Strange as it may seem, certain attributes of Prague – its Gothic-novel grotesque, its links to astrology, the relics of its junk dealers – coincide with the predilections of the Surrealist movement to which Nezval belonged. From this point on, Prague poets will be caught up in his reliquary of mouldy Marché aux Puces bric-à-brac.

Unlike Josef Čapek's *poutník*, who observes events like a cold, lethargic, pensive bird, Nezval's *chodec* lacks the "joy of meditation";[3] he rushes restlessly through the wonders of Prague without lingering to probe or judge. Yet Nezval feels a link between his pedestrian and the limping pilgrim (whom he also calls the *hrbatý chodec*, "hunchbacked pedestrian"),[4] if only in that they both equate the miraculous with the fleeting quality of existence. "The task of the pedestrian may in fact seem such a high ideal *because* life is fleeting."[5] Everything in his exploration of Prague breathes of the miraculous, and everything is like the butterfly held prisoner in the crystal ball he contemplates together with Breton in Přemyslova Street in the display window of a cleaners, a disquieting object combining lepidopteran futility (the Čapeks' mayflies again) with the magic of prognostication, and connected in Nezval's mind with the birth of Aube, the child Breton conceived in Prague.[6]

20

"Prague was more beautiful than Rome," Jaroslav Seifert states at the beginning of his poem "Světlem oděná" (Arrayed in Light, 1940),[1] using a comparison that has occurred to a number of visitors, including the sculptor Rodin.[2] The poem describes the drunken foray of an enchanted pilgrim through Prague during the days of the Nazi occupation: from Saint Vitus' Cathedral to the Golden Lane, Belvedere, the Charles Bridge, all the way to the Jewish Cemetery and back through Malá Strana to the Castle. Despite frequent allusions to the suffering and malaise of those woeful times, Seifert provides us with the rare image of a luminous Prague woven of melodious strands of light and dancing on point. Throughout Seifert's verse Prague is a symbol of spring blossoming anew, a tree eternally rejuvenating and sprouting fresh foliage.

Seifert reaches back in time to the period preceding the Poetist avant-garde, to Vrchlický and his cycle *Pražské obrázky* (Prague Pictures), in which the city on the Vltava is synonymous with springtime, "a sea of greenery and flowers",[3] all frenzied chirping. Vrchlický, who makes a brief appearance in Seifert's poem "Hradčany při západu" (The Hradčany at Sunset) complete with "walrus moustache" and "nicotine-yellowed fingers",[4] also poses as a *poutník* before whose eyes, in the glimmer of twilight, the Castle "emerges from the darkness like a fata morgana".[5]

For Seifert the theme of spring is a pledge that Prague will endure despite the passing of time, the mutability of the things of this world, the fell tyranny of its Calibans. There is, however, another motif pervading the frames of this tracking shot: that of return, a return to Prague as a refuge for the afflicted and harbour for castaways. This is a frequent motif in Czech poetry during the German occupation. It occurs, for example, in Josef Hora's melancholic verse epic *Jan houslista* (Jan the Violinist, 1939), whose hero returns to his native land, the places of his youth, overcome by longing. During those years poets who had previously been enamoured of foreign "wonders" suddenly saw a bed of roses in every Bohemian shrub, royal gold and purple in every rag. The swallows return to the nest. After adventures in the labyrinth of the world, Seifert, champion of a generation advocating exoticism, flights to Paris and beyond (his Poetist friend Biebl roamed as far as remotest Java), found the paradise of the soul in the oppressed city of Prague. For it is written: "I shall die in my nest" (Job 29:18).

21

The years of the Nazi occupation saw another pedestrian stalking Prague, the *vratký kráčivec* (unsteady walker) of Vladimír Holan's poem "První Testament" (First Testament, 1940).[1] So thin that he "could sleep inside a hair", the *kráčivec* or "the everyday personified" (*všednost sama*) crisscrosses the distressed metropolis throwing sweet crumbs to the birds. He is ominous and somnambulist like a creature brought to life by Doctor Caligari, and although he winds a scarf tightly around his neck "he does not suppress his guttural sobs". As he moves forward, the lethargic "seeming dead" awaken and come down to the street. In the throng the *kráčivec* picks up bits of conversation, mangled discourse, trite abuse, greetings, the cries of news vendors and street hawkers: *Abfälle der Umgangssprache*, verbal detritus that piles up into a kind of *Merzdichtung*. Following his morning walk the sad *kráčivec* returns to his "tomb". This gloomy specimen, who has his origins in the dances of death of the Bohemian Baroque, fits well into the frightening *Panoptikum* Holan painted during the war, into his chilling cinema of ghosts and lemurs, his "infernaliana" projected by the smoking mushroom of a crooked oil lamp.

There is a close relationship between Holan's *kráčivec* and the *noční chodec*, the "nocturnal pedestrian", an important figure for the poets and painters who came together in Group 42 during the occupation. One comes across the *noční chodec* fleetingly in Nezval's poem "The Devil" as early as 1926. Now, however, he becomes the protagonist of an entire period in Czech art and letters. The poets and painters of Group 42 resolved to describe in obsessive Surrealistic detail the most desolate aspects of the metropolis, placing special emphasis on the sordid existence in the industrial slums ringing the city where the houses are lost amid swamps and weeds.[2] No more wonders like those discovered by Nezval on the eve of the Great Darkness, only dense air and malaise in the outlying districts of Holešovice, Dejvice, Košíře, Nusle, Podbaba – the desperate grief of Prague under the constraints of the Protectorate. František Gross paints the Libeň gas reservoir, an evil thing wedged between barrack-like tenements, as a huge, poisonous mushroom looming over the city.[3]

Picket fences, shanty towns, crumbling slum dwellings, walls pockmarked like tarantulas, deserted tram termini, aqueducts, slaughterhouses, street lamps atop high poles, huge depots of refuse and *tandlmark* odds and ends, love hotels, rat-trap taverns, tarred urinals, *réclames* smeared across rundown buildings – such is the grey landscape of the Group's pictures and verses. Only one painter, Kamil Lhoták, does not follow their lead; he goes back to the beginning of the century in his imagination, re-evoking jalopies ripe for the graveyard, motorcycles with sidecars, montgolfiers, biplanes, petrol advertisements and old-time race cars with the passion of a collector. He depicts aerostats with such fervour one would say he belongs to the brotherhood of balloonists in Jules Verne's *Robur le conquérant* who fiercely defend their "ballons dirigeables" against the supporters of flying machines.

The nocturnal pedestrian is represented most often in the paintings of František Hudeček.[4] A mysterious messenger in the cold, starry winter night, he enters the military uniformity of the tenements. A dim light seeping from street lamps painted blackout blue, electric torch beams and starlight all converge on him; they spray him with the twinkling glitter of Christmas tree sparklers. He is trapped and hidden as in a puzzle, a geometrical spell, a web of beams tracing occasional broad circles, the target of a shooting match of nocturnal lights. The outlying districts become the theatre of a gloomy yet luminous sea, a cosmic mystery, and the pilgrim-pedestrian, party to the magic of the night – as if just down from Mount Sněžka in Mácha's "Pout' krkonošská" – seems himself a jumble of shooting stars and refulgent trails. The long rows of street lamps with metal lids tower over him like the candelabra held above the head of Karl Roßmann by the liveried servants in the winding corridors of Pollunder's country house in *America*.[5] He harbours something of the old Prague belief in the stars and their influence on the fate of man.

Hudeček's stellar pedestrian is similar to the nocturnal pedestrian of the poet Jiří Kolář, who is also called *ranní chodec* (morning pedestrian), *kolemjdoucí* (passer-by) and *svědek* (witness).[6] Since he moves within surroundings of dismal poverty, amidst slum blocks where "long mouldy tablecloths . . . hang from the sky in shreds",[7] one can imagine him as tiny as Holan's *kráčivec* sucked dry by witches. Many of Kolář's long polyphonic odes came into being during his night-time walks or as dawn broke along the ugly, filthy, starving working-class districts, which he invokes, litany-like: "sad hungry dog torn from the chain and howling at the sky".[8]

The "Stations of the Cross" of his pedestrian, an insignificant out-sider, are the pubs, dance floors, waiting rooms, goods-train stations, "tat-tered curtains of advertising posters",[9] bridges, "hollow lyre strings of slum dwellings".[10] He bursts into the heart of these wretched dwellings making them transparent, revealing their shoddy goods and threadbare chattels.

Kolář's harsh, rough-hewn style – scraps of dialogue, digressions, ejaculations and drastic metaphors – wonderfully expresses the seediness, the teeming of the amorphous masses which, in both Kolář and Holan, evokes associations with food: "Invisible hands knead the dough of pedestrians on the pavement's pastry board."[11] Yet musical analogies, bursts of imagery and hosts of angels – perhaps alighting from apothecary signs, perhaps brothers to Halas's angels of death – worm their way into the trivial fabric. Kolář is capable of striking sudden transcendental sparks with his *Poesie der Banalität*. A concert of angels accompanies his depictions of broken marriages and marital infidelity among the poor, his walks through a shabby, rank world, and it is of little consequence that the angels are often crude fairground souvenirs. The squalor of the settings does not prevent him from intensifying the mystery, the space of night.

Prague pilgrims of the occupation period wander and gesticulate wildly. In the paintings of František Gross the pedestrian is transformed into a "man-machine" (*člověk-stroj*), an Arcimboldesque Meccano, a fren-zied collection of levers, wheels, pistons and bolts, a leaden figure lacking the lightness of Hudeček's pilgrim, a coil of stellar rays in which the arcane sextants of Rudolfine astrology seem to return to life. In some of Ivan Blatný's poems the pedestrian becomes a *kolemjdoucí*, a passer-by, an automaton, a minor clerk clumsily sauntering about the city like a slapstick comic, a grey being given to pausing in front of shops and dreaming, with an occasional touch of eccentricity or madness.[12]

But to return to the images of Hudeček and Kolář, I begin to doubt that all the motion, the zigzag is anything but an illusion; I wonder whether the pedestrian, drugged by the damp, heavy fumes of the outskirts, suspended in a knot of stellar rays, is not actually standing still in deathly silence, blocking the streets like the *nehybný poutník*, the immobile pilgrim depicted by František Janoušek, one of the favourite painters of Group 42. Nezval's pedestrian gleaned the iridescent foam, the glitter of eternal beauty of the threatened city, while the nocturnal pedestrian passes through the sordid "labyrinth" of the outlying districts without illusions, without wonder and, like a fallen angel, without any hope of "paradise". Pilgrimage and pov-erty have become a tautology. There is no redemption. There are no spectacles to turn a dunghill into a mountain of joy, a slum into a palace.

22

The long rows of towering street lamps, the emaciated oil lamps in the hovels of the poor, the glow and cold reflections of light in the slums play a prominent role in the paintings and poetry of Group 42 (and in the photographs of Miroslav Hák, who was a member). "The dawn crushes the bedbugs of the lamps' bleary eyes,"[1] Kolář writes in one poem, and in another: "The lamps' tongues have grown wooden."[2] Blatný speaks of "the gas lanterns' yellowed autumn teeth"[3] and ends a landscape description with: "It is a Saturday evening from the age of gas lamps/as in a picture by Kamil Lhoták/with a sleepwalking girl gazing at the ball of the moon."[4] In several series of photographs by Jiří Sever – who was close to Group 42 and took pictures of shanties, ramshackle buildings and fence slats – and especially in the series *Maskovaná Lucie a jiná setkání* (Masked Lucy and Other Encounters, 1940–2), we find swooning lamps enveloped in mist, lamps projecting from desolate walls, hearse lamps and long lamp shadows – the blacked-out lights of wartime.[5]

One could write a study of Prague writers' treatment of their city's ambiguous lighting, its glow softened by abundant fog, its chthonic phosphorescence. "The lanterns on the bridge/chatter their glass teeth," says Jiří Wolker in his poem "Návrat" (Return, 1921).[6] In "Description of a Struggle" Kafka writes, " . . . for the Moldau and the quarter on the further bank lay together in the dark. A number of lights burning there teased the eye."[7] Then there are the gas lanterns that shine with a dying refrain in Paul Leppin's "Prager Geisterroman" *Severins Gang in die Finsternis*: "Outside, the storm split the rattling glass of the lanterns in two . . . An early lantern shone in front of the Kreuzherrnkirche, filling the air with glassy colours . . . The electric lamps, already glowing, hung over the trees like moons."[8] In Leppin's novel not only Prague has lanterns but the Prague sky as well: "The late summer stars burned like red paper lanterns."[9]

Severin, the protagonist, belongs to the family of nocturnal pedestrians wandering in amazement through a mysterious, infernal city aglow with faint *Gaslaternen*. "It had grown dark and Prague spread before his feet with weeping lights . . . The city lay beneath him in a valley. Light shone here and there like the eyes of a distant sleepy animal."[10] Severin is twenty-three years old, has left school and works every morning in an office where ill humour and cold steal their way into his body. He returns home exhausted in the afternoon, throws himself on his bed and sleeps until evening. Then, *as soon as the lanterns are lit*, he roams through the Chinese shadow pantomime of the streets in the midst of beckoning, unwholesome apparitions, all of which could wear a label saying *absonderlich/Made in Prague*. Pale, restless, tormented by fears, moving with the wind like a reindeer, he wanders from place to place, from *Nachtkaffee* to tavern, finding no peace.

There is something tired, fragile and hopeless, a boundless, sobbing *Zärtlichkeit* in the brittle fabric of the novel. There is also a link between the feverish, unsettled quality of Leppin's protagonist and the ephemerality of his loves, the anxiety and immoderate curiosity with which he wanders about the "labyrinth" in exhausting nocturnal perambulations and the volatile sensuality that drives him from woman to woman, the glow of intoxication and the hopeless melancholy that inevitably ensues.

According to Max Brod, Leppin is "the true singer of the Old Prague passing away in pain . . . a poet of eternal disillusionment".[11] His "pedestrian" is a frightened shade in a shuddering, haunted city full of nocturnal miracles and glowing lanterns, afraid of the light of day. For, as Mácha says, "the candle has its thief in the sun".[12]

23

The Comenian pilgrim encounters all kinds of astronomers and astrologers along his journey through the labyrinth of the world, men who plot horoscopes and make prophecies by studying the conjunctions and oppositions of heavenly bodies. Mr Ubiquitous leads him to a balcony where they are setting ladders against the sky and catching at stars to measure their orbits with rulers, twine, weights and compasses. The pilgrim is delighted by this game, yet he soon notes that when the stars do not dance to the stargazers' tune they complain of the *anomalitas coeli*.[1]

Astrology is a constant attribute of the nature of Prague, especially during the age of Rudolf II. Mikuláš Dačický z Heslova mentions falling stars, tailed phantoms, winged dragons and strange fires in the firmament a number of times in his memoirs of the period between the late sixteenth and early seventeenth century.[2]

The age of Rudolf II teemed with meteorists, astrologers and "diviners of clouds"[3] who deduced presages of disaster from the stars, catching the scent of the future like hunting dogs. Prague offered refuge to Tycho Brahe and Kepler. The passage of melancholy but fiery phenomena across the heavens announced plagues and complications, collapses, routed armies and depopulation of the countryside.

I will never have my future read by the wax doll of a fortune-teller who swells her chest, shakes her head and looks me over with a hostile eye from a glass case in Pigalle. Yet Rudolf II's courtiers all burned to know their "nativity", which the astrologers often devised with the most obvious of tricks. The Emperor himself was impatient to learn the meaning of the fiery vapours that streaked across the sky, hanging over the threatened city like arrows in Klee.

In Jiří Karásek ze Lvovic's drama *Král Rudolf* (King Rudolf, 1916) Rudolf's mistress Gelchossa characterizes the sovereign as a "dreamer whose nature/is deception of the senses/a dreamer to whom/only the stars and faraway voices speak".[4] And Madách, in the eighth scene of *The Tragedy of Man*, has Rudolf, who has just awoken from a bad dream, ask Kepler to draw up his horoscope. Madách's Kepler, who appears as one of the many reincarnations of Adam in the history of mankind, does in the end undertake the vain profession of soothsaying with the aid of his *famulus* Lucifer to satisfy the lust for gold of his frivolous wife Barbara (the reincarnation of Eve), who then betrays him with Rudolf's courtiers.

24

Rudolfine astrology is permeated by an anxiety, a sense of instability that tormented the period. The following lines by Seifert might serve as its epigraph: "The telescopes are blind for fear of the universe/and the fantastic eyes of the astrologers/were drunk by death."[1]

The king's mantle is a mirror of the stars in the firmament. The two court astronomers seem to have caught the Emperor's ill humour, his uncertainty, his tainted soul, his melancholia. Max Brod emphasizes the gloomy anxiety of one of them in his novel *Tycho Brahes Weg zu Gott*. Tycho, a Chagallian patriarch, arrived in Prague at the Emperor's invitation, tired and ill and with a host of students, family members and servants, after wandering the length and breadth of Europe.

Rudolf II and his two astronomers shared an apprehension of the mutability of fate as well as a yearning for the unknown and awe at the supreme harmony of creation. Each of them could have repeated the words of Nezval's "wondrous wizard":

> I saw life in infinite metamorphoses
> and blessed the human desire
> to hasten after new stars
> flaring up and going out
> behind the glass window of night.[2]

The love of "curiosities" and arcane phenomena increased the longing of Rudolf's age for the dark signs concealed in the movements of the fiery celestial bodies and, consequently, a burning interest in the "speculative arts". In Karásek's *Král Rudolf* the Emperor asks Arthur Dee, who has recently returned from a journey abroad, "Are there any new discoveries in the occult sciences? Have you brought me the most recent interpretations of the symbol of the salamander? Have you found out anything new about the magnetic stone, the *asemos*, about the rim of the sun and the moon?" He adds, "I have been told that in Saint Vitus' Cathedral mysterious fires flare up and move in the darkness of night. What enigmatic times we live in! What wondrous events are drawing near! How I wish to know the inscrutable Unknown that shrouds us and sends us signs like those distressing, terrifying fires."[3]

The chronicles of the period give accounts of nocturnal suns, talking cats, bells that refuse to ring, streams of boiling water bursting into chancels and meandering their way to the altar. "A strange thing has come to light in Bohemia," Dačický records. "A Jewess in Prague gave birth to an animal, a live bear, which creature ran about the room and scratched itself behind the ear and died."[4]

People feared the imminent end of the world and worried about the progressive expansion of the earth's limits. "Some Dutchmen from the Netherlands," Dačický notes, "sailed very far along a new, hitherto unknown course; they saw great empty expanses of land and water, running into a sea of ice, through which they had to cut a path, and facing great danger fighting white bears. Unable to continue owing to the ice and cold, they returned to their country, albeit not all of them and without profit. Only the Lord GOD knows where and when we will come to the end of the world!"[5]

"Und die Komet strahlte blutrot am Himmel und in Böhmen war Krieg." Frequent cawing of the raven forecasts rain; comets announce long series of wars. The constant wars, constant plagues, the Turkish menace, the religious persecution – they all made life seem more ephemeral, fleeting, and increased the hunger for divination. One need only point out Wallenstein's passion for horoscopes, his belief in the influence of the stars.

25

In *Román Manfred Macmillena* (The Novel of Manfred Macmillen, 1907) Karásek ze Lvovic expresses the longing of the Rudolfine period in the following terms: "The race of the astronomers is extinct; the alchemists' fires have gone out. Nor does Tycho Brahe or Kepler draw up horoscopes for the tormented Rudolf any more."[1]

The astrologer is a central character in the mythology of Prague, a character who at times becomes one with that of the alchemist. Even if they do not walk through fire and descend to the shades below, these prognosticators, like shamans, investigate the conjunctions of the stars and extract responses so obscure that even the Sphinx or Oedipus would be hard put to interpret them. Their elixirs and plague remedies border on downright fraud and reveal the cunning of con artists.

In Svátek's novel *Astrolog* the swindling toady alchemist Scotta claims the ability "to read the destiny of men in the stars" and pro-claims himself "disciple of the divine science of astrology".[2] He invents nativities for Don César de Austria, the illegitimate son of Kateřina Stradová and Rudolf II, and for Zuzana, the daughter of the nobleman Korálek z Těšína.[3] In the tragedy *Král Rudolf* (King Rudolf) by Vítězslav Hálek, a "telescopist" (*kukátkář*) warns the Emperor against his brother Matthias.[4]

The Dadaist clowns Voskovec and Werich parodied the Rudolfine astrologer in their musical comedy *Golem* (1931) in the slapstick figure of Břeněk, who fashions an artificial woman for his sovereign (of the race of golems and Prague robots, that is, in alembics), an (alas!) frigid "materialized moonbeam" named Sireal.[5] In a story by Věra Linhartová entitled "Polyphonic Pastime", Dr Altmann, a shady psychiatrist and Hoffmannesque wizard who wanders about Prague as if it were a foggy metaphysical insane asylum, treats a set of patients including Verlaine and Rimbaud, Dylan Thomas, Nijinsky, Billie Holiday and Charlie Parker plus a heavy drinker named Hamilton, an astrologer funambulist who observes the sky from a building atop a vertiginous spiral staircase on Petřín Hill and tied to a balustrade "with a system of ropes and pulleys" to keep him from falling.[6]

The meanderings of nocturnal pedestrians in a city perpetually men-aced by death-portending comets are a reflection of heavenly trajectories, drunken orbits, a floundering in the void, a constant fear of flying off track, vertigo, falling.

26

Of all the astrologers and professors of sorcery, Tycho Brahe (1546–1601) has most coalesced with the demonic nature of Prague, where he arrived in 1599 at the behest of Rudolf II. Little is changed by the fact that he spent most of his time in Benátky, eastern Bohemia, at a hunting castle converted into a lavish observatory similar to the one at Uranienborg (Arx Uraniae) on the small island of Hveen in the Øresund, which King Frederick II of Denmark had given him during better days.[1]

If a merganser diving into water means rain, then the name Tycho heralds the deluge of mist called Prague. The German humorist Albert

Brendel (1856) called him Tichodejprág.[2] He is part of the mystery of Prague not only because he moved within a setting of astrolabes, hourglasses, armillary spheres and sextants but for his large artificial nose, which lent him the sinister appearance of a rhinoplastic manual's dummy. According to Max Brod, the nose was a prosthesis of silver and gold, replacing the one he lost in a duel over a lady while a student in Rostock. Tycho liked people to feel it, and his opponents insinuated that he used it as an alidade for his astronomical observations,[3] as if his face consisted of astronomer's instruments in the manner of Arcimboldo's paintings. A further grotesque detail is the legend that he died at a banquet of a burst urinary bladder.[4] The "loquacità di Ticone" referred to by Galileo also seems to coincide with the nature of the city on the Vltava.[5]

Tycho's tombstone in the Gothic Týn Church glimmers like a source of magic in many stories with Prague settings: the red Slivenec-marble sculpture of the goateed student of the stars shows him in a somewhat loutish light wearing heavy armor, gazing upwards with a crick in his neck, resting his right hand on an armillary sphere and gripping a sword with his left.[6] "Cette église contient la tombe de l'astronome Tycho Brahé,"[7] the Wandering Jew Isaac Laquedem whispers to Apollinaire as they walk through the Old Town. Karásek ze Lvovic's Manfred Macmillen roams in the faint light of the Týn Church near the tomb.[8] In *The Witch of Prague*, Crawford's Wanderer contemplates the grave twice: at dawn when the church is filled with pale, mournful-eyed people, and at sunset in the empty church, when he meets the sinister Keyork Arabian near the tombstone.[9]

In Brod's telling Tycho's mystery is increased by the presence of a dwarf who follows him everywhere, a pale redheaded hunchback named Jeppe (of the sort found in a Boito libretto), a mite who jumps about his master yelping like a bloodhound and whom the astronomer saved from being roasted alive by a gang of *Landsknechte* in a Gipsy camp. During the austere banquets, Jeppe, dressed in a scarlet buffoon costume, sits curled up at Tycho's feet, waiting to be tossed a morsel.[10] A mysterious bond unites the pustulous cripple to the astronomer with the false nose.

27

Walking up Thunova Street towards the Castle Steps, "anyone who knows the history of Prague", Jiří Karásek states in the novel *Ganymedes*, "involuntarily recalls the melancholy reign of the moribund Rudolf II, who buried himself alive beneath the heavy shadows of astrology, magic and alchemy".[1] In actual fact, Rudolf II (1576–1611) transferred his residence to Prague Castle seven years after ascending the throne.

The ravings of alchemists, birthday horoscopy, the elixir of life and the philosophers' stone, Tycho Brahe and Kepler, the Golden Lane, the animal and vegetable physiognomies of Arcimboldo, Rabbi Loew and his homunculus Golem, the fearful, misshapen Ghetto, the old Jewish Cemetery and the Emperor's *Kunstkammer* – these are the images, the components of that bewitched kaleidoscope we call Rudolfine Prague.

Residence of the King of Bohemia and Hungary, Lord of Austria and Holy Roman Emperor, Prague enjoyed every advantage civilization and wealth could offer. A host of distillers, painters, alchemists, botanists, goldsmiths, astronomers, astrologers, spiritists, soothsayers, conjurers and professors of the speculative arts swarmed round Rudolf. Charlatanry was rampant. The city teemed not only with would-be sages who talked stuff and nonsense and sold turpeth and rhubarbe-hermodactyl pills in wooden hovels but also with hired thugs, swordsmen and cut-throats from every land under the sun. For them Prague was a land of milk and honey, a Brueghelian *Luilekkerland*. The adventurers and rascals attracted by the Emperor often landed in the dungeon of the White Tower overlooking the Stag Moat.[2] A band of Italian thieves was apparently in cahoots with the conniving grand chamberlain Philipp Lang z Langenfelsu.[3]

As late as 1884 the novelist Alfred Meissner lamented that the Rudolfine Age still lacked its Walter Scott.[4] It was indeed an age worthy of ballads, with the smoke of sorcerers, the obfuscation of mountebanks, the gentle bubbling of alembics and the grim glances of dwarfs. Giordano Bruno paid a visit to Prague in 1588, twelve years before he was burned at the stake. Legend has it that Faust lived there as well. The *Englische Komödianten* arrived in Central Europe at about this time, and their clown, known as *Pickelhering*, began to jest in German.[5] The influx of so many foreigners made the city a melting pot of languages. I only hope the Italian spoken there[6] was less false than what the mealy-mouthed, supposedly Rudolfine characters in crude Romantic tragedies like Josef Jiří Kolár's verbose *Magelóna* (1852) spouted forth.

28

Who was Rudolf II, this patron of luminaries and impostors, at whose court I seem to have lived? "A sage clown and mad poet", according to the ironic formula of Voskovec and Werich?[1] In any case, he inhabited a world of gloom, of abnegation, and one confronts it as one confronts a *finstere Bootsfahrt*, a gloomy voyage.

Rudolf's father Maximilian (1564–76), the son of Ferdinand I, married his cousin Maria, that is, the daughter of Charles V, Ferdinand's brother. Rudolf was therefore the great-grandson of Joanna the Mad by double lineage. Towards the end of 1563, at the age of eleven – he was born on 18 July 1553 – he was invited to Madrid by his uncle Philip II (his mother's brother) to learn the cold, hard ritual of the Spanish court.[2] This court was very different from Maximilian's, where freedom of thought was not quelled and Protestants were held in a certain respect.

Here, in seven years, Rudolf became a perfect "Spaniard", acquiring the customs and masks of that dissembling monarchy. Bigotry, intrigues, religious pomp, suspicion, persecution of heretics, the Inquisition's funeral pyres, the illusion of boundless majesty, vainglory on land and at sea – such was his school.[3] Odd preparation indeed for someone who was to reign in a country jealous of its religious freedom and infected by the disease of heresy. The sullen dynastic system, permeated as it was with subterfuge and suspicion, exerted a fatal influence on the young prince's character: it heightened his morbid shyness, his yearning for solitude, and planted the seeds for the megalomania and persecution complex that later so oppressed him.

Although he was instructed in orthodox Catholicism and the rigours of the Spanish court and although Spanish manners remained in force throughout his reign, Rudolf was a tolerant monarch, perhaps because of his father's example or his love of peace or his certainty that the Catholic party was still small as compared with the Utraquists and the Bohemian Brethren. It is no accident that Rabbi Judah Loew, one of the great sages of Judaism, was his friend and that he received Johannes Kepler, who was persecuted for his Evangelical faith, at his court.

Moreover, the older generation of Catholics was not nearly so implacable and bigoted as the young men of high birth educated by the Society of Jesus, which had arrived in the country in 1556[4] with the fanaticism of the Counter-Reformation. But while the reformers and defenders of tolerance split into small clashing factions, the Catholic group – well-organized, closely knit and supported by the court, the Papal nuncio and the Spanish ambassador – acquired tremendous power.[5] Marriages between the Bohemian and Spanish nobility also played a role in the process. In Bohemia fervent Catholics were known as "Spaniards" (*španělé*).[6] A Prague Spain was born.

29

Rudolf II never ceased reading the Latin poets and spoke a number of languages: German and Spanish best, Czech less fluently. An accomplished amateur in alchemy, the natural sciences, physics, astrology and magic, he spent his time among paintings, objets d'art, cupels, luted crucibles, glass jars, armillary spheres and alembics in the company of alchemists, painters and fortune-tellers, and loved to paint, weave and dabble in inlaying and watchmaking.[1]

He attended sessions of the court council unwillingly and only occasionally; he neglected affairs of state, often entrusting them to the plotters and machiavels of his entourage. He hid from strangers, withdrawing for long periods to the innards of Prague Castle as if it were the Escorial. Reflected a hundred times by pitiless mirrors in candlelight, his wan face – the eyes downcast, the mouth muscles drooping and weary – made him resemble, in the words of Max Brod, "a god in need of help".[2] "He attends mass in a hidden oratory completely enclosed by gratings," his chamberlain Rumpf says of him in Karásek's drama *Král Rudolf*. "He walks only along corridors whose windows are walled except for narrow slits."[3]

It was impossible to distract him from his retorts and superstitious observations,[4] and living a solitary existence he believed the slander of evil tongues, the *ignavum pecus* of the courtiers. Loath to grant audiences, he would keep foreign ambassadors waiting for months in antechambers which, like barber shops, proved hotbeds of gossip. Yet makers of horoscopes, magic mirrors and homunculi had free access to him, even notorious swindlers like Jeronymo Scotta. He sometimes descended from his rooms into the central wing of the Hradčany above the Stag Moat (*Hirschgraben*) to admire the tulip hedges, the acacia-lined walkways, the orangery, the greenhouses, the fountains, statues, arbours, exotic birds and, most of all, the African lion, whose death – according to an oracle – would serve as prelude to his own demise.[5]

Black humour and black thoughts were Rudolf II's downfall. Although he disdained the affairs of government, he was jealous of his power and inclined to invent nonexistent, vindictive persecutors, pouncing suddenly on anyone who aroused his suspicion, exploding in savage outbursts of rage, weaving illogical plans to stamp out presumed enemies and show the others his still undiminished might.[6]

Horoscopes, horoscopes. We see Rudolf in a twisted posture that heightens his frenzied gestures. Mad, he shifts to a diagonal position. Long, menacing shadows, shadows of one obsessed with shadows, chase him dressed in the Spanish fashion – in a black frock of smooth plush trimmed with gold lace and a white ruff – through the corridors of the palace.[7] His was a gloomy penitent's life concealed behind the horrid masks of anger and duplicity.

He enjoyed plunging his devotees from the zenith of favour to the nadir of misfortune. On the night of 26 September 1600 he attacked his chamberlain Wolfgang Rumpf, whom he suspected of plotting to deprive him of the throne.[8] Rumpf rotted in prison for the rest of his life. The same fate awaited another grand chamberlain, Jiří Popel z Lobkovic, and the energetic protestations of the Catholic faction were to no avail in freeing the unlucky man.[9] In *Král Rudolf* Hálek hypothesizes that not even Eva z Lobkovic, whom Rudolf loved, succeeded in obtaining freedom for her father.

After each morbid fit he would fall into state of apathy, withdrawing increasingly into himself and forsaking his duties as ruler in favour of alchemy, the arts and the stars. Meanwhile, the Empire was beset by theological controversies, an insurrection of Transylvanian princes and constant incursions of the Turks. Indeed, all through his fourteen-year reign Moslems and Catholics slaughtered and pillaged one another, as is attested with great passion by the memoirs of Mikuláš Dačický.

In Jiří Karásek's drama the chamberlain Rumpf gives the following description of Rudolf:

> I have known His Majesty ever since he was a child. I accompanied him to the Spanish court of King Philip. I can therefore say that there is no sadder and lonelier creature on earth. We tarried in dark cathedrals until nightfall. I saw him pray fervently. Heaven, it would seem, could only bend to such an assault. Yet he prayed in vain. No sooner did we leave the church than he was unhappy again. He doubted his salvation and feared the punishments of Hell. Here in Prague he seeks refuge as in a monastery. Fearing people, he goes out only at night. He speaks to no one; no one has ever seen him smile. He dresses only in black, and his soul is ever gloomy. Were it not for his fascination with the occult arts, were it not for art, statues, paintings, books, gems and fabrics, all of which he collects with insatiable greed, he would waste away to a most incorporeal shadow.[10]

The hereditary insanity of the family, the effects of the stifling Spanish apprenticeship, the incurable tumour of mistrust, the complex of lese majesty, the fear of the Turks, of his ambitious brother Matthias and of divine forces all combined to magnify the melancholy that blackened and inflamed his blood.

A prey to lust, he sought rapture and relief in the arms of voluptuous courtesans.[11] Irresolute,[12] he never married; moreover, a horoscope had predicted that a legitimate heir would rob him of his throne. He consoled himself with a harem of concubines. Kateřina Stradová, daughter of the court antiquary Jacopo Strada, persevered the longest in his bedchambers, bearing him six children. One of the three boys to whom she gave birth,

Don Julius, is said to have perished at the age of twenty-three at Krumlov Castle after a lascivious and violent life.[13]

A vessel of infamy – and thus a choice morsel for Romantic melodramas – Don Julius (or Don César de Austria or Marquis Julio) is remembered for the bestial murder of his last mistress, the daughter of a barber-surgeon from Krumlov. Having run her through and slit her throat, he chopped her corpse into pieces and flung them about the room. He then gave her a solemn funeral, following her to the grave with the clergy and servants in mourning.[14] "Your soul wallows in the slime of revolting passions," Rudolf cries to him in Kolár's *Magelóna*, "a gloomy host of a hundred crimes teems over you like green lizards in the devil's skull."[15]

30

Rudolf's paranoia grew progressively worse. His choler produced the blackest of moods, and all the apozems, aperients, tinctures of tartar salt, crayfish eyes and powdered stag horn were of no avail. He was suspicious of the Papal nuncio and the entire curia, whose concern for his succession he found intolerable; he was irritated by the chanting of the Hradčany Capuchins, whom he believed to be agents of his persecutors.[1]

He also feared the Jesuits and every kind of religious order because a horoscope had predicted that like Henry III of France he would be killed by a monk. He spoke ill of the Pope, avoided masses and church ceremonies and became hysterical at the sight of a cross.[2] Hence perhaps the constant motif of the agony and disquieting beauty of Christ nailed to a hard wooden cross in Czech literature and Prague culture. Rumour had it that he was possessed by the devil and bewitched by the magic potions of his concubines. That is why, in *Magelóna*, his speech is filled with words of exorcism such as "Patibulum, Patibulum".

Literature has magnified the wickedness of the courtiers surrounding him. Its rancour falls especially on the overweening Philipp Lang z Langenfelsu, a converted Jew of humble origins who did not balk at using a band of highwaymen to carry out his wicked intents. He also maintained an alchemist's laboratory, though his riches came not so much from transmutations as from gifts extorted from petitioners and valuables removed from the Emperor's coffers. Yet even the craftiest of thieves gets caught. Lang was imprisoned in the White Tower on 7 May 1608, where he died a violent death a year later.[3] In the action-filled novel *Pekla zplozenci* (Spawn of Satan, 1862) Josef Jiří Kolár makes Lang (whom he calls Jáchym instead of Philipp) evil incarnate. Coveting the treasures of the deceased alchemist Kurcín (who keeps them in Prague in the Faust House), Lang hatches a plot to eliminate Kurcín's twin sons Jošt and Vilém. He sends hired cut-throats to kill Jošt, then accuses Vilém of having committed the deed at the prompting of the Florentine Sibilla Rezzonica. The plan is unsuccessful at first because Jošt is saved by the prior of Na Slovanech Monastery and Vilém, though already hanging – it really does go too far! – slips alive from the noose and finds refuge in the home of a dolt by the name of Scotta, whose satanic ceremonies happen to attract Rudolf. Lang finally succeeds in having the two Kurcíns – the eponymous "spawn of Satan" – slain, yet he who sows a wind will reap a whirlwind: the horrible dungeons of the White Tower await him. In the comedy *Rabínská moudrost* (Rabbinical Wisdom, 1886), Jaroslav Vrchlický sets Rabbi Loew's austere erudition against the iniquity of Lang, a libertine and prevaricator who steals and dissipates the Emperor's treasures with the help of accomplices and toadies.

But let us return to Rudolf. Melancholy devoured his constitution like a fever. Every word provoked him; every cutting remark infuriated him. He raged wildly, vowed revenge and made a number of attempts at suicide. He spoke only of dying. "He avoids all contact with people," Rumpf says in Karásek's play:

> He whiles away the time alone in his rooms. The golden chalice that he engraved with his own hands lies abandoned among his things . . . He gazes apathetically at tables overflowing with unattended documents of state. There are rumours afoot that Rudolf has died and that the news of his death is being kept from the people. He has not been seen by anyone for the longest time. He does not so much as show his shadow in the chapel. Some say he has gone mad. They remind us that he is the great-grandson of mad Juana of Castile.[4]

After expelling his few loyal ministers over the years, he entrusted the affairs of state to the hands of scullery boys, grooms, trabants and other menials he deemed incapable of removing him from power. Now wholly at the mercy of his servants, he loathed them: they had to look the other way when he undressed. All this weakened the already ailing Empire.

But there is also a strong link between Rudolf's melancholy and the turbid *logos*, the black nature of Prague. In Karásek's *Král Rudolf* the Emperor, walking to the window in the moonlight, dreams of Prague, "sister of mystic souls", being renamed "Rudolf City".[5] In Hálek's tragedy Rudolf rails against the "ingrate city" when, deserted by all, he is forced to relinquish rule to his brother Matthias (23 May 1611).[6] In *Magelóna* Kolár has the Emperor accuse his capital of having become a den of iniquity, a sanctuary of infamy, and imagines it filled with gallows,[7] as though Prague were nothing more than the landscape of scaffolds in Brueghel's *Triumph of Death*.

31

Rudolf kept a number of noted painters and sculptors on whom he lavished gifts, estates and various favours. Arcimboldo, Bartolomäus Spranger, Adriaen de Vries, Johann Hofmann, Josef Heintz, Joris and Jacob Hoefnagel, Pieter Stevens, Ägidius Sadeler, Hans von Aachen, Daniel Froeschl, Roelant Savery, Matthäus Gundelach and many others (mostly from Germany and the Low Countries) constituted a kind of cosmopolitan *École de Prague* around the emperor, its common characteristic being Mannerism.[1] They arrived in groups and were bound by ties of friendship and blood. New masters took the place of those who died or left for other courts and there was a constant bustle of miniaturists, medalists, sculptors, landscapists and painters of *kontrfekty* (fakes), religious tableaux and hunting scenes. Oddly enough, they grew more numerous about 1600, when the ruler's melancholy deepened and his decline grew worse.

Rudolf's desire to embellish his court with artists stemmed from his compulsion for collecting, for accumulating valuable objects, rare items and naturalia. For collecting and hiding his treasures from envious eyes. For caressing them, watching over them jealously, taking pleasure in them like a miser.

Jakub de Strada (Jacopo Strada), superintendent of the Imperial collections, says in Svátek's *Astrolog*:

> The Emperor considers the collections his private property and therefore guards them like the apple of his eye. Only a few visiting crowned heads, a few famous artists have been admitted to these rooms . . . The Emperor regards the picture gallery as his exclusive property, which no one is permitted to touch.[2]

We cannot agree with certain scholars[3] who claim that the paintings adorning the Castle exerted no influence on the development of Czech art if it is true that Karel Škréta, the greatest painter of the Czech Baroque, knew them as a young man.[4]

Rudolf's grandfather Ferdinand I, his father Maximilian II and his uncle Archduke Ferdinand of Tyrol were ardent collectors and archaeologists. Rudolf, however, was unequalled in his passion. He spent huge sums of money on his *Kunst- und Wunderkammer*. He dispatched special commissioners and occasionally the *Hofmaler* themselves all over Europe to purchase paintings, jewelry and exotic implements for him. He ordered the artists in his entourage to make copies of the canvases he was unable to obtain. To prevent damage to *Das Rosenkranzfest*, the Dürer his agents had bought in Venice, he had the painting carried across the Alps by four powerfully built men.[5] His favourite painters were Dürer and Pieter Brueghel.

The *šacmistr* (treasurer) of his collections was, as we have mentioned, the Italian antiquary Jacopo Strada, who had held a similar office at the court in Vienna. The fact that his fair daughter had long since won the Emperor's sullen heart helped Strada to obtain high positions at the Castle for himself and his family, and when he died, in 1588, his son Octavio became director of the collections.

Josef Svátek claims in his novel *Astrolog* that even Strada was allowed to enter the *šackomora*, the precious cabinet of Rudolfine curiosities, only in the presence of the Emperor or with special permission,[6] but his exaggeration can perhaps be explained by the ambiguous role he assigns to the old antiquary as a front for cunning Scotta, king of the *Quacksalber* and swindlers.

32

In Max Brod's novel, the ill, doubt-plagued ruler tells Tycho Brahe that he is seeking *"perfection in stone and metals and on painted canvas"*.[1] And indeed, all the items in his collection – clocks, jewels, even astronomical instruments and freaks of nature – bore the mark of skilful refinement that makes them valuable *objets d'art*.[2] He combined a longing for fullness and the sublime with a love for strange, exotic, "Indian" things, for the gaudy and for baubles with a trace of adventure and wonder.[3]

Rudolf's predilection for the miraculous coincides with the Mannerist taste of the age. Collectors were excited about the merchandise seafaring caravans brought back from the Indies: Cocus de Maledivia, conch-shells, ivory hunting horns, exotic fruits and seafood, earthenware from Cathay, ostrich eggs, feathers of exotic birds, Japanese paintings on paper and silk – they were all called *indianisch*.

The *Kunst- und Wunderkammer* was a goldmine of minute objects put together with microscopic care: minute ivorywork on nutshells, cherry pits and shells, delicate ornamented enamelware. A splendid painting by Joris Hoefnagel may serve as an emblem of Rudolf's great love for tiny things: in it the artist heaps flowers, fruits, butterflies, Eurasian water voles, toads, snails, a locust and every species of insect around a white rose,[4] the kind of withered rose found centuries later in Halas's poems.

Goldsmiths at the Prague court inlaid sharks' teeth in gold as serpents' tongues. Stone polishers chiselled rough crystals, *Handsteine*, into miraculous landscapes, crucifixion scenes and models of mines. Anything odd or outlandish could be considered a "dream" talisman, a pretext for analogizing. Thus people looked at a pointed narwhal tooth and saw the horn of a lovesick unycorn or a clot of amber or a congealed mass of luminiferous ether or the secretion of a mysterious animal. They saw the bone of a giant in the bone of an extinct animal, the claws of a griffin in the horns of an African antelope.

Rudolf imagined stones and plants with strange animal shapes and unusual colours to be sources of supernatural power much as the Incas believed in *huaca*. He had a large number of cameos and rare stones:[5] *Donnersteine* (prehistoric flintstones), two nails from Noah's Ark, double-headed monsters, a crocodile and specimens of bezoar (calcium deposits from the intestines of chamois and ibexes), amulets and bracelets skilfully fashioned from gallstones possessing miraculous powers.

Among the many peculiar objects he collected I might mention the knife swallowed by a peasant during a bout of guzzling and removed nine months later, in 1602, by the barber Master Florian; an iron chair (*Fangstuhl*) that held whoever sat in it prisoner; a musical clock with a gilt lid decorated by a hunting scene of leaping stags; an *Orgelwerk* that performed "ricercars, madrigals and canzoni" by itself; stuffed ostriches; rhinoceros chalices for boiling poisonous potions; a votive medallion of Jerusalem clay; the lump of soil from the Hebron Valley out of which Yahweh Elohim formed Adam; and large mandrake roots (alrauns) in the shape of little men reclining on soft velvet cushions in small cases resembling doll beds. Incidentally, the magical powers of the mandrake, a plant of the potato family, was greatly enhanced when placed under a scaffold. Alrauns, vegetable puppets of the Prague theatre, belong to the same family of man-like figures as the Golem, robots and Kafka's *odradek*.

33

Rudolf II stacked the precious items of his collection at random on shelves and tables, in innumerable cabinets and strongboxes.[1] To acquaint the reader with some of the other objects populating that *verzauberter Raum*, I shall compile an unsystematic inventory and thereby reflect the collection's confusion.

Plaster casts of lizards and reproductions of other animals in silver, *Meermuscheln*, turtle shells, nacres, coconuts, statuettes of coloured wax, figurines of Egyptian clay, elegant mirrors of glass and steel, spectacles, corals, "Indian" boxes filled with gaudy plumes, "Indian" containers of straw and wood, "Indian", that is, Japanese paintings, burnished silver and gilt "Indian" nuts and other exotic objects the great carracks brought from India under full sail, a skin-coloured plaster-covered female torso of the kind the Prague Surrealists so loved, amber and ivory boards for playing dice, a skull of yellow amber, amber goblets, bagpipes, "landscapes" of Bohemian jasper, a small table of enamelled silver, shells of agate, jasper, topaz and crystal, a silver picture in an ebony frame, a bas-relief in oriental alabaster, painted stones, mosaics, a small silver altar, a crystal goblet with a silver lid, a topaz carafe given to Rudolf by a Muscovite delegation, a carafe of "starstone", a glass jug of Bohemian agate with a gold handle, a large topaz drinking vessel in the shape of a lion, ruby-inlaid gold tableware, clay pitchers (some of which are covered with red velvet), a coral ship with figurines, a ship of gilt wood, a tiny ship of silver-plated Cocus de Maledivia, a jewel casket of rock crystal, a casket of mother of pearl, a silver lute, lamina of lapis lazuli, rhinoceros horns, ivory hunting horns, gaudy knives inlaid with gold and gems, porcelain, scraps of silk, globes of various guise including a silver one atop a hypogryph, armillary spheres, measuring instruments, Venetian glassware, an ancient head of Polyphemus, Deianeira and the centaur in silver, medals, maiolica in many colours, anatomical specimens, harnesses, spurs, bridles, rough wooden saddles, domed pavilions, doublets and other booty left by the Turks during their mounted forays, hunting gear, banners, muzzles and collars, every kind of plate, ostrich-egg goblets, sabres, cut-throat daggers, muskets, stilettos, sword canes, mortar pieces, pistols and verdugas. And automata and musical clocks. Clocks, clocks and more clocks. In the shape of a silver boat or a tower with trumpeters . . . [2] I recall the dream Kubin has in Perle in *Die andere Seite*:

> And then I heard all about me a multifarious ticking, and I became aware of a great number of clocks of every size, from church clocks and kitchen clocks to the smallest of pocket-watches. They crept through the meadow like turtles on short stubby legs to the accompaniment of an excited ticking.[3]

Rudolf's collection did in fact include a small turtle containing a clock-work.[4]

From Bohemian garnets to nose saddles, from sea corals to carafes of rhinoceros horn, from treacherous blades with ruby eyes in their handles to *ushebtis* and humming-bird feathers – what stimuli to the imagination! This inventory of jewels, artefacts, silverware, utensils and useless baubles embracing the realms of nature and faraway lands, this mishmash, this convivial properties room strove to be an *orbis pictus*, to reflect the book of God. Moreover, the indiscriminate mixing of various regions and climes corresponded to the picturesque melting pot of Rudolf's city. Nor should we forget the ancient and modern statues, the numismatics, the masses of paintings or the horses Rudolf collected with great fervour, if only to have himself painted in the saddle all heavy armour and martial mien.

34

Tycho Brahe, who visits Rudolf's *šackomora* in Max Brod's novel, shudders at the depression and anguish produced by this "uncontrollable accumulation of objects". "The emperor too seemed frightened in the midst of his treasures."[1]

Rudolf's obsession with objects derived from his longing to fill the void around him, to suppress his fear of solitude, but also from thanatophobia: by assembling a forest of rare gadgets, he hoped to stave off death. If it is true, as Gogol says in "The Portrait", that an auction is like a funeral – think of the gloomy voice of the auctioneer when he bangs his hammer – there is something funereal about Rudolf's prodigious collections, and his galleries are more tombs of the dead than rooms for the living.

Yet the immobility, the immutability was only apparent. The dead objects were relentlessly sinister. They glowered at him from their cages like animals in ambush, and the ones he looked at too often took on his features, mirrored his hypochondria.

A change of climate does wonders for hypochondriacs: it fortifies the brain, cleanses the nerve fluid and rectifies the enzymes as well as the bodily fluids. Yet Rudolf is unable to escape the objects holding him captive. He returns to them at night in the dark glow of large candelabra. And behold, he turns into one of the men-objects of Bracelli's *bizzarrie*, whose bodies are made of sections and boxes for concealing goblets, gems and necklaces. The frog-like creak of the cabinets, the gleam of the crystal and amulets, the sanctimonious idiocy of the *abinzoar*, the fearful eyes of the portraits, the oily sheen of the fabrics, the whisper of the stones interest him far more than affairs of state. In that *huaca* storeroom, in that *Traumland* of fetishes he deciphers the mysteries of the universe as from cucurbits and horoscopes.

In Jiří Karásek's drama Rudolf is a Hamlet, a *král-snivec*, a dreamer king, loath to make decisions, avoiding inquisitive glances and daylight, a wretched shadow in a repository of rarities and antiques, who in the end feels dead among the dead objects surrounding him: "Like the phantom of a king, I play a shadow play with the crown/which destiny has pressed upon my tortured head/like the blossom of a passion flower/nature has impressed the instruments of torture . . . "[2]

35

> And His Majesty dust
> settles lightly on the abandoned throne.
>
> Jaroslav Seifert[1]

Rudolf's collections had an ill-starred destiny. His band of courtiers began to abscond with them during his lifetime. Philipp Lang z Langenfelsu, master thief, master of subreption and well acquainted with the saying that white silver draws black lines, pilfered old coins, jewels, jasper vases and "Indian" rarities every chance he got.[2]

Dačický relates in his memoirs that following the death of Rudolf II on 20 January 1612, one of his chamberlains, the wicked Jeroným Makovský, hoping to be released from prison, revealed the whereabouts of many treasures the Emperor had "hidden and immured". "No one knows where those precious objects, those rediscovered treasures have gone to," Dačický adds, "because during all the strife in Bohemia there was a constant *dryps-draps* . . . "[3]

The collections were abandoned after Rudolf's successor Matthias moved his residence to Vienna. The Thirty Years' War, which began in 1618 with the Second Prague Defenestration, dealt them a number of further blows.[4] Following the Battle of White Mountain, Duke Maximilian of Bavaria took no fewer than one thousand five hundred cartloads of gold and valuables from the Castle as compensation for the assistance he had given Ferdinand II when he withdrew from Prague on 17 November 1620. The Kurfürst of Saxony filled another fifty wagonloads with booty when his army occupied the Bohemian capital in 1631. *Dryps-draps.* Anyone who passed through Prague relieved the Hradčany of a portion of Rudolf's curiosities. Once Jonah had departed the chapel-cave of its innards, the enormous whale supplied whole cartloads of meat, hide and blubber to foreign plunderers.

The worst came when the Swedes captured the Castle and Malá Strana on the night of 26 July 1648. Samson's foxes sowed less ruin in the Philistines' corn than Königsmarck's mercenaries in Rudolf's galleries. It was as if the Swedes had come only to rob the treasures of the hypochondriac sovereign for their queen, Christina, who coveted them. In the course of an unparalleled orgy of theft which, *longe horrendior quam ignis,* also included the palaces of the Czech nobility and the Rožmberk and Strahov libraries, Königsmarck did not forget to take fifty cartloads of gold and silver for himself. *Dryps-draps.* The stolen wealth was carted to Wismar, then shipped to Stockholm. The commission created to draw up the losses after the thieving finale of thirty years of war found only bits of statues, empty frames and a few damaged paintings, including Dürer's *Rosenkranzfest.*

The subsequent fate of the collections, scattered all over Europe,[5] is too involved to go into here. Some survived in spite of everything, however, as if the *huacas* had multiplied by magic. The Archduke Leopold Wilhelm, brother of Emperor Ferdinand III, reassembled a fine group of Rudolf's paintings – consisting largely of the Buckingham Collection auctioned in Antwerp at the end of the war[6] – which was highly admired throughout the seventeenth century and influenced the works of the Baroque painter Petr Brandl.[7]

Beginning with the reign of Charles VI (1711–40), a mediocre sovereign and fanatic religionist, the Habsburgs considered the Castle Gallery a repository and reserve of Vienna's art collections (in the name of centralism) and began to purloin paintings in a new *dryps-draps* that slowly depleted the recently restored collections.[8] In 1749 Maria Theresa lightheartedly sold a number of paintings to the Dresden Gallery to improve her financial situation,[9] and in 1757, during the Seven Years War, when Frederick II of Prussia bombarded the Castle, what was left was piled up in the cellars in such a hurry that a large amount of statuary, porcelain and crystal was broken.

In 1780 Joseph II decided to use the ancient building, pride of the Bohemian people, as an artillery barracks, and canvases and other old, rotten, useless objects had to be removed to make room for ammunition. An auction was announced and a frivolous inventory took place. The best paintings (including Dürer's *Rosenkranzfest*) and those least damaged were valued at a gulden or two, while the inconspicuous or more damaged brought estimates of a few kreutzers. Furthermore, as the statues were appraised according to weight and state of conservation the famous *Ilioneus* – for which Rudolf had paid ten thousand ducats – together with two marble torsos was assessed at thirty kreutzers.[10] The announcement of the auction stated that purchased items were to be removed at once – anything to get rid of what to the cold utilitarianism of the day looked like a pointless agglomeration of junk.[11] The ignominious auction, an event no less devastating than the pillaging of the Swedes, was held on 13 and 14 May 1782.

What about the remaining items, the rubble? The day before the auction the Castle servants heaped bits, shards, plaster casts, fossils, shells, statuettes, damaged coins, medallions and stones of little worth into panniers and baskets and tossed them from the Powder Bridge into the Stag Moat. The refuse heap that piled up at the bottom of the moat proved a treasure trove for Prague children during the next fifty years.[12] So it was that an immense fortune, an endless list of splendours was reduced to a heap of gimcracks and gewgaws. The eternal presence of the *tandlmark* in the Prague dimension.

The affront of Joseph's auction rankled in the Czech mind throughout the nineteenth century. As late as 1862 the painter Karel Purkyně grieved that Rudolf's wonders graced the galleries of Vienna, Munich, Dresden and Stockholm, while the Prague Castle was bare.[13] In that archive of lost glories there now echoed, to use Seifert's words, "the fanfares of silence".[14] For the proponents of the Czech National Revival that magnificent suite, enclave of hated Habsburg rule, represented a robbed strong box, a foreign mausoleum.

Yet not everything had been sold at the infamous auction. Like truncated roots the *huaca* repository sent out new shoots. An inspector dispatched from Vienna in 1876 discovered a number of items hidden in inaccessible places, paintings that had escaped theft and looting as if by magic.[15] So the *dryps-draps* began anew, the most valuable canvases being quietly packed off to Vienna a few at a time, and the Prague pilgrim, the eternal outsider, was none the wiser.[16] But Rudolf's wondrous strange picture gallery must truly have possessed as many lives as a phoenix, because despite the bloodletting of the last impoverishment some valuable forgotten paintings have been found in the Castle cellars in recent years. Final remainders, final consolation.

The astounding history of the *šackomora* seems to symbolize both the untold losses and the capacity for survival of a country "where the blossoming tree of the mirage/quickly turns to sand".[17] Here jewel caskets turn into flea-market bric-à-brac, the falcon's hauteur melts into the owl's dull melancholy and all that remains of great dreams is a profusion of ashes. But enough of these insane collections. I have tired of pursuing their glitter.

36

When Lieutenant Lukáš asks Švejk whether he has ever looked at himself in the mirror, he answers, "At the Chinaman, Staněk's, they once had a convex mirror and when anybody looked at himself in it he wanted to spew. A mug like this, a head like a slop pail, a belly like a soz-zled cannon, in short a complete scarecrow."[1] Arcimboldo's composite portraits bring to mind "scarecrows" reflected in the magic mirrors of a large metaphysical fair booth. His faces of fruits, vegetables, birds, game, roasts, books, kitchen and cellar utensils and farm implements also contain something of the essence of Prague – "the mosaicist of dreadful things conjoined", the supreme attainment of the "fashioning of the grotesque" that Daniello Bartoli speaks of in his essay "La ricreazione del savio".[2]

Giuseppe Arcimboldo (1527–93), "the most ingenious of fantastic painters",[3] assumed the post of court portraitist left vacant by Jakob Seisenegger during the 1560s when the latter's eyesight failed. Ferdinand I (1526–64) was ruler at the time. Arcimboldo remained in Vienna during the reign of Maximilian II (1564–76). He then followed Rudolf II to Prague, where he became so integral a part of the atmosphere at court that he was identified with the mythology of the period, taking on something of the magical ambivalence and saturnine melancholy characteristic of the alchemists. We see it clearly in his self-portrait, which shows him hieratic and severe, wearing a black overcoat and conical hat, his beard framed by a starched ruff. In the comedy *Rabínská moudrost* (Rabbinical Wisdom) set during the age of Rudolf II, Jaroslav Vrchlický makes him (under the name Arcimbaldo) a scoundrel, a bohemian adventurer who discloses the secrets of Rabbi Loew's sorcery.[4]

37

Arcimboldo's art, then, is closely linked to Rudolf's preferences: his love of *Automaten* (mechanical dolls and artificial men like the Golem), his alchemistic sense for the amalgam of disparate bodies and especially his collection mania.[1] There is an intimate relationship between Arcimboldo's mixed portraits and Rudolf's *Kunstkammer*, a cabinet of naturalia, rarities and anomalies. Arcimboldo's figures are themselves collections, agglomerations of objects, fruits, flowers and animals. It is no accident that Arcimboldo took part in enriching the Emperor's collections, and after retiring to Milan in 1587 as an old man he continued to acquire "curiosities" for Rudolf's great museum.

The Four Seasons, for example, is a veritable stockpile of vegetal elements. *Summer* (1563): a profile of fruits and vegetables with grapes for teeth, a pear for a chin, the cheek an apple, the nose a cucumber, the ear an ear of corn and the hair a luxuriant still life. The choice of fruits and vegetables for the parts of the head "is so ingenious that the astonishment one feels must approach wonder".[2] The portraits *The Cellarer* (1574) and *The Cook* (1574) are also collections, the former a confusion of kegs, casks, bottles, glasses, corkscrews and taps, the latter of pots, bowls, pans, a colander, egg shells and snails in the manner of a *Bauernhochzeit*, a nobleman's parody of peasant mores.

The passion for collecting is especially evident in *The Librarian*, a caricature of the Imperial historian Wolfgang Lazio (1514–65), himself a collector of books, folios and coins. The painting is an inlay of books: an open book for hair, a book nose, a head of books, ribbon bookmarks for ears, a chest of bound books and weighty digests. His model is Sebastian Brant's *Narrenschiff* (Ship of Fools, 1494). The description of the library in Comenius' *Labyrinth* also comes to mind when one looks at this "scarecrow", an apothecary library with medicines for the ills of the mind, in addition to boxes as books, box-books, an apothecary of boxes and learned men who eat their fill of books.[3] Arcimboldo's librarian, who is square like a box, recalls the geometric figures and square robots of Luca Cambiaso and Giovanni Battista Bracelli, other leading Mannerists. Nor should we forget that of the characters Švejk encounters in the insane asylum,

> the wildest was undoubtedly a gentleman who pretended to be the sixteenth volume of *Otto's Encyclopedia*, and asked everybody to open him and to find the entry "Cardboard box stapling machine", otherwise he would be done for. He only quietened down when they put him in a straightjacket. Then he was happy, because he thought he had got into a bookbinder's press and begged to be given a modern trim.[4]

Arcimboldo's passion for curiosities goes hand in hand with the feeling for detail characteristic of many painters at Rudolf's court. Bartolomäus Spranger, Pieter Stevens and Roelant Savery lavished attention on every hair, every branch, every stem, every pebble in their landscapes, menageries and "nature manuals". In Comenius' *Labyrinth* one of the orderlies of the queen of the world Marnost (Vanity), Úlisnost (Suavity), wears an inside-out wolf's skin instead of armour and a wolf's tail as halberd.[5] Like Comenius, Arçimboldo uses animals as allegories of character defects, passions and the dismantling of the spirit. All the animals constituting the head of *Earth* have allegorical meaning, which the Mantovan canon Gregorio Comanini explained in the dialogue *Il Figino ovvero Del fine della pittura* (1591).[6]

It is no simple matter to find one's way in this dense cluster, in this intarsia of animals, in this interlacing of ears, tails, hooves and horns that makes *Earth* into a kind of Noah's Ark, a bestiary similar to the landscapes of Roelant Savery, these oppressive jumbles of turkey-cocks, baboons, amphibians, stags, birds and wild beasts. From the back of the neck to the brow the head is all monkey, ibex, horse, wild boar, bear, mule, stag, deer, leopard, gazelle, dog, camel and lion. The fox, "slyest of animals", is the brow, its tail the eyebrows. The ear and cheek are a bashful oliphant supported by a donkey. The rabbit, unwary but with an excellent sense of smell, forms the round nose with its back. The open mouth of a wolf makes up the eye. The mouth is a ravenous tomcat. The chin a tiger's head held by the oliphant's trunk. An ox reclining next to a roebuck represents the neck.

38

Kokoschka is wrong in claiming Arcimboldo's art to be "anti-magical, devoid of all superstition".[1] Comanini points to the dreamlike quality, the "artifice", the miraculous aspects in his works. One of the interlocutors in *Il Figino*, Guazzo, states in a discussion with the three "ministers of Sleep" Morpheus, Phobetor and Phantasos:

> If they were not mythical creatures I should say that all three ministers of Sleep are familiars of Arcimboldo, as he knows how to perform their arts and transformations. Indeed, he does more than they, for he transforms animals and birds and snakes and knotty branches and flowers and fruits and fish and herbs and leaves and ears and straw and grapes into men and the garments of men and women and the ornaments of women.

Another interlocutor is even more enthusiastic:

> Arcimboldo's powers of imagination are most lively, because, having brought together images of the tangible things he sees, he shapes them into strange fancies and visions, . . . joining them with great skill and transforming them into what he wishes.[2]

Although Arcimboldo depicts objects with painstaking realism, they have the haunted, frightening vitality of ghosts, of dead remains: jumbles of fish, piles of overripe fruit beginning to spoil. There is something amorphous, flaccid and revolting about the menagerie face entitled *Earth*; it is a hunter's nightmare, a sinister muddle of beasts. *Water* (1566), a monstrous head of bug-eyed fish, octopuses, eels, tiny sea animals, conch shells and snail shells, is the triumph of slime, my idea of Lovecraft's horrid giant squid head of the sea god Cthulhu.

Winter (1563) exudes boundless desolation; it is the fearful, grotesque mask of a prickly, hairy old man bent by decrepitude, a mass of knots. A gnarled tree trunk forms his head, twisted branches and small leaves his hair; his nose is a bare, broken, barkless branch jutting out of the trunk. Twigs make up his beard and eyebrows; moss-covered larch agarics serve as his swollen lips. His wrinkled neck is wrapped in a reed mat, and a lemon and an orange hang on a branch sprouting from it.

And what is there to say about the ghastly horror of *Fire* (1566), with its ancient military fury about to set conflagrations and lead mounted forays recalling Maximilian II's campaign against the Turks?[3] The figure has hair of restlessly flickering flames, a brow and mouth of fuses, the eye of a candle stump, a nose and ears of sword handles, a candlestick and torch for a neck, emeralds and metal studs for a collar and a chest of mortars and blunderbusses.

As the painters of Surrealism have shown us, meticulous attention to detail need not exclude ambiguity. One need only recall *The Cook* with its reversible head consisting of pieces of roasted meat between two trays that act as helmet or metal collar depending on how the painting is held. There is an unmistakable link between the cool Pop Art imagery of a Claes Oldenburg (with his vegetables, bright pastries and sandwiches) and Arcimboldo's all but odoriferous roasts, fruits and game; indeed, the exaggerated imitation of the most minute details of reality can be so realistic as to become unreal.[4] Yet Arcimboldo's whimsical brush produces other demonic effects. By placing together random objects, of similar origin or not, he creates a chance magic, a diabolical hybridization.

Perhaps this is why his figures evoke primitive cultures, the tattooed men of the Marshall Islands, the cranial deformations of the Belgian Congo's Mangebetou tribe. The miscellany of fish in *Water* reminds us that the Melanesians conceive of their gods as sharks, and *Summer*, a kaleidoscope of fruits and vegetables, is not far from the painted face of a Polynesian.[5]

39

A painted face, a face made of a number of random objects, is a special kind of object, an *objet d'art*. It makes man the catalogue, the sum of the instruments he uses, a puppet constructed from the tools of his trade. None of Arcimboldo's paintings contains bodies, yet one must imagine them to be stiff and puppet-like. Their entire humour is summed up in the head, which is a riddle, a jigsaw of objects wedged one inside the other, of plants flourishing together in seeming harmony – grape vines with elms, olive trees with myrtles – of wild animals united in docility.

Life is replaced by an inanimate patchwork, an ensemble of devices. Arcimboldo's dreamlike visions help to pave the way for Čapek's robots. They aspire to schematicism, tend towards mass production, the limbo of duplification. The marionette-like stringing together of utensils, birds and fruits shows the beauty of the Face on the decline. Having relinquished its claim to the semblance of God, it becomes slimy and ugly, reduced to a repository, because man is the slave of the tools that he thinks he controls but that actually consume him to the point of penetrating his features.

Arcimboldo's composite faces exhibit two contrary aspects: enticing inanity, a *menetekel* of horror, a somber sense of dissolution and death on the one hand and, on the other, irony, farce, a fair-booth *lächerliche Anatomie*, a carnivalesque, vulgar world, a Celionati world. Features resembling soft pies of cathartic fruits for the prevention of hypochondria, the idiotic, hedonistic grin of loutish *Summer* with its puffed-up cheeks and an artichoke-bedecked chest and even the visage of *Spring* which, though a floral mosaic, turns out upon closer inspection to be afflicted by the stiffness of age – it all smacks of carnival.

Besides, even the marvellously jocund can turn diabolical, as in the monstrous, bug-eyed faces in *The Cook* or *The Cellarer* or *The Jurist* (1566), the latter a portrait "of a certain Doctor of Jurisprudence," that is, the Imperial Vice Chancellor Johann Ulrich Zasius (1521–70), "whose entire physiognomy was devastated by the malady of France, which left only a few tiny hairs on his chin"[1] – an ugly likeness made of fish and bony bird's legs, so disgusting it seems to belong to an arch devil, whose mouth emits a stench of asafoetida.

40

Do the parts of these portraits really join together in a single clockwork, or does each part live its own life in a kind of anatomical breakdown like the parts of the face in a Gogol story? And do not the various parts of the face have their own individual souls, as some primitive tribes believe?[1]

The ugly, deformed noses affixed to the bloated faces by Arcimboldian plastic surgery are disturbing. If they were tickled to produce resounding sneezes, they just might come unglued. What if one of them were to start strolling through Prague? In any case, they immediately recall another figure of Prague demonology: the astrologer Tycho Brahe, who sported an artificial nose of gold.

The composite mugs – especially those in the *Season* cycle – also have something in common with the rustic masks of the Czech Baroque theatre: Lucek with its long, monstrous beak; wide-eyed goat and horse figures with names like Brůna, Perchta and Klibna; and finally Smrtka (Death), a straw doll wrapped in a chain of egg shells.[2] Arcimboldo's faces use the materials that traditionally adorn these folk characters: egg shells, straw, sack cloth, bear skins. *Summer* wears a straw jacket with sheaves sticking out of the collar, *Autumn* a shirt of rough barrel staves – so many figures for the folkloristic processions of an avant-garde director like Emil František Burian.

Although most of Arcimboldo's idols were stolen by the Swedes in 1648, I still seem to make out their fetish-like subjects in a carnivalesque crew along the streets of Prague-Bamberg as brought to life by Celionati-Arcimboldo. Furthermore, Arcimboldo is often attributed with organizing masked balls, torchlight processions, carousels, tournaments and mythological processions (for example, the 1571 wedding of Archduke Karl of Styria, the brother of Maximilian II, to Maria of Bavaria in Vienna), in which hybrid creatures similar to his composite head were on parade.[3]

I think I can make out his *Autumn* in the Prague fog, with its *Landsknecht* mien of apples, musk melons, vine shoots and clusters of grapes, the uncouth paragon of a churlish harvest and utterly lacking in *tesklivina*, the melancholy humour typical of *Autumn* in Halas's verse. And *Air*, a bundle of beaks and tiny birds' heads and restless birds' eyes, with a peacock's tail chest and more eyes. *Spring*, whose face, white gorget and dark Spanish dress are all densely embroidered with flowers. And *Flora*: all vine leaves, stem and bindweed lace trimming and petal bands, an arcane botanic creature, yet too plump to be compared to the tiny floral doll Dörtje Elverdink, who sleeps in the calyx of a tulip in E. T. A. Hoffmann's *Meister Floh*. Moreover, if we wish to become one of Arcimboldo's innumerable imitators we could, using his strategy of "metaphorical transference",[4] make other composite heads, that of an alchemist, say, a composition of flasks, cucurbits, retorts and alembics. One could easily imagine Prague as an "Inventio Arcimboldi", a wholly anthropomorphic city with the trees on Petřín Hill as hair, the Hradčany as brow, the palaces of Malá Strana as eyes, the Charles Bridge as nose and the Old Town Square as mouth.

And who is the "boss" of these spirits descending from the Castle galleries? Rudolf II himself, human jigsaw, Rudolf-Vertumnus, as depicted by Arcimboldo, an exuberant collection of fruits and vegetables: the brow a musk melon, an apple and a peach for cheeks, one eye a cherry, the other a blackberry, a pear for a nose, hair made of shoots, grapes and spikes of corn, two hazelnuts the lips, a prickly chestnut shell the beard,[5] the head larger than an "Indian" pumpkin, a triumph of drupes and pulps exuding a buffoonish, smug foolishness, a schizoid, sardonic grin from bursting cheeks.

41

Arcimboldo's fascination lives on. The barber-shop-window wax dolls the Surrealists loved so dearly are direct descendants of his composite heads. There is an intense affinity between Arcimboldo's waxworks and the works of Jindřich Štyrský, who gleefully amassed every kind of "curiosity" and put together figures out of asparagus and an old woman's shoe or an old divan and an advertisement for a device to increase breast size.[1] There is an Arcimboldesque element in Karel Teige's collages and in realizations of the Nezvalian theme of "woman in the plural": female nudes made of randomly detached and reattached parts of the body (breasts for cheeks, eyes on legs) and interlaced with mirrors, columns, amanitas and royal agarics.

Arcimboldo's technique, however, lives on most of all in several characters from Nezval's *Absolutní hrobař* (The Absolute Gravedigger, 1937). In the first of them, "Muž, který skládá z předmětů svou podobiznu" (The Man Who Makes His Portrait Out of Objects), Nezval replaces the static quality of Arcimboldo's pictures with a kind of evolutionism.[2] His objects alternate with time and whim in such a way that the man goes through a series of "bodily phantasmagorias" or, rather, conjurer's tricks. First he wears a "hat in the shape of a small coffin" he spotted in the window of a junkdealer's shop; then he has a "cactus head" covered with "thorns of biting thoughts". At the dentist's he finds two grindstones in his mouth, and as they grind "the glass eye of his cannibalistic desires" he notices his tongue is "shaped like a mole". His neck is "a small bunch of Havana cigars" held together by a high collar and a tie that is "a tame swallow". On the days when he feels older, his hair looks like "white wood shavings".

But the strangest of Nezval's figures is that of the title: the absolute gravedigger. If El Lisitzky's undertakers in the costume sketches for the electromechanical spectacle *Sieg über die Sonne* (Victory Over the Sun) are dancing coffins wearing top hats, music-hall caskets shaped like *prouny*,[3] Nezval's is a nauseating bugaboo, a gluttonous larva, a Gargantuan creature engrossed in devouring "one of his daily putrid lunches" in a dilapidated tavern. The absolute gravedigger combines gastrimargy with decomposition. His left eye, "a pickled hard-boiled egg", is pointed "at a cadastral map formed by a spider on a mould-covered salami; his right eye, "all fly larvae", emits an occasional "button-sized flesh fly". His soft palate, "coated by a membrane of saliva and dust", contains "a miniature cemetery turned mixed grill". Even Halas's "merry gravediggers" (*veselí hrobaři*) pale next to this scab-, mucus-, slime- and lichen-covered bear, though Halas also has a face whose mouth is a "morgue of strangled voices".[4]

Nezval's emphasis on the outlandish dimensions of the nose is a direct reference to Arcimboldo's paintings. "Like the fin of ocean cyclones", "covered with nettles and cheese-like islets as large as semolina", it is a "fan protected by *Secession* nostrils", a "snail of decay" under which a swallow builds its nest. This "metaphysical stirrer of the bran in an absolute cesspool", this Golem stuck together with graveyard scraps is wonderfully suited to the essence of a city that draws much of its witchcraft from an unsettling graveyard: the Old Jewish Cemetery.

Arcimboldo's devices also reappear in the caricatures of Adolf Hoffmeister. Each *podoba* (likeness) is a synthesis of the person represented, his calling and the symbols with which he surrounds himself. Thus Chesterton sails through the air like a montgolfier with an antenna the shape of a cross on his nose. Max Ernst, his body a run-down English manor, wanders among the columns, phantoms and plants of his collages. Teige becomes an integral part of his typographical geometries. Sergei Tretyakov is a long rectangle of Chinese characters, George Bernard Shaw a prickly potted cactus. In these burlesque portraits, as in his imaginative book illustrations (Verne's Fix has glasses made of two clocks, the Cheshire Cat has claws that look like owls' heads) and in his *cartes drolatiques* of Europe for the Liberated Theatre, Hoffmeister transposes Arcimboldo's scurrility into a frivolity and clowning typical of the Poetist era.[5]

42

> And in the stillness of rosy evenings
> the glass foliage tinkles
> the fingers of alchemists grazing it
> like the wind
>
> Jaroslav Seifert, "Praha"[1]

When Rudolf II moved his court to Prague in 1583, the city became an academy of the occult. Like gnats to sweet wine alchemists flocked to Prague from all over Europe. In the hope of replenishing coffers drained by the acquisition of so many rarities and of obtaining an elixir to prolong his life, Rudolf surrounded himself with a crowd of eccentric distillers, whom he extolled and showered with gifts only to throw them into a cramped cell once they disappointed him.[2]

The luted vessels, the flasks, the hermaphrodites, perturbations and marriages, the coupling of elements, the katabasis into infernal regions, the coitus of King Sulphur and Queen Mercury for the generation of philosopher's gold, the oneness of the sufferings of metals in the alembics and the passion of Our Lord, the gripe's egg, the glass spheres, the hollow trees, symbol of the athanor – all this alchemical magic kept Rudolf from affairs of state and stirred his imagination to a frenzied pitch.

Legend has it that Rudolf was himself an adept of the teachings of Hermes and that round his neck he wore a small silver casket covered with black velvet and containing a worthless elixir of life. After his death the chamberlain Kašpar Rucký z Rudz stole the casket along with a selection of treasures and tinctures. Captured and thrown in prison, he hanged himself by a silk cord, but when his ghost took to wandering, the corpse was drawn and quartered and the ashes strewn over the Vltava.[3]

Alchemy fits perfectly into Rudolf's world and its predilection for the occult, for Mannerist freaks, hybrids, curiosities, composites and clay androids. Similarly, his pathological, saturnine melancholy, which anticipates the lugubriousness of the Baroque and Mácha, corresponds to the nigritude, the deep black of decomposition, during which the matter of the Magnum Opus assumes the colour of death; it is the melancholy of the adept waiting endlessly for the results of his admixtures and coctions.[4]

The agents Rudolf set loose in foreign lands in search of *objets d'art* also had a mandate to track down alchemists and entice them to his court with gifts and promises.[5] For the charlatans – who travelled the length and breadth of Europe like the *Englische Komödianten* and *commedia dell'arte* companies – Bohemia was something of a California of the spagyric art. A symbolic copperplate engraving of those years might have depicted Prague as a dim sun in the shape of the head of Rudolf II, Hermes Trismegistus the Second, hanging in a sky blackened by sulphurous vapours, its Imperial gardens ablossom with metal trees and populated by black ravens, a flotilla of outlandish athanor vessels plying the Vltava, frightening gulls and ducks, while Brueghel's hag, dressed all in iron, scuttles down from the Castle on her way to Hell.

The proof of the pudding is in the eating, which is why Rudolf had his court physician Taddeus Hagedecius (Tadeáš Hájek z Hájku) examine an alchemist before taking him into his service.[6] Still, a goodly number of sharps managed to gull both Rudolf and his chief physician with sleights of hand. They hid gold powder in the clay or wax double bottoms of their crucibles. Or they stirred the liquid in the hot crucible with a hollow wand containing a few ounces of gold under a layer of wax. Or they placed coals containing shavings of the precious metal covered by black wax, which melted when heated.[7]

Rudolf often raved about imposters who led him by the nose with their endless *coniunctio* of sulphur and mercury, of volatile and stable substances. He was not the only one. The aristocracy and wealthy burghers delighted in coagulations and sublimations and spent huge sums on alchemical ovens in their palaces and manors. Though robbed blind by one mountebank after another, they persisted in their dream of cheap gold and perennial youth like the fool in the fairy tale who waits for the master's donkeys to defecate gold and rubies. The *lapis philosophorum* captivated them like an evil spirit.

As a result, Prague was invaded by hordes of swindlers, quacks and ointment makers, all mumbo jumbo and magic mirrors. A sizable number of adventurers struck it rich, boasting expertise in making mercury fly and sulphur gleam, and then bolted – that is, if ill fortune did not first hurl them into the "Caucasian depths" of the White Tower or hang them in their gold sequins from a gilt noose. And just as the clown's grin can turn into an outcast's grimace of anguish, so the other side of the alchemist's vulgar mask is mourning and grief.

43

Tradition has it that the alchemists of the Rudolfine era lived in the tiny houses of Golden Lane (Zlatá ulička, Alchimistengäßchen, Goldmachergäßchen), a dreamy, lilliputian street on the periphery of the opulent Castle. Meyrink, who according to Max Brod had himself sought the philosophers' stone,[1] gives this description of it:

> A narrow, winding lane with crenels, a snail's path barely wide enough for one's shoulders to pass. I am standing in front of a row of small houses, none of which is taller than myself. Were I to stretch out my arm I could touch the roofs. Here during the Middle Ages disciples set the philosophers' stone aglow and poisoned moon beams.[2]

Oskar Wiener writes:

> It is actually a cheerful street that looks as though it had been built from a toy-box. The bright doll's houses, the largest of which is hardly more than four square paces, are stuck against the wall enclosing the Stag Moat. Although the queer little cul de sac is currently inhabited by the poor, the tiny rooms, each of which constitutes a house in itself, are kept scrupulously clean, and geraniums and carnations blossom in the windows, of which there are never more than two.[3]

According to legend, Rudolf, who was suspicious by nature, kept a close eye on his long-haired alchemists in Golden Lane. Each of them received a *Puppenhaus* as a home and laboratory and was required to wait around the clock for transmutations. A *Landsknecht* with a halbert patrolled the little street night and day. One golden morning, intoxicated by the song of the first spring birds weaving their nests, several of these charlatans clamoured to be allowed out for a walk in the Stag Moat.

But noble friends of the Emperor happened to be hunting there, and uncouth alchemists could not be permitted to mingle with such a select company. To protest their sequestration, the *Wundermänner* cut off their Assyrian beards, smashed retorts, flasks and bellows, hurled them into the Moat and went on strike: not one more grain of gold for the court. The supercilious Rudolf decided to satisfy their request in his own way: he had them dragged to the Moat and flung into iron cages hung from the spruce trees, where they perished a wretched death by starvation. He did so because an alchemist must never leave his smoke-filled kitchen unattended,[4] and thus treated the wizards of his "harem" much in the manner of Saturn, who devours his own children, and antimony, *lupus metallorum*, which corrodes metals.[5] Meyrink even goes so far as to claim that Rudolf's bears in the Stag Moat "lived off the flesh of adepti".[6]

The legend claiming that the alchemists resided in Golden Lane goes back, like the Golem legend, to the late Romantic period. In fact, Golden Lane came into being during Rudolf's reign because the Castle, a city within a city, was not subject to the laws governing the rest of Prague, and a rabble of shopkeepers, unregistered craftsmen, pedlars and persons of ill repute took refuge within its walls. The row of toy houses grew up alongside the Stag Moat – clinging to the complex organism of the Castle like a parasite – with the tacit consent of the authorities. The street's name came from the fact that there were goldsmiths among the original inhabitants, but archers, Castle guards and gaolers also made their homes here. Craftsmen, merchants and even archers amassed considerable profits from selling provisions, beverages and objects of use to the prisoners in the two towers that delimit the Lane: the White Tower, where alchemists were often incarcerated, and the Daliborka.[7]

The latter took its name from the knight Dalibor z Kozojed, who was imprisoned there at the end of the fifteenth century for supporting the peasants of the Litoměřice region in their revolt against a cruel squire. Fearing that the solitude and endless silence in the remote dungeon, from which he could not see so much as a patch of sky, would drive him mad, Dalibor had a violin brought him, and practised so much that he attracted the curious from all over Prague. In spring the prisoner's sad trills competed with the birds chirping in the Stag Moat, nor did the violin cease its sobbing until Dalibor died beneath the executioner's axe in 1498. Every legend is to some extent based on fact, and in fact the heartrending music was none other than the cries of Dalibor being tortured on the rack or "violin" in hangman's jargon. Which of course does not prevent him from playing in the haunted tower on moonlit nights.[8]

Even if the belief that there were alchemists among the tenants of Golden Lane may stem from the fact that its tiny houses were inhabited by goldsmiths, the historical explanation is no less fascinating than the legend, because it provides us with a Kafkaesque picture of a parasitic world at the perimeter of a mysterious Castle. It is no accident that in 1916 Kafka lived for a time at number 22 of this little street.[9] Nor is it accidental that more than a castle, the Castle is "only a wretched-looking town, a huddle of village houses" in his 1922 novel.[10] Of course, no one can erase the legendary connection between the alchemists and the small, narrow street. We can say along with Nezval:

> In the Golden Lane in the Hradčany
> time almost seems to stand still
> If you wish to live five hundred years
> drop everything take up alchemy
>
> When that simple miracle comes to be
> our rivers will exhale their gold
> Farewell farewell charlatan say hello
> for us to the coming century[11]

In the narrow kitchens behind the tiny windows our imagination still makes out adepts and attendants eager to discover, as Cencio says in *Il Candelaio* (The Candle Bearer), "purest and most veritable gold in the bottom of the glass cucurbit, reconstituted *luso sapientiae*" (I.xii.).[12] We see them in our mind's eye shut up in those little houses as in luted vessels, absorbed in carrying out innumerable distillations, repeating the same process for weeks and months on end, choked by smoke, burnt by fire, blackened by pitch, nodding for want of sleep and with a patience that goes well with the infinite, proud patience of Prague. We hear them grumbling as in Comenius' *Labyrinth*:[13] one at the disfavour of the stars, another at the mud in his mercury, yet another at some cucurbits that have exploded because the flame was too high or at a coction that has failed because the flame was too low; this one is unable to continue calcining because there is too much smoke; that one's nitrogen has evaporated. We repeat after Seifert:

> Alchemists, boil your poisons,
> mumble an obscure formula,
> write the signs of a secret alphabet,
> and the devils will obey you.[14]

The Golden Lane, then, though a scanty architectural complex that seems conjured by a magic wand, acts as the backdrop for the dramatic miracle of transmutation. Much of the demonic nature of the city on the Vltava emanates from its houses. In Karásek's drama *Král Rudolf* Arthur Dee confesses to Rumpf:

I love wondrous Prague, which is as unique and enchanting as its melancholy king. Believe me, this gloomy city plants a glow of madness in the brain of those who make it their own. The Golden Lane, where Rudolf has placed his alchemists' forges, is the city's soul. So much energy, so much magnetism of occult forces is concentrated there that experiments which fail elsewhere will succeed there.[15]

To complete the picture we must mention the fact that the Polish writer Stanisław Przybyszewski, idol of the Czech decadents, was unsuccessful in his efforts to settle in Golden Lane[16] and that the renowned Prague fortune-teller Madame de Thèbes lived in one of the houses – number 4 – before the Second World War.[17] Three worn-out cards, three cards on the heavy tablecloth, many yellowed photographs on the walls and a magnificent view of the Stag Moat. As in the dark fortune-teller's booths in Josefov, a plump tomcat with a belly like a drum prowling the small room when not curled up, like Beardsley's black cat, in his mistress's basket-like coiffure.

44

In August 1584, two English magicians arrived at the Castle. They had come from Poland.

John Dee conversed with spirits by evoking them in a magic mirror, a sphere of smoky quartz given to him by the angel Uriel.[1] He was aided in his tête-à-têtes by the necromancer Edward Kelley. Alchemists' biographies are typically a morass of enigmas, intrigues, murky details and miracles. Nonetheless, if chronicles describe John Dee (Jan Devus), an astrologer born in London in 1527 and a favourite of Queen Elizabeth I, as a highly learned man, the sources unanimously call Kelley a *Jahrmarktsdoktor*, a greedy mountebank whose soul lacked the balm of honesty, a windbag adventurer who, according to Svátek, "deserves a place in a Czech *pitaval* rather than in the Pantheon of Rudolfine scholars".[2]

Kelley's dubious nature and diabolical aura were heightened by the fact that he had a hook nose, mousy eyes and no ears (the Lancaster executioner had cut them off in 1580 as punishment for forging documents).[3] Meyrink describes him as "a charlatan with severed ears, a seducer, a medium".[4] His real name was Talbot, and he was born in Worcester in 1555. After his bout with the hangman he let his hair grow long, changed his name to Kelley and wandered all over England. In the course of these peregrinations he came across a mysterious manuscript in a Welsh inn, a document that had been discovered in the grave of a sorcerer-monk along with two ivory phials: one containing a red powder, the other a white powder. The opuscule was written in an indecipherable language. Kelley was convinced that it contained the formula of the philosophers' stone and hurried off to Dr Dee in Mortlake on 22 November 1582 in the hope that the spirits, invoked by the magic mirror, would provide the key to its decipherment.[5]

Though a drunkard and swindler, Kelley managed to gain the trust of the Queen's astrologer and became his assistant. Their transmutations, exorcisms, angelology and conjuring tricks attracted the curious and, it would seem, Elizabeth herself to the Mortlake "chapel". When the Palatine of Sieradz, Olbracht Łaski, Bruno's *prencipe Alasco polacco*,[6] travelled through England in June of 1583, he did not fail to visit Dee's laboratory. On 26 June a spirit summoned via the mirror predicted that he would ascend the Jagellonian throne upon the death of King Stefan Báthory.[7] Łaski, who in fact aspired to the throne, was so enchanted that he invited the two magicians to Poland. After an adventuresome journey John Dee arrived in Cracow together with his wife Jane Fromond, son Arthur and the braggart Kelley and continued producing the Chagallian apparitions that had so enthralled Łaski.[8] Stefan Báthory, also a connoisseur of horoscopes and astrology, had the heavenly messengers appear in his residence as well.[9]

In August 1584 two English magicians presented themselves at the Prague Castle. They had come from Poland. John Dee, who understood the language of the birds and could speak the idiom of Adam the protoplast, ingratiated himself with the hypochondriac sovereign by turning mercury into gold and bringing his crystal ball to life with a whole theatre of spirits.[10] After all, what piece of equipment could better have suited Rudolf's whims and the curio gallery, the *boutique à merveilles* that is Prague, than a magic mirror? A talking mirror, an abyss of angels, a mad object worthy of a place in the arsenal of Prague illusionism alongside the top hats of Tichý's jugglers and the triangle time machine in Jakub Arbes's novella *Newtonův mozek* (Newton's Brain).

Although they were received at court with full honours, the two magicians ran with the hare and hunted with the hounds. They abused the support of another alchemy fanatic and gull, Vilém of Rožmberk, Lord of Krumlov and Margrave of the Kingdom of Bohemia, by promising him the Polish throne with the help of the providential sphere. Wonder-workers, soothsayers, distillers, companies of cutpurses and swindlers converged on Rožmberk's laboratories in Krumlov and Třeboň in hordes and impoverished the House of the Five-Leaf Rose with a thousand frauds and artifices. An adept from Meissen had Rožmberk give him eighty florins, which he then planted in the Krumlov Castle garden and watered with an alchemical tincture. One night while Rožmberk was patiently waiting for them to send out golden shoots, the swindler dug them up and disappeared with his loot.[11] This anecdote illustrates the tendency of believers in the spagyric art to consider metals living organisms able to grow, ripen and multiply like grain if sown in fertile soil,[12] as well as the knavery of the alchemist-sower who hoodwinks his patron (because he who sows kindness reaps ingratitude).

Like Łaski, Rožmberk eagerly took part in spiritualistic seances. He placed the Krumlov blacksmith at Dee's disposal and ordered him to seek the philosophers' stone *for him alone*; he hid Dee in his castle in Třeboň when Rudolf, hounded by the Catholic party and the Papal nuncio, who accused the English magician of necromancy and commerce with Satan, banished Dee from the Czech lands.[13] When Báthory died in 1586, the Swedish prince Zygmunt III Waza, nephew of the last of the Jagellonians, ascended the Polish throne, leaving Rožmberk and Łaski empty-handed, and Dee chose to return to England even though the Mortlake rabble had burned down his house and valuable library. In the meantime, he continued to keep records of his appointments with the angels, albeit without Kelley's assistance. Elizabeth died in 1603, and her successor, James I, was not well disposed towards him. Dee, following the advice of the seraphim, prepared for another journey abroad. He fell ill before his departure, however, and died at Mortlake in September 1607.

In Prague literature John Dee is often portrayed as a scrounger and cheat, though not so coarse and impudent as Kelley. In Jiří Karásek's drama *Král Rudolf*, John Dee and his son Arthur pretend to distill *aurum potabile*, preparing instead a lethal potion with which to poison Rudolf. They are betrayed by Dee's daughter Gelchossa (with whom the emperor has fallen in love) and buried alive in the White Tower. Gelchossa tries to dispel the melancholy (the seat of evil spirits) from Rudolf's soul and replace the vain books and deceit, the fraudulent magic and alchemy with her love.

The main character of Meyrink's novel *Der Engel vom westlichen Fenster* (The Angel from the Western Window) is a modern reincarnation of John Dee. Meyrink's hero relives the journey of the English magician to the city on the Vltava, his visit to the gloomy Emperor, his debate over alchemy and angels with the wizened, almost mummified Rabbi Loew. Are there any points of contact between Dr Dee and Meyrink's Maharal? The alchemists' *magisterium* was called Adam because the matter of transmutations was the quintessence of the universe, and the Golem is a copy of Adam because it is made of clay.[14] The creation of the Golem and the search for the philosophers' stone thus converge. Dee's mirror anticipates the future in the same way that gulls anticipate storms; the Maharal's cinema brings the patriarchs back to life from the distant past.

Was John Dee's spiritism nothing more than charlatanism, leger-demain and *Jahrmarktsgaukelei*? If he used deception to invoke super-natural beings, why did people fail to notice they were being duped? Is it possible that their overheated imaginations actively wished to be fooled by the tricks of the *kryształowa tarcza* or *magické zrcadlo*? Had Elizabeth, who held him in such esteem, not been informed of his *tours d'adresse*, his frauds? Though if he was a genuine prognosticator, soothsayer and alchemist, why did Elizabeth allow him to seek his fortune with foreign sovereigns and potentates rather than keep him at her own court?

It has been surmised – and the surmisal is not to be discounted – that Dee and Kelley were secret agents of Albion's queen, that they wished to prevent the Habsburgs from seizing the Polish crown or that they were trying to raise support for the struggle with Philip II of Spain. This hypothesis would seem confirmed by a certain coolness on Rudolf's part towards John Dee and by the two sorcerers' constant trips between Bohemia and Poland; it would mean that the whole business of mirrors, omens and archangels was simply a camouflage for political intrigues and the diary in which Dee recorded his conversations with the heavenly messengers a cover or memorandum in code.

45

It is, however, contradicted by the subsequent fate of Kelley, also known as Engelender. Kelley also enjoyed the esteem of Vilém of Rožmberk and carried out his costly distillations in the margrave's laboratories at Krumlov and Třeboň. When Dee was banished from Prague in 1586, Rudolf II summoned Kelley to the Castle in spite of the fact that Vilém did not wish to let him go.

Kelley presented the sovereign with a remedy for his hypochondria and transmogrified mercury into gold in his presence with a drop of blood-red oil. Rudolf, convinced he had found a pearl of an adept, the bright sun amongst his torches, rewarded him with great gifts and honours, appointed him Imperial Counsellor and in 1588, because Kelley claimed to be descended from Irish nobility, raised him to the Bohemian knighthood (*rytíř z Imany*).[1] Kelley began to strut about like a sage with the essence of the universe in his pocket.

Occasionally he travelled to Třeboň, where John Dee was hiding under Rožmberk's protection. He took walks with his old associate; they went hunting in the woods and fishing in the numerous ponds. One autumn day a drunk coachman landed them in a ditch and the local fishermen were barely able to pull them out again.[2] Meanwhile, both the Emperor and Rožmberk waited in vain for Kelley to produce the philosophers' stone. And if Rudolf had promoted him to the rank of knight, Rožmberk gave him two fiefs near Jílové – Libeřice and Nová Libeň – each together with the neighbouring villages.[3]

Using his earnings and the dowry of his wealthy Bohemian wife Johanna, Kelley bought a brewery, a mill and some houses in Jílové and, bit by bit, gained a monopoly over the food trade in the region. As one of the highest magnates in the kingdom he raised prices at will, ignoring protests on the part of the citizenry. Meanwhile his younger brother arrived in the promised land, passing himself off as an Irish knight, taking a rich noblewoman to wife and buying two estates from the Earless One with her dowry.[4]

In Prague, where he divided his time between orgies of wine and orgies of women, Engelender bought two houses. One of them, in Dobytči trh (Cattle Market) is, according to Romantic tradition, the house in which Dr Johann Faust lived.[5] Faust is also an obligatory charlatan of the city of Rudolf II. In the *Faustbücher*, the earliest of which is dated 1587, the sorcerer travels throughout Europe atop Mephistopheles, who transforms himself into a horse with wings "like a camel" and soars over Prague.[6] The Faust House (Faustův dům) could hardly be located in a more haunted place than the Cattle Market – we shall have occasion to return to it later – a square associated in the popular imagination with plots, prisons, executions and men buried alive, a necromancer's paradise, all mandrakes and gallows.[7]

According to the legend, which made the Czech Romantics swell with pride, Faust was a Czech who practised the black arts, that is, necromancy and printing. His name was Šťastný, that is, Happy, that is, Faustus. During the Hussite Revolt he emigrated to Germany, where he took the name Faust von Kuttenberg after the town of his birth (Kutná Hora in Czech). In other words, he was none other than Gutenberg, the inventor of the printing press.[8] In the poem "Labyrint slávy" (The Labyrinth of Glory, 1846) Jan Erazim Vocel recounts how the defeat of Prokop Holý's Taborites in 1434 led the Bohemian baccalaureate Jan Kutenský (Johann Kuttenberg) to devote himself to the spagyric art, to which end he sold his soul to the devil Duchamor. After his beloved Ludmila sacrificed herself to free him from the devil's clutches, he settled in Mainz, where he invented the printing press to the eternal glory of the Slavs. In Czech folk puppet plays, the *pimprlata* theatre,[9] Faust is the more conventional figure of the *Faustbücher* even if, when conjuring up "Alexander the Great with the cloak of a Czech duke and the fair Helen in Turkish dress" at the court in Lisbon, he comes dangerously close to the Czech Punch – Kašpárek by name – who mistakes devils for owls.[10]

Although Kelley's fame and fortune continued to grow for a time, he eventually got his comeuppance. Even the Land of Cockaigne has its death masks. In April 1591[11] Kelley killed a courtier, a certain Jiří Hunkler, in a duel. The emperor, enraged and tired of waiting for the philosophers' stone, issued a warrant for his arrest. Kelley tried to reach Třeboň and refuge in Rožmberk's El Dorado, but the police caught up with him at an inn in Soběslav where he was waiting for fresh horses. He drew his sword, but was overpowered and taken to the Chuderka Tower at Křivoklát Castle.[12]

Kelley raged like a wild animal in captivity; food had to be pushed in to him through a narrow slit. Then he stopped eating and fell ill. Rudolf, fearing that Kelley would die before revealing the formula, sent a renowned court physician to cure him, but as the prisoner refused to divulge the mysteries of his retorts the Emperor imposed harsher incarceration. Rožmberk's attempts to intervene on behalf of his protégé merely increased Rudolf's venom. The castellan of Chuderka Tower received orders to extract the secret formula from him at all costs, even torture, yet Kelley held his tongue.[13] When Rudolf impounded the Englishman's property in the autumn of 1591 and entrusted it to two Imperial commissioners (who plundered it), his wife went heavily into debt to ease his imprisonment.

Kelley remained in Křivoklád for more than two and a half years. Having given up all hope of mercy or a regular trial, he resolved to flee. One night he bribed a guard and lowered himself from a window of the tower with a rope, but the rope snapped and Kelley fell into the moat. He was found the following morning unconscious and with a fractured leg. Rudolf took pity on him and allowed him to be brought back to Prague by his family, but the leg had to be amputated and was replaced with a prosthesis.

Thus Kelley's peg-legged, earless figure joins Tycho's noseless one, Arcimboldo's ugly mugs and the ranks of limping pilgrims. Kelley was no longer admitted to Court, where other cozeners now shone. His property was returned to him, though the commissioners had so vandalized it that his wife had to sell her jewellery to restore it to its former glory.[14] There was no more money to be made in alchemy. Vilém of Rožmberk had died in 1592, and his brother Petr Vok preferred a harem of exotic beauties at Třeboň to dubious distillations. Kelley's story is proof of the saying that the alchemist's purse is made of chameleon hide for it contains nothing but air and wind. Kelley was unable to satisfy his host of creditors even by selling his many houses and estates, and Rudolf, using his debts as a pretext, had him thrown into the dungeon of Most Castle in November 1596. His wife, who had refused to renounce him and retire to a nunnery, moved to Most with their two children to be close to him.

Kelley sent the emperor his treatise *De lapide philosophorum* from prison with a cover letter protesting his innocence and stating that it would always be the way of mankind to set its Barabases free and crucify its Christs. His only answer was more severe treatment. Thus does a charlatan become a martyr, a would-be saviour. Ladies and gentlemen, instead of the opulent spectacle of luted vessels, hollow trees and glass spheres in which the elements mate, we shall now witness the fall of an arrogant alchemist – not the plunge of an Icarus in a Brueghelian sea of opalescent darkness but the crash of a scoundrel in the cold hell of a Bohemian prison. If tortured metal reenacts the sufferings of Christ, then the earless charlatan suffered great tortures in his alembic jail. Moreover, whereas the substances in the athanor know only a temporary death (for they shall be resurrected in sublimation), there is no glorious rebirth for the earless charlatan, there is but death with no return.

In the summer of 1597 Kelley's wife requested an audience with the Emperor only to be threatened with imprisonment and banishment of her children to a monastery. Once more Kelley attempted flight. He even managed to arrange for his brother, who had come from Prague, to wait for him with a carriage at Most Castle. But cruel fate! The rope broke again, and Kelley tumbled back into the moat, this time breaking the other leg. Dragged back to his cell, he took his own life by drinking a potent poison his faithful wife had smuggled to him. The date was 1 November 1597.

46

Another alchemist whose name is linked to sorcery in the city on the Vltava also lived a life full of suffering: the Pole Michael Sendivogius.[1] His biography abounds in such ill-assorted vicissitudes, it seems a collage of many lives.

When Sendivogius passed through Prague in 1590 after a tour of Germany, Kelley, who was at the height of his power and feared competition, kept him at a distance from the Imperial court in one of his houses in Jílové,[2] but it was a simple matter for Sendivogius, who passed himself off as a nobleman and comported himself accordingly, to find patrons in the Bohemian capital. He quickly managed to dupe the physician Mikuláš Löw z Löwensteinu and, later, the wealthy patrician Ludvík Korálek z Těšína. The latter was like Cencio, the protagonist of Giordano Bruno's *Il candelaio*, a fanatical devotee of the spagyric art. His shrewish wife, who did not tolerate her husband's alchemistic eccentricities, could have repeated the angry words of Cencio's wife Marta:

> He is so obsessed with finding the philosophers' stone that he cannot eat and grudges going to bed, the nights seem longer to

him than to a girl with a new frock to don in the morning and everything annoys him, depresses him. His only pleasure is his furnace. [I.xiii.][3]

Sendivogius first won over Korálek by dipping a nail and a clothes hanger in a liquid and holding them over red-hot coals until they turned to pure silver. He then promised to make him live to two hundred. Korálek lost his head, forcing money and presents on Sendivogius against the objections of his wife. When the alchemist cured him of dropsy and his daughter of smallpox, Korálek waxed so enthusiastic that he signed over a house in the New Town to him complete with household effects, two beds and bedclothes, a cartload of coal for his experiments and a white-plumed hat. When a child was born to Sendivogius, Korálek sent him puerperal sheets and pillows, two kegs of wine and butter from his own estate.[4]

After healing Löw z Löwensteinu's seriously ill son with his panacea, Sendivogius came to be considered a wonder-worker.[5] He could not have had much faith in his own physic, however, as he fled Prague for Saxony when the plague broke out in 1594, and despite appeals from his patron did not return until it subsided. He also requested funds to buy one of the Jílové houses that Kelley's wife, in financial straights, was forced to sell. Korálek, whose own purse was almost empty, contracted large debts with the wealthy Jew Maisl, which sent his wife into such a rage that she fled to her mother. Shortly thereafter the simpleton patrician, who combined an obsession for alchemy with an over-fondness for drink, suffered a relapse. This time Sendivogius was unable to save him, either with sun tincture or moon salt or tincture of sudorific antimony. Korálek died in 1599 at peace with his Xanthippe and shouting "Hic est ille Lapis tuus philosophicus!" at the Polish alchemist.[6]

Madame Korálková accused Sendivogius of having poisoned her husband with his electuaries and ordered him to return the monies the dearly departed had lent him. He was arrested in Jílové, yet was able to prove that the emulsions and mixtures he had administered were harmless: Korálek had died of intemperance. After paying a portion of his debts, Sendivogius was released from prison. He disappeared in the general confusion following a renewed outbreak of the plague.

Enter the mysterious figure of Alexander Seton (Setonius), an itinerant alchemist known as the Cosmopolitan, who performed miracles with red powder. Seton appeared like a meteor in various parts of Europe executing dazzling transformations only to steal away immediately afterwards. Everything went well until he was captured by the Prince-Elector of Saxony, Christian II, who had him incarcerated and tortured in the casemate of Königstein Castle in the vain hope that he would reveal the formulas of his distillations. Seton's shadow steals in and out of the destiny of more than one alchemist who passed through Prague Castle. That of the Strasbourg goldsmith Filip Jakub Güstenhöver, for instance. When Rudolf learned that Güstenhöver was in possession of a vial of purple tincture given to him by Seton during one of his fleeting visits, he immediately sent a chamberlain to Strasbourg to persuade the goldsmith to come to Prague. Güstenhöver reluctantly accepted, and the journey turned out to be a fatal one indeed, for the vial was not Robert-Houdin's *bouteille inépuisable* and was soon empty. The sovereign suspected fraud and sent the goldsmith to rot in the White Tower.[7]

Michael Sendivogius arrived in Dresden while Seton was languishing in the murky darkness of his cell in Königstein. He had met him during his wanderings through Germany as a young man. With his elegant manners and sleight-of-hand tricks, which included turning a live trout into crystal and crystal into a trout, Sendivogius won the favour of Christian II, then wheedled permission to visit Seton and walk with him around the fortress, claiming he could talk the Scottish alchemist into divulging the formula to him.[8] After that it was a simple matter to bribe the guards and flee with Seton to Cracow. *Zu spät!* Weakened by his chains, tortures and the escape, Seton died a few months later without revealing the formula to Sendivogius, though he did leave him his notebooks and a red powder he had hidden before his capture and retrieved during their flight.

Sendivogius returned to Prague with Seton's tincture and delighted Rudolf by allowing him to carry out a transmutation by himself. According to Meyrink, he feigned astonishment at the sight of his tincture's wondrous effects (to keep the sovereign and notables from asking him for a secret he did not know), claiming he had purchased it from a *Marktschreier* in Cracow for a few coppers. Yet Rudolf's heart was so overwhelmed that he ordered the following inscription to be engraved in marble: "Faciat hoc quispiam alius, quod fecit Sendivogius Polonus."

As Sendivogius' fame soared, so did the intrigues against him. On a trip to Prague from Cracow he was attacked by cut-throats hired by the Moravian nobleman Kašpar Macák z Ottenburku and thrown in prison, from which he escaped using a rope made of strips of his own clothing. He ran a far greater risk when he went to perform transmutations at the palace of Duke Frederick in Stuttgart. Although he managed to win the Duke's goodwill, his success aroused the jealousy of the court alchemist Müller von Müllenfels. The Swabian barber Ignaz Müller, who had learned a bag of *Quacksalber* tricks on his wanderings through Europe, had also spent time at Prague Castle, where he had aroused pensive Rudolf's enthusiasm by performing a fake transmutation with a double-bottomed crucible and allowing himself to be shot with a bullet made of an amalgam that disintegrated in flight. The Emperor granted him nobility.

It is understandable that this mediocre, uncouth alchemist or, rather, carnival tout should have been jealous of the well-mannered and most gracious Sendivogius, who had jeopardized his position at the Stuttgart court. On the one hand, he whispered to the Duke that Sendivogius had lied about having accidentally bought the blood-red tincture from a market crier; on the other, playing the Machiavel, he urged the Pole to disappear before the Duke had him hanged in his effort to extort the secret from him. With Seton's fate still fresh in his mind, Sendivogius retreated, but the vulgar barber's ruffians, disguised in heavy coats and comical false beards, assaulted him as he fled, stole the miraculous tincture and cast him into the deepest dungeon of a dank tower. Müller then boasted that he too had discovered the formula, but the overjoyed Duke took the vial and tried to extract the secret from him with merciless questioning. It was like squeezing oil from cork or wine from pumice.

Sendivogius, who like an alchemical Houdini always managed to escape from the most difficult prisons, had meanwhile fled the tower. (Meyrink embroiders upon his escape, making his rescuer a fair young Gipsy girl, Fiametta [sic], worthy of a story by Mácha. Enamoured of Fiametta, the alchemist plans to take her with him to Strasbourg, but she replies, "The children of Egypt do not betray their blood"[9] and bids him adieu in a romantic scene.) When Duke Frederick learned of his beloved distiller's fraud, he turned him over to the executioner, and the ex-barber, dressed in a gold-sequined suit, swung like a marionette from a gilt gallows.

Sendivogius never regained possession of the red powder.[10] Without it he was finished. He took to wandering through Poland selling letuaries and syrups of sheep's sorrel and verjuice syrups and squeezing lolly from the gullible Polish *szlachta*. (Meyrink imagines that, after many more adventures, the alchemist retired with his fair Gipsy girl to a crumbling farmhouse atop an inaccessible mountain in the dense Black Forest, far from the hurly-burly of the world, to study the occult arts.) He died in 1646 at the age of eighty.

In Prague literature Sendivogius also bears the mark of an evil intriguer and rogue. *Magelóna*, a Romantic tragedy by Josef Jiří Kolár overloaded with turgid turns of phrase, Latinate syntax, alchemical terminology and in general the most arrant nonsense, shows Sendivogius – astrologer, "maker of gold" and sorcerer – in cahoots with mad Don César, the illegitimate son of Rudolf II. The Pole hatches daring frauds, clever thefts and hellish plans, but ends on the gallows, a fitting finale for a scoundrel of his ilk. The oddest aspect of the work is that Don César, who outwits the Spanish noblewoman Magelóna Trebizonda, figures as the fruit of an affair between Rudolf and Sendivogius' wife.

47

Rudolfine Prague, then, was an abode of charlatans, knaves and blow-hards, in short, people who make their living by cheating other people out of their purses. My account cannot ignore the Greek Mamugna of Famagosta, who arrived in the city on the Vltava with two black mastiffs, indeed black devils (much as in Tichý's canvases the satanic Paganini arrives in Prague in a rickety pitch-black coach wearing a scaly stove-pipe hat). Mamugna passed himself off as the son of the Venetian Marco Antonio Bragadin, who had been captured and skinned alive by the Turks during the fall of Famagusta. He had himself addressed as *conte serenissimo* and gave opulent soirées with the gold he extracted from his Prague patrons. Kelley's enmity placed limits on his success, however, so Mamugna fled. He met his end in 1591 on a gilt gallows in Munich and landed in a pauper's grave together with the carcasses of his demon mastiffs.[1]

The champion adventurer during the era of Rudolf II was, however, the Italian Geronimo (or Alessandro or Giovanni) Scotta (or Scota or Scotti or Scoto), astrologer and distiller, but most of all ne'er-do-well and toady.[2] Dačický writes in his memoirs under the year 1591: "A certain Italian living in Prague, who deceived and tricked the people with his sinister cunning, was especially known for his diabolical leg-erdemain. His name was Scotta."[3] Scotta seems to have been born in Parma. He too criss-crossed Germany, where he pulled an end-less series of roguish tricks, especially marriage swindles. Arriving in Prague on 14 August 1590 with three red velvet carriages drawn by forty horses and with a large train of liveried servants, his mous-tache lightly twirled, his hand arched on his hip like a bow, the raised brim of his hat forming a sail on his head, Scotta radiated splendour.

He took ostentatious lodgings in an Old Town inn, but soon wormed his way into the Castle, where he was initially taken for a thoroughbred. Kelley, however, who was mortally afraid of any other alchemist, allowed him to practise only astrology. Scotta's luck did not last long: by 1593 he was back in Old Town Square in a wooden booth selling salves, stag-horn jelly, vitriol of Mars and cassia pulp.

Scotta figures in Prague literature as a leech, a schemer adroit at duping the great brotherhood of simpletons and fools. Not surprisingly, he occupies centre stage in the highest achievement of Prague horror-tale kitsch, the Gothic novel *Pekla zplozenci* (Spawn of Satan) by Josef Jiří Kolár. Kolár tosses together gallows, alchemy, mandrakes, witches, occult rites and nocturnal machinations. His stereotyped atrocities are so vulgar they make one roar with laughter. Kolár's Giovanni Scotta, alchemist and barber surgeon, "great necromancer and halberdier of the Most Serene

Prince Satan", beggars all description. "A demonic sign or brown wart like a garden spider stood out on the convex bridge of his aquiline nose, which had the peculiar property of turning fiery red when wild desires or savage lust or mad passion sprang to life in the depths of his soul."

Scotta dwells in a horrid, smoke-filled, smoke-blackened house, all buckled walls and crooked overhangs, a hovel with a decrepit wooden turret on an ogee roof and a garden in which he keeps magpies, ravens and – most important – wolves (in iron cages), whose rabid spittle he collects for his experiments. The pride of his laboratory is an athenora of gold and crystal and several caskets containing an array of outrageous objects: roots of the sidrikma plant – the seven-herb plant – which fuels the athenora, a capsule with flesh butchered by the glow of the planet Jupiter, a capsule with the stingers of queen bees, a green bottle with the froth of hydrophobic wolves, a small case with the anachytis stone for capturing rays from the constellation of the Pleiades, a stone stolen from the priests guarding the bull Apis in the Temple of Isis and Osiris in the ruins of Memphis. An incredible mishmash. The household chores are performed by a thin, wrinkled woman, an old witch whom the necromancer summons with a whistle:

> What a strange creature this Abigail was! A small hunchbacked figure in a garment of dark brocade with a long, purple face like a mummy's and a bonnet whose long ribbons hung down to either side of her waist. She bore more than a passing resemblance to a vampire (a Phyllostoma Spectrum, to use the naturalist's term), the creature that lies in wait at night for sleeping men and animals to suck their blood with its pointed tongue.

Later in the novel we learn that this harridan, "supreme miracle of occult pneumatology", has taken Scotta as her second husband and born him a daughter, Lukrecie, alias Fair Devilkins. Her first marriage, with the since deceased alchemist Jakub Bartoš z Kurčínů, produced the twins Vilém and Jošt, whom a perfidious chamberlain of Rudolf II, the notorious Lang (here called Jáchym Lang), seeks to destroy. Lang accuses Vilém of having killed his brother (though it is, of course, Lang • who tried to kill Jošt) and sends him to the gallows. But believe it or not, on the stormy night of 25 May 1593 Vilém frees himself from the noose and finds refuge in Scotta's house, by which time everyone thinks his corpse has been desecrated by the hangman and dissected by the *anatomáci*, that is, the dissectors. Vilém becomes Scotta's disciple, a follower of that "ignominious occult and true pneumatology that made many sharp minds behave like madmen during the age of Rudolf, and led them into the quagmires of the will-o'-the-wisps". He returns with Scotta and Rudolf himself to his place of execution to look for the mandrake which, as is well known, grows underneath the gallows. He fondles it like a doll, washes it in red wine, dresses it in a tiny shirt and keeps it in an ebony casket lined with red velvet.

Scotta wishes to make Vilém immortal so he can marry him to the mysterious Sempiterna. Once more we have the extended life motif that Crawford dealt with in *The Witch of Prague* (where the warped necromancer Keyork Arabian and the witch Unorna contrive to prolong the life of a Methuselah by transfusing the blood of a seriously-ill youth by the name of Israel Kafka into his veins). Scotta maintains that man can attain immortality only if he is quartered, placed in the athenora and reassembled into a new structure. The emphasis on *anatomace*, dissection, can be traced to the fact that the first public autopsy in Prague was performed in 1600 by Dr Jan Jessenius. "In Prague", Dačický writes in his memoirs,

> a certain doctor, a foreign medicus, desiring to know perfectly the nature of man, requested from the authorities a criminal sentenced to death and, killing him with poison, cut him in two and opened all his limbs to observe what was in his body, especially the veins, which art physicians call *anatomace*.[4]

Vilém is on the operating table under Scotta's knife when Abigail rushes in to rescue him, a whip made of serpents in her right hand, in her left a mandrake. She is possessed like Brueghel's Dulle Griet. Scotta deluges her with "his entire pack of snow-white cats", "a host of large, foul frogs and toads", "an infinite multitude of flittermice, which nimbly flap their wings". Dishevelled and enraged, Abigail defends herself with the mandrake, while Scotta devours a snake to regain his strength. Abigail holds out, so he tears off the scarlet cloth draped over the lower part of her body: one leg is shining metal, the other is that of a donkey, confirmation that Abigail belongs to the race of witches. This Grand Pandemonium of toads, frogs, cats and noctules closely follows the mêlée between the archivist Lindhorst and the hideous, toothless witch Lisa in E. T. A. Hoffmann's *Golden Pot*. Hoffmann's shrew surrounds herself with bats, owls and a black cat, and exhibits her repulsive nudity to the student Anselmus in a crystal bottle.

Voskovec and Werich parodied the chimeric language, dubious settings, foreboding spirits and false Rudolfine atmosphere, in short, Kolár's whole preposterous thriller in their musical *Golem*. Court alchemist Jeroným Scotta, "necromancer and minister of Satan", who in the novel is the despicable chamberlain's adversary, plays his accomplice in the comedy. He is a nasty, decrepit old man who despite asthma and sclerosis draws strength from daily doses of an elixir of life. Scotta hatches behind-the-scenes plots, steals the *shem* from the synagogue, strangles the astrologer Břeněk with his beard (the kind of long white beard found in slapstick comedy) and hangs him from a noose, but the gallows snaps exactly as it does for Vilém in *Pekla zplozenci*, and Břeněk falls to the ground alive.[5]

In Josef Svátek's novel *Astrolog* (1890–1), the court alchemist Alessandro Geronimo Scotta is less diabolical, more Cagliostresque. Unctuous, cloying, sly as a fox, versed in worldly cunning, a tactician of intrigues in league with spiteful courtiers, he spews honey from a tongue more bitter than colocynth and bamboozles the naive with baneful intrigues. Svátek links him to Sendivogius's patron Korálek z Těšína and shifts facts from the lives of Kelley and John Dee to him, creating an unparallelled gallimaufry in the process.

Svátek's Scotta wields a magic mirror found 150 years earlier in the tomb of a Welsh bishop skilled in alchemy. One day the "miraculous glass sphere" that "reveals things far away" falls into the hands of the German (!) alchemist Setonius, who passes it on to Scotta. Zuzanka, daughter of the simpleton Korálek, is pining for the love of her betrothed, Oldřich Rabštejnský z Čihanova, who has travelled to Spain on orders from Rudolf II. Since the mountebank from Parma wishes to become the wealthy patrician's son-in-law and thus lay his hands on Zuzanka's dowry, he shows her her beloved embracing an angelic Madrileña in his catoptromantic globe and Zuzanka expunges him from her heart.

Yet how Svátek debases the equipment meant to create prognostic ectoplasms! A pitiful crystal ball magnifying a lifeless picture clumsily painted by Scotta! To make his character an even greater blackguard, Svátek relates a swindle Scotta pulled off with the antiquarian Jakub de Strada. Scotta hides a coffin containing a Pharaoh's mummy in the forests of Brandýs on the Elbe, then exhumes it in the presence of Rudolf to prove that there was an Egyptian burial ground in ancient Bohemia. But when the shipping slip of the agent who sold the mummy to the Imperial collections falls out, Scotta lands in the White Tower. Released after three years, he turns to hawking herbal juices, salves and pain-killing potions.

The character of Scotta unites necromancy with the brazen guile and criminal vice of the highwaymen and desperadoes who plundered Rudolfine Bohemia. He is the prototype of the Italian swindler stranded in the city on the Vltava. Svátek uses every opportunity to call him "treacherous Italian", "Italian knave", "fatuous Italian", "Italian adventurer" and to emphasize his "diabolical Italian cunning". In this regard I should recall that during Rudolf's reign Prague contained a band of Italian thugs who killed on contract using pistols called in Czech *bambitky* or *panditky* (from the Italian *banditi*). To put an end to the looting and slaughter, Rudolf had three wooden scaffolds erected, three gallows from which many a scoundrel swung.[6]

Scotta also served as the model for a number of impostors in Prague literature. In the previously mentioned poem by Vocel the devil claims to belong to the Italian house of Duca del'amor and is vexed that he has ended up an ointment seller (like Scotta) with the name Duchamor (Pestilence of the Spirit). He calls himself an Italian Master before an august assembly and boasts of having taught "at the glorious academy of Bologna".[7] Scotta's influence also makes itself felt in the wily Vocilka from Tyl's stage fable *Strakonický dudák* (The Bagpiper of Strakonice, 1847), a university drop-out, tramp, scrounger, will-o'-the-wisp and sycophant.

In the end, all that remains of these innumerable adepts and hucksters is a vague, unsettling impression alongside the image of Golden Lane and its dwarf-like houses. Because of their similar fates they come together in a single shapeless charlatan-alchemist puppet-giant hopping over Prague with a knavish smirk on its face. O the blindness, o the stupidity, o the madness of greed! All the clownish fever, the devilish razzle-dazzle have vanished into nothingness, leaving behind only lead and smoke and a Saturnalian melancholy. None of the elixirs prolonged life. And if there was indeed a bit of gold to be found, it was to be found on the gallows.

48

Jan Amos Komenský writes in Chapter Twelve of *The Labyrinth of the World and the Paradise of the Heart*:

> That which has the potency to change metals into gold possesses other most astounding properties: for instance, it can preserve humans to the end of life and ward off death for two or three hundred years. In fact, if men knew how to use it, they could make themselves immortal. For this stone is nothing less than the seed of life, the kernel and quintessence of the universe, from which all animals, plants, metals and the very elements derive their being.

In Vladislav Vančura's comedy *Alchymista* (1932), we see Emperor Rudolf II before an assembly of astrologers and distillers (John Dee, Sendivogius, Kelley, Bragadino, Kepler, Hájek, Tycho Brahe and others) breathlessly imploring the alchemist Alessandro del Morone (a variation, perhaps, on our Italian mounteback Alessandro Scotta) to keep him from ageing, save him from the murky abyss, restore his youth.

The alchemy that flourished in Prague during Rudolf's reign and the search for the philosophers' stone also provided the idea for Karel Čapek's play *Věc Makropulos* (The Makropoulos Secret, 1922).[1] Hieronymos Makropoulos, one of the many quacks and distillers who thronged to Rudolf's court, and a blusterer in the mould of Scotta and Mamugna, prepares an elixir capable of keeping the sovereign young for three hundred years. Rudolf, afraid of being poisoned, has the alchemist's sixteen-year-old daughter test the *aurum potabile*. In this way another Prague motif, that of the spagyric art, enters into Čapek's repertoire alongside that of the Golem.

As the play begins, the alchemist's daughter is a famous singer named Elena Marty and has lived longer than three hundred years under a number of different names: Elina Makropoulos, Ellian MacGregor, Eugenia Montez, Ekaterina Myshkina and Elsa Müller. Čapek makes a point of her beauty, but she is "beautiful enough to drive one mad", "cold as ice", "cold as a knife", as if from the grave. She emanates a fascination, a perverse magnetism that infatuates and ensnares the men she meets, yet her perennial youth is in fact a disguised old age and she finds it difficult to hide the irritation of memory, the weary cynicism of experience. A wrinkle, an involuntary twitch, and out might come her real face: all her charms, shamelessly caked over with make-up – wrinkles artificially smoothed, cheeks red with wax, hair yellow with dandruff, a glass eye perhaps – would vanish, leaving only a fashionable hat.[2]

There is something both metaphysical and witchlike about the singer, a sullen magic heightened by the play's dry, legal-office setting. The formula for immortality she carries round her neck is reminiscent of the Golem's *shem*. Though coveted by many, it proves a terrible burden: Elena Marty is mortally weary of immortality. It undermines moral values and dries up feelings. The joy of life comes from an awareness of its brevity; too long a life produces boredom and revulsion.

> No one can love for three hundred years. Or hope, create, observe for three hundred years. It is impossible. One grows tired of everything. Being good and being bad. One grows tired of heaven and earth. And then one realizes that nothing in fact exists. Nothing. Neither sin nor pain nor even the earth: absolutely nothing.

The protagonist of Jakub Arbes's novella *Newtonův mozek* (Newton's Brain, 1877), a talking automaton, states before a learned assembly that human life prolonged through medical advances will eventually decline. Longevity, then, is a form of punishment. The Struldbrugs in *Gulliver's Travels* are not to be envied.

Leoš Janáček accentuates the ghost-like quality of the singer in his operatic version of *Věc Makropulos* (1925). Elena Marty has become haughty, aggressive, despotic and ultimately empty.[3] "It is a terrible thing, the feeling that man has no end," the composer wrote. "It is sheer grief. She wants nothing, expects nothing."[4] "A beauty three hundred years old and eternally young, but with dried-up feelings! Brrr! Cold as ice . . . "[5]

Like Helena Glory in *R.U.R.*, here too a woman, Kristina, destroys the formula by fire. Elena Marty's end is that of a Golem stripped of his *shem*. If mankind massacred by robots in *R.U.R.* stirs in Čapek a hymn to life, in *Věc Makropulos* the fall of life immortal inspires in him an *apologia* of death. Yet the moral is the same: the order of existence must not be upset. In the great ontological dilemma tormenting the world, death is necessary if only to give life beauty.

49

The focal point of Prague's magic was the Jewish Town (Židovské Město), also called Josefov after the late eighteenth-century Emperor Joseph II, the first ruler to ease religious and racial discrimination, and, during the nineteenth century, the Fifth Quarter (Pátá čtvrt). It is a mysterious district of which very little remains: several synagogues – principally the Staronová (Old-New) – the cemetery and the town hall with its famous clock, mentioned by Apollinaire ("the hands of the Jewish Quarter clock run backwards")[1] and Cendrars ("and the world, like the clock of the Jewish Quarter in Prague, desperately revolves backwards").[2] It is a district where to this day one feels the presence of the Golem because, as Nezval says, the Rabbi Loew's *shem* is on home ground, "under the tongue of all things, even of the pavement, though made of the same stone with which all Prague is paved".[3] The slanted architecture of the Ghetto sets one to dreaming, and one soon imagines the crooked houses moving, bunching together, driven by the *sheymes* stuck in the maws of their disturbing ogee doors.

According to Jewish tradition, the origins of the Prague Ghetto go back even farther than the founding of the city itself. Some legends claim that Jews came to Prague immediately after the destruction of the Temple in Jerusalem; others place their arrival during the eighth or ninth century. In Romantic novels their coming is foretold by no less than Libuše, yet the chroniclers are likely to confuse matters. Václav Hájek z Libočan claims in his Bohemian chronicle (1541) – as does the Jewish annalist David Gans in *Zemach David* (The Descendants of David, 1592) – that the Jews were granted permission to settle in Prague between 995 and 997 as a reward for having helped the Christians to repel the infidels.[4] It is, however, a proven fact that caravans of Jewish merchants established warehouses there earlier in the tenth century during their long journeys from the Orient to the West and that these way stations eventually formed the nucleus of a Jewish colony, which grew up during the twelfth and thirteenth centuries.

Since Gothic times, the Jewish Town was a plexus of crowded dwellings enclosed by a gated wall,[5] a wall within walls, which gradually expanded as Jews purchased houses along its periphery. (Following the Battle of White Mountain, for example, a number of houses abandoned by the Evangelicals were incorporated.)[6] The wall was torn down during the nineteenth century (despite the objections of fanatical rabbis who preferred isolation) and for a time replaced by *šňůry* and *dráty*, ropes and wire.

Adherence to tradition was so great that despite blazes, floods and attacks by the Christian mob, despite the oriels, turrets, porticos and roof terraces added during the Baroque, the Ghetto retained its original topography and medieval appearance until almost the mid-nineteenth century. Until then there were more houses made of wood (which was prohibited) than of stone.[7] Following each bout of destruction (like the terrible fire of 1689) everything was feverishly rebuilt as it had been.[8] Thus while Prague changed styles and grew, the Ghetto remained a heap of wretched medieval structures with scattered Baroque additions.[9]

Wedged into a narrow area between the Old Town and the river behind the "gallimordium", the old brothel,[10] the teeming Ghetto – with its ever-increasing population,[11] its crumbling, rat-infested houses – was the smallest of all Prague districts. Its 93 000 square metres made it one-ninth the size of the Old Town, which was tightly packed with churches, markets and monasteries, and one-thirteenth as large as Malá Strana, which consisted mostly of the gardens and palaces of the nobility.[12] The only trees to spread their branches in the Ghetto were those *painted on the walls*. There was but one garden: the garden of the dead. Yet for all its asphyxiating closeness the Ghetto had one synagogue for every ten houses.[13]

The picturesque aspect of the Ghetto (as we see it in yellowed photos and in the paintings of Jan Minařík, Antonín Slavíček and other artists from the beginning of the twentieth century) was a result of its daredevil architecture, the dense interweaving and overlapping of misshapen, damp, run-down, tainted hovels, nests for the King of Mice and his subjects. It was a bizarre labyrinth of filthy, unpaved alleyways as narrow as mine shafts, where sunbeams rarely swept away the refuse of the shadows: ugly, fetid alleyways running through the belly of a dilapidated tenement only to end like bats on a blind wall; alley-ways like crevices criss-crossed by patches of mould and foul smells; zigzag alleyways with streetlamps on the corners, cesspool-like puddles and arched wooden doors; alleyways, whose bends and curves lent them a certain drunken, wobbly, dreamlike quality.

The Ghetto had a large number of courtyards and galleries, galleries inside courtyards with twisted outside staircases, teetering old roofed-in staircases. If it was impossible to build a gallery in the courtyard, it was simply stuck onto the façade.[14]

The decrepit houses burst with inhabitants, who were often squeezed four to a room with straw mattresses in each corner. Despite the sickening heap of bodies, however, there were always coops for doves and geese.[15] Thus the hovels of the Jewish Town share the cramped quality of the dolls' houses in the alchemists' Golden Lane.

I feel I lived in that Ghetto long ago; I see myself as a Chagallesque Jew at Succoth with an *etrog*, a yellow cedar branch, in my hand or at Chanukkah, lighting an eight-armed menorah with a *shammes* candle, or as one of the *shammosim* in the many synagogues, or wandering through the foul, *gespenstisch* darkness of the narrow streets.

We are used to seeing the Prague Ghetto through Expressionist eyes and especially the descriptions of Meyrink, whose novel *Der Golem*, to use Kafka's words, "wonderfully reproduces the atmosphere of the old Jewish quarter of Prague".[16] Meyrink turns the Prague Ghetto into the *Schauplatz* of a demonic *Zwischenwelt*, a land of nightmare, whose spectre-like nature seems to symbolize the weariness and emaciation of Europe early in the century. His book tells us of the treachery of the Ghetto hovels, a treachery that increases at night when the doors open wide like screaming throats. In Paul Wegener's film *Der Golem* (1920) the slanted, angular houses have thatched Gothic spires articulated rhythmically as if to match the high conical hats and pointed beards of their tenants.[17] Expressionism closely follows the gloomy, *unheimlich*, medieval decay of the Fifth Quarter, the unruly ghosts who live here. Given its winding lanes, crooked, shrivelled houses, lop-sided windows and blotches of shadow, the city in *Doktor Caligari* may be based on the Prague Ghetto. Carl Mayer and Hans Janowitz apparently wanted to have the sets done by Alfred Kubin,[18] a German Bohemian from Litoměřice known for drawings evoking nightmares, sorcery and grotesque monstrosities and for his novel *Die andere Seite* (The Other Side) featuring the mouldy, decrepit houses of the city of Perle, which also recall the Fifth Quarter's rat-holes.

The golden age of the Prague Ghetto coincides with the reign of Rudolf II, when Rabbi Jehuda Loew (Liwa) ben Bezalel, a gold-mine of wholesome teachings, and the renowned benefactor and financier Mordechai Maisl (Meysl or Mayzl) lived there. Both were the subjects of many legends. Maisl (1528–1611), whose wealth was attributed to the spells of two dwarves (*trpaslíki*), was the *roysh-hakol* of the Jewish Town and built three synagogues – one of which bears his name – public baths, the town hall and a hospital and supported the *beth hamidrash*, the Talmudic school founded by Rabbi Loew. He clothed the poor, gave trousseaux to destitute brides and even lent money to Rudolf for his collections and campaigns against the Turks.[19]

Yet the history of the Prague Jewish Town, like that of all ghettos, is above all the history of the haunted little man: persecution, taxes, pogroms, expedients and subterfuges. The Ghetto did not live from moneylending and trade alone. There were craftsmen of every profession and a famous butchers' guild that supplied meat to Christians. There was once a butcher who weighed himself along with his wife every Saturday night and distributed the combined weight in cuts and quarters of meat to beggars.[20] And how strange that the Jews, who were excellent fire fighters, hastened to extinguish blazes in neighbouring quarters, the springboard for incursions that destroyed their own houses.[21]

Black-bearded Jews wandered among the decaying hovels of the Ghetto wearing pointed yellow hats whose tips were often decorated by a strange ball and caftans with yellow cloth circles.[22] But the picturesque is more than outweighed by misery and degradation: the instant they left the Old Town Ghetto, Jews were attacked by the rabble with rocks and snowballs like the puppets in a *jeu de massacre*, the pointed hats – later replaced by top hats – rolling on the ground.

50

Unlike the hats, the serrated triangle of the Old-New Synagogue spire did not roll; its grim, blackened, oblong quadrilateral, a storehouse of angelology, has stood firm since the late thirteenth century.[1]

The hero of the novel *Gotická duše* (A Gothic Soul, 1905) by Jiří Karásek takes a stroll one night along the dirty lanes of the Ghetto and happens to enter the synagogue,

> dead as if buried under the mould of graves, a wan beam of light falling from the narrow Gothic windows like a weak glimmer of the present . . . Through the oil lamps' suffocating stench came the voice of the cantor singing in the almemar, his drawling voice like a lament for the dead past and a people living in vain. The congregation, heads bowed, dully bewailed the destruction of Jerusalem . . . It was so desperate and mournful he had to leave to keep from choking in sadness . . . [2]

Another visitor, Hans Christian Andersen, notes more prosaically in 1866, "The ceiling, the windows and the walls were filthy with smoke, and the smell of onions was so foul I had to go back into the open."[3]

Today the synagogue bears the lifeless patina of a museum, but as late as the nineteenth century, buried between the crush of the surrounding hovels, it aroused fear with its ogee architecture, the mournful light filtering through its small windows, the Gothic grating enclosing its almemar, the dusty attic in which the remains of the Golem were said – yes, even then! – to lie, the grimy walls covered with stains shaped like morays or lampreys and spattered with the blood of Jews slaughtered as far back as the massacre of 1389, commemorated in the famous lament of Rabbi Avigdor Karo.[4]

"Tausend Jahre zählt der Tempel schon in Prag," Else Lasker-Schüler wrote in a poem.[5] The Old-New Synagogue is said to be older than Saint Vitus', than any church in Prague. There are a number of legends concerning its origin: that it was built with stone from the destroyed Temple in Jerusalem and brought to Prague by Jews fleeing Palestine; that community elders dug into a hill indicated by an old soothsayer and came upon the Synagogue completely built; that angels transferred the rubble of the Jerusalem Temple to Prague (much as the House of the Virgin – the Santa Casa – was "flown" from Nazareth to Loreto), where they rebuilt it with the injunction to alter nothing. Whosoever attempted to tamper with that dark naved and aisled cell was visited with misfortune and death. During a blaze in the Jewish Town a host of angels (themselves creatures of fire, according to the Talmud)[6] would appear on the spire – the Synagogue's pointed hat – in the guise of white doves to save it from the flames.[7]

51

A group of olive-complexioned, bearded men in long, black, white-ruffed robes and tall, black, moth-eaten hats makes its way along the narrow lanes of the Ghetto. They are members of the Funeral Brotherhood (*Pohřební bratrstvo* or *Chevra kaddisha*), an august confraternity engaged in works of charity: comforting the ill, succoring the dying, conducting funeral services and maintaining cemeteries. Membership was considered a great honour. At the annual banquet held to name the head of the Brotherhood, members drank from mugs decorated with funeral scenes.[1] Their doleful mien and grave gait contrasted sharply with the pranks of the *badchanim*, the Purim jesters. And here they are with silver combs to card the locks of the dead, silver brushes to clean their fingernails, mounds of earth to prop their lifeless heads. Sullen masks, they wend their way to the Old Jewish Cemetery.

A misreading of certain headstones has placed the origins of this necropolis in the distant past. In point of fact the earliest stone, that of the poet and rabbi Avigdor Karo, bears the date 23 April 1439. When in his lament for the pogrom of 1398 Avigdor states that not even the graves were spared the wrath of the Christian rabble, he is certainly referring to another, older burial site. The latest headstone bears the date 17 May 1787. Burials in the Old Jewish Cemetery were discontinued during that year by order of Emperor Joseph II to prevent the plague from spreading through so densely populated an area.[2]

Compressed into a strip of land between the Klaus, Pinkas and Old-New Synagogues, the Cemetery was originally surrounded by bordellos, soaking pits, tanners' booths and huts inhabited by executioners, outcasts and dog catchers.[3] A confusion of tombs piled one on top of the other, it reflects the mania for crowding together people we find in the hovels and for heaping together objects we find in the Ghetto's junkshops. There was so little space that new soil was simply sprinkled over old graves, and because parts of the Cemetery have as many as twelve layers of tombs the ground is extremely uneven.[4] Dense clusters of crooked, broken gravestones protrude, leaning like Brueghel's blind men, sinking, soon to be swallowed by the damp black earth.

The gentlemen of the Brotherhood struggle along the narrow paths, their contorted shapes like those of the shaky gravestones. Stones deformed like pulled teeth, wrinkled stone tiaras stuck in the mud, slabs that crawl like *culs-de-jatte* over inextricable detritus, stelae laid bare by the writhing of the dead and the bulges in the soil perform a mysterious ballet. Rabbi Loew's grandson Samuel, who died in 1655, wished to be buried near his grandfather's grave. The plots on all sides were full, but with a little push here and a little pull there the Rabbi's tomb was shifted to make room for him.[5]

Spiderwebs hang from tomb to tomb like scraps of crêpe. Visitors, descendants and the devout leave small piles of pebbles as a token of respect for the deceased, as the Jews did in the desert during Biblical times for lack of flowers. The only vegetation in this garden of the dead consists of bare, eroded, shrivelled and bent elder shrubs, which seem to imitate the slant of the tombstones. In spring the air is filled with a pungent smell and a riot of corymbs in bloom, and the populous family of stunted, crippled slabs seems to draw comfort from their white blossoms.

Holunderblüte (Elder Blossoms, 1863), a novella by Wilhelm Raabe, tells the story of a lazy student who travels from Vienna to Prague, where he meets a girl in the Ghetto, the granddaughter of the Cemetery caretaker and a descendent of Rabbi Loew. Her name is Jemima, "like Job's daughter". The student spends the entire summer taking walks with her amidst the gravestones and elder shrubs, listening to her legends of the dead. Like the dying Marinka, the daughter of a street musician in the 1834 Mácha tale that bears her name, Jemima has a beauty out of keeping with the poverty and haunted grime of the environment in which she lives.[6] Jemima senses the proximity of death: she has a heart ailment like the delicate ballerina Mahalath who perished in 1780 in the blossom of her youth, the last person (according to Raabe) to be buried in the Cemetery.

"You will forget me as one forgets a dream," Jemima says to her beloved, adding: "Remember the elder blossoms!" In May of the following year, 1820, the student returns to Prague, "which itself is like a dream", in time for the elder blossoms. While the city prepares for the festival of Saint John of Nepomuk with wreaths, carpets and greenery, a gloomy silence hangs over the Ghetto. The student learns that Jemima has died. With the enticing scent of its elders, with its centuries of decay, its slanting tombs and the stern glances of its evil fetishes, the Jewish Cemetery suffuses a pernicious melancholy, a mortal blackness. "And they call this place Beth-Chaim, the *House of Life!*" Raabe exclaims.

This theatre of stone seems to resound in the "Prayer of the Stone" by Vladimír Holan, where a rock mass speaks – it matters little whether the rock represents a menhir or dolmen or massebot or the Prague stelae – in an abstruse catacombian language of its own:

> Paleostom bezjazy,
> madžnûn at kraun at tathău at saün
> luharam amu-amu dahr!
> Ma yana zinsizi?
> Gamchabatmy! Darsk ādōn darsk bameuz.
> Voskresaet at maimo šargiz-duz,
> chisoh ver gend ver sabur-sabur
> Theglathfalasar
> bezjazy munay! Dana! Gamchabatmy![7]

Holan's prayer can be interpreted as the eulogy of a dead man, if we assign the word *voskresaet* (Russian for "resurrects", "rises") a role similar to that of *shalom* in the ancient Graeco-Hebrew epitaphs in Palestine.[8] In his diary *Lemuria*, Holan calls the gravestone *aktinolit*, that is, "light-stone" (from the Greek ἀκτίς, "splendour, brightness").[9]

The gentlemen of the Brotherhood wander amidst the immense blackened herd of headstones – immense in so narrow an enclosure, where one can barely squeeze one's way through. There are eleven thousand of them, from the most simple and coarse made of sandstone – square or oblong with a flat, curved or pointed top – to the more refined and ostentatious in red Slivenec marble or limestone, which date from the sixteenth century, to the sarcophagi of the seventeenth century such as Rabbi Loew's, which can take the form of a tabernacle or ark (*ohel* or, in Yiddish, *hoyslech*, "little house") and reflect the influence of Baroque architecture.[10]

52

The gravestones have a rich symbology. Blessing hands are the sign of *kohanim*, the priests; pitcher and basin are their assistants, the *leviim*. Scissors indicate the grave of a tailor, tweezers the grave of a doctor; a mortar and pestle represents an apothecary, a lute an instrument maker, a book a printer and an *etrog* a vendor of greenery for the Succoth festival. Grapes signify wisdom and fertility; a scene in Paradise means that the name of the woman in the grave is Chava (Eve), a rose that her name is Rose; pictures of animals (stags, bears, wolves, lions, roosters, foxes, doves, carp, geese) designate people with animal surnames.[1] A headstone depicting Adam and Eve contained a young couple slain on their wedding night by the angel of death; a headstone graced by two chickens pointing their beaks at a woman's head marked the resting place of an adulteress whose eyes were pecked out. There is a legend that the carcass of a dog that had been thrown over the wall to desecrate the graveyard was buried in a corner by Rabbi Loew.[2]

In addition to the name and title or profession of the deceased and the date on which they died and were buried (reckoned in relation to the beginning of the world) the gravestones contain sobriquets, stereotyped eulogies, wishes for eternal life in verse and rhymed prose, lists of the deceased's merits and formulaic lamentations from the Bible and rabbinical literature.[3]

I sense the letters on the headstones in this lugubrious ballet ready to spring to life like the words in the *Book of Ibbur*, which a slanty-eyed stranger presents to Athanasius Pernath in Meyrink's novel. The square letters of the Hebrew alphabet (perhaps by analogy to those of the old Ghetto printers' shops) come together in optical poems with the other funeral symbols, visual alphabets analogous to the old Prague shop signs whose praises Josef Čapek sang in *Nejskromnější umění* (The Humblest Art, 1920). It is no accident that Hoffmeister depicted the Jewish Cemetery in almost alphabetic collages where even the elder shrubs take on the appearance of Hebrew characters.[4] Headstones and sacrophagi, shrubs and men of the Brotherhood – they all seem to have metamorphosed into dancing letters whose fantastical permutations constitute a mad Talmudic exercise in acrology.

These "strange hieroglyphics", as Raabe calls them, have fascinated a number of writers. In a short story by Kafka, Josef K. dreams of a cemetery – surely the graveyard of the Fifth Quarter – where he meets an artist with a velvet cap (perhaps a colleague of Titorelli's). The artist writes "Here Lies" on a tombstone (under which Josef K. will soon disappear) in gold letters with an ordinary pencil. "Every letter was clear and beautifully formed, deeply incised and all of the purest gold."[5]

In Jiří Karásek's novel *Ganymedes* (1925), the Englishman Adrian Morris, a "human sphinx" as enigmatic as Crawford's Wanderer, walks about the Jewish Cemetery seeking the grave of Rabbi Loew and interpreting the inscriptions and emblems that grace the headstones.[6] In *Hobby* (1969) by Jiří Fried, the narrator takes a stroll with an insane old copyist at the melancholy sunset hour to contemplate the tombstones of a graveyard, perhaps that of the Prague Ghetto. The old man transcribes the Hebrew epitaphs thinking they are secret formulas, though he does not understand them.

Where is the mathematician Joseph Shalomo ben Elijahu Delmedigo de Candia? Where is the annalist and astronomer David Gans? Where the butcher David Koref? Where the Rabbis Zeeb Auerbach and David Oppenheim? Where Rabbi Judah Loew ben Bezalel? And Mordechai Maisl? And Frumeta, his second wife? And Hendel, the wife of the *Hofjude* Jacob Bashevi of Treuenberk,[7] in whose tomb a Polish queen was said to rest in peace? Where are the gentlemen of the Brotherhood who were here just now, so black and so emaciated that they looked like orioles in their broad, flat hats? Swallowed by the mire, they lie crushed beneath the stones, slush and moss – shadows of memory.

"The shadow enters darkness and man enters earth," Jaroslav Seifert says softly in his poem "Světlem oděná" (Arrayed in Light) during his walk through Prague towards evening. He quietly approaches the walls of the Jewish Cemetery whence the pestilential breath and evil eye of the Golem spreads.[8] And not only of the Golem. For the necropolis teems with phantoms. Beneath a tombstone depicting a woman between two roosters lies a Catholic priest, a renegade Jew who wished to be buried alongside the Jewess he had loved in his youth. And every night a skeleton ferries him across the Vltava to Saint Vitus' Cathedral so he can play penitential psalms on the organ.[9]

53

The Jewish Cemetery has captured the imagination of many Czech painters (Antonín Mánes, Jaroslav Čermák, Vojtěch Hynais, Jindřich Štyrský, Adolf Hoffmeister) and several foreign writers (including Andersen and Liliencron).[1] During his stays in Prague the Polish writer Przybyszewski took walks here with Jiří Karásek,[2] an authority on Golemic legends and master of graveyard effects, as in the novella *Zastřený obraz* (The Veiled Picture, 1923), featuring a crumbling Malá Strana graveyard (in the Košíře section) complete with melancholy ash trees, rusty iron crosses and Empire-style angels.[3]

Visitors are struck by the centuries-old sadness of the place, the accumulation of the dead of many generations in so small an area, sunken, to quote Raabe, "as in a bottomless, voracious swamp", the intense vitality of the crowd of lopsided stone, their mystery increasing in the feeble winter light when they jut out of the snow and the icy wind shakes the slender branches above them. Rudolf Lothar describes in "Der Golem" (1904) the desolation of the place when the whirling snow drapes the tombs in ermine stoles and spreads a shimmering carpet over the narrow paths. The gravestones in the veiled light of a winter afternoon reminded Crawford of the ranks of a great routed army; the consumptive bushes suggested a forest of skeletons extending their bony hands. Remember the elder blossoms!

The ghostly atmosphere explains why Raabe, Karásek and Crawford set mysterious scenes here. In *Ganymedes* Karásek uses it as the meeting place for the eccentric Englishman Adrian Morris and the Danish-Jewish sculptor Jørgen Møller, an occultist who tries to extract the secret of the Golem from the epitaph engraved on Rabbi Loew's coffin. The necromancer has a nose "hooked like the beak of a bird of prey" and perfidious eyes bloodshot "as if dripping dark red mulberry juice".[4]

In Crawford's creaky hearse of a novel *The Witch of Prague* the witch Unorna hypnotizes the fanatical young Jew Israel Kafka in the Cemetery of the Fifth Quarter, forcing him to relive all the torments suffered by Šimon Abeles, a boy who, according to legend, was tortured and killed by his father because he had renounced the Jewish faith. This legend, encouraged by the propaganda of the Counter-Reformation, created an uproar during the Baroque. In September 1693 twelve-year-old Šimon Abeles fled the Ghetto for the Klementinum, the Jesuit seminary, and asked to be baptized. He was, however, returned to his parents. His father, assisted by a certain Löbl Kurtzhandl, tortured and killed the boy on 21 February 1694. When the crime came to light, Lazar Abeles was arrested. He hanged himself by his phylacteries in the Old Town Hall prison. The executioner dragged the body outside the city gate, drew and quartered it, tore out the heart and crushed it to a pulp. Kurtzhandl, condemned to death on 19 April 1694, was broken on the wheel, where he agreed to convert in exchange for the privilege of being administered a coup de grâce by the executioner.

Egon Erwin Kisch, who studied the Inquisition-like proceedings, was convinced that the Abeles case was a monstrous show trial staged by the Jesuit politburo.[5] The boy's body was exhumed from the Jewish Cemetery and placed on display for an entire month in the Old Town Hall. The curious came and dipped their handkerchiefs in the fountains of fresh blood that gushed from his wounds. At last, after an opulent funeral cortège in March 1694, the mortal remains of Šimon Abeles were laid to rest in the Týn Church not far from the tomb of Tycho Brahe. Students, nobles and the bells of every church in Prague honoured the martyr as a candidate for sainthood. There was a fearful silence in the Ghetto.[6]

According to Raabe, there is no sky so black during a storm as the sky over the cemetery of the Prague Ghetto. "The old elder shrubs sigh and groan like living beings in great tribulation, and the ground gulps the torrents with a sinister gurgle as they stream down the headstones crammed one on top of the other." Gentlemen of the Funeral Brotherhood, let us leave before the storm tinges the sky the colour of ink, let us leave this place. It does not lift my spirits. For it provides shelter from everything but death.

54

When the walls and gates were torn down at the beginning of the nineteenth century, all that remained to mark the boundary between the Ghetto and the Old Town were tangles of metal wire, *dráty*. Well-to-do Jews gradually abandoned filthy, overcrowded Josefov as their wealth increased through speculation and business, and moved to modern houses.[1] By the beginning of the twentieth century the area around Vrchlický Gardens (the Stadtpark) and the residential district of Bubeneč was a plexus of splendid villas built by wealthy Jews.[2]

But the petite bourgeoisie of accountants, junior clerks and commercial travellers, who loved the dignity of their white collar, also left the *eyrev*, the enclosed Fifth Quarter. Only the destitute and the fanatically Orthodox remained. In return, Christian beggars and other anti-social elements – swindlers, whores and ne'er-do-wells, the suspicious and the lost – swarmed in. Indeed, the Jewish Town, called "Za drátem" (Behind the Wire) after the wire that still hung loosely at a few points during the seventies,[3] became a refuge for criminals and the down-and-out, a promised land for thieves and vagabonds, a den of iniquity.

"It is as though the jurisdiction of the world had ceased and the lonely traveller were left at the mercy of other invisible, hidden and malevolent powers."[4] In Karásek's novel *Ganymedes*, walking through that area the Englishman Adrian "felt the humiliation of the old Ghetto, now demolished, the filth and defilement of its peeling buildings, its winding streets and lanes teeming with inhabitants emerging from their oppressive, ugly caves . . . "[5]

The rotten cobblestones stank of refuse, stagnant puddles and foul rivulets. Rats were everywhere. In the entrances to the hovels half-naked women relieved themselves in plain view – the quarter had neither latrines nor sewers – and during the sweltering heat they left their suffocating houses to delouse their children (as they used to do in Sicilian villages when I was a boy: I still remember the crunching sound of lice being squashed between thumbnails). On hot evenings, when the residents sat out in front of their foul-smelling shanties and bantered with neighbours across the alley, family secrets flew from door to door, from balcony to courtyard.[6]

In the poem "Z ghetta" (From the Ghetto), Jaroslav Vrchlický depicts a woman who on a scorching summer afternoon reels along this "winding network of crooked houses", this "mingling of refuse and rubble"; a bedraggled woman with a yellow tinge to her face, goose down in her ruffled hair and the "weight of motherhood beneath a veil of threadbare rags", followed and mocked by the rabble.[7]

But let us look inside these cold, musty hovels, these stinking dens, these fetid holes: rooms a few metres square divided by strings or chalk lines on the floor; persons of different age and sex who had met in a tavern or in prison, hardened petty thieves and bankrupts who had once owned flats lined with plush carpets in other Prague districts packed together indiscriminately – every room, then, a kind of Dark Hole, a den of rotten straw mattresses and tables used as makeshift beds in which sick old people, passionate couples, prostitutes and children huddled between ghostly chalk lines and women gave birth in the presence of strangers, a Dark Hole in which the crowding increased towards evening as the beggars returned from their rounds. The crush of the maids and helpers in K.'s overheated Brückenhof room in *The Castle* may well reflect the heaping of tenants into the filthy cubicles of Josefov.

The main source of income for the wastrels who came together in the Ghetto and the Jews who had remained behind was the barter of every kind of junk. Odd-looking peddlers, tiny men with shrewd faces in bowler hats exhibited their *Trödelwaren* on stands and in the entrances of dark shops, trying to lure the idlers who came to the Ghetto out of curiosity. Apollinaire recounts in "Le Passant de Prague": "We walked through the Jewish Quarter with its stalls of old clothing, scrap iron and other nameless objects."[8] At every step, at every corner, flocks of junk dealers squabbled to sell off the rummage the *handrlata* had turned up for them in the city.

55

The *handrlata*[1] were itinerant junk men who went from house to house with sacks over their shoulders buying up rags and rummage. They were as much a part of the Prague streets as the Slovak *dráteníci* (tinkers) and the *opánkáři* (sandalmakers) with their broad round hats.[2] They were old, very old and as transparent as if made of straw – constables of Methuselah, vezirs of the Christmas Witch. Bundled up in long, filthy overcoats like the caftans of the Polish Jews, bent over by the weight of their sacks, they entered every courtyard, croaking in a drawling, plaintive voice, "Handrle-handrle vu"?[3] A mob of street urchins would tease them – "Handrle-handrle vu?" – and they would swing their sacks at them, vainly shooing them away.

A curious head pops out from one of the windows along the galleries, and the *handrle, dieu-clochard* that he is, calls out squinting slyly, "Nix zu handln, nix zu chahrn?"[4] Mrs Hlochová makes a sign to him from the second floor: she has piled together her husband's old things in her narrow kitchen: shoes with worn-through soles, threadbare vests, opera hats so crumpled they make your hair stand on end. The *handrle* buys it all, forcing down the price as much as he can: you have to ask three times what you want, then make gradual concessions. Offer shoes and he wants clothing; offer clothing and he wants shoes. In fact, he is equally eager for both, though he swears he is not interested in either and takes them only because he "doesn't want to have climbed the stairs for nothing". He strikes his bargain and asks, "Is that all, missus?" and Mrs Hlochová removes a flotilla of white starched collars, gloves, bowler hats and parasols from a chest. The *handrle* buys everything: razors, combs, lamps, scissors with broken ends, spurs, albums, locks without keys and blonde locks from a mane miraculously luxuriant thanks to Anna Csillag's Hair Lotion. There is only one thing he turns up his nose at: ladies' hats. Mrs Hlochová takes out a very old one, glistening with naphthalene. The *handrle* starts, knits his brow as if he had seen a *másik*, a demon, and cries out with disdain, "I am not a milliner, missus!" But then he notices the black ostrich feather. "I'll take the feather, but you can keep the hat." The dithering goes on for hours. More than once the emaciated little man flings the sack over his shoulder, opens the door and pretends to leave, yet before long back comes his head like a puppet's through the curtain: "One florin eighty, missus; I swear to God I can't give you more . . . "[5]

Everything the *handrlata* bought during their peregrinations through the courtyards of Prague ended up in the *tandlmark* of the Fifth Quarter. Crushed mortars, bent graters, wooden spoons, hammers and chisels, broken tools, unrecognizable machine parts and mousetraps lay piled high in the cavern-like depths of warehouses or spread out on street stands. Unmatched muddy horseshoes, ladles, frying pans and coal rakes, buttless guns, rusty daggers, dress swords with mother-of-pearl handles, timepieces without dials, "Schwarzwald" cuckoo clocks without striking mechanisms, knives without blades, forks without teeth, hiltless swords, bottomless sieves, triggerless muskets and tongueless scales.[6] Plus a *kudlmudl*[7] of dusty tomes it was a joy to rummage in, to say nothing of worn-out shoes, pipe bowls, umbrellas and wrinkled suits reeking of sweat.

Thus, the Ghetto became a kind of *Merzbau*, a Babel-like drydock of trifles and tatters scrounged from all over Prague. It was as though the flotsam and jetsam of creation had converged there. If silver dominated Rudolf's *Kunstkammer*, rusty scrap iron dominated the Fifth Quarter. Both of Prague's great stockpiles – high art and base realia – seem to have been governed by the apotropaic power of metals.

Early photographs show the dark junk shops of the Ghetto crammed to the ceiling with merchandise, goods spilling out of the doors, piled on stools and along the floor, small men wearing bowler hats and baggy clown trousers, the junk dealers, as dignified as Georgian *kintos*, standing under the shop sign, in front of clocks, bird cages and petroleum lamps. In *The Golem* Meyrink enumerates the shoddy items for sale in one of them: "the battered metal cornet without keys, the incredible portrait of still more incredible military men in red coats, painted on a paper background yellow with age; rusty spurs stuck in a circle round a mildewed leather strap and antiquated furniture of every kind and description."[8]

In the Fifth Quarter broken and wobbly objects got back on their feet: clock faces found their dials, guns their triggers, blades their handles. Any *pištuntál*,[9] any trifle, represented a potential fortune. This microcosm of the business world was especially animated on Sundays. Sellers and customers haggled, all cries and oaths, their arms flailing. It was a true spectacle, a Bohemian kermis worthy of a Bohemian Brueghel.[10]

56

The most dedicated drinkers and whoremongers converged on the Ghetto at night. "Vous allez voir," Isaac Laquedem says to Apollinaire, "pour la nuit, chaque maison s'est transformée en lupanar."[1] Taverns, brothels and every manner of enticement flourished in the narrow streets of the Fifth Quarter. There were smoke-filled bars smelling of mildew and decrepitude, the regulars jammed together beneath an oil lamp that cast a yellowish glow over their bloated bellies;[2] there were bordellos which, following an 1862 decree, displayed a long iron pole with a red lantern,[3] red like the light of the honky-tonks and saloons in the Storyville section of New Orleans during the early days of jazz.[4]

Had you, an ambiguous shade, wandered through the Ghetto's maze at night by the flame of the sparse gas lamps, you would have run into masses of tarts – *flundry, fuchtle* and *bludičky*[5] – tempting passers-by with their crudely made-up mouths, their come-hither eyes, their raised skirts and *zeisiggrün* stockings.[6] In some streets almost every house was a house of prostitution[7] with moth-ball bawds winking from the doors and windows, their huge wrinkled breasts hanging down to their elbows. "At each door, standing or seated, was a shawled matron muttering the call to nocturnal love."[8]

Siskin-green stockings, sinister red-potion lamps, blind harpists, luxurious "salons" (like the Salón Aaron described by Paul Leppin) with wall-to-wall mirrors in which languid, opulent whores worthy of a Pascin – *jeptišky* or "nuns", as they are called in some Prague songs[9] – lazily trailed *secese* dresses across thick carpets. The provincials who ended up in the Fifth Quarter in search of amusement ran the risk of awakening parted from their wallets, watches or rings.[10] Criminals and knaves often hid out in the taverns and houses of ill repute, bringing the plumed police in their wake.[11]

Oddly enough, the houses of the remaining Orthodox Jews, austere individuals who observed the holy days in the traditional fashion, survived almost to the end of the Fifth Quarter alongside the bordellos. It was not uncommon for the din from the *Tanztavernen*, the shouts of the drunks in the streets and the uproarious laughter of the whores to mingle with the drone of Sabbath chants issuing from the synagogues.[12]

The ambivalence and eccentricity of Josefov was intensified at the end of the nineteenth century by a number of bizarre characters: tiny, well-dressed, clean-shaven Herr Wehle, who was known as "Wehle mit dem Paraplüh" (Wehle with the umbrella) because he always carried an umbrella and a parasol, and walked the lanes, followed by a crowd of hooting urchins, with one open over his head and the other closed under his arm, depending on the weather; or melancholy Chaim Paff, who was known as "Paff mit der ledernen Flinte" (Paff with the leather rifle) and would run away screaming if anyone yelled "piff paff" (bang bang) at him.[13]

Lovelorn servant girls, ladies in rustling silk, people hoping for a glimpse into the future came from all over Prague to consult the Fifth Quarter's many fortune-tellers and sorceresses. These soothsayers were accessible only through a tangle of galleries, corridors and rooms overflowing with tenants who scrutinized the intruders with acrimonious glances. Their cramped quarters were filled with cards, chalk, bottles of murky liquids and books on geomancy, and many of them kept big black cats with owl-like heads.[14]

57

The stench, the filth, the dilapidated, teeming hovels, the lack of sanitary facilities and drinking water, the narrow alleyways with neither air nor a ray of sunlight, the poverty, prostitution and crime all led the municipal authorities to demolish the Ghetto.[1] As a result of the *asanační zákon* (Slum Clearance Law) of 11 February 1893, the entire Jewish Town, with the exception of a few synagogues, the town hall and the cemetery, was razed to the ground.

The crooked hovels, the dance halls, the brothels, the public houses, the salons and the dives – Lojzíček, Luskovic, Jenerál (The General), Stará paní (The Old Lady), Denice (The Morning Star), Tři kapři (The Three Carp), U Lišků (The Liškas' Place), U chytrého zvířete (The Cunning Beast) – all disappeared. The entire Babylon of vice into which the charlatans, pimps and outcasts had sunken was suddenly gone.[2] Valid as the reasons for demolition were, the process was more ruthless than it need have been. If we did not know that building speculation played an important role in it, we might presume it was the desire to do away with the humiliation of its inhabitants that fed the destructive fury of its demolishers, who turned its alleys into Parisian-style boulevards, its shanties into luxurious *secese* palaces the better to satisfy the desire for splendour on the part of the *haute bourgeoisie*.[3]

True, the Slum Clearance Law did not affect the Jewish Quarter alone. Other districts that failed to meet the hygienic requirements of a modern city – Na Františku, for example – were levelled. Such merciless devastation aroused the wrath of many cultural figures. On the initiative of Vilém Mrštík, author of the novel *Santa Lucia*, a number of writers drafted a manifesto entitled "Českému lidu" (To the Czech People) on 5 April 1896 in defence of threatened landmarks.

In 1897 Mrštík published a fiery pamphlet entitled "Bestia Triumphans", excoriating all those who would mar the city's character in the name of urban renewal, who would destroy distinctive examples of its architecture and replace them with dreary *Wohnmaschinen*. Mrštík accused the barbarous, anti-humanist Bestia, a figure he borrowed from Nietzsche's *Dawn*, of blinding and brutalizing its followers and inciting them to deface the city on the Vltava with acts of vandalism. He denounced the efforts of the Municipal Council as "a policy of deception, a circus of Pharisaic masks" in the service of the Bestia.[4]

For Mrštík, who came from the as yet untouched Moravian country-side, the destruction of Prague, this "paradise of the heart", resulted from the decay of a national culture that was repudiating traditions, folklore and patriarchal customs in its mania for modernism.[5] Other writers picked up Mrštík's theme. Jiránek saw the removal of the "splendid branch of a centuries-old chestnut tree in Letenská Street" and the division of an old garden into lots as evidence of the fearful advance of the Bestia Triumphans.[6] Vrchlický lamented the disappearance of "old corners", "old temples", "narrow winding lanes", the "mystical Ghetto", "old embankments," the "city ruined by the modern age" in the poem "Stará Praha".[7]

Poets voiced the melancholy of that vanished world many times over. In the story "Das Gespenst der Judenstadt" Paul Leppin describes a beautiful, ailing prostitute Johanna who flees the hospital one night to return to the "salon" in which she worked only to find it levelled in the name of progress.[8] Vrchlický, who laments the disappearance of the Ghetto, sings the praises of the blackened, collapsing synagogues that survive: "You are like widows, you grey synagogues,/in tattered garments, ashes on your head,/yet when the night comes to earth in a black tallis,/I see your windows shine, all flame and porphyry."[9]

Although the zeal of the Slum Clearance crusaders put an end to the musty smell, the unhealthy atmosphere and the mystery are still present in Prague's heavy air. As Kafka said to Janouch:

> In us all it still lives – the dark corners, the secret alleys, shuttered windows, squalid courtyards, rowdy pubs and sinister inns. We walk through the broad streets of the newly built town. But our steps and our glances are uncertain. Inside we tremble just as before in the ancient streets of our misery. Our heart knows nothing of the slum clearance which has been achieved. The unhealthy old Jewish Town within us is far more real than the hygienic town around us. With our eyes open we walk through a dream: ourselves only a ghost of a vanished age.[10]

At certain magic hours the atmosphere of the destroyed Ghetto seems to spread to every corner of Prague like the smell of stale beer, like the dampness of the river. Nezval noted that from time to time, "especially during the days in which the sky brews a storm but the storm does not come", the spell of the Jewish Town spread "like a wing extended too long in flight in one of the old museums".[11] Nezval also remembers a nocturnal walk with Jindřich Honzl in the troubled old Josefov district whose – his words – "De Chiricoesque vistas" provided him with the key to a different emotional interpretation of Prague.[12] The dense crush of feverish ratholes is thus transformed into the nostalgic rarefaction of Metaphysical Painting.

58

What is a Golem? An artificial man made of clay. Like the orderly Švejk, the servant Golem is a key figure of Magic Prague. The Hebrew word *golem* (*goylem* in Yiddish) in the 139th Psalm indicates a rudiment, a sprout, an embryo, or, better still, "imperfect substance":[1]

> My substance was not hid from thee,
> when I was made in secret, and curiously
> wrought in the lowest parts of the earth.
> Thine eyes did see my substance, yet being imperfect . . .

The reference to earth inclines one to presume that as early as Biblical times *golem* meant a mass of clay.[2]

The concept of *golem* thus implies something unfinished, coarse, undeveloped. In the Talmud a woman who has not yet conceived and a jug requiring polishing are termed *golem*.[3] It is but a short step from the meaning of "imperfect" and "rough" to that of a dim-witted, clumsy man.

The creation of the Golem, that rabbinical diversion, follows the myth of Adam, the only man who did not issue from his mother's womb, being formed instead from the dust of Elohim (Genesis 2:7).[4] One could say that the ancient protoplast was also a formless mass of soil (virgin soil), a Golem, until Yahweh Elohim breathed the breath of life into its nostrils and made it the gardener of paradise; conversely, one could call the Golem an Adam without the breath of life, an incomplete creature of clay, its aphasia proof that it lacks a soul (though certain mystics claim that while lacking *neshumah* (the light of God) it does possess *ruach* and *nefesh* or, at least, like animals, a vegetative soul.[5]

All the many variations on the *Golemlegende* depict the mute mud puppet as a surly but dim-witted servant, a leaden fool. Its stature is that of a giant, and it has two sewer-like nostrils and a mouth as large as a millstone. Three motifs recur throughout the flamboyant palette of variations: servitude (the *Knechtmotiv*), rage (which culminates in rebellion) and the return to dust (whence it came).

How does one make a Golem? First one must purify oneself, the oldest formula being contained in the commentary of the imaginative Eleasar of Worms (1176–1238) to the *Sefer Yezira*, the Book of Creation, a text one must know thoroughly before attempting to begin.[6] Then one forms a puppet from virgin earth and walks it in a circle while reciting the letters of the tetragram in various permutations. One of the variations prescribes 462 turns.[7] To make the Golem move on its own, one writes the word *emet* (truth) on its forehead or places the *shem* (*shem hameforash*, a slip of paper inscribed with the unutterable name of God) in its mouth. Just as the signs of the alphabet – together with numbers and *sefiroth* – play an essential part in the creation of the universe, so the word is central to the modelling of artificial man, an imitation of divine creation; indeed, the magic power of the alphabet – and especially that of the tetragram – is what infuses instincts and impulses into the base clay.

How does one destroy a Golem? By walking it in a circle in the opposite direction while reciting the alphabet backwards as a curse, paying close attention to the number of turns, the combinations of letters and the way one walks. Otherwise one will end up like the students of a mystic who, after walking backwards with the wrong gait and mumbling the letters in the wrong order, sank into mud up to their navels and would have died had the rabbi not intervened.[8] There are, however, simpler means to weaken and dissolve a Golem that turns – heaven help us! – insolent. One removes the *shem* from its mouth or, if it has the word *emet* on its forehead, erases the first letter so that only *met* ("death") remains, and the creature will go limp and revert to a mass of soft mud. But one must take care lest one meet the fate of Rabbi Elijah of Chełm, called Israel Ba'al Shem Tov, a famous gaon and miracle worker of the sixteenth century, who by means of a ruse had the puppet bend over and scrape off the first letter of the word *emet* only to be crushed to death when the immense heap of clay collapsed upon him.[9]

59

There once was a time when no self-respecting town in East-Central Europe lacked a *Golemlegende* of its own or a rabbi who did not dream of fashioning androids and automata with the help of the *Sefer Yezira*. The most prominent Golem makers are the previously-mentioned Rabbi Elijah of Chełm and Rabbi Jehuda Loew ben Bezalel, who created his Golem in the Prague Ghetto.

Loew (also Loewe or Liwa) was born in Worms or Poznań between 1512 and 1520 and led congregations in Mikulov (in Moravia), Poznań and, finally, from 1573 on, Prague, where he died in 1609.[1] A respected authority on mathematics, physics and astronomy, a penetrating exegete of the *Haggadah* and a sworn foe of Talmudic casuistry, the Maharal[2] was considered one of the most profound scholars of the age.[3] "His fame," Rudolf Lothar writes in the story "Der Golem", "has spread throughout the world. Emperors and kings speak of him, and all learned men are his friends. What he writes is as precious as gold and precious stones, and what he says enters his mouth from God."[4]

Yet why does the Golem legend adhere to a sage completely outside the Cabalistic tradition and whose biography provides no real basis for the myth of the pernicious monster?[5] Perhaps the answer lies in the demonic atmosphere of Rudolf's Prague – a breeding ground for androids and spirits – of which he was a prominent figure. Legend transforms Rabbi Loew into a Cabalist and magician learned in the diabolic arts, that is, a typical representative of a time in which swarms of mountebanks and parasites who deserved to sink into the deepest bowels of Hell held their own against eminent scholars and in which there was a great belief in supernatural forces; legend grants him extraordinary miracle-working powers as conjurer, distiller, *Totenbeschwörer* and all-round master necromancer. It is no accident that in Vrchlický's comedy *Rabínská moudrost* (Rabbinical Wisdom), Lothar's story "Der Golem" and Wegener's film *Der Golem* his study is a veritable hotbed of alchemy replete with athenor, alembics, signs of the Zodiac and occult library.

60

The most important event in Rabbi Loew's life was the audience Rudolf II granted him on 16 February 1592.[1] Several historians claim they discussed problems of the Jewish community; legend asserts that Rudolf, burning with the desire to penetrate the secrets of the universe, queried the magician on the Cabala and related mystical matters. The reason their talk has so appealed to the imagination of later generations is that it remains shrouded in mystery and that a Jew (a Jew of high station but a Jew nonetheless) was deemed worthy of holding forth with the Emperor.

Both legend and literature have magnified the ties between Rabbi Loew and the court, court scholars, astronomers and especially Rudolf – ties that could have guaranteed Imperial protection for the Jews of Prague. In *Rabínská moudrost* the perfidious minister Lang complains that the Maharal enjoys Rudolf's highest favour thanks to the support of Tycho and the "charlatan" Kepler.[2] Max Brod imagines a meeting between Tycho Brahe and the rabbi in the Emperor's antechamber. He also has Tycho draw an analogy between his own nomadic life and the destiny of the Jewish people, which maintains its faith in the face of constant persecution.

The legends tend to turn the rabbi into a kind of Jewish Faust. According to one, Loew approached the Emperor on the Stone Bridge to implore him to revoke a decree ordering the expulsion of the Jews from Prague. When he stood before the magnificent carriage, it immediately halted as if by magic; when the rabble pelted him with rocks and lumps of clay, they turned into flowers; and when the rabbi, covered with flowers, fell to his knees, Rudolf pardoned the people of the Ghetto and invited him to court.[3] There he agreed to call forth the spirits of the patriarchs Abraham, Isaac, Jacob and his twelve children for the Emperor and his courtiers in a remote hall of the Castle on condition that no one should talk or laugh. Red-hot coals billowed coils of smoke in the darkness. Summoned by the magic words of the rabbi, the great figures of Genesis appeared, one by one, on the wall. But when Naphtali, one of Jacob's twelve children, a hunchbacked, freckled carrot-top, freed himself from the smoke with outlandish somersaults against a background of fields of flax and grain, Rudolf and his enchanted courtiers burst into uproarious laughter. The vision immediately disappeared, and with a crack the roof started caving in on the terrified dignitaries. It would have crushed them to death had Loew not stopped it with a few choice Cabalistic formulas.[4]

In Wegener's film ballad *Der Golem*, on the other hand, it is Ahasuerus who provokes the laughter and the falling ceiling is held up by the Golem once the frightened Emperor has promised clemency for the Jews he intended to banish. Meyrink claims that Loew summoned "the phantoms of the dead" with a "laterna magica"; Karásek evokes the "miracles of the magic lantern" in *Ganymedes*.[5] We too might be tempted to place Loew among the earliest precursors of the cinema along with the Jesuit Athanasius Kircher, who first described the *laterna magica*[6] in 1654, if we did not recall that Johann Faust summoned the noble spirits of Alexander the Great and his consort from the realm of the shadows for Charles V in Innsbruck in a *Volksbuch* dating from as early as 1587.[7] Moreover, there were a number of Cabalists – one need mention only Isaac Luria (1534–72) – who conjured spirits from the hereafter and held discourse with Biblical patriarchs.[8]

One day Rudolf decided to visit Loew in the company of his retinue.[9] Following Faust, who had made a stately castle appear for the Count of Anhalt, the rabbi transformed his ramshackle house into a magnificent dwelling decorated with marble, tapestries, carpets and paintings, much like the castle of the Queen of the World, Marnost (Vanity), in Comenius' *Labyrinth*, that is, he transformed a hovel wedged between the crumbling rat-holes of the Ghetto into a sumptuous palace with a salon (*mázhúz*) surrounded by suites of brilliant rooms, all mirrors and crystal chandeliers, where the tables sparkled with golden goblets and costly porcelain, with clarets, candied fruits and other dainties, and the banquet he hosted quite outshone the feast Faust held in his imaginary castle.

Some commentators believe that Rabbi Loew was able to transform his house by projecting the entire Hradčany Castle onto his study by means of a "camera obscura".[10] In Vrchlický's comedy the "camera obscura" becomes a "bizarre toy", a rotating box inside of which Loew, "wizard and sorcerer", as the painter Arcimbaldo characterizes him, hides his daughter – to the displeasure of his jealous wife Perl – from the clutches of Philip Lang z Langenfelsu, as usual the vessel of archvillainry. This inner-sanctum device is not merely a secret laboratory for studying light or searching for *aurum potabile*; it is a hiding place and an illusionist's prop.[1] "My room," Loew declares,

> is the belly of Jonah's whale: in it my servant Yechiel has secretly prepared a great many toys, including an iron lion that walks and, until recently, a metal figure called the Golem, which, once the proper mechanism is triggered, opens its mouth and imitates human language.[12]

Note that Vrchlický replaces the clay dummy with a *metal automaton*.

The *Wundermann* Judah Loew long held Death at bay with his Cabalistic powers. One night during the plague, as he was walking through the cemetery, he happened on an emaciated woman wearing a veil and clutching a slip of paper. He tore it from her hand and ripped it to shreds: it was the list of those doomed to die and contained his name written in red ink. Several times he managed to escape death by similar feats of guile. Once, however, his little granddaughter gave him a magnificent rose for his birthday. Enchanted, he began to sniff it and in no time fell down dead: Death was hiding in its calyx.[13] Death in a rose. Alas, Death in a rose. For Nezval the figure of Rabbi Loew filtered through legend becomes one with poetry:

> You sought poetry and found legend
> so they *are* good for something the stories about Rabbi Loew
> it is your story poetry
> it is your story how could I mistake you
> you reach out to me from faraway centuries
> it was you who ventured onto the Stone Bridge
> to obtain an audience with the Emperor
> the mob greets you with stones but on your clothes
> flowers fall not mud
> your house is not like other dwellings
> you are lion and you are grape
> you bring things of clay to life, and make them wilful creatures
> into each of their mouths you place the *shem*

its power lasting a century or a week
needing renewal every Friday
and yet poetry why did you kill the Golem
it is terrible to wipe the mysterious sign from one's forehead
and be carried to the attic and crumble into dust
jealous you lie in wait for Death and take from its hand
the letters that list your name amongst the doomed
once you escape but in the end you too poetry will find
Death hidden in a rose.[14]

61

Listen closely, for now you shall hear how Rabbi Loew fashioned the Golem. One night in 5340 (1580), after he had taken the ritual bath in the *mikve*, recited the tortuous 119th Psalm and read passages from the *Sefer Yezira*, the rabbi (air), his son-in-law Isaac ben Simon (fire) and the Levite disciple Yakob ben Chaim Sasson (water), wrapped in white hoods, proceeded by torchlight to a place on the banks of the Vltava where there were saltpeter quarries and ample silt.[1] There they formed the Golem from mud (earth), whereupon Isaac on the right and Jacob on the left circled the figure six times chanting combinations of letters (*tsirufim*) and impressing the redness of fire and the dampness of water into the clay body. Then the rabbi placed the *shem* – a strip of parchment bearing the name of God – in its mouth and ordered the Golem to stand and obey him blindly as a servant. At dawn the three returned to the ghetto along with Yossel Golem where, to avoid bothersome questions, Loew told his nagging wife Pearl that he had picked up the poor mute stranger off the street out of pity.[2]

What did Loew's android look like? In the legend it is dressed as a *shammes*, but we find it impossible to imagine it other than Wegener did in his film *Der Golem*: tall with puffy features, helmet-like hair, heavy buskin shoes, a jacket of pressed parchment like a jazerant or, rather, like the armour of padded cotton hardened in salt water Aztec warriors wore. In the film the puppet is created in a laboratory by an act of *schwarze Kunst* as it were, by the conjunction of the stars and by the occult sciences. Loew traces a circle of fire, evokes Astarte, goddess of the Canaanites, and a grim mask, a *Totenkopf*, which looks like nothing so much as phosphorescent jelly, appears in a burst of flame and sulphurous vapours. This ghastly face gives the rabbi the magic word, which he writes on a strip of parchment. He then conceals the parchment and a Star of David in the Golem's chest.[3]

The clay man sits rapt in a corner awaiting the Maharal's orders. It executes his every wish with sheep-like docility. According to Meyrink, the rabbi built the homunculus "to help him ring the synagogue bells"; according to Vrchlický, it assisted the rabbi in his "Cabalistic kitchen".[4] As Yossel Golem must refrain from all work on the Sabbath, Loew removes the *shem* from its mouth (or forehead or chest) every Friday at sunset, thus preventing it from moving.

Once, however, he forgets. He is in the Old-New Synagogue officiating at the Friday evening service when the Golem starts foaming at the mouth and raving as if possessed. After smashing household articles and slashing mattresses, it runs out into the street, strangles chickens and cats and flattens house fronts. It is as ugly as sin and bloated like a huge toad with rage. People run headlong out of its path, screaming, "Yossel Golem has gone mad!" The huge shapeless body advances clumsily through the terrified Ghetto shooting flames from its bloodshot eyes and twitching violently. When the rabbi learns what is happening, he immediately interrupts the singing of the 92nd Psalm. Had he waited a moment longer he would have risked destroying the entire universe, for had the Sabbath begun he would not have been able to stop the berserk automaton. He rushes up to the Golem with a cloud on his brow and tears the *shem* from its mouth. The wild servant, smeared with blood, dirt and feathers, topples unconscious to the ground. Immediately the Psalm resounds again from the synagogue.

Some versions of the legend explain the rabbi's forgetfulness as a result of his concern over an ailing daughter, Esther.[5] In Wegener's film the Golem leaves the Ghetto for a sunny field where unsuspecting children wearing garlands of flowers are gamboling about. At first they run away in fear, but eventually they pluck up their courage and return. One of them jumps into the Golem's arms and steals his star in jest. The huge servant goes limp and falls with a crash. Thus the innocence of children saves mankind from the monster's wrath.[6]

And what does the rabbi do after rendering his creation harmless? With his two assistants and the *shammes* Chaim he makes seven counter-clockwise turns around the android while reciting his Cabalistic formulas in reverse order. Yossel Golem then returns to a pile of clay and to the attic of the Old-New Synagogue beneath a clutter of battered books, old *talesim* and vests decorated with *tsitsis*.[7] Although Loew is said to have forbidden anyone from entering the attic, a rabbi gaon clad in a *taleskotn* with *tefillin* once tried to explore it. He immediately came down white as a sheet and shaking like a leaf.[8] When Egon Erwin Kisch boldly made his way up to the attic, all he found were moth-eaten chests, tallow-encrusted candelabra and nondescript bric-à-brac beneath layers of filth and cobwebs.[9]

According to another legend, the *shammes* Abraham Chaim, who had helped the Maharal to destroy the Golem, disregarded the rabbi's injunction and brought it back to life. One night he and his brother-in-law Abraham Sachariach, himself a *shammes*, crept up to the attic like thieves and moved the pile of clay to the basement of Chaim's Cabalist brother-in-law Asher Balbierer in Cikánská Street. While they were trying to return the figure to life, the plague broke out and divine justice was done: two of Balbierer's five children perished. The *shammesim* hurriedly threw the grim abortion into a coffin and buried it outside the Ghetto walls on Calvary Hill near the Old Town Gate.[10]

62

What are the main characteristics of the Golem? Legend justifies its creation as a means of defending Jews against the pogroms unleashed against them by Christians accusing them of ritual murder, and legend has it that the most implacable foe of the Prague Ghetto was a certain Thaddeus, a fanatical friar so foul a schemer that hanging would have been too good for him.

From this standpoint the Maharal's Golem is a hero of the constantly threatened Jewish Quarter. Especially during the period between Purim and Pesach he wanders though its crooked lanes driving away suspicious shadows, making sure no vagrant is hiding the bodies of Christian children in Jewish houses. One night he surprises the thickset butcher Havlíček carrying the exhumed body of a baby hidden in the belly of a slaughtered pig into the house of wealthy Mordechai Maisl, his creditor.[1]

It is for such deeds that Yossel Golem possesses superhuman strength and can thwart every snare, crush the ribs of the iniquitous with its hands and rout the spiteful mob. What is more, a doeskin amulet covered with Cabalistic formulas – one of the talismans discussed by Eleasar of Worms – can render it invisible.[2] Thus equipped, the Golem requires no intelligence; it is utterly submissive, a dolt, a blockhead. While Loew is said to have spoken of the Golem in terms of an "automaton that obeys its builder",[3] it also has something of the fairy-tale rogues who keep ending up in ridiculous situations as a result of following all commands to the letter.[4]

When *der dumme Hans* (alias Golem) is sent to buy apples at the market, he drags the vendor and her stand and her baskets of fruit through the streets of Prague[5] like the servant who uproots an orange tree and carries it to his master because the latter tells him, "Bring me an orange". When Yossel is sent to fetch water, he inundates the courtyard.[6] When Pearl, who much resembles the absent-minded *rebbe* wives of Chassidic tales,

sends him to buy a carp, Yossel flies into a rage against a fish that hits
him in the face with its tail, tosses it into the river and returns home
empty-handed.[7] Nor is it a good idea to give him household chores: he
is simply not cut out to set the table or clean the kitchen.

Loew's omniscience and miracles and the cunning with which he
directs his servant-defender transform him into a kind of *tsadek* and
Wunderrabbi of the breed of bizarre wizards who populate Chassidic
stories. It is no accident that the bloodsucker Friar Thaddeus, who
never ceases to hatch plots against the Jews, accuses Loew of being a
necromancer and that Yossel saves the rabbi from the poison the accursed
Thaddeus has mixed into the unleavened bread.[8]

Whereas a Polish *Golemsage*, revolving around Rabbi Elijah of Chełm,
makes its appearance as early as the seventeenth and eighteenth centuries, the Prague legend goes back no further than Romanticism. It occurs
for the first time in a collection of myths, anecdotes and curiosities of
Jewish life brought out by the Bohemian Jewish publisher Wolf Pascheles
in German between 1847 and 1864 under the title *Sippurim*. No earlier
document (neither David Gans's chronicle of 1592 nor the 1718 biography
of Rabbi Loew) mentions a Golem moulded by the Maharal. All previous
references to *goylemes* are to the clay puppets of Galician rabbis. Every
subsequent reteller of the legend, from Vrchlický to Karásek, Jirásek and
Meyrink, draws on the five-volume *Sippurim* collection. Rabbi Loew's
letter concerning the creation of the Golem dated 1583 – though actually
written not earlier than 1888 – and the *Volksbuch* entitled *Wunder des
Rabbi Löw* (*Niflaoth MHRL*, 1909), falsely attributed to a contemporary
of the great gaon, are clearly forgeries. Chaim Bloch's monograph *Der
Prager Golem* (1920) gives an exhaustive treatment of these manipulated
"sources".[9]

Thus the saga of Rabbi Loew has been blown up to the point of
eclipsing the Chełm legends, and Prague has become the Golem's main
Schauplatz. The Prague legends graft echoes of the deeds of Faust – the
Faust of the *Volksbücher* and the Czech puppet plays – onto the Maharal's
biography, but most of all they bring him into line with the Chassidic
tradition. The elementary magic that pervades them, the presence of
anecdotal character sketches, a certain *meshuge*, zany quality on the part
of the rabbi, as well as the interruption of the service all point to the
legend's Chassidic origins. Nor is it terribly important that the gloomy
Prague atmosphere and the surly disposition of the mud *panák* exclude
the ambivalent gaiety that is so constant a Chassidic feature. Yet there is
an abyss separating Loew, the incarnation of high knowledge and (if we
believe the legend) Cabalistic guile, from Israel Ba'al Shem Tov, miracle
worker of Podolia, uncouth exorcist, hawker of talismans and medicinal
herbs and totally alien to anagogic disputes and Talmudic casuistry.

The Prague cycle extends the motif of the clay body's sudden insanity threatening annihilation on Sabbath eve from the Jewish community to Prague itself and beyond. The *shem hameforash*, fuel of life and sustainer of devastating rage, becomes a magic tool, a tool-character like the winder of the golden skein in the Erben ballad, a safe conduct for the miraculous, a devil's trap. The Prague *Golemlegende* also touches on the revolt of the automaton against its creator, of brute force against wits and intelligence, of servant against master. And finally, considering the close connection between Loew and his android, the Golem can be seen as its creator's alter ego, his frightening *Doppelgänger*. I do not wish to imply that the Golem merely played Mr Hyde to Loew's Dr Jekyll, but there can be no doubt that both loutish *Knecht* and master are messengers of Lemuria, the land of ghosts.

63

Golemic literature alternates between the Polish motif (of the *emet*) and the Prague motif (of the *shem*). A virtually endless stream of Czech and German writers has recounted the deeds of the Golem in plays and ballads in which the monster is a dim-witted knave who hates his creator, a mixture of beast, blustering lackey and agent of Beelzabub with a pyromaniac's thirst for revenge, that is, in which the tricks and trumpery of the *Schauerromantik* run rampant.

At times the Golem's creator grows presumptuous, rivalling God, aspiring to the Nietzschean ideal of a Superman, but divine retribution soon comes to shatter his titanism; at times he seems little more in his exuberant arrogance than a *Menschlein*, a runt unaware of his own limitations.

Vrchlický's ballad "Golem" depicts the creation of the clay monster as an act of pride on the part of its creator, an attempt to vie with the Creator though "but a gnome" (*pouze trpaslík*). He puffs himself up and raves like a demon with flaming eyes, yet were it not for Yahweh, who reduces the figure to a dust heap with a thunderbolt, the rabbi would be lost. Thus does the Lord give the arrogant puppetmaker a taste of the torment he suffered from having to hurl his first creatures, the angels, into Hell.[1]

Liliencron's ballad "Der Golem" describes the rabbi's bizarre dance to restrain the raging flunky. "Hopsa, hopsa, what leaps!" His ludicrous Golem is made of "carved wood" and kicks and rears like a horse. He is an indefatigable servant entrusted with "sweeping, cooking,/rocking the babies, cleaning the windows,/polishing boots", but when he gets the urge he "uproots trees,/tosses houses into the clouds,/hurls people into the air" and even "puts the Hradschin on his head" like a wig. More ludicrous than even the Golem hobby-horse is the rabbi who, though "very much at home/in the arts and sciences,/especially the black ones,/and in the difficult Cabala", must toil and moil and endure all sorts of torment to pull the *shem* out of his mouth. "All-too-clever," the poet concludes, "is sometimes all-too-stupid."[2]

Liliencron's comical ballad is not far removed from the Dadaist comedy *Golem* by the clowns Voskovec and Werich. Its "Píseň strašlivá o Golemovi" (Fearsome Song of the Golem) exhibits the combination of artlessness and cunning typical of *kramářské písně*, Czech broadside ballads. Poking fun at the stupidity of both master and servant, it tells of a Loew who is annoyed with his aunt for having pinched his old-new trumpet and fashions a monster to scare her. But the Golem falls in love with the attractive, passionate aunt and slays a junior cavalry officer when he finds him in her arms. The raving lump of clay commits other crimes as well, but in the end is driven to suicide after holding out in an old mill for nine months and nine weeks against an entire regiment.[3] Thus the Golem saga is turned into a frolic, and the presumptuous magician and his simpleton servant join the fraternity of clowns.

Loew was also allegedly concerned that "the Golem be created without a sex drive, for had he had one no woman would have been safe".[4] Yet how could the story of a clay android do without love interest? In a moralizing, rather feeble ballad by the Prague poet Hugo Salus, Loew's daughter, the frivolous Rifke, "silly as a goose", falls for the dark "clay Hans" her father has created. To cure her of her infatuation, the rabbi orders the Golem to embrace her. He squeezes her so hard that her bones crack and she is nearly crushed to death.[5]

Things take a woeful turn when the idiot himself falls in love. A whiff of cunnus arouses even clay, and the monstrous rod rises in the beast's trousers. Yet when regardless of her name – Esther or Miriam or Abigail – the rabbi's flirtatious daughter stirs the Golem's carnal desire, does it not mirror a spiritual desire to escape his monstrous condition and be granted a human soul?

In Arthur Holitscher's drama *Der Golem* (1908) the leaden android Amina takes a fancy to Abigail and is furious at finding itself less than a man. Yet its passion is so absurd that Abigail jumps out of the window and it tears the *shem* from its neck, turning back, thereby, into a sad lump.[6] In Wegener's film the Golem's coarse clay face breaks out in pustules when Miriam prefers the blonde Junker Florian, a well-groomed ladies' man exuding an ingratiating languor. In retribution the Golem burns down Ghetto hovels, hurls pedestrians to the ground, drags the prodigal daughter, unconscious, back to the rabbi and tosses the dandy, his antithesis, from a terrace.

Rudolf Lothar, author of a *Maskenspiel* entitled *König Harlekin*, complicated matters even more in his story "Der Golem". Loew's daughter Esther rejects the ugly Elasar, whom the Rabbi has chosen as her husband. Loew then transfers the soul of the slumbering Elasar into the Golem. The monster falls in love with her; Esther returns its feelings. Coming home from the Sabbath service, Loew cringes at the sight of the Golem holding Esther in its arms of clay. He raises a hammer against it, and lo! a storm breaks out, the Golem bolts into the Jewish Cemetery and melts away. When Elasar reawakens, his soul reenters his body and Esther realizes she feels the same emotion for him she felt for the android.[7]

Lothar injects an unusual element into the Golem saga: the transitory transmigration of the soul, a kind of temporary *gilgl* from a sleeping person into a clay puppet. The operation recalls the way fakirs and shamans use hypnosis, their spirits perambulating through the cosmos while their bodies lie in a deep, death-like sleep. Misshapen Elasar's pure soul takes on a new glow when encased in the mortal frame of clay. Uttered through the Golem, his tender words eventually win over his at first unwilling bride, who forgets by magic that Elasar is short and stooped, "almost a dwarf, with a disproportionately large head from which two large eyes glowed".[8] Here the Golem is an inducement to love, a go-between. Moreover, Lothar's childlike android is welcomed by the angelic hosts, as his final flight into the storm makes abundantly clear.

64

Thus the Golem is not always unattractive. Lothar writes that unlike the depressing deformity of the fiancé his angel-golem is a model of youthful grace and vigour, that the rabbi was surely inspired by a "Greek marble statuette of Apollo".[1] The Golem created by the Danish sculptor Jørgen Møller in Jiří Karásek's *Ganymedes* also contains a shimmer of classical beauty.[2]

It is worth dwelling briefly on this novel, which reworks the Golem saga in *fin-de-siècle* style. Karásek handles the motif with the solemnity of those Decadents who loved to celebrate life (like Franz von Stuck, who donned formal attire to work at the easel and was proud of being called the "Maler im Gehrock").[3] Karásek's Danish Jewish sculptor Jørgen Møller, as famous as Thorwaldsen, gives up art because he is unable to breathe life into his statues.

Obsessed with the idea of creating a Golem who, unlike Loew's, has the gift of speech, he moves to Prague. After five years of unremitting study in the Jewish Cemetery, he discovers that the life-giving formula is contained in a cryptogram in the epitaph the Maharal composed for his own tombstone. To instill life in a Golem, one must extract the rays concealed in the letters of the alphabet, but only a wise man who is also just, a *tsadek*, can perform the operation.[4]

Møller, who is so ugly he has never been loved, fashions not a brutish, bumpy-faced servant but a handsome youth with the lineaments of a classical statue: a Ganymede who is both friend and master and can satisfy his every desire. Enter the theme of homosexuality in the Golem legend. (I should also mention such female *goylemes* in literature as the Gipsy Isabella created for Charles V by a Polish Jew in a tale by Achim von Arnim that inspired the Surrealists. In addition to the female Golem the tale contains a tiny root man, an *alraun*.[5])

If Loew had a hard time keeping his scullery lad under control, how can the consumptive Møller deal with a creature whom he regards as his master? He trusts that the shared passion between man and android will prove stronger than the powers of evil and will not hear of turning Ganymede back into clay no matter how he rants and raves.

The product of a lesbian mother and misogynist father, Møller models his Golem on Radovan, a languid adolescent whose swooning effeminacy is reminiscent of a Beardsley figure. Then he powders his face and makes up his eyes to attract the eccentric Englishman Adrian Morris, who drives him mad with passion. Although he could use wax, "commonly known to absorb fluid in the ritual of black magic",[6] Møller also uses clay, mixing it with pure water (whereas, according to Karásek, Loew soaked it in the blood of animals, as evidenced by the bestial frenzy that grips the android whenever baleful stellar powers come into play).

The motif of perfect identity between puppet and model may derive from Villiers de l'Isle-Adam's *L'Ève future*, in which Edison creates (with *électro-magnétisme* and *matière radiante*) the *andréide* Miss Hadaly, a puppet, "créature nouvelle, électro-humaine", who reproduces down to the most minute detail the features, skin, shining eyes and gestures of the elusive, cold Alicia Clary for Lord Ewald, who loves her.

In a deserted house in a field outside Prague Møller moulds his Ganymede, intoxicated by the soft body of the naked model, whose slender limbs exude "the stimulating voluptuousness of languor and death".[7] Little by little, however, he loses interest in Radovan, who seems plain and lifeless in comparison with his Ganymede. Moreover, as the statue nears completion, Møller gradually loses his strength:

> The more lifelike Ganymede grows, the closer death comes. I feel that at the moment he comes completely to life *I shall die*. The tragedy of it all is that I shall not survive to gaze into the living pupils of my Ganymede or hear his vibrant voice, that in giving him life I create my death.[8]

After countless attempts he succeeds in infusing motion into his graceful Golem, but the effort drains him completely. As he dies, he implores Morris to destroy the creature – who is lying on a soft marital bed in a room draped in white fabrics and scented with myrrh – and bury him that night in his tomb, but Morris lacks the courage to reduce the android to dust with seven ceremonial circles and resolves to take him home.

Radovan enters Morris's house that night through a dormer window. The house smells of candles and funeral wreaths. Suddenly Radovan sees himself – that is, Ganymede – laid out on Morris's bed. Terrified by the resemblance, he involuntarily brushes the *shem* against the clay dandy's lips whereupon the latter opens its eyes, rises from the marital bed and embraces him so hard that he suffocates. Thus the Golem's rebellion is a revolt of the reproduction against both model and creator. Morris finds Radovan dead with the crumbled android on top of him. Refined, androgynous, fragrant and well-groomed, the mud figure is still a source of perdition.

65

Strictly speaking, the eponymous hero of Meyrink's *Der Golem* (1915) has very little in common with Rabbi Loew's strapping bogeyman; it is more an elusive phantom, a *Spuk*, an enigmatic spectre that reappears in the Ghetto every thirty-three years to spread chaos. Lurking among the unsuspecting inhabitants of the *Judenstadt*, it assumes physical dimensions under the influence of favourable stellar forces and sidereal conjunctions.[1]

Meyrink's Golem, then, is a symptom of an epidemic of the spirit that can spread like wildfire, the incarnation of an underlying ferment in the suffocating confines of the Ghetto, a buried psychosis that bursts forth on occasion to spread unspeakable ruin. In other words, the Golem is brought to life by the fears and deep-seated anxieties of the persecuted Jew. It is an extension of the poisoned atmosphere of the Fifth Quarter, of its crumbling hovels and greasy stones. Every thirty-three years the apparition staggers its way through the squalid alleys bathed in an ambivalent *Zwielicht*, a stranger with a yellow face and mongoloid features dressed in a faded, *altmodisch*, suit.

The spirit's Oriental cast (Wegener's Golem also has slanted eyes, high cheekbones and a pug nose)[2] is meant as evidence of the sinister forces at work within the walls of Prague. Feverish Asiatic eyes often stare out of the general gloom in Meyrink's stories. A haunted house leaning against the grassy Castle Steps "like a dead watchman" accommodates the macabre laboratory of Dr Mohammed Darasche-Koh, taxidermist and "Persian Satan".[3] There is an equally frightening house in nearby Thunova Street, a narrow, shrivelled, forbidding structure in which the mysterious Egyptologist Dr Cinderella cultivates pitcher plants, drosseras and other carnivorous flora covered with swollen veins and bulging eyeballs.[4] Max Brod recalls in his memoirs how fascinated Meyrink was by the arcane worlds of Buddhism and the Cabala and by the possibilities of exploiting them amidst the silhouettes of Prague's palaces.[5]

One of the many inscrutable tall tales in *Der Golem* is that of the immense treasure of the Order of Asiatic Brothers ("who presumably founded Prague") buried beneath a large grey stone in Golden Lane and guarded by Methuselah to keep Satan at bay. The embalmer Keyork Arabian in Crawford's *Witch of Prague*, a dwarf with the face of a basilisk in a misshapen skull, stands out among the Oriental doormen to Hell concealed in the cracks of the city. I shall return to him presently.

Kubin went further than Meyrink in *Die andere Seite* (The Other Side, 1907), a novel similar to *Der Golem* in many respects. Instead of transferring the Asiatics to Prague, he moved Prague, renamed Perle, beyond Samarkand into the heart of Asia. Oddly enough, he gave the protean, flabby, slimy and elusive despot who rules and oppresses the crumbling capital of the Dream Kingdom the Prague name Patera, the name of the popular Café Union waiter who befriended so many writers and artists.[6]

While Meyrink's Golem has much in common with the Wandering Jew Apollinaire met in Prague at the beginning of the century and while its periodic return echoes to a certain extent the Ahasuerus myth, the period between its appearances, thirty-three years, evokes the age of Christ.[7] In addition, then, to symbolizing aspects of the Jewish soul and the suffocating atmosphere of the Ghetto, the Golem contains elements of Christology.

What makes Meyrink's novel Expressionistic is its spectral, nocturnal quality, the garish makeup of its wax-museum characters, the doubles, the sorcery, the feverish style. It also revels in the arcane – in Yoga and Indian philosophy in general, in the Talmud, occultist doctrines, curiosities from the Cabala and every manner of black magic. Note, however, that Meyrink, who was a student of theosophy, falsely ascribes to the Cabala everything with an exotic ring to it: the origin of tarot, for example, and the *Ibbur*, a book as nonexistent as the *Necronomicon* discussed by Lovecraft, though the title derives from a word used by Jewish mysticism to denote the "fecundation of the soul" (*Seelenschwängerung*), that is, the accretion of a second soul.[8]

The notion of the Golem as a spirit wandering where the rat-holes of the Ghetto once stood reappears in *Ganymedes*. The sculptor Jørgen

Møller, "delirious shipwreck in the depths of the Past",[9] claims that one can meet the clay ghost (in the form of a tall, ingratiating youth) in the broad boulevards laid out after the *Assanierung*, because here and there the spirit of the vanished Jewish Town still pulsates. Then there is the legend that the Holy Rabbi will rise and give new life to the puppet of clay through the formulas of the *Sefer Yezira*.[10]

66

Prague literature and culture abound in dummies, *goylemes*, marionettes, wax statues, mechanical dolls and automata.

Josef Jiří Kolár's novel *Pekla zplozenci* (Spawn of Satan) a gold mine of grand-opera deviltries, features, as we have seen, the Italian necromancer Scotta, who wishes to dissect the young Vilém and fuse him back together in the athenora oven, there to wed him to the immortal Sempiterna. But alas and alack! Vilém takes advantage of the absence of the presumptuous metaphysicaster and sneaks into the athenora, where he finds his betrothed lying motionless on a sofa. When he realizes that Sempiterna has a bald wooden skull beneath her wig and that her mechanical clock of a soul keeps her from stretching out her arms to him unless she is wound up, he flies into a rage, turns Scotta's hellish laboratory inside out – the nerve of the rogue, trying to saddle him with a *dřevěný tajtrlík*, a literal blockhead! – and flees to the Faust House, followed by his bride, her springs and gears creaking "like a corpse plucked from the gallows".[1]

Orpiment is as yellow as saffron, and the dwarf Keyork Arabian in Crawford's novel is no less horrible than Scotta. Convinced that the human body can resist the wear and tear of time like the granite of the Egyptian pyramids, the embalmer crams his Prague laboratory with stuffed men and animals, the skulls and mummies of all races and a variety of barbaric weapons, African masks, idols, sacred drums and other items suited to an ethnographic museum. Like Herbert West in the Lovecraft story, Keyork tries to stimulate dead cells and bring the mummies back to life with elixirs, extravagant machines, glass hearts and electrical charges; his only response from the embalmed, however, is a fleeting grin, a perfidious glance.

Meyrink too delights in a swarm of mummies and hideous wax faces. His junkdealer Aaron Wassertrum – he of the "goggle fish eyes" and harelip in *Der Golem* – keeps "a life-sized wax doll" in his shop under a pile of peeling objects. The sinister Persian demon Mohammed Darasche-Koh, who appears in several of Meyrink's stories, owns a stuffed blond head by the name of Axel that resembles the *terafim* of the Cabala (human heads dried, pickled and given *shem* under their tongues).[2] The head hangs from the ceiling by a copper bar stuck in its crown, the eyes bulging, the neck wrapped in a silk shawl, the exposed reddish pulmonary lobes and heart twitching at the command of a battery attached by gold wires.[3]

One of the many living mummies of Prague is the hero of Jakub Arbes's novella *Newtonův mozek* (Newton's Brain, 1877), a conjurer who falls at the Battle of Hradec Králové and reappears in Prague one night to give a magic show for an audience of scholars, nobles and other notables. He opens his act as an embalmed cadaver in officer's garb, but gradually grows more animated as electric current turns him into an automaton. He climbs out of the coffin and down from the catafalque and, after a moment of darkness, returns in his old black conjurer's costume. He then removes the top of his skull (cracked by a Prussian sword) like a beret and informs the astonished assembly that he has replaced his brain with Newton's, which he has stolen from an English museum.

There is no end to these disturbing Prague puppets, the mummies peopling her waxworks, the dummies gracing her shop windows. Foremost among the latter was the large stuffed tiger in the shop of a furrier by the name of Procházka in Ferdinandova třída. The padded feline became an integral part of the city at the end of the last century. The German poet Friedrich Adler devoted a poem to it; Leppin mentions it as well. The beast was wrapped in furs, clutched a fashionable muff in its open jaws and wore a rakish beaver beret on its head. Mr Procházka often lent it to the organizers of masked balls, *šibřinky*, who placed it prominently among the rushes, palm trees and Indian temple ruins of the bargain-basement Oriental setting.[4]

Odradek, the star-shaped spool of thread that gets up on its feet and takes a walk in Kafka's story "The Cares of a Family Man", also belongs in the company of Prague automata. The Prague connection is underscored by the name, which is not abstract *Klangmaterial*, like Blümner's Ango Laina but a Czech word derived from the verb *odraditi*, "to dissuade". One could base an entire *rêverie* on this tangle of wire wound in a ball, half puppet and half obscure object, which emits a sound "like the rustling of dead leaves": Is it a mechanical *alraune* of the kind Meister Abraham makes in *Kater Murr* or a piece of junk bought at the *tandlmark* that obeys secret impulses like the two striped celluloid balls jumping capriciously around the room of the ageing bachelor Blumfeld?

I would also place the Prague Christ Child, the *Jezulátko* – a wax doll dressed in silk, gold brocade or other costly materials depending on the season and displayed in the Baroque Carmelite Church of Our Lady Victorious – in my imaginary Museum of Prague Puppetry. The small figure was brought to the city on the Vltava from Spain during Rudolf's reign, when the ties between the Spanish and Bohemian nobility were close. If the massive Golem, even reduced to clay, was a harbinger of disorders and disasters, the *Jezulátko* – an exquisite rag doll and model of delicate fabrics – was a salubrious balm cheering the spirits of the disheartened, a physician for both body and soul. And the fact that the principal patron of the dark church where it lies and where the mummies of the Carmelite Order's protectors lie in sumptuous open coffins was the cruel Spanish general Baltazar de Marradas (who commissions the *Jezulátko* in his death throes from the sculptress Flavia Santini in Julius Zeyer's legend "Inultus" [1895]) is of scant significance.[5]

In the tale "Nämlich" (In Fact, 1915) by the Prague German Paul Adler, the protagonist, a lunatic with a simpleton's imagination, says of the *Jezulátko*:

> I also very much like the Child Jesus, though I am a little afraid of His mother because she is made of old porcelain. His cheeks are red and His hands hold a wand. The Child Jesus likes to play with a big smooth ball. The Child often plays rocking horse with me. I am always the horse and the Child of God rides on my back.[6]

I have placed the statuette of the *Jezulátko* here as a talisman to defend and protect me from the frightening magic of all the *goylemes* and wax dummies I have so recklessly evoked.

67

The brass duck and Vaucanson's flute player, the chess-playing Turk of Baron von Kempelen,[1] the clockwork idols, the machines chock full of reels and wheels, the talking heads, the moving wax dolls of the "mécaniciens d'autrefois"[2] are nothing but worm-eaten sideshow puppets, innocuous street-singers, compared with the cruel robots devised by Karel Čapek in the drama *R.U.R.* (Rossum's Universal Robots, 1920).[3] "Robot", android, artificial worker, is a Czech word Čapek derived from *robota*, or "corvée", the labour due to a lord from his vassal.[4]

Čapek's automata belong to the same family as the Golem, and although they are manufactured on a distant island their roots are in the humus, the witchcraft of Prague. But if the Golem is a clay figure brought to life with the aid of the *shem* – the slip of parchment containing the name of God – robots consist of a chemical substance that acts like protoplasm, an "organic gluten", as Josef Čapek calls it,[5] discovered by the philosopher and scientist Rossum (from *rozum*, "reason"), an "old eccentric" and "mad visionary" of the mad scientist type popular during Expressionism.

Like the Golem, the robot is a *Knecht* and perhaps a *knouk*, to use

Beckett's term, that is, an obedient but grim, sly servant who cannot wait to take revenge on his master. Moreover, in Old Slavonic *rob* had the meaning of "slave". The robots, technologically sophisticated automatons who feel neither pain nor emotion nor fear of death, provide an ideal source of labour; indeed, their endurance, strength and low cost make them the perfect replacement for the imperfect human machine, a carcass with great ambitions but limited strength.

If we stretch our imagination a bit, we can even try to make something of the assonance between "robot" and "rabbi". Yet unlike Rabbi Loew's glum clown, the robot possesses an "extraordinary rational intelligence" and an "extraordinary memory". The resilience of these bondsmen insensitive to breakdowns and accidents brings to mind another source for the idea and even name of the robot: Jules Verne's Robur-le-Conquérant, who features "an iron constitution equal to all challenges and astonishing physical strength" and resembles a huge spheroid head grafted onto a trapezoid with "geometrical shoulders".

R.U.R. has been called a "Golems-Marionetten-Kömodie".[6] But as Čapek said to Jules Romains in 1927, the struggle with the Golem was much simpler: all one had to do to tame the rebellious brute was remove the *shem* from its mouth. What can you do to tame a robot?[7] There is only one Golem, and if it goes out of control it can be brought back in line by a ritual act, whereas robots constitute a compact, obstinate mass that – horror of horrors – no one is able to restrain. There is no comparison between the sudden madness of a man of clay that foams at the mouth and grinds its teeth and the orchestrated, implacable hatred of an enormous band of *goylemes*. It is as though the rabbinical puppet were to multiply into an endless series. As Dr Gall says in the play, "We have given the robots faces that are too identical. A hundred thousand identical faces turned towards us. A hundred thousand expressionless bubbles. It's like an awful dream."

Expressionless bubbles. The same can be said of the ugly newts in Čapek's novel *Válka s mloky* (The War with the Newts, 1936). These slimy aquatic devils – cross-bred amphibian shades, half seal, half green lizard, with little children's hands, worthy of the underwater city R'lyeh inhabited (in Lovecraft's stories) by the Great Cthulhu – reproduce uncontrollably, growing into an enormous homogeneous mass, a horrible mucilage, a scourge that undermines and eventually disintegrates the human race. Like robots, newts "do not on the whole require any of those things which man needs to find relief and solace from his metaphysical terror and existential *Angst*. They manage without philosophy, without life after death and without art; they do not know what imagination is, or humour, or mysticism, or play or dreams".[8] But Čapek renders his "lizards", *tapaboys*, soft moving "things" more eerie than robots by the "tap-tap" they make when they come out of the damp mud at night and the "ts ts ts" they use to call humans. It makes one's blood run cold! Their apocalyptic sounds still rings in my ears, like the "buch buch buch" of the vampires in Czech Romantic ballads.

Certain motifs besides the mechanical servant link *R.U.R.* to the *Golemlegende* motifs of sudden madness and breakdown, of the convulsions that attack and disable the robots from time to time, reducing them to shells ready for the junk heap. Another idea associated with the legend (and one voiced with loathing by the character of the wet nurse) is that the manufacture of abominable homunculi is a demonic act, an act of sacrilege against divine creation. Furthermore, the insurrection of the robots against their creators recalls variants of the Golem saga in which the clay monster's rage stems from his hatred for the rabbi who gave him life (though in tune with other mass dramas of the time the revolt of the undifferentiated colloids in *R.U.R.* also reflects social unrest and the stifled rage of the oppressed).

It is the unmitigated wrath, the hard-hearted collective hatred, the obtuse gravity in the robots' grim, bubble-like faces that made Čapek's play so powerful. Unlike Fritz Lang, who later arranged the crowds of slaves and machine-like men in *Metropolis* (1926) into decorative groups with an element of Expressionistic geometry,[9] Čapek makes no attempt to stylize his mob; indeed, he magnifies our revulsion with intentionally dry language. He himself was appalled by the spirits he had unleashed:

> While writing, I was seized by a terrible fear: I wanted to warn against mass production and dehumanized slogans, and I was suddenly seized by the fear that things would be like this one day, soon perhaps, and that my warning would no longer be of any help. Just as I, the author, had led my dull machines in whatever direction I pleased, so someone would one day lead mass man against the world and against God.[10]

In *R.U.R.*, as in its twin play *Věc Makropulos* (The Makropoulos Secret), a woman destroys the presumptuous formulas contrived by the excessive ambition of men. Here the destruction of the Formula by Helena Glory, a rather wooden character with a suffragette-like or, rather, Salvation Army humanitarianism, is basically a diabolical act: by trading the secret of how to build the robots for life itself, she deprives the last humans of their sole chance to survive. In the glow of the fire consuming the Formula, Helena becomes the devil's handmaiden.

Before long the robots realize that with no humans left to build them their race faces extinction. Yet Čapek raises a tree of life upon the ruins of the apocalypse. "I wasn't feeling well, Olga," he wrote to his wife, "which is why towards the end I searched almost frantically for a solution in the spirit of love and compromise. Do you think it is believable, darling?"[11] Human love with all its jealousy, vanity and dedication carries over to two androids of the highest category: Helena and Primus. In the last analysis, then, Čapek's finale reworks a theme from the Golem saga: the sexual awakening of the *goylemes* and their dream of becoming true human beings.

In this "Science-Nonfiction-Horror-Story"[12] as in the later novels *Továrna na Absolutno* (The Absolute at Large, 1922) and *Krakatit* (Cracatite, 1924), Čapek appropriates a scientific discovery as the basis for a vision of the end of the world. Whether robot, cracatite or carburettor of the Absolute, the discovery eludes human control and causes monstrous upheavals, mass annihilation. Moreover, man is entirely to blame: his laziness and inefficiency encourage the robots; his arms and wars allow them to triumph. "No Genghis Khan ever built so enormous a mound of human bones." What holds for robots holds for the newts: because humans exploit them as cheap labour and cannon fodder, swarms of them – they reproduce uncontrollably – undermine and eventually smother the human race. Man himself "is financing this End of the World, this whole new Flood".[13]

Thus *R.U.R.* attempts to warn technological society to heed the abyss into which it is about to fall. Not that the men on Rossum's island shine in comparison with the brutal rabble of the robots. I am irritated by their coldness, their calculating imperturbability, the way they flirt with Helena during the robots' attack. But most of all I am puzzled by the fact that in the midst of all this futuristic engineering they have only pistols and high-tension wires and not so much as a small plane in which to escape.[14]

Though perhaps Čapek meant to emphasize the foolishness of inventors incapable of ridding themselves of the monsters they have created. If so, their blatantly archetypal names – Domin (Dominus), Busman (Businessman), Alquist (Aliquis+Alchemist), Fabry (Faber) and Gall (Galenus)[15] – are ludicrous. By extension, however, the robots themselves symbolize humanity reduced to a servile, overburdened mass. There is an obvious affinity between the mechanized men of Zamyatin's *We*, who wear grey-blue "unifs" with gold number plates, and Čapek's robots bundled into cloth cassocks with brass numbers.

Čapek imbues *R.U.R.* with his aversion to collectivist rhetoric, class hatred, totalitarian ideologies and revolts that tear the world asunder in the name of illusory transformations. If the spread of the newts reflects the expansion of the Nazi beast, the agitation of the robots clearly refers to the Russian Revolution. If the savage caricatures of representatives of the Habsburg Monarchy in Hašek's *Švejk* reflect the influence of the grotesque distortions of Soviet posters, the aggressive pronouncements of Čapek's androids parody Bolshevik edicts and propaganda slogans.

The Čapeks touched upon the proletarian revolt in the story "Systém" as early as 1908.[16] It features a pompous capitalist and plantation owner named John Andrew Ripraton who brags about the infallible coercive "system" he uses to control and deplete the working masses in his barracks-like Hubertstown: "The worker has to be turned into a machine that works and nothing else. Every thought is a violation of discipline." In the end, however, the workers awaken and rebel, destroying his factories and family.

That Čapek was at variance with the selfishness, greed and arrogance of the bosses, profiteers, *nouveaux riches*, the blatant inequalities of capitalist society and the narrow-mindedness of wealth comes out clearly in the entomological "morality" *Ze života hmyzu* (The Insect Play, 1921), in which he and his brother Josef satirizes the human vices of the post-World-War I period, transferring them to butterflies, ants and coleoptera. He did not, however, believe in lofty reforms promising bright futures. He was convinced that their fanatical proponents would make far greater errors than those made by the classes they sought to replace, and did not therefore share the intoxication of the avant-garde, which sensed the clarion call of rebirth in the stamping feet of revolution. Slogans, revolts and miraculous discoveries were, he felt, the way to disaster.

Instead he favoured common sense, balance, the happy medium – an inclination that might rankle were it not for the fact that too many experiments, too many vain hopes, too many soaring Superman illusions have made us wiser and led us – albeit with the regret of doffing our attractive Romantic cloaks – to admit that he was right in the end. Alquist, Čapek's alter ego, says, "I believe it is better to lay a single brick than to plan huge projects." And at the end of *Krakatit*, God, a white-haired gentleman who carries the world around in a covered wagon – a peep show lit by an oil lamp – says to the inventor Prokop, "You wanted to do things that are too great, and you will end up doing small things. It is better that way." And Busman, in *R.U.R.*, says that what makes history are the small needs of unimportant men, not great dreams. The trouble is that the rejection of bumptious heroism, mass upheaval and castles in the air can easily turn into the smug provinciality of the concluding banquet in *Továrna na Absolutno*, where country folk go on about trust and tolerance over mounds of sausage and sauerkraut.

Confronted with the menace of Čapek's dreary automatons – a menace that excludes all fair-booth tricks, every ambiguity – one longs for the wax museum. True, Čapek presents the apocalypse with the detachment of reason, but his androids have their roots in Prague sorcery and are as demonic as harlequins, no matter how clear the opposition between the two *Urgestalten*.[17] Though the chief of a host of the dead and a chthonic shade with *Unterwelt* connections, the harlequin is still a tightrope walker, a conjurer, a superclown, a sail of multicoloured patches; Čapek's dark, Dies Irae robots are idols of a sullen technological civilization, managerial and dry, supercilious Lenten figures and champions of a mechanization process that destroys humour and imagination. To quote Ariosto:

> che ben fu il piú crudele e il piú di quanti
> mai furo al mondo ingegni empii e maligni,
> ch'imaginò sí abominosi ordigni.[18]

> [This is the worst device, in all the years
> Of the inventiveness of humankind
> Which e'er imagined was by evil mind.]

68

Another Rave

I am writing from the city you love to tell you that in these turbulent times Prague is swarming with *goylemes*. There is not a chestnut tree, not a courtyard, not a roof or bridge or door left that does not bear the mark of their crude clay paws: Malá Strana, Loreta, your corner on Kampa Island, Petřín Hill, Belvedere and Olšany Cemetery. Bands of "shapeless lumps" huddle together in this ship of fools whose prow is the Hradčany and stern Letná Plain.

The entire city lives in darkness and terror. Even the glutinous clay resorts to camouflage, changing into microphones, informants, ferrets, oversized ears, huge bundles of files, Kafkaesque insects. The bestowers of fraternal aid claim they wish to refresh us with their charms and protection, though in reality they are ready to tear us to shreds, to unleash huge metallic toads on us with treads for paws.

The stench of the Golem is everywhere – the odour of rotting compost, servility and stale goat sweat. By now it is too late to shore up the walls, shut the doors and dig trenches. The infernal stew has seeped through everything to such an extent that your poet friend, the Madman of Pampeluna, could compose a gloomy golemiad. They have invaded our very houses, these clay men, scratching, laughing, eating, drinking and brushing their bad teeth.

The people themselves – even the most innocuous, the most trustworthy – are slowly turning into *goylemes* for having made too many pacts with the devil. The sausage sellers, the tram shunters, the tapsters, the waiters at the Café Slavia, the regulars who leave the Barbora at dawn – they all have something Golem-like about them. Of course the more loathsome members of the brotherhood flaunt their golemnity. Oh, the airs, oh, the indignities, injustices and lies they use to ensnare the fearful and trembling. Women mate with the *goylemes* without fear of turning into dolls and issuing strips of earth and chips of sticky mire from their split bellies.

During the last century our homes were hives of musical devices and gewgaws: snuff boxes, jewel- cigar- or sewing-boxes that played a jingle the instant the lid popped open; musical mechanisms hid in the bottom of beer mugs and tankards and table lamps, on chairs and in daguerreotype albums; tiny checkered windmills moved their vanes at the pull of a string, playing a delicate waltz, very often the "Maximilian Waltz".[1] Today there is nothing that does not conceal a facet of the Golem. Whatever you say – whisper, memory, tender word – it is all recorded on invisible reels; every sentence you speak can be used by them to set loathsome machines of slander and ruin in motion against you.

This is why silence reigns, why all you hear is the gnawing of mice who have caught scent of the marl. But from time to time vehement conflicts flare up, and sons accuse fathers of having surrendered the country. The *goylemes* will record their every word. Caught in the Golemic vice, we let everything go to ruin: we make no effort to halt the process; we care only about pacifying them. We're in for it if they lose their tempers. "What will happen tomorrow?" your poet once asked prophetically. "The walls will have ears . . . "[2]

Our only consolation will be to wake up one morning and see the clay remains of the *goylemes* in the refuse bins. But now for every Golem that crumbles a hundred others spring up in its place and the best of us are dying of heartbreak or forced to lead a miserable existence somewhere else in the world. There must be redemption. There is nothing on this earth that does not totter and fall. But when?

Part Two

Part Two

69

On 18 June 1621 the Prague executioner Jan Mydlář received an order to erect a scaffold for the execution of twenty-seven Czech dignitaries (nobles, knights and burghers) condemned to death for having led a revolt against the Habsburgs.[1] That very night, working by torchlight in the Old Town Square, the executioner's assistants began construction of a *theatrum* four ells high and twenty-two paces long and wide. It was enclosed by a wooden railing, linked by a narrow bridge to a balcony of the Old Town Hall (which served as a backdrop) and covered to the ground with black cloth.

At *five o'clock* on 21 June, a day of infamy in Bohemian history, the Castle cannons gave the signal for the ignominious spectacle to begin. The *theatrum* emerged as the tentative light of dawn relieved the darkness. Two detachments of light cavalry and three infantry companies had been summoned to keep the throng at bay. One of Mydlář's assistants, his head draped in black, set up a crucifix in front of the block, next to which Mydlář himself waited with bared sword and a face as hard as cold quince. The coffins stood ready beneath the scaffolding as in a crypt. Haughty magistrates clad in black sat on the Town Hall balcony, three of them walking back and forth from the scaffold to summon the condemned one by one.

The drums rolled and the trumpets blared throughout the execution to prevent the mob from hearing the groans and last words of the executed men, whose heads continued to twitch on the sand-covered floorboards after being separated from their torsos. Six servants of the executioner, the *holomci*, wearing black masks and black cloaks, carried off the truncated cadavers so the executioner might avoid touching any of the wretches he had dispatched with his sword. "An atrocious spectacle," Dačický writes: black scaffold, black dress, black masks. The square, as Machar later claimed in a poem, was a true Golgotha.[2]

The executions went on for four hours, the infallible executioner using four swords to decapitate twenty-four notables. As a kind of interlude, a respite from his labours, he hanged the other three: one from a gallows erected in the centre of the square and two from a beam jutting out of a Town Hall window. In the aforementioned poem by Machar, the hangman, worn-out and thirsty, recounts the details to his wife, cynically boasting – while waiting for a servant girl to bring him a mug of beer at the Green Frog Inn – of having severed each head with a single blow. Josef Svátek, on the other hand, maintains that, tormented by having to slaughter Czech patriots, Mydlář donned black mourning garb instead of the usual flame-red hood and did his utmost to lessen their suffering by beheading them as efficiently as possible.[3]

Svátek wished to transform the Prague executioner into a legendary figure similar to the Parisian hangman Charles Sanson (whom Pushkin once called a *svirepyi figliar'*, "a wild clown").[4] Following the example of the Sanson family's alleged memoirs, which cover a number of generations, he invented a whole dynasty of Mydlářs and composed (1886–9) fictional memoirs for them, concentrating on the crimes, trials and executions of the age of Rudolf II and the Thirty Years' War.[5] The germinal idea comes from the fact that executioners were allowed to marry only executioners' daughters and executioners' sons were forced to follow in the bloody footsteps of their fathers. Hence their lineage (*rody katovské*) in Bohemia, as in other countries, formed a unique, closed caste.[6] Svátek's memoirs abound in Romantic anachronisms, and he turns the bloody events into lachrymose melodrama, the hangmen into loving, sentimental and, therefore, suffering outcasts.

Even prior to Svátek, however, Josef Jiří Kolár had gone further. In the tragedy *Pražský žid* (The Jew of Prague, 1872) he posits that Mydlář refused to execute the twenty-seven notables and was therefore replaced on the scaffold by another hangman, unrecognizable as such underneath the traditional red hood.[7] The plot, which teems with horror, hyperbole, high-flown distortion and pettifogging jargon, has Master Mydlář flee Prague with Rabbi Falu-Eliab and Verena, the daughter of Count Thurn, leader of the defeated Czech army, both of whom he has freed from prison. When they reach the Silesian border, he hangs the evil prosecutor Přibík Jeníšek, a one-time quacksalver who played the leading role in the blood bath.

In point of fact, Jan Mydlář not only swung the sword and tightened the nooses but embellished upon the proceedings by chopping off the right hand of Ondřej Šlik, Bohuslav of Michalovice, Jiřík Hauenšild and Leander Ripl, and hacking out the tongue of the rector of Prague University, Johannes Jessenius, before delivering the *coups de grâce*. It is this "ghastly amputation" that most troubles the rector, friend of Tycho Brahe and defender of numerous dreamers and eccentrics during the reign of Rudolf II in Vrchlický's poem "Jessenius".[8] As Machar writes, "it was painful to see/the bloody mouth whose truncated tongue/yearned to speak . . . " (Jessenius' headless corpse was moved to the field outside the Horská brána – the gate to the road for Kutná Hora – where it was quartered and impaled on posts.)

Shortly before noon Mydlář returned to the ill-fated *theatrum* to collect twelve heads, which he carried in iron baskets to the Stone Bridge to expose them to ridicule on the cornice of the Bridge Tower – six facing Malá Strana, six facing the Catholic Church of the Holy Saviour. He nailed the severed right hands of Count Šlik and Dr Hauenšild to their heads and Jessenius' tongue to his.

Except for the skull of Count Šlik, which was returned to his family in May 1622,[9] the heads remained suspended in their iron baskets for a decade. Not until a band of Czech émigrés entered Prague with the Protestant Saxons in 1631 were they removed from the Tower and interred in Týn Church with due ceremony.[10] Yet even though in 1766 a coffin containing eleven skulls was exhumed in the church, popular wisdom has it that the heads were buried in a secret place in the Protestant Church of the Holy Saviour and that every year on the anniversary of the execution they rise and visit Old Town Square to make certain the hands of Master Hanuš's astrological clock have not stopped: when they stop, doom is nigh.[11]

Thus on 21 June 1621 one of the bitterest tragedies in Bohemian history was played out. The executioner Jan Mydlář, instrument of the vengeance and treacherous bigotry of Ferdinand II, secured the rout and subjugation of a people of rebels and heretics with his unerring swords. How odd, then, that through the years Romantic distortions should have transformed him into a melancholy hero forced to slaughter against his will. I shall never tire of crying out against all the Mydlářs who have raged and still rage in Prague: *In ignem aeternum, in ignem aeternum!*

70

When Matthias ascended the Imperial throne in 1612, having forced his brother Rudolf II to abdicate the Bohemian crown in the previous year, he moved the seat of the Empire to Vienna. Meanwhile, tension was mounting in Prague between Protestants and Catholics. Instances of intolerance indicated that the religious liberty granted by Rudolf's Royal Charter of 9 July 1609 was on its way out. Finally, Protestant leaders, incited by Count Thurn, resolved to confront the Habsburgs head-on. On 23 May 1618 a small group of the most radical among them went to the Castle to request an audience. Following an exchange of insults and affronts the Protestants threw the two *locum tenentes* Jaroslav Bořita z Martinic and Vilém Slavata and their secretary Filip Fabricius out of the window. Although all three survived the long fall, the time for sabre rattling had past; this was open revolt.[1]

A thirty-member directorate was formed. Count Thurn raised a mercenary army of sixteen thousand. After scoring initial victories in skirmishes against Generals Dampierre and Buquoy near Pelhřimov and between Veselí and Lomnice, after pushing the Imperial troops back as far as the outskirts of Vienna, the Czechs, plagued by indecision and lack of resources, failed to exploit the situation. In the meantime, the machinery of mêlée went into gear. When the ailing, oscillating Matthias died in 1619, he was succeeded by the young Archduke of Styria, Ferdinand II, a sanctimonious, unyielding product of Jesuit schools who was convinced that any compromise with the Protestants would be an offence against Almighty God. But on 19 August the Prague Diet deposed Ferdinand as King of Bohemia (a title it had frivolously granted him a few years before) and set in his place the twenty-three-year-old Frederick – Elector of the Palatinate, son-in-law of James I of England and head of the German Protestant League. Frederick, whose Calvinism came close to the faith of the Bohemian Brethren, arrived in Prague at the end of October with his wife and court, and was crowned King of Bohemia on 4 November.

Ferdinand II immediately began elaborate preparations to do away with this Protestant kingdom so dangerous to the Habsburgs and in the very heart of Europe. The Catholic League sent him a large, battle-hardened army under the command of Maximilian, Duke of Bavaria; the King of Poland dispatched a Cossack regiment; Spain, France, the rest of Catholic Europe and even the Lutheran Elector of Saxony, eager to annex Lusatia, sided with the Emperor against the Calvinist King of Bohemia. The German Protestants, the English king and Holland all enthusiastically supported the Czech cause, yet refused to commit themselves materially. The only monarch to send troops was the adventurous Prince of Transylvania Gábor Bethlen. Negotiations with the Turks came to nought.

The balance of power turned when the thirty thousand men of the Catholic League, led by Maximilian and General Tilly, joined Buquoy's Imperial forces in June 1620. The decisive engagement between the Catholics and the Czechs, led by Christian von Anhalt, took place on 8 November 1620 at Bílá Hora (White Mountain, so called because of the chalk marl extracted there), a hill with a commanding position of the Bohemian capital.[2] Although it was a minor encounter of minimal importance for the rest of Europe, it spelled ruin for Bohemia, marking the end of ancient glory and the onset of a decline that was to last for centuries.[3]

Shortly after noon – it was Sunday – Imperial troops, exhorted by the fanatical Carmelite monk Dominicus a Jesu, attacked the left wing of the Czech army, Count Thurn's light cavalry squadrons. At first the "heretics" held their own, but when the reinforced Imperials forced them to give ground, chaos spread from detachment to detachment. A charge by Anhalt's young son, who briefly managed to penetrate Imperial ranks, proved futile. One regiment after the next, the Czech army split and then disintegrated under Catholics' constant hammer blows. The result was not so much retreat as full-scale flight, a crush in which arms and impedimenta of all kinds were abandoned. The Hungarian cavalry also fled before the Polish Cossacks, who rode with the reins between their teeth. A single company of Moravian infantry held out to the last – and was wiped out. The battle was over by two in the afternoon.

When the Prince of Anhalt saw that all attempts to assemble the troops were to no avail, he set off for Prague, making his way past the press of baggage wagons at Strahov Gate and galloping to the Castle. There he encountered King Frederick, who was just on his way to the battlefield with his guard: he had been delayed at the Hradčany giving a lunch for the English ambassador. Prague was teeming with armed men and could have been defended. The "Winter King", however, left for Silesia the following morning at dawn with his family and retinue, and by noon the Protestants had unconditionally surrendered to Buquoy and Maximilian.

While solemn masses of thanksgiving were celebrated in Vienna and hell and brimstone hurled at the "heretics" from the pulpits, a special court presided over by Karl von Liechtenstein condemned to death the twenty-seven notables who, hoping for clemency, had refused to flee. Ferdinand II confiscated the property of the rebels who had either fallen or fled or been executed and, after the farcical "general pardon" of those who had sided with the "Winter King", bestowed it upon the victorious commanders. Thus it was that a group of speculators, careerists and *malefikanti*[4] from a number of lands (Buquoy, Liechtenstein, Wallenstein and Marradas) amassed enormous wealth at the expense of the Czechs. Meanwhile Ferdinand set about reconverting the country to Catholicism, depriving Lutherans, Utraquists and other Protestants of all rights, driving their pastors and preachers out of the Czech Lands and entrusting schools, the university and the censorship of books to the Jesuits.

Thousands of burghers, nobles, artists and intellectuals (including Comenius) emigrated and continued the struggle abroad for several decades, some with the pen, others with the sword in the ranks of the Saxon, Swedish and other armies that fought the Habsburgs. There were Czech contingents, for example, among the troops of Gustavus Adolphus, a sovereign in whom the exiles placed great hopes. And while the Catholic nobility that remained behind was Germanized under the influence of the Viennese court, the impoverished and oppressed peasantry persisted in "heretical" Protestant traditions for years, strengthening its faith by reading old religious books behind the Jesuits' backs.

Between White Mountain and the end of the Thirty Years' War in 1648 the Czech Lands were raped and defiled by one army after the other. "There is nothing in Bohemia but 'grab it' and 'give it here',"[5] Dačický cries out in anguish. Enraged peasants hanged marauding soldiers from the trees like puppets among the smoking ruins.

The curious fact that Prague, which failed to repel the Imperial troops after White Mountain, stood up to Königsmarck's Swedes in 1648 may be explained by the not so curious fact that instead of playing the role of liberators they too indulged in plundering and atrocities.[6] The Peace of Westphalia put an end to hopes for the restoration of the Kingdom of Bohemia, which the roar of musket-fire, the cannonades, the pillaging, the depredations and the listless acceptance of it all had in any case turned into a deserted province. Prague lost its royal splendour; a mournful silence overlay its streets. The Castle of the Bohemian sovereigns was left empty and mute, a relic of past glories. Thus began the temporary situation that persists to this day.

71

Many foreign pilgrims have seen the city on the Vltava as sullen and suffering, a plexus of dead arteries, the lifeless eye of a land prostrate and somnolent since the Battle of White Mountain. It was as if a dense, indissoluble mist had descended upon its body after the defeat.

When Caroline de la Motte-Fouqué visited White Mountain beneath a white wafer of a moon and a delicate, shroud-like mist on a cold night in 1822, she shivered at the thought of standing where the fate of the Czech nation had been sealed.[1] Visitors have been struck by the frailty of the joyless, eternally pouting city, its suffocating, defenceless lethargy, its deposed-sovereign majesty, the pallor, the morose resignation of those who walk its constricted streets, a dungheap of ancient glories.[2] But most of all it is the writers of Prague, both Czech and German, who bear the anguish of the rout, the curse of White Mountain, the affliction of the *finis Bohemiae*.

"Prague! Prague! My country's heart of stone! . . . Unhappy land, unhappy mother!" Karel Hynek Mácha cries in an 1834 prose poem expressing the malaise, the decay, the dejection of the Czech people, unable to shake off the evil spell of the disastrous battle.[3] "Walk up White Mountain," Karásek wrote later,

> and you will feel you have never been closer to death. In the distance you will see the dying city, the tragic queen, Prague. She is dying of exhaustion, and the agony that has weighed upon her for three centuries is a wound that can never heal. When here on White Mountain the scarlet sunset slowly bleeds and down below in the darkling blue basin all the bells of Prague ring out, it is like a grandiose requiem.[4]

The definition of himself Kafka gave to Gustav Janouch fits this sorrowful setting: "I am a jackdaw, a *kavka*. I am grey, like ash. A jackdaw that longs to vanish between the stones."[5] *Švejk* too – with its black humour, its obsessive barroom badinage, its apocalyptic visions and its insane asylums – is part of that gloom.

The black moods of Rudolf II, the hypochondria of the alchemists, the lack of an outlet to the sea, the execution of the twenty-seven notables, the morbidity of the Baroque, the grimness of the Jewish tales – in short, the principal productive elements of Prague's sombre side – have in the course of time fused into a single symbol: White Mountain. The threads of its melancholy wind round the spool of that cataclysm of defeat.

Bohemia is landlocked. It is surrounded by water only in Shakespeare's *Winter's Tale*, where (in Act Two, Scene Three) Lord Antigonus arrives on a deserted Bohemian shore from Sicily by ship. A character in one of Jan Neruda's *Tales of Malá Strana* constantly complains that his country is not washed by the sea. Mr Rybář is an elderly retired civil servant who wears a wig and a top hat, a white waistcoat, shoes as cracked as the roof of a hackney cab, white stockings fastened with silver studs, black trousers to the knees and a green gold-buttoned dress coat with long flaps that strike against his thin calves. The green coat – which evokes the aquatic demons of Czech folklore – his name (*rybář* means "fisher") and his peevish longing for the sea lead people to call him a *hastrman* or water sprite. When he learns that the stones he has collected all his life are worthless, his simple, limited disappointment becomes one with a desperate regret that Prague does not lie on the sea, a springboard for escape, for broadening the soul.[6]

The Baroque replaced the Czech army, brought to wrack and ruin on the infamous hill, with a cohort of saints, of troubled statues yearning for heaven and dancing Moorish dances in opulent churches and on the parapets of the Charles Bridge. The point of intersection between the mourning for White Mountain and the theatricality of the Baroque gives rise to the unmistakably grotesque, feverish atmosphere of Prague literature, always a refuge for agitated, visionary characters, little men with whims as eccentric as a tarot pack gone wild.

The grim memory of White Mountain, then, permeates the works of Prague writers; it provides at least a partial explanation of why so many books about Prague are set at night against a backdrop of ceruse moonlight. Jakub Arbes has innumerable descriptions of the dark, empty, rain-drenched streets of Malá Strana in his *romaneta*: run-down alleyways where the dull light of gas lanterns swaying in the wind creates mysterious, bloodcurdling silhouettes. German and German-Jewish writers are especially good at capturing the enervation, the fetid atmosphere that vanished with the Slum Clearance Law. I think of Paul Leppin's novel

Severins Gang in die Finsternis – a work that casts the dim light of a shuddering, frightened Prague, all mist and dying lanterns – and the story "Beschreibung eines Kampfes" (Description of a Struggle, 1904–5), in which Kafka treats the Bohemian capital as a virtual city of the dead, a wintry Bruges on the Vltava: "The Moldau and the quarter of the town on the farther shore lay together in the dark. A number of lights burning there teased the eye."[7] The Vltava is an accomplice to the witchcraft of "Prrrague", as Meyrink writes. To a foreign fool it may at first seem as mighty as the Mississippi, though in fact it is "only four millimeters deep and full of leeches".[8]

Prague has the rhythm of slow, endless mastication (like that of Gregor Samsa, chewing on a bit of food in *The Metamorphosis* for hours on end),[9] a catatonia from which it at times awakes with a burst of energy that immediately dies down. Visitors have noted this phlegmatic quality; it effects them as well. Albert Camus renders the anxiety, the dull dismay of the Rudolfine city with crystal clarity in the essay "La mort dans l'âme":

> I became lost in the opulent Baroque churches, trying to find a native land, only to leave emptier and more desperate at the disappointing tête-à-tête with myself. I wandered along the Vltava cut into sections by seething weirs. I spent endless hours in the deserted, silent, huge Hradschin district.[10]

Gide's *Journal* defines Prague, with a cadence of old fanfares, as a "ville glorieuse, douloureuse et tragique".[11]

To this day the grief of *finis Bohemiae* lies stagnant in the crooked byways, the splendid churches, the old palaces; it is the rancour of a culture constantly interrupted by the brutal meddling of arrogant neighbours. The rare outbursts of violence are followed by day after day of ashes, beery torpor, laceration and mourning. Traces of the Prague atmosphere extend as far as the Ostbahnhof in Vienna. One senses it in the leaden grey passenger trains waiting to leave at night for a lost Bohemia, in the advertisements which, like fools and owls, repeat one and the same message: *Der billige Verkauf geht weiter*, The clearance sale continues.

72
(Written in Bruges)

The spell of White Mountain brought time to a standstill in the city on the Vltava, changing it into a storeroom of ancient glories, curios, statues and monuments, of flaking rubbish, votive offerings, encrusted candelabra, rusty clock springs – in short, a city of relics. Prague sleeps curled up in its opulent past like a restive animal. Heavy brewery horses tread back through the centuries towards a single point: White Mountain. Alas, the splendour of the edifices does not ease the mourning; the beauty of the dressing does not dull the pain.

The protagonist of Karásek's novel *Gotická duše* (A Gothic Soul, 1905) feels as spent and defenceless as Bohemian culture. He identifies his haunted existence with the haunted quality of his city, a den of antiquated glories, a people grown lazy, broken by ill luck. When he climbs Petřín Hill at sunset, the peal of bells from many periods evokes the ups and downs of Prague's sad history. Their dark metallic strokes resounding to "the tiles of the roofs, the lopsided chimneys, the rotten frames, the walled-up panes, the blackened chimney-pots, the crumbling cornices" awaken the music of past events in the still air of twilight.[1]

Every cranny in Prague, Karásek says in *Román Manfreda Macmillena* (The Novel of Manfred Macmillen, 1907),

> is steeped in the past. It thrusts itself upon you at every turn, breathes upon you from the green shadows of extensive leafy gardens, envelops you from a dark portal, from the depths of a palace entrance. You are in an ancient city that retains the soul of those who lived there before you, the stifling proximity of the tombs of those who lived there in previous centuries.[2]

"I know nothing," Francis says to Manfred,

> of the city's present. All I seek here is the past. If I wish to experience being laid out in a church in a crystal casket, if I wish to view life through the glass of my coffin, I go to Prague: it has an oppressive atmosphere because of all the tragic events that have taken place there. I see the Hradčany, Malá Strana, Old Town Square, and feel that only the Past is present in Prague . . . In Prague everything is over and done with; it matters as little who is living there now as it matters who lives in a crumbling old palace once the dynasty for which it was built is extinct. I like to walk through Prague at night. I feel I can catch every sigh of her soul. In rare bursts of clarity I see the glorious necropolis rise up only to plunge again into the sad, dark mirror of its ruinous futility.[3]

When Jørgen Møller goes to Morris's Malá Strana house in *Ganymedes* (1925), Karásek comments,

> Here in the heart of the town they seemed the only living beings; the ancient streets around them were deserted. Here nothing recalled

the world, the present. Here there were only intimations of the Past and its resurrected mysteries.[4]

Strolls through Prague by his characters give Karásek the opportunity to sketch a doleful portrait of the city, whose proud palaces grow dark beneath the widow's weeds of the centuries.[5] It is an unreal city made for mysterious encounters, a funereal *theatrum mundi* in which the black-draped drums that drowned out the execution of the twenty-seven notables still roll. Manfred says,

> We wandered through the streets at twilight and at night, when in the deceptive moonlight everything was magnified enormously. We gazed down from the embankment at the Vltava – which flows through the city with an imposing, mournful air – and up at the sombre silhouette of the Castle, which breathed the melancholy of a ruin. The long, empty edifice, dark as a prison, had a depressing effect upon us: it symbolized the hopelessness of a land that has outlived its glory.[6]

In Karásek's drama *Král Rudolf* (1916), the sovereign invokes Prague while leaning against a Castle window in the moonlight: "sarcophagus . . . plunged into shadows . . . enveloped in mystery . . . "[7] Karásek merges the myth of White Mountain with the typical penchant of the Decadents for mysterious, dead cities.

Before Karásek, F. Marion Crawford called attention to the tangle of glutinous mists and coal smoke dominated by ashen-grey afternoons with only the rarest flashes of sun. In his *Witch of Prague* (1891) it takes on the appearance of a graveyard cowering in sullen torpor, a veritable Böcklinian isle of the dead. "It is a city," mutters Keyork Arabian, "for old men. It is saturnine. The foundations of its houses rest on the silurian formation."[8] Both Crawford and Karásek run into swarms of breathless pedestrians advancing through the winding lanes with doleful expressions and an automaton-like gait, exchanging only whispers, more spirits than bodies. To these spirits we might add the ones that return after death, the revenants who pay the poet a call in Holan's verses. "The entire city is extinct,/lying like an empty tomb." Thus Karel Hynek Mácha, the great Czech Romantic. In Mácha even the moon is permeated with mourning for White Mountain, and a number of motifs refer to this source of desolation, including the obsessive harp motif: "harp without strings/hung in ancestors' crypt . . . harp of times gone by/cradle of sweet sounds", harp with a "curved womb".[9]

Malá Strana is ruled by the past. As Rilke writes in the story "König Bohusch",

I know my little mother Prague to her very heart, to her very heart, [Bohusch] repeated as though someone had called his statement into question, because her heart is the Kleinseite and the Hradschin. The heart always keeps the deepest secrets, and there are many secrets in these old houses.[10]

When Karásek's exotic Adrian Morris walks through Malá Strana, he instinctively feels that "extraordinary things could happen in the depths of the old houses" and that what had once been hidden here would eventually come to light.[11] In Neruda's stories, set little more than a hundred years ago, Malá Strana – with its palaces and gardens, its vast churches, its narrow streets running uphill to the Castle, its yellow street lamps reflected in puddles – was a sleepy provincial town. Incidentally, if you look today at the enchanting conglomeration of tile roofs, roof terraces, dormers, chimneys, chimney-pots and towers from the greenery of Petřín Park and the Castle, you will still see what seems a town lost in sleep, untouched by the hustle and bustle of life; its houses, to quote Arnošt Procházka, are "refuges for solitary souls and jewel caskets for forsaken hearts".[12]

In the period described by Neruda, plump, orange cats stuck their heads between window-sill geraniums, tufts of grass peeked out of side streets, wind-blown garments and striped, flowered pillow cases hung from the windows, odd little men – usually pensioners – passed their days smoking pipes and telling anecdotes in inns or at front doors. Sloth was everywhere.

No place seems to have so many old men as Malá Strana, and since old people like to put their hands in their laps and avoid haste, the entire quarter has a gentle meditative quality about it, its streets are curiously quiet.[13]

The melodious rustling of the leaves, the stones and the coats of arms of the façades – everything harks back to a time long since vanished. The delicate emblem on the Three Violins House[14] in Nerudova Street could serve as the symbol of the district's sedative-like musicality, the music of its silence, its stillness serving to intensify the insecurity, the cyclothymia of the city as a whole.

Perle, the capital of the Dream Kingdom (*Traumreich*) in *Die andere Seite* (The Other Side, 1909) by Kubin, a rotting, hellish, grey city draped in funereal crêpe and older than the Sybil, is a facsimile of Malá Strana: "The sky above was always cloudy; the sun *never* shone, *never* were the moon or the stars visible at night."[15] The mist streaked with faint yellow flashes of gas flames, the murky, dull air, the Negro River, from which it rises, black as ink, the heaps of decrepit houses and the sleep-sickness that afflicts its inhabitants in epidemic proportions all reveal how close this opaque metropolis of lethargites, of faint echoes with no light of its own is to crestfallen post-White-Mountain Prague.

"What I remember about Prague," writes Albert Camus, "is the smell of pickled cucumbers that they sell as a snack on every street corner and whose sour, pungent fragrance aroused my anguish."[16]

Here, in Bruges, I thought of you, Prague. Along the putrid, lethargic canals, in the fields where flocks of white swans with the letter B on their beak crowd together, before the Memlinks at the museum, in the quiet of the Béguinage, in the market place that recalls the wasteful arrogance of Flanders, in front of the maisons-Dieu in the Street of the Blind Ass, on the Quai du Miroir, in the shops with their piles of candelabra, lace and copper trifles, I thought of you, Prague, with your stone glories and your chests overflowing with rusty junk, of your pickled cucumbers, whose pungent smell arouses anguish. The rotten waters of Bruges come close to the musty smell on Kampa Island, home of Vladimír Holan, the great piper of ghosts and spirits.

Perplexed and as prickly as a purple thistle by Tichý, I hurled a tightrope from Flemish Spain to the Spain of Bohemia. On days dripping with mire, when the damp green of the surrounding polders exudes melancholy, when the Gothic houses of Bruges (which Hanuš Schwaiger painted so well) are as disquieting as the mysterious Sibyl Sambetha painted by Memlink, I thought of your parks, Prague, of your bewitched palaces, of your taverns reeking of spilt beer; I thought of evenings when I stared down from Kampa's walls at the Vltava splashing its shores with angry waves, frightening a large water rat, identical to the rat that gnaws away at Ophelia in Holan's poem; I thought of the evening drizzles in which a foolish tow doll of a moon played hide-and-seek with chestnut trees, mist-maned horses, the verdigris-green dome of Saint Nicholas', and the bridge towers. Here, in Bruges, as in your crooked streets, I, Señor Rodenbach y Karásek, felt the melancholy of a buried pride, a prestigious past, a vanished greatness. You resemble each other in your death throes, your foul humours, in the Good-Friday light, you rotten, you detestable, you most Ophelia-like of cities. From afar I heard the whistling with which you, Prague-Josephine, gather your humble race of mice.

73

Keyork Arabian the hunchback claims that the Czech metropolis has the same convolutions as the human brain, "full of winding ways, dark lanes and gloomy arches".[1] Evil-looking houses squat at every turn, stained with black pustules, cartilaginous carcasses. In Malá Strana, at the Castle and throughout the squiggles of the Old Town a fluid resin of sticky shadows trickles along decrepit walls. Crumbling old houses with large staring eyes and throats as coated as Kafka's leave their impression in the pitch-black wax of mist. No visitor has failed to note the perfidy and infirmity of the houses of Prague.

Tight-fisted, consumptive old houses with doltish façades and inside – tangles of tunnels, gales of draughts. A Kafkaesque lair. Shadowy rooms along impossibly narrow lanes, rooms bundled in heavy, fringed *secese* drapes; anaemic, ill-groomed rooms with abandoned combs on tables set with cloths fried in grease; rooms with mirrors covered as though reflecting menstruating women, with oval portraits of ancestors in Austro-Hungarian uniform, with chests full of bowler hats and starched collars, with mousetraps and mouseholes whose eccentric inhabitants have tow hair that glows phosphorescent in the dark like the wigs in Tichý's clown paintings. Myopic corridors, attics crammed with trinkets, fans, albums, oil lamps, galleries, toilets on landings, tortuous, daredevil stairs and banisters with oracular dignity. As the Prague poet Leo Heller put it:

> In meiner Heimat gibt es dunkle Gassen,
> die irr und eng sind und wie traumverloren,
> und Häuser gibt es, alt und lärmverlassen,
> mit blinden Fenstern und mit morschen Toren.[2]

> [In my country there are dark lanes,
> twisting and narrow and lost in dreams,
> and there are houses, old and far from din,
> with sightless windows and rotten portals]

Reader, do you remember the Ghetto hovels in Meyrink's *Golem*: "the discoloured buildings, standing side by side in the rain like a herd of derelict, dripping animals, erected without plan, as fortuitously as so many weeds poking up from the ground . . . "? Meyrink describes "something hostile, something malicious" about those wretched houses, their

> quiet, barely perceptible mimicry, as though at certain hours of the night and early morning grey they took mysterious counsel together . . . Strange sounds would creep along the roofs and down the gutters . . . The front doors: wide open black maws with rotten tongues, chasms that could blurt out piercing screams at any instant, so piercing and malignant that they would chill us to the

very core of our being . . .   A window: its panes obscured by drops of moisture that have made it an unhealthy blister on the wall."[3]

In Meyrink Malá Strana houses are no less treacherous than those of the Ghetto; they are steeped in a terrifying *Todesstille*.

> The air in Malá Strana is more sinister than any other in the world. It is never clear and never wholly night. A dull, faint ray of light comes from somewhere, seeping from the Hradčany onto the rooftops like a phosphorescent mist. One turns into an alley and sees only lifeless darkness, then suddenly a beam of light from a crack in a window pierces one's pupil like a long, evil needle. A house emerges from the mist, a house with amputated shoulders and a receding forehead, and stares dully from empty dormer windows into the night-time sky like a dead animal.[4]

Meyrink is fond of comparing Prague houses to lurking beasts.

Equally horrifying are the warped, flayed, mud-caked, rat-infested houses Kubin portrays in *Die andere Seite*. Woe unto you if you venture near them at night. You will hear stifled groans (a strangling or worse) through the barred windows. "Gateways yawn as though eager to swallow each passer-by."[5] When the Dream Kingdom finally breaks up with an apocalyptic din, the houses bunch together in a drunken pile painful to behold, screaming frightfully in their "obscure, incomprehensible language".[6] These vistas of perpendicular lines, these rebellious old objects, this architectural teratology may well be the source of the crooked houses, slanted windows, warped frames and wedge-shaped doors in *The Cabinet of Doctor Caligari*.[7]

Crawford had hinted at the preternatural quality of Prague architecture by placing Unorna the witch in the Karlova Street house known as The Golden Well (U zlaté studně) and wicked Keyork Arabian in the Celetná Street house called The Black Mother of God (U černé Matky boží). The whimsical Golden Well façade of black stucco saints was meant to protect the house from the plague, and the house itself was once a bastion of spirits. Popelka Bilianová (1862–1941), a prolific writer of mawkish, tear-jerking novels, wrote that the high-walled spiral staircase was so narrow that when a fat man climbed it not even a mouse could pass. Were a ghost to appear in front of you, you could not escape. It is anyone's guess how the furnishings were moved in, but the dead were lowered through the window. On Good Friday the water in the basement well shone like yellow sequins: a pile of gold was hidden at the bottom. It was guarded by the white elbow of a maid who had drowned trying to fetch the beguiling metal.[8]

Little of what takes place behind these closed doors leaks out. And what does take place in the gloomy Malá Strana house of the "Persian Satan" Dr Mohammed Darasche-Koh? "A human stomach floated in a bluish liquid in a glass bowl atop a sideboard . . . The inside door handle was a human hand adorned with rings, a dead man's hand, its white fingers clutching at the void."[9] In the house of the Egyptologist Dr Cinderella, also in Malá Strana, there was a collection of luxuriant carnivorous plants, all throbbing veins and eyeballs with repulsive blueberry-like protuberances. "I bumped into bowls of whitish bits of fat sprouting fly agarics with translucent skin, fleshy red mushrooms that burst at the touch."[10]

Meyrink's interiors resemble the chamber of the old master in Arbes's *Ethiopská lilie* (The Ethiopian Lily, 1886) with its skeletons and herbaria, stuffed animals and anatomical specimens,[11] and the study of Keyork Arabian, a museum of mummified corpses. Møller's laboratory in *Ganymedes*, a medieval forge full of religious tracts, mysterious electuaries, parchments covered with Cabalistic symbols, is located in a "sorcerer's cave" outside Košíře near the stream where Rabbi Loew is said to have found the clay for his Golem.[12] Adrian Morris lives in Thunova Street along the slopes of the Castle in a dwelling once inhabited by one of Rudolf's concubines.[13]

Prague literature contains an abundance of sinister old houses. Leppin writes that when his Severin looks at Prague houses through closed eyes they take on strange shapes: "Was the city to blame with its spent passion, its dark façades, the silence of its large squares? He still imagined invisible hands brushing against him."[14] Where could the mad hero of Arbes's *Svatý Xaverius* (Saint Xavier, 1878) live but in a Malá Strana shack in Umrlčí ulice (Dead Man's Street)?[15] And what a horrid view of the houses and churches of the gloomy Dobytčí trh (Cattle Market) there is in Karolina Světlá's *Zvonečková králova* (Queen of the Bells, 1872): "Black as graveyard earth, heavy as a coffin lid, they looked like graves without shape or contour, indiscriminately heaped one on top of the other in a single odd pile." One of these houses boasted an illuminated balcony with a red strip that pierced the darkness like a trail of blood from a winding sheet.[16] If you walked past it at the midnight hour, dear reader, your legs would tremble. The windows of the Malá Strana Bonneval Palace in Josef Svátek's novel *Tajnosti pražské* (The Mysteries of Prague, 1868) are always closed, and its luxuriant garden blocks the view of the lamenting skeleton that stalks the grounds by night. These dens of spectres and spirits with their dark spiral staircases, huge empty spaces and endless corridors provide the perfect backdrop for the hackneyed devices and trite horrors of late Romanticism.

Decrepitude magnifies the houses' powers of sorcery. Witness

Kubin's grim Perle, the jumble of crumbling, old buildings that the tyrant Claus Patera has bought in Europe. Patera's Asiatic Dream Kingdom is an "Eldorado for the collector",[17] a heap of *tandlmark* rubbish: "Only objects that have been used can pass its gates."[18] Even the clothing its inhabitants wear is absurdly out of date. If Lovecraft's Innsmouth issues a stench of fish, slimy seaweed and mire, the stench of a "mixture of flour and dried codfish"[19] pervades the streets of Perle. More than the Asiatic city it purports to be, Perle is a Central European metropolis with its musty courtyards and black chimneys, out-of-the-way garrets, wooden or tile roofs and profusion of bizarre chimney pots.[20] When "a disease of lifeless matter" ("eine Krankheit der leblosen Materie")[21] covers the houses with cracks and rust and the walls slowly crumble, one feels a specific reference to Prague.

Among the most illustrious examples of Prague's disturbing architecture are the oppressive buildings in Kafka's *Trial*. The tribunal Josef K. is summoned to one Sunday morning is held in a typical Prague *barabizna*, a cross between a workers' tenement and a ghetto hovel, a maze of dark stairs, stifling corridors, galleries and storerooms. A combination warehouse, office and laundry, with small shops below the street level and windows full of mattresses and tenants shouting to one another, it shares characteristics of both the proletarian district of Žižkov and the Jewish Town. Also typical of Prague is the filthy *činžák*, the tenement in whose attic the hack painter Titorelli lives, with its narrow, airless staircases swarming with insolent little girls. And we could go into great detail about the oppressive Prague-like nature of Josef K.'s rented room. Even Kafka's *America* is modelled after Prague: we need only recall the tenement with its innumerable staircases, landings, balconies and corridors and the cramped room where Brunelda, the shady soprano, lies on her sofa in a red dress and thick white woolen stockings.

To this day, every evening at five, Franz Kafka returns home to Celetná Street (Zeltnergasse) wearing a bowler hat and black suit. The houses in which Kafka lived with his family in and around Old Town Square all had something mysterious about them, especially Zu den Heiligen Drei Königen at 3 Celetná Street, where he lived for ten years beginning in 1897. This old building huddled directly against Týn Church, from which the sound of the organ and choirs and the odour of incense filtered through a large perforated window into the square courtyard, a dark well wound round with galleries.[22] To this day, every evening, Jaroslav Hašek proclaims to his drinking companions in one or another dive that radicalism is harmful and wholesome progress can be achieved only through obedience to authority. Hašek too was affected by the houses of Prague. As his indigent parents moved from one hole in the wall to the next, he spent his childhood and adolescence in cold, dank rooms, deafened by the screams of children in the courtyards and the babble of women on the galleries. It may well have been the agony of childhood poverty, the squalor of those rooms that aroused in him an unrestrained yearning for the road.[23]

So we have leprous façades, stifling rat-holes, stones as smooth as slabs of fat,[24] palaces marked with a grief tears cannot redress, nightmarish houses rubbing their muzzles against us from afar. No wonder Prague has such a keen awareness of confining, hope-killing walls. As Paul Adler says, there is "room enough for the unknown" within the walls and between the houses "room for hackney cabs and processions of fools".[25] The Dream Kingdom is surrounded by a huge wall with a gate that constitutes "an enormous black hole".[26] Kafka's description of the irregular, inconsistent construction of the Great Wall of China may well come from the walled-in feeling so common in Prague writers. Walls – hideously cracked, crumbling slates, enigmas, incubi, "the longing to break through to the miraculous"[27] – recur with special frequency in poets and painters of Group 42, in the works of Orten and Holan.

74

Anyone familiar with Prague literature will have the impression that its characters are components of the buildings,[1] extensions of the architecture, fragments of the walls of palaces and hovels, the naves of opulent Baroque churches, "the broad pages of roofs".[2] Churches are immensely prominent in the Logos of the city on the Vltava. "There are as many churches as days in the year. In this respect Prague rivals Rome."[3]

Following the example of the Decadents, who were largely responsible for the magic image of the Czech metropolis, we have concentrated not so much on its architectural splendour as on its lugubrious backdrops, dank darkness, mouldy old age. Karásek transformed every church into a melancholy *Panoptikum*, dwelling on the decay of the altar flowers, the languor of the statues outlined by garments of glossy creased silk, the infirm penumbra of the sanctuaries and the White Mountain dirges. When the Decadents used churches to exalt the corruption of the flesh, the ecstasy of martyrdom and the rapture of sainthood, they were simply indulging in a predilection for the Baroque, a Prague constant. The city on the Vltava goes to outlandish lengths to indulge its Baroque fantasies: in the Hradčany district it invents the Barnabite Monastery and Saint Benedict's, whose monks revere the blackened mummy of the Blessed Electa; in Loreta it sculpts the statue of Saint Starosta on the cross with splendid garments but a man's beard;[4] and at Saint George's, again in the Hradčany quarter, it creates the awesome statue of Saint Brigitte, a putrid combination of toads, snakes and lizards.[5]

Two passages from *Román Manfred Macmillena* will provide us with the mirror of the morbidity, malevolence and madness Karásek feels in the churches of Prague. In Saint Henry's the gold statues of one altar

> looked like cataleptic ghosts who had just risen from their graves and taken cumbersome shape. Deeply affected by their chilling, grotesque spectrality, I began to tremble. The morbid terror excited within my innermost self an arcane relationship with the beings who had decayed here beneath the church floor and in the surrounding cemetery, which had long since ceased to exist.[6]

In Saint James':

> All the melancholy objects I have viewed until now with antiquarian pleasure wear a mocking sneer. Christ stares at me from the glass cabinet. Several deathly pale statues come to life in the frames of the reliquaries; several bones and tibias threaten as if ready to grab and strangle me. Everything is cruel and grotesque; everything seems distorted, conceived by a madman . . . [7]

Karásek painted the mystery of Prague's sanctuaries in even bleaker colours in the novel *Gotická duše* (A Gothic Soul). The hero, the last scion of a noble line with a long history of insanity, is a Rudolf-like hypochondriac. Fearing he too will go mad (he does in the end – and dies in a mental hospital), he retreats into solitude, his greatest delights the smell of incense and wilted flowers, the sight of "glass coffins containing embalmed cadavers atop the altars".[8] He also feels drawn to the Barnabites or Discalced Carmelites, who live like moles in the darkness of mystical reclusion. Their lugubrious cloister near the Castle was shrouded in wildly imaginative legends.[9] People said that before taking vows each novice had to remove the ring from the shrivelled hand of the terrifying mummy of the Blessed Electa at midnight. During mass the faithful heard the chanting voices of those buried alive coming from the bowels of the church and saw the flickering of troubled eyes behind its rusty gratings. "The altars rose like shapeless catafalques."[10] "Only the main altar, covered with candles beneath the image of Saint Teresa, fervent in her devotion to Christ, shone like a great pyramid of liquified gold, glowed like an immense *castrum doloris*."[11] That church deranges the Gothic Soul; it drives him mad. The by-then jejune motif of the haunted basilica acquires new vigour in the myth of lifeless, funereal Prague.

Tereza Manfredi (1884), a stilted novella by Julius Zeyer, also features the Barnabite theme. Princess Manfredi, rejected by the painter Benedikt, withdraws to the Barnabite Convent. When Benedikt spies her sleepwalking in the pale-green moonlight along the winding rooftops towards his nearby studio, he burns with love, but it is too late: Tereza will die even as she takes the veil. Again Zeyer's shades are shaped by the architecture, by spirits emanating from the "labyrinth of blackened roofs, proud towers and majestic domes".[12]

In the novella *Svatý Xaverius* (Saint Xaverius, 1878) Arbes tells of the baleful power of a painting by František Xaver Balko in Malá Strana's Saint Nicholas' Church, a painting depicting Saint Francis Xavier expiring by a river bank on a coarse reed mat. A fanatical Rudolf-like youth named Xaverius, whose face is as similar to Balko's Xavier as if he had posed for it, steals into the deserted church at night and searches desperately for the enigma hidden in the canvas. After long investigation he finds that when superimposed on a map of Prague a series of dots in the painting indicates the route from the house in which Balko lived to the Malvazinka vineyards outside Smíchov in which a treasure is said to be buried. One night Xaverius goes there with the narrator to dig it up, but a match falls into the grass igniting some bits of red arsenic, and when in the sinister glow he sees the saint's livid ghost he flees in terror. The tin box he manages to get his hands on contains nothing but worthless minerals. Here motifs of sorcery and cryptographic symbology merge with that of Jesuit fiendishness – a common theme in Prague literature – and the magic of the nocturnal, spirit-breeding church.

Churches exert a fatal attraction on Prague fiction's morbid characters. Leppin writes of his Severin that "something always compelled him to tarry in the darkness of side altars where the statues stood austerely in their niches and the eternal light flickered in its red glass".[13] Nor should one forget the important role Saint Vitus' Cathedral plays in Meyrink's *Golem*. Having taken the hat of a stranger there by mistake, the hero runs through the life of Athanasius Pernath, "the most esteemed stonecutter of his day",[14] as if in a dream. Only Meyrink would think of placing the clownish mistaken hat act in Saint Vitus' Cathedral and in the soft light, the blurred focus in which Prague literature is wont to describe its houses of worship:

There I stood in the darkness, the golden altar gleaming at me like a veritable rock of peace, through the blue-green shimmer of the fading light that drifted down onto the praying-stools through the multicoloured windows. Sparks crackled from red glass lanterns.

The enervating smell of tapers and incense.[15]

Neruda's tale "Svatováclavská mše" (Saint Wenceslas' Mass, 1876) is set in the mother church of the Bohemian diocese. The author recalls the night when at the age of nine, shivering with terror, he took part in an imaginary service performed by Saint Wenceslas. Neruda brings to life the spectral quality of the church at night, the spell of its ornaments, vestments and statues in the dark, the bumping noises and sharp shadows: "The columns and altars seemed hung with the blue altar cloths used on Good Friday, their long folds enveloping everything in a single hue or, rather, pale monotony."[16]

This is the place to recall the great Cathedral section in Kafka's *Trial*, where the bare style glazed in a paper-thin, pettifogging sheen echoes the crystalline essence of Saint Vitus'. The inclement weather (it is a damp, cold, foggy day, nearly as dark as night), the gloom of the Cathedral rendered by the glimmer of a "large triangle of candles" on the main altar, the immense, oppressively empty space, the pulpit as narrow as a niche – everything ties the section to the previous spine-chilling church descriptions in Prague literature. In fact, there are surprising parallels to the scenes in *Svatý Xaverius* based on the interplay of light and shadow in the basilica of Saint Nicholas.[17] And if the mystery of *The Trial* is heightened by the parable of the guardian of the law and the man from the country told to Josef K. by the priest, here too Arbes's *Xaverius* comes to mind: suffering from hallucinations in the sinister church, Xaverius dimly sees a hydrocephalic homunculus with the face of the painter Balko climbing over the altar and incoherently haranguing two women in mourning – his mother and grandmother. Again the similarities are of a generic nature; they stem from the common humus of the city. One last comment: the guardian in the parable "in his furred robe with his huge pointed nose and long, thin, black Tartar beard"[18] seems to come from Meyrink's repertoire.

After so many exercises in spiritism I long for the *Tanztavernen*, but I still have something to say on the topic of cathedrals (though pausing in cold churches on these damp days will only make my cold worse). Prague fiction is characterized by an oppressive recurrence of the Spanish-derived image of the crucifix, a gloomy tangle of wounds and rent limbs, a fountain of gushing blood, a spiritualist vision and source of terror. Here are two examples from Karásek. In the Church of Saint Henry:

> No sooner did my eyes fix on the cross hanging on the wall than I felt behind me the presence of a living being. I was seized by terror, for now even the cross at which I had been gazing assumed a ghostly appearance: it was no longer hanging on the wall but suspended in the darkness.[19]

And in the Barnabite Convent:

> The large Christ covered with bleeding wounds that glowed in the darkness like mystical signs descended from the arms of the cross and slowly approached the altar.[20]

Above the bed of the pious humbug Nepovolná, in the previously quoted novel by Karolina Světlá, hangs an enormous rough-hewn crucifix with a golden crown of thorns on its head and large pomegranates in its five wounds.[21] In the novella *Sivooký démon* (The Grey-Eyed Demon, 1873) Arbes sketches a terrifying crucifix embedded in a Malá Strana palace like an evil fetish, a restive, unbridled Christ twisted like a cripple with clots of blood black as coal and plague-like boils.[22] No painter could have conceived a more frightening figure.

The sacred cross upon which Our Lord died is the principal motif in another saturnine Grand-Guignol Arbes novella, *Ukřižovaná* (The Crucified Woman, 1878). The mind of the young protagonist of this web of horrors, the narrator's schoolmate, is deeply unsettled by the repeated apparitions of a crucifix with a female face disfigured by a thick black beard. The face corresponds to the features of a Jewish girl from Tarnów crucified by rebellious Polish peasants and to the bearded Saint Starosta on the cross at the Loreta Church. The demonic instigator of these ravings is the deformed, monkey-faced catechist Schneider, who has clouded the boy's mind with his own haunted memories. He is a murky mishmash of Golgotha, trichophilia, fire and brimstone and visions of hell, of impaled flesh and insanity.

The theme of the cross is dominant in *Tři legendy o krucifixu* (Three Legends of the Crucifix, 1895), especially the Prague legend "Inultus", by Julius Zeyer. It is twenty years after White Mountain. The Charles Bridge is teeming with beggars, symbols of the anguish and want of Bohemia. One of them, Inultus, is a young poet with a Nazarene mane. Disheartened by the decline of his oppressed country, he is no longer able to write. "His genius had fallen silent with the anguish of his land. Every living thing in that period was stunned, paralyzed and petrified like the land itself."[23] When the proud, unfeeling sculptress Flavia Santini from Milan notices Inultus one evening, she invites him to her palace in the environs of the Castle. She is working on a large clay Christ and hopes to give its face the genuine pangs of a man struggling with death. She uses Inultus as a model and binds him naked to the cross. The poet hangs for days without food or drink on the fearsome rood. Sadistic Flavia slashes his face, twists the ropes tightly round him, thrusts a crown of thorns on his head and, finally, plunges a dagger in his heart. Even as her model writhes in his death throes, she puts the final touches on the sacred figure. She then goes mad and hangs herself.

Zeyer is making an indirect allusion to the torturous drama of Baroque statuary, the brilliance of Baroque art in moribund Bohemia. He is also drawing a Messianic comparison between the Passion of Our Lord and the calvary of the Czech nation, the horror of the crucifixion and the catastrophe of White Mountain. Inultus, the Unavenged, deludes himself into believing he can redeem his martyred land by mounting the cross and experiencing the sufferings of Christ, as though the fact of being crucified were ontologically sufficient to transform him into a redeemer. Zeyer's ghastly story is accompanied throughout by the mournful music of the Vltava, the "great, tragic lamentation of Prague, which lies at the foot of the gloomy Castle like a queen in chains".[24]

75

The Cattle Market (Dobytčí trh), now Charles Square, was a vast breeding grounds for demonic deeds and black spirits, an infernal maze of charlatans' booths and rickety shacks, the site of the Faust House, the Chapel of Corpus Christi and the Church of Saint Ignatius.[1] It was built around a mysterious rock, which was topped by a cross and used for illegal executions, the corpses falling through a trap door into a tangle of underground passageways, torture chambers, hideouts and *cubicula* in which prisoners sentenced by secret tribunals were walled up alive.[2]

In the novel *Tajnosti pražské* (The Mysteries of Prague) by Josef Svátek, the members of the secret society Mladá Čechie (Young Bohemia) meet in those skeleton-cluttered catacombs, and one of them, the physician Ludvík, actually finds the bones of his mother, who was held prisoner there by masked thugs.[3] Prague stories are often plunged into dark underground rooms. In a farcical novel by Svatopluk Čech the beer-drinking philistine Mr Brouček goes on about having passed through a number of them beneath the Na Vikárce Inn during his fictitious trip to the fifteenth century.[4] Karel Chalupa tells the story of a cooper who had his shop in the former monastery of the Knights of the Cross and would get lost looking for hoops in a maze of pitch-black crypts crammed with stinking bone-filled coffins.[5] To quote Holan: "What would be a knot in a coffin/when the moon hardens over the city."[6] Outbreaks of Romantic infections, relapses of neurasthenia and carpenters' workshops full of a veritable armada of coffins – that is what Prague literature is made of.

A number of Prague dwellings share the honour of having accommodated Doctor Faust during his stay along the Vltava: the Teyfl (Teufel?) House in Sirková (Sulphur) Street, which has its name from the legend that the necromancer left behind the stench of Hell; Sixt's House in Celetná Street, not far from the mansion of Korálek z Těšína, the patron of distillers; a run-down shanty in the Coal Market; and, most of all, the Faust House (Faustův dům) in the Cattle Market, which is especially apposite given its location, bizarre architecture and the fact that Kelley the alchemist kept his kitchen there.[7] In a previoulsy mentioned narrative poem "Labyrint slávy" (Labyrinth of Glory), Jan Erazim Vocel transforms the Faust House into a sumptuous, highly attractive palace with tall columns, taffeta hangings, gold-framed windows and ceilings of smooth, polished cedar.[8] Josef Jiří Kolár, in *Pekla zplozenci* (Spawn of Satan), surrounds it with a garden of exotic plants, wondrous fountains and cages of hyenas, basilisks, wolves and leopards.[9] Prague legend would have us believe that the house was Faust's final dwelling place on earth, the scene of his last encounter with the devil, and that after Faust's disappearance, when the house was shunned by all, Satan appeared through a hole in the attic to carry off a poor student who had had the extraordinary courage to take up residence there.[10]

Hotbed of superstition in the sinister Cattle Market was the Jesuit preserve of the Chapel of Corpus Domini. Whosoever walked nearby at night, especially if the wind brushed his face and drops of rain kissed his hands, would hear chinking chains and groaning voices and see figures in white sheets, ghosts in priestly garb, hangmen draped in red overcoats. There were those who swore that Jesuits put their opponents to death beneath the oratory. Indeed, in local folklore and the Bohemian Romantic imagination Jesuits are diabolical beings. This is not surprising, for as Charles Patin, a French traveller who visited Prague in 1695, noted, if London had the honour of sustaining thirteen hundred apothecaries, the city on the Vltava wallowed in the bliss of two thousand Jesuits.[11]

The novel *Zvonečková královna* (Queen of the Bells) by Karolina Světlá is set in this hallucinatory market and shot through with anti-Jesuit zeal. A sullen and highly sanctimonious widow, Nepovolná, lives with Xavera (the feminine form of Xaver), the daughter of a daughter of hers who died insane, in a house called U pěti zvonečků (The Five Small Bells) because the head of Saint John of Nepomuk painted on the façade is encircled by silver bells that quiver with a diabolical sneer. Completely under the control of the Jesuits, particularly the insidious, machiavellian Father Innocence, Nepovolná machinates against Freemasons, *philosophes* and sympathizers of the French Revolution (we are at the end of the eighteenth century) under the guise of taking up collections, attending processions and adorning the churches of Prague. Fair Xavera, queen of the bells, bred to piety and Jesuit duplicity, falls in love with Klement Natterer, a young conspirator and leader of a secret society. She warns him of the danger hanging over him, and when he refuses to take her seriously she flies into a rage and denounces him to her grandmother and her confessor as a rebel and heretic. When Natterer is executed before her very eyes near the accursed chapel, Xavera goes mad and spends the rest of her days in rags on the street where Klement ascended the scaffold.

What ludicrous goings-on, what blood-stained Romantic trash this puppet show of Jesuits, ghosts, conspirators, necromancers, skeletons and hangmen, this infernal theatre replete with ghoulish props.

76

Macabre city in which one eats sweets that both look like and are called little coffins (*rakvičky*), where coffins slide off hearses and Doctor Kazisvět (Spoiler) brings Councillor Schepeler back to life during his funeral.[1] City of alchemists' elixirs, where the pale, wrinkled young Ismena becomes as fair as a Madonna by Murillo after taking arsenic (though the poison kills her soon afterwards).[2] Haunted city where a piece of opal heralds bad luck once it loses its sheen.[3] City of miracles where an improbable flower, an Ethiopian lily, works its way into the fates of men from the herbarium where it lies drying.[4] In short, a city where ghosts roam restlessly and multiply like weeds.

> Skeletons and skulls and crossbones with "Keep Smiling" written across them, headless corpses and weeping ladies in white, transparent nuns and dried-up conventuals, gallows victims and gallows escapees, haunted pinchpennies and unbaptized infant corpses, howling villains and haughty, blue-blooded hussies.[5]

Penitent souls, shells engulfed in flames, bleeding corpses with daggers in their chests, beheaded cadavers and witches, bogeymen and monsters in various guises, lemurs of the apocalypse, diseases incarnate, divine retribution in the flesh, heraldic spirits and heralds of the Plague wander incessantly through the foggy streets of Prague,[6] through the winding lanes that branch out from Jánský vršek on the slope of Hradčany Hill, through corridors of palaces with illegible coats of arms,[7] through crypts and devastated cemeteries, through long-since desecrated monasteries (especially of the Dominican persuasion), through oddly-shaped houses like The Golden Well, through huge deserted buildings like Černín Palace, where Princess Drahomíra plummeted to Hell accompanied by a powerful stench of sulphur. In the face of these insalubrious demonoplectic projections even the sturdiest of innards will tremble.

Like crickets and frogs on a summer's evening, Prague's ghosts screech in unison along the margins of these pages. To keep them from becoming a nuisance, I shall admit but a few of their pestilential though legendary hosts. The former Dominican Monastery in Karmelitská Street, which was for a time converted into a theatre, is haunted by an actress known as Headless Laura. Laura once flirted with a wealthy count, and when her husband, a humble bit player, learned of her infidelity he severed her fair head and sent it to the nobleman in a parcel. Headless, she took to wandering the convent's corridors in a rustling, pink silk dress, with bracelets on her wrists and pearl necklaces on what was left of her neck.[8]

In the Malá Strana Church of Saint John on the Washing, a hospital for the poor and a laundry, there lived a mean widow who hid her nest egg in a crypt. Every night the ghost of a black monk – in other versions a bloodthirsty parish priest – begged her for a thaler because he had stolen money from the house of God and needed to assuage his guilty conscience. The widow resisted for a time by painting a circle around her place of rest in holy water, but in the end, having gone without sleep to the limits of her endurance, she threw him the thaler as one tosses a coin to a beggar, whereupon the monk jumped into a black carriage drawn by two black goats and set off through the church gates, which opened with a deafening roar. But the coin was counterfeit, and the monk returned the following night to strangle the old skinflint. Every night since then a flaming carriage drawn by infernal billygoats has burst from beneath Saint John's, barrelling through the neighbourhood and making a racket with its wheels, whips and brays. Ghosts beget ghosts, and the old crone's spirit wanders through the church with the counterfeit thaler branded on her forehead.[9]

In Liliová Street in the Old Town, near the Saint Laurence Monastery, a headless Knight Templar appears every Friday after midnight riding a fire-breathing white charger and wearing a white cape emblazoned with a red cross, his reins in one hand, his skull in the other.[10] Every night a one-eyed Black Spaniard leaves the Benedictine Monastery in Hybernská Street sporting a ruff, a sombrero pressed deep over his eyes, a pointed beard in the shape of a mouse's tail and long, flowing hair and riding a three-hooved old nag.[11] Saint James', on the other hand, produces the mute ghost of a pale Latvian swordsman with a red scar in the middle of his face, a tilted red hat and a disdainful gaze.[12] Every night, at Jánský vršek, a headless skeleton rides by in a fiery wagon[13], to say nothing of the headless Premonstratensian horsemen, the nuns out on a spree, the skinflint millers criss-crossing the city in a four-horse carriage[14] and all the rest of Prague folklore's gloomy riffraff.

In Kozí náměstí (Goat Square) a fat woman with a starched, bell-shaped skirt drifts about with a large ring of keys. While alive, she delighted in badgering seamstresses and servant girls who failed to make her crinolines as fluffy as she wished. Now she blows at pedestrians until they puff up like balloons.[15]

An alluring Jewess with jet-black hair and pitch-black eyes suddenly emerges at night from the Ten Virgins Brothel in Ozerov to entice night owls by undulating her body into lascivious poses. Anyone who ventures close enough is smothered in kisses and whirled in a dance until he faints.[16]

Then there is the languorous temptress who steps down from a silver carriage every Friday at midnight and wanders through the cemetery next to Saint Martin-in-the-Wall singing sadly to herself. Once a lad began to accompany her on the guitar from a window across the way, and she gazed at him with grateful, melting eyes, stole his heart and lured him into the carriage with her, after which he was never seen or heard from again.[17]

Another damsel of the trap-setting sort arrived in Prague during the 1870s covered with paste necklaces and jewels, her face hidden by a black veil, her torso wound in shiny silk. The dubious lady, who found lodgings at The Black Horse, offered dinner and fifty thousand florins to any young men who agreed to spend a night of ecstasy with her, yet all the would-be gallants fled her room in a cold sweat once she removed the veil to reveal a monstrous skull.[18]

One Christmas a pastry cook with a shop in The Golden Well made gingerbread figures of two headless Spanish ghosts, a knight and his spouse, who were rumoured to roam the ramshackle house at night. The two outcasts then appeared to him with their heads on their shoulders and begged him to add their real faces to the sugar dolls he had fashioned and exhume their bodies from the basement where their slayers had hurled them. The confectioner obeyed without a whimper and gave them a proper burial, in exchange for which he received the considerable sum they had hidden in the plasterwork.[19]

When the plague carried off the owners of The Black Cat in Panská Street, an evil servant murdered their children in order to seize the family's belongings, but a large black cat (or hobgoblin in cat's clothing) with curved hooks for claws scratched his chest night and day and the maddened servant would run through the streets imploring people to remove the infernal encumbrance from his chest. In vain: the creature was invisible.[20]

And who is that imposing old man with the plumed hat and spurred boots leaving the Jesuit Church of Saint Bartholomew and fending off a rabid mastiff with a dagger? Why, Count Deym, who enjoys no peace in the grave because while on earth he turned a man into a dog, which dog will not rest until it is restored to human shape. The trouble is that as a corpse the Count can no longer work miracles.[21]

Emauzy (Emmaus) Monastery is haunted by a rogue of a monk who spent alms on women and drink and went so far as to steal hosts from the tabernacle. He was beheaded.[22] We are fairly besieged by greasy cowls, filthy frocks, headless torsos begging for the deliverance of a decent burial.

There was also a time when the appearance of ghosts foretold scourges. One snowy March night in 1713 the Great Plague arrived in Prague in aristocratic garb on a wobbly black nag. He dismounted at an Old Town inn. His face was the yellow of wax, his lips purplish and dry; a large black plume hung from the tangle of his gilt braid. But beneath it all was a skeleton. The first victim of the pestilence, which was soon to infect the entire country, was the inn's charming chambermaid, whom he clutched to his chest and kissed with his foul maw while she was making up his room.[23]

Some ghosts are impossible to get to the bottom of. In December 1874 there was a persistent trumpeting in the house of a Mr Procházka in the Podskalí district of Prague, a house that may have belonged to the Jesuits. The trumpeting was accompanied by tremors, groans and the din of falling china. An entire cordon of police was summoned to keep the curious at bay. Some claimed they saw a Jesuit hat fly through the air; others were certain the trumpeter was the ghost of someone who had wiped out the man's family. Little old ladies lit candles and sprinkled the area liberally with holy water. Just as the barking of a single dog makes all the neighbours' pets howl, the blasts called forth bedlam in the surrounding area. After three tumultuous weeks the trumpet ghost, who had in the meantime inspired a street ballad and a polka that entered the repertoire of the café-chantants and the balls, ceased its concertizing as suddenly as it had begun.[24]

In those days all Prague flocked to the Bergheer Ghost Theatre, a wooden pavilion, to witness revenants, skeletons, *mátohy* and other assorted spirits (produced by mutual reflections in large mirrors and an ever thick haze of smoke), which a performer tried to behead with valiant strokes of the sabre.[25]

The street ballads (*kramářské písně*), the *pitavaly*,[26] Popelka Bilianová's tear-jerkers, the bloody penny dreadfuls (*sensační krváky*) and the illustrated magazines greatly swelled the ranks of Prague ghosts. They received a new boost from the Surrealists, who positively revelled in spine-tingling texts. Nezval had a special weakness for cheap horror and murder stories, the "mysteries of Prague", the thrillers chock-a-block with gruesome crimes and published by a number of less than respectable publishers, primarily Alois Hynek, at the end of the nineteenth century for readers who would believe anything.[27] As Nezval himself puts it:

> Although large portions of them are unreadable today, there is much genuine poetry, much genuine love for Prague lurking behind their outmoded exterior . . . Prague has mysteries of its own. I am certain there will come a time when its hidden Romantic chiaroscuro will be of great help to poets.[28] The rapidly growing interest in thrillers has revealed Prague to me in an increasingly magic light, the old part of Prague, the part that least belongs to this century.[29]

City of waxworks and wax statues, city of short-lived events, zodiac of spectres, city where proud, bewigged countesses had their cooks fashion slippers out of bread dough, elegant short-pastry pumps, and held magnificent banquets until the Devil demolished their mansions with a thunderbolt, sucking them alive into Hell.[30] Even during the war, during the blackout of the German occupation, popular gossip created an apparition in Prague, a little man on springs by the name of Perák, a gaunt unseemly fellow, an *odradek*, who escaped Nazi persecution thanks to his agility.

While some of the ghosts have vanished or been granted redemption and a few remain hidden, dejected, as helpless as chicks in tow, there are still so many left in the Czech capital that, according to Eduard Bass, they would be worth exploiting for the tourist industry with slogans like: "Visit old Prague, playground for the spirits! Every midnight a first-rate witches' sabbath!"[31] Twentieth-century additions to the masquerade of monsters and infernalia include the phantoms swarming around the Legion Bridge in Nezval's *Edison* and Holan's dead angels. I should also like to add the ghost of an acquaintance of mine who plays the piano every night in a crumbling hole in Ostrovní Street surrounded by mountains of faded newspapers tied with string. This spirit, the thin and witch-like Mrs Hušková, plays the instrument just as she did during her prime, when marriage to a bank employee prevented her from going on the concert stage.

77

The executioner, lord of the noose, is clearly central to the Bohemian metropolis. Nezval considered Jan Mydlář, the hangman who put to death the twenty-seven notables, a "man worthy of his future thrillers".[1] Wrapped in a black cape with a lining as scarlet as waxwork plague boils, clad in a red leather waistcoat and floppy black breeches, shod in soft leather boots and sporting a dirk at his waist,[2] he joins the great procession of alchemists, *goylemes*, Švejks, pilgrims, hops dolls, Arcimboldesque heads and Merlinesque wizards that has been parading through the city on the Vltava for centuries. In Prague the Lord of the Gallows is not merely the master of ceremonies and solo performer in a macabre spectacle that attracts crowds of spectators; he is a magician, unguentarian and orthopedist: he mends limbs as well as breaks them.

Hangmen had their heyday in Bohemia first during Rudolf's reign and then during the Thirty Years' War, when the entire country became, to use an expression of Aloysius Bertrand, "a hanging gallows that holds out its hand to passers-by like a one-armed beggar".[3] Booty-hungry deserters dangled everywhere from trees. Peasants were beheaded for having cut snippets of genitals or scraps of clothing from the poor devils to concoct love potions for themselves or anti-perspirants for their pack animals; hangman's assistants collected the blood and slaver of the executed – a cure for the falling sickness – in gleaming brass basins. But there were also extravaganzas, where the hanged man was a "military officer in a costly, magnificent uniform with gilt spurs".[4]

Hangmen could supplement their income by selling noose strips as amulets, supplying cadavers to dissectors, catching rabid dogs, clearing the streets of carrion and cleaning sewers. As the compilations of confessions extorted on the rack demonstrate, it was a hangman's paradise. These "pitch books" (*knihy smolné*) feature tales of witches concocting philtres and potions, unwed mothers feeding their offspring to the pigs, stepfathers seducing their stepdaughters, simpletons raping goats, tales of blood-curdling tortures and executions by wheel, fire and tongs, of hangings, beheadings and live burials, tales that Hrabal considers close to the *morytáty*, "which were meant to arouse horror and fear of the crime in the listeners".[5]

The most sensational execution held during the reign of Rudolf II was that of the Imperial Marshal Heřman Kryštof Rosswurm (or Christian Herrmann Freiherr von Rußwurm), a noted strategist and philanderer, who on 25 (or 29) July 1605 at the instigation of the Milanese scoundrel Giacomo Furlani challenged Count Francesco Barbiano di Belgiojoso to a duel. The servants of the contending parties intervened, and Belgiojoso was killed in the ensuing broil. Rosswurm was arrested and attempted to exculpate himself, but the perfidious Chamberlain Philipp Lang z Langenfelsu (Lang again) tore up his petitions and convinced Rudolf that the Marshal was conspiring against him with the support of the Turks. Thus it was that at dawn on 20 (or 29) November Rosswurm was decapitated and laid out on the bare ground in a monk's habit in the Hradčany Town Hall. Thanks to Lang, the Imperial pardon arrived an hour after the execution.[6] Golden days for hangmen.

When Chamberlain Kašpar Rucký z Rudz, alchemist and swindler, imprisoned for stealing treasures from the late Rudolf, hanged himself in his cell in the White Tower in 1612, the executioner transported his cadaver to Strahov Gate, chopped off the head, sawed off the arms and legs, ripped out the heart, crushing it like catfood against his mouth, quartered what was left of the torso and flung the carcass piece by piece into a ditch filled with quicklime. But when the Chamberlain's ghost – which did not lack a certain sense of black humour – took to roving through Prague on a flaming cart, the executioner was forced to exhume the body, commit it to the flames and fling the ashes into the Vltava.[7]

Rudolf's connection to the funereal theatre of the gallows is evident from an ordinance dated 9 February 1608, in which the Sovereign's chancellery asks the notables of Kutná Hora for "a bit of the moss that grows under the scaffolds on the bones of the men who leave this world for their misdeeds . . . especially the kind that grows on human skulls".[8] Thus Kolár is not exaggerating when he imagines Rudolf disguised as an assistant hangman searching (by night and the dim light of a smoking lantern with Doctor Scotta, the black dog Damnausta and Vilém) for mandrakes beneath the gallows that Vilém escaped unscathed. "Here," Scotta says, "in illustrious, wondrous Prague, in this seat of the occult arts and all human knowledge, the flower of the unique, genuine, living mandrake has blossomed."[9] With the hauteur of a customs officer Kolár describes the bizarre ritual of finding the hairy alraune root, a root he also calls *šibeničníček*, "little gallows", from the Czech *šibenice*, "gallows".

All the metaphysics of the Prague executioner comes back to life in the grand finale of Kafka's *Trial*, when in the moonlight of a typically Romantic execution scene two hangmen, two "pallid and plump" ham actors, two frock-coats, two top hats lead Josef K. to the "small stone quarry, deserted and bleak" of Strahov.[10] Arbes, in his *D'ábel na skřipci* (The Devil on the Rack, 1865), had earlier described a dog being killed "in the empty stone quarry outside Strahov Gate".[11] "Wie ein Hund!" ("Like a dog!") are Josef K.'s last words as one of the actors plunges a knife into his heart.[12]

78

Thus Kafka too was aware of the theatrical element in the executioner's ceremony. Josef K. surmises that the two gentlemen in black who accompany him to his execution are "tenth-rate old actors", enquires which theatre they are connected with and finally deduces from their double chins that "perhaps they are tenors".[1]

If the word *pendu* occurs ten times in the verbal miniatures of Aloysius Bertrand, how often do the words *gallows* and *hangman* recur in this *Praguerie* of mine? And how can I possibly overlook Jan Křtitel (John Baptist) Piperger, the city's penultimate official executioner. Piperger lived in a nondescript little house in Platnéřská Street with the following nameplate sneering from the door:

> ## JAN KŘTITEL PIPERGER
>
> Master Executioner of the Kingdom of Bohemia

He was a quiet craftsman, an upholsterer or cabinet maker, short and stubby, crippled by the gout, yet able when called upon to turn into a demonic virtuoso of the noose. No wonder Death, a strolling musician in a black frock-coat, black bowler and white carnation, often lured passers-by to the foul tavern opposite the house with his fiddle.

A journalist by the name of Kukla has described the horror he felt at visiting Master Piperger in his lair in January 1888 shortly before the latter left for Kutná Hora to execute two criminals, August and Karel Přenosil, who had killed the young police private Kašpar Melichar in the woods.[2] Piperger was born in 1838 to an executioner in Steyr, one of the first in his profession to exchange the sword for the noose (all sixteen of his brothers served as "master executioners" in various parts of the Habsburg Empire), but next to his sack of hooks and knotted ropes in the dark cubby hole of a dwelling was a black case with the sword that his father – God rest his soul! – had used for his last decapitation: in the eyes of old hangmen a sword possessed the powers of a talisman.[3]

By the time Kukla visited him (overcoming his fear of the catacomb-like corridors that made even his gentle steps ring out), Piperger was a doomed man. He was suffering from heart trouble; he shivered from the cold and gasped for breath when he spoke; his hands shone transparent in the red light of sunset. And thus, looking for all the world like one of Meyrink's ghosts, he predicted that the Kutná Hora execution would be his downfall. Then with a sardonic grin on his yellow, sunken-eyed face he played a macabre jest and slipped the noose round the horrified Kukla's neck.

According to Kisch, Piperger was deeply depressed towards the end of his life. Local gossip claimed that in 1872 he had poisoned Jana Wohlschlägerová, a widow he had married in Croatia a decade earlier. Who would have deemed an executioner innocent, especially as he was known to be an expert in magical herbs and spells? Yet Kukla depicts Piperger as a pathetic figure, a suffering demon. He writes, for example, that the old hangman paled, shook and burst into tears when, on 21 June 1866, he had to hang his friend Václav Fiala – tapster of Ve sklípku (The Small Cellar) and the gallant of many a waitress – from a high post on the Žižkov plain for having killed his mistress Klára Žemličková.

It was Piperger who strung up the Gipsy Josef Janeček in a Plzeň square. Janeček was the highwayman Švejk evokes at the divisional court in order to comfort a downhearted teacher-soldier: "You mustn't lose hope. It can still change for the better as the Gipsy Janeček said in Pilsen when in 1879 they put the cord round his neck for double robbery with murder."[4] Janeček was led to the gallows to the deafening pealing of bells and surrounded by the Thirty-Fifth Infantry Regiment. The crowd was so large that a number of people were trampled in the crush. Hundreds of Gipsies were rumoured ready to descend on the city, burn it down and save the rogue from his punishment, but the corpse hung from the scaffold until the following night and the mob showed no signs of dispersing.

Piperger reluctantly performed the execution at Kutná Hora (Kukla gives the date as 12 January 1888, while Kisch claims it was 11 June), plagued by a fever and grave foreboding. And in fact, no sooner were the two criminals hanging from his slipknot than he collapsed into the arms of his stepson, who had been his assistant since the Janeček hanging. The stepson, Leopold Wohlschläger, immediately put him on the train to Prague, where he died four days later. A *morytát* insinuates that when the Almighty summoned Piperger to heaven the hangman balked for fear of ending up in Hell along with those he had hanged.[5] The strolling musician with the flower in his buttonhole continued to fiddle opposite the decrepit house long after its tenant had died.

Piperger's stepson and successor, appointed *Scharfrichter für das Königreich Böhmen* on 24 June 1888, lacked the slightest trace of mystery. Whereas Piperger had haunted dives, especially the Černý pivovar (The Black Brewery), where he would frighten the patrons with tales of the gallows, Wohlschläger led a secluded life, a pipe-and-slippers existence, between executions, devoting himself to goldsmithing and his family. Yet Wohlschläger, who Švejk claims would hang a man for four florins, had the ambition to become hangman in Vienna.[6] Unfortunately for him he fluffed his trial execution there. He was put in charge of hanging a woman who had slit her daughter's throat, but the noose got tangled and the condemned woman jerked convulsively like an octopus for a few seconds before dying. So much for that position! Wohlschläger blamed his failure on the poor quality of rope used in Vienna.

79

At this point I should like to acquaint the reader with Mácha's "Křivoklát" (1830), a work of splendour, sonorous echoes and tongues of fire, a fragment originally intended as part of a long novel to be entitled *Kat* (*The Executioner*) and to consist of four "stations", each bearing the name of a Gothic castle in Bohemia. Mácha's text, so full of dramatic substance and dialogues that it tempted E. F. Burian to adapt it for the stage,[1] centres on the bond between Wenceslas IV and his executioner. The chroniclers of the period abhorred their sovereign, the only king to whom Nezval claimed to be attracted;[2] indeed, they claimed he frequented the taverns of Prague with his hangman (whom he called his crony), fraternized with the rabble, drowned priests, beheaded noblemen, roasted bad cooks on the spit and had his wife mauled to death by a wild dog.[3] He is similarly belittled in Mácha's version:

> In the morning King Wenceslas or, as the denizens of Prague call him, Wenceslas the Lazy, condemns anyone he considers guilty, at noon his crony dispatches the culprit from the world of the living, and in the evening the two of them weep over a glass of wine for the dead man and continue to mourn until their tongues stop obeying them and they are taken off to bed dead drunk.[4]

In light of the poet's obsessively detailed description of his tormented gaze, flaming pupils, grimaces, sneers and the transformations of the executioner's face, the entire story could be regarded as an essay in metoposcopy or facial *chiaroscuro*. The king (in white trimmed with silver) and the executioner (in black with a red cloak) seem to fuse into a single, insane two-faced figure, consumed by the same somnolent sadness, the same restlessness, the only difference being that the king, ashamed of his majesty, yearns to descend to the rabble, while the hangman, ashamed of his villainy, yearns to escape his base state. As it turns out, the executioner is in fact the bastard grandson of Wenceslas III, the last of the Přemyslids, and has chosen his nefarious profession out of a burning desire to deride mankind and suffer humiliation. Mácha poured himself, his desperation and his hypochondria into the hangman, who stares into the distance tormented, dreaming, a virtual Pierrot, and conceals his grief with grimaces and outbursts of uproarious laughter.[5]

The royal lineage of the hangman and his foul moods, the love of a girl (Miláda) for the hangman who has executed her father, the sad songs Miláda plays on the harp, the girl's decline and death, the castles, the dungeons, the catafalque on which Miláda lies in white with the executioner's sword on her heart – all the settings, props and motifs of the tale come straight from the Romantic repertoire. The key prop, the sword, recurs obsessively: if the hangman represents the degeneration of regal pride and the decline of ancient glory, the sword, symbol of majesty, is reduced to an executioner's tool.[6] "O Sword! My image!" the hangman exclaims at the end when he finds it lying on dead Miláda.[7]

The metamorphosis of dynast to executioner or outcast is closely connected with the theme of a violated Bohemia, of the period following White Mountain, of the prostration and dejection of the Czech people, whose music resounds in the leitmotif "O King! Good night!", a piercing sign of exhaustion, *zaklinadlo* (magic spell) and plaintive greeting that sums up the fates of the executioner, the king and Miláda and stands for the transience of life, the precariousness of power, the *finis Bohemiae*.[8]

O King! Good night! Romanticism exalts the figure of the executioner. In his play *Pražský žid* (The Jew of Prague) Kolár links the vicissitudes of Rabbi Falu-Eliab after White Mountain with those of Jan Mydlář, attributing the same persecution and abjection to them both. To lend the executioner dignity, he transforms him into a saviour. Thus the patriot hangman Mydlář, eager for redemption, refuses to slaughter the twenty-seven notables and delivers the rabbi and Verena, who have been accused of witchcraft and rebellion against the Habsburgs, to safety.

O King! Good night! Emulating the mawkish novelettes of High Romanticism, Prague writers transformed this walking sword, this avenging filthy scoundrel, this first-born of Satan into a poor pariah, a wretch kept in constant quarantine from his fellow man, an outcast who pronounces death penalties yet flees the outcome like the plague and is therefore more to be pitied than despised.

Lachrymose as these tales are – they fairly fret over the fate of the hangman – there is in all honesty something moving about him. For the executioner did live like a beast; he was in fact banished from normal human contact. Caught in the tangles of the ropes, hooks and harpoons he employed to grab carcasses soaked in blood and bilious humours, he spent sleepless nights on intimate terms with the ghosts of those he had sent to their Maker with a jerk of the rope or a vigorous chop. He entered the city through a special passageway at an out-of-the-way point in its walls, he had a remote niche set aside for him in Saint Valentine's Church, he had his own table and filthy glass in the tavern, and when he danced with his most gracious wife, himself paying for musicians who accompanied every note with grimaces and sneers, the hostess would quickly sweep and scrub the floor, in spite of the proverb that he who sweeps gets dust in his eyes. Anyone who went to a hangman's funeral – and not even gravediggers were eager to do so – walked in front of the coffin: to follow it would have been a disgrace. Gentlemen took care not to be grazed by his stinking hands during executions.[9] And although he was praised for a skilful knot or clean blow, Heaven help him if he missed his mark: the rabble aroused does not forgive a clumsy executioner. Dačický relates how two hangmen were stoned to death in Prague in 1588 when they failed to behead their victim by the third blow.[10]

O King! Good night! Mácha's executioner still rides from Křivoklád to Prague, his red cloak fluttering like a blaze in the evening sun.[11] A picturesque image, a theatrically picturesque image, a piece of bloody buffoonery turned spectral, turned ghastly. Earlier this century invisible hangmen raged through Prague's greasy mists with torments of fire, blinding lights, ice-cold water and injections of scopolamine; now, after an all-too-brief yet intoxicating truce, they are swarming back to life from their swamps of hatred, deciding who shall live and who shall die, as during the period of fanaticism when, in Kolář's words, "even the rope was ashamed of the noose".[12]

Once more the city on the Vltava is sunk in the oblivion of sleep beneath a gloomy, insalubrious sky, once more closet Mydlářs slither through its sewers, cavities and crypts. It is a city that sits and watches the card game others play on its flesh. A huge emporium of ropes and hemp. A city where in every tavern the slimy ghost of a police spy, a Bretschneider, has his ear cocked to the chatter of the drunks and the desperate. A city with donkey-ears on its head and a yoke round its neck. A city in which a flicker of rebellious thought paves the way to foul dungeons, filthy cells and the bread and water of tribulation.

Yet often, when every human comfort has flown, the hangman is the innocent prisoner's only friend and sustenance. With threats, blows, drugs, sleepless nights and gruelling interrogations he convinces the prisoner of the truth of the accusations and persuades him to confess the most fantastic of crimes, thus speeding his death sentence and freeing him from torture, madness, delirium, utter isolation.[13] What then is the guiltlessly guilty Prague pilgrim to do? As Jiří Orten wrote during the days of the Protectorate: "Take pity on the hangman, go straight to the gallows and sing, sing to the end!"[14]

80

The Baroque came to Bohemia in the first half of the seventeenth century, during the Thirty Years' War.[1] Its appearance coincides with events ruinous for the Czech Lands, that is, with the victory of Ferdinand II at the Battle of White Mountain (1620) and the Peace of Westphalia (1648). Once the "abominable rebellion" (*ohavná rebelie*) was crushed, the Counter-Reformation did its utmost to uproot the detestable plant of heresy and outlaw the wiles of the Antichrist, the rites of Satan.

The Habsburgs, as we have seen, used their limitless power to force anti-Catholic nobles and intellectuals out of the country, then confiscated their possessions, dividing them among a handful of generals and their followers, who suddenly found themselves fabulously wealthy. Thus, while Czech culture was being eradicated like a pernicious weed, rapacious soldiers and predacious speculators acquired vast estates. The common folk, down to their last penny after the lootings and burnings by foreign troops, had to slave for the greater glory of their new masters, their *robota*, or agricultural servitude, growing progressively more severe. Meanwhile, swarms of Carmelites, Jesuits, Servites, Barnabites, Knights of the Cross, Brothers of Mercy and Spanish Benedictines overran the subjugated land.

Initially, then, the Baroque thrust itself, a foreign body, upon the Czechs. It was the pacifying, propagandistic art of the oppressors, an aggressive symbol of the Counter-Reformation, of subservience to the Habsburgs, the scorn of the Church Triumphant at the anguish of a defeated nation. Initially, then, the Czechs viewed the Baroque with hostility, like a narcissus born of a rotten onion.

The lot of the vanquished was hard indeed: anyone who did not attend mass was branded a heretic, fonts of holy water rose to the heavens, souls agonized under the burden of divine offices, sermons and penances. Churches changed face. The Church of the Holy Trinity in Malá Strana, a bastion of Lutheranism, was transferred to the Spanish Discalced Carmelites in 1624, who remodelled it (1636–44) with a Baroque façade and consecrated it to Our Lady Victorious, protector of the Habsburgs at White Mountain. A sanctimonious and convoluted Spanish bias worms its way into the heart of Prague, symbolized not only by the Infant Jesus, the *Jezulátko*, which had its home in that church, but also by Don Baltazar de Marradas, Imperial field marshal and commander of the Prague garrison, who provided the funds for the reconstruction.

Before long the desire on the part of the usurpers to assert their authority and flaunt their power stimulated a major building boom. Together the Emperor's faithful commanders and the Church's faithful orders tore down entire districts, replacing them with massive whales of structures, imposing thrones to vainglory.

The imaginative Machiavellian generalissimo Albrecht Václav Eusebius Valdštejn (Wallenstein) did not hesitate to demolish twenty-six houses, three gardens and a brickworks in the heart of Malá Strana to build (1623–30) his ostentatious two-story palace with five courtyards and a garden. It is an oppressively massive structure, an enormous edifice, whose façade is laid out in a tiring series of symmetrical windows and wrinkled eye-socket dormers. Valdštejn, "Admyrall of the Atlantic Ocean and the Baltic Sea", was so averse to noise that he could not endure a sparrow chirping. Though accustomed to the din of battle, he demanded strict silence in his colossal, empty palace, the officers of his retinue not daring to open their mouths or speaking so softly that, according to Girolamo Brusoni, they were like "penitents at confession".[2] A host of pages and orderlies kept Noise, or Life itself, at bay before his rooms.

The Jesuits razed thirty-two houses, three churches, two gardens and a Dominican monastery to build (1653–79) the Klementinum Seminary, a huge block wedged between Old Town shanties. It was a stout stronghold, a rusticated redoubt, provocative and pretentious, an emblem of supremacy and harsh indoctrination. The monotony of the vertical fascias connecting the windows of the façade from one floor to the next and alternating with a row of mighty squared columns corresponds to the endless corridors in a Kubinesque nightmare.

The palace of Count Humprecht Jan Černín z Chudenic in the Hradčany district (1669–92) also makes a display of excessive dimensions, seeming to challenge the Castle in stubborn arrogance. It is a sullen, unyielding structure without a spark of passion, cold as ice and with an enormous façade divided at the window level by a row of thirty huge Palladian demi-columns supported by tall ashlar socles.

With its tendency to exaggeration, obsessive repetition and gigantism, early Prague Baroque reflects the authoritarian overweening nature of its creators, who considered themselves a chosen people. The horizontality of the building material, articulated by monumental columns and pilasters, asserts the new owners' implacable longing to take possession of vast spaces, take root over a wide area, dominate. Their severe residences oppose all playfulness; they are more fortifications than palaces, citadels in enemy territory.

At the turn of the eighteenth century, however, conditions began to change. The nobles started loosening their ties with the Viennese court, the Czech clergy took to reviving local customs and shoring up the cult of John of Nepomuk with illuminations, tridua and pilgrimages: the festivities celebrating his beatification (1721) and sanctification (1729) bolstered Bohemia's importance in the Catholic world.

As the eighteenth century progressed, the patricians and the clergy engaged in a kind of intense building competition, commissioning artists from all over Europe to build churches, charterhouses, shrines, palaces, gardens, statues, chapels, columns to the Virgin and columns in commemoration of the plagues. Prague became a city of architectural wonders. But tears and blood combined with the mortar in her Baroque churches. The powerful portal atlantes by Braun supporting the balcony of the Clam-Gallas Palace (1713–25) seem to allude to the Czech people, burdened with privations and bowed under the weight of so much pomp.

Gradually the Baroque freed itself from grim Imperial austerity and fused with Bohemian culture. What had initially been a despotic foreign import and reminder of subjugation became the life blood, the very genius of the recatholicized nation. Despite its political dependence Bohemia regained the inspiration it had enjoyed during the Gothic age. With the late Baroque, then, Bohemia both returned to the European context and enriched it with its own characteristic resources and variations. The palaces of Malá Strana, the paintings and frescos of Karel Škréta, Petr Brandl and Václav Vavřinec Reiner, the statue gallery on the Charles Bridge, Braun's sculptures in Kuks, the churches of Giovanni Santini-Aichl and Kilián Ignác Dienzenhofer – they all bear witness to the amazing fervour with which the Czech milieu appropriated Baroque stylistic premises as it recovered from its humiliation.

Indeed, the late Baroque exploded in Bohemia with irrepressible exuberance, as if the country wished to make up for time lost in privations and the plague. Within a few decades it constituted the dominant element in the Prague panorama, its stylistic key, its *basso continuo*. Prague has corners where to this day one can breathe a Baroque atmosphere unspoiled by later centuries. With its thirst for theatricality and optical effects the Baroque fairly transformed the cityscape, harmonizing buildings with vegetation and modulating the uneven terrain with ramps and staircases, with roof terraces adorned by statuary. It replaced the staccato of the Gothic houses with an unbroken fugue of palaces merging into a single façade of delicate stuccowork, and created charming little squares from tortuous spaces left over from the Middle Ages.

The landscape along the left bank, elevated by nature like an amphitheatre and visible in all its glory from the Charles Bridge, offered special possibilities for the newly vibrant architecture. While the Stag Moat retained a medieval character and the smell of alchemy, Malá Strana and the green slope of Petřín Hill were converted into a sort of *boîte à perspective* or *boîte d'optique* in which each part fitted marvellously into the whole and fine buildings were graced with terraced gardens – like those of the Fürstenberks and the Vrtbas – from which the nobility looked out over Prague as if from dress-circle loges. Nestled at the foot of this striking prospect, this rolling declivity, is an edifice that provides the Prague panorama with one of its focal points: the immense sculpted mass of Saint Nicholas and its glowing dark-green Dienzenhofer dome (1750–2). Kafka provides a fitting description of Kokoschka's view of Prague "with the green cupola of Saint Nicholas in the centre": "In that picture the roofs are flying away.

The cupolas are umbrellas in the wind. The whole city is flying in all directions."3

The music of Prague Baroque architecture is an unending melody of convex and concave forms. As Giordano Bruno writes: "The spherical cannot enter into the spherical because they touch at one point; the concave, however, can enter into the convex."4 In Dienzenhofer's Saint-John-on-the-Rock (Svatý Jan na Skalce, 1730–9) the convex balustrade of the staircase forms a single oval with the concave material of the façade, whose concavity is further emphasized by the slant position of the two spires with their high lanterns. A wave-like instability recalling Borromini agitates the façades of a number of Prague churches, like Saint Ursula's (Svatá Voršila, 1702–4) and Saint Nicholas' (Svatý Mikuláš, 1703–11) in Malá Strana. In the latter the wings curve concavely, while the stone at the centre describes a convex motion that immediately retreats, frightened, into three secondary concave waves. All feeling of density is destroyed by a persistent surging of protrusions and eddies, of reliefs, of holes trapping the light. The contrast between the timidity of the concave and the arrogance of the convex on the façades of the churches and statues of Prague corresponds to the plays on words and the oxymorons of the Baroque poetry of a Bridel and the neo-baroque verse of a Holan.

In the early decades of the eighteenth century, then, Prague architecture loses the angry ascetic rigidity, the autocratic horizontality that had blighted life in the city on the Vltava from the time of White Mountain. The churches of the late Bohemian Baroque – evoking as they do endless reveries with their heaven-bound domes, their ecstatic verticality, their constantly shifting planes and vertiginous perspective – belong not to the Philistines and Theatines who wait, eyes glued to the ground, to be blessed with holy water, but to dreamers, lovers and poets. For, as Holan writes, "without pure transcendentalism/no palace can rise".5

Then too, more intensely than in other countries, the Baroque in Bohemia pursued its ties to the Gothic, a Today eagerly seeking its Yesterday. Many monastic orders – especially the Premonstratensians, Cistercians and Benedictines – attempted to revive the religious tradition of the Bohemian Middle Ages. The result is a mixture of two styles. Whether the movement stemmed from a desire to touch the hearts of the people, evade directives from Vienna or ease the suffering of the peasantry (by proving that Catholicism was not alien to the Czech Lands), the fact remains that confraternities of friars gave new life to the canons and customs of the Gothic.

This return to the Middle Ages is most apparent in the votive structures. If many churches built between the thirteenth and fifteenth centuries retained their Gothic core beneath the Baroque surface, the morphology of newly built churches represents a blending of the Gothic and Baroque. Giovanni Santini-Aichl's monastery churches outside Prague (Sedlec, Kladruby and Želiv) and especially the Cistercian church in Zelená Hora near Žd'ár on the Sázava (1719–22) are splendid variations on Gothic themes, on the verticality of the *Hallenkirche*, a terpsichorean display of pinnacles, acute-angled forms and reticular vaults in which ribbing seems to quiver, matter to dissolve.

The period's persistent historicism, which simply leaps over the age of Hus, its imaginative combination of Baroque bombastic spirituality and Gothic upward rhythm, is not the exclusive province of architecture; it pervades the legends, poetry, homiletics, panegyrics and liturgy of Bohemia of the late seventeenth and early eighteenth century. A character in a dialogue by Miloš Marten goes so far as to speak of the "restored Gothic of the Counter-Reformation".[6] Thanks to a number of scholars (Vilém Bitnar, Josef Vašica and, most of all, Zdeněk Kalista), the expression "česká barokní gotika" (Bohemian Baroque Gothic) is now widely accepted.

Thus the continuity of a land ravaged by wars and depredations was re-established by the mingling of two styles. It makes no difference that the Dienzenhofers, Brokofs, Brauns and Santini-Aichls were foreigners or descended from foreigners. The fascination of Prague and Bohemia has always derived from a mixture of heterogeneous, even clashing elements. Besides, the foreign artists who gathered there in great numbers during the age of Rudolf II quickly assimilated the Bohemian tradition, and by immersing themselves in the Bohemian capital they imbued it with their fantasies, their dreams and the temper of their works.

81

Prague is peopled with an army of statues. At the turn of the eighteenth century ecstatic figures longing for heavenly glory, more numerous than the distillers of the Rudolfine Age, appeared on the gables, loggias and the façades of churches and monasteries. Pulpits were transformed into lush sculptural vegetation. Contorted statues, statues *in cymbalis* adorned confessionals, altars, balustrades, chancels, chapels and organ balconies. They assembled in theatrical groups to represent scenes from the Passion. They occupied terraces and bridges, columns to the Virgin, staircases, verges, gardens, alcoves and corbels, the façades of opulent palaces. Distinguished members of the League of Caeli Caelorum – divine secretaries and angelic warriors, soaring cherubim, patron saints, Jesuits, devils, doleful Madonnas, evangelists, jurisconsults, holy lawgivers – to say nothing of the hosts of atlantes, giants and other mythical creatures, eagles and Moorish slaves.

During the first quarter of the eighteenth century Prague could boast more than twenty studios of master sculptors vying with one another in a creative fervour that seems to have animated their restless statues. Two complementary artists stand out: Ferdinand Maximilián Brokof (1688–1731) and Matyáš Bernard Braun (1684–1738).

Brokof: majesty, monumental unity, logic, in dense, concentrated expressivity shunning all dramatic impulse; reflection, solidity and the search for pure sculptural values prevailing over the usual extremes of the Baroque.

Matyáš Bernard Braun, on the other hand, breathes a disquietude, an unrestrained excitement into his subjects, capturing them in moments of anxiety, even paroxysm. He tends towards hyperbole, outbursts of the senses, passionate distortion: with a whirlwind of fluttering clothes ruffled by jagged points and pleats twisted like knots he heightens the agitation and anguish of his labile, violently mobile spirits. Their fiery Berninian dynamism has a reverse side of desperation, as if the exuberant gestures were attempting to cover a presentiment of nothingness. Braun made the dramatic substance and impatience of Prague wholly his own. "He was born in the Tyrol," Oskar Kokoschka wrote, "and there can be no doubt that had he remained there he would have been nothing more than one of the innumerable woodcutters whose crucifixes are so admired by visitors to the Austrian Alps."[1]

Prague's Baroque statues are accents in space, rhythmic signs of the cityscape. The Prague pedestrian takes active part in their dealings and chatter. And if one of them ups and takes flight? "My last dear illusion," Holan writes, "is that when your pedestal is removed you will remain for an instant in the air."[2] In April, when even stones fall in love, the pedestrian has the illusion that they are stirred by the warmth of spring and their lips whisper sighs of love, as in Baroque *alamódová poezie* (poetry à la mode).[3] "Love! That's the thing!" – again it is Holan speaking – "Even statues would take their first steps."[4]

Modern Czech poetry is full of sculpture. Halas speaks of "statues' motionless anguish".[5] Seifert says that "the statues have merged with the dark/waving the weight of their garments".[6] And Holan: "The plane tree on Kampa was relentless/for untold centuries, and the statue on Opyš/was never banished to the plaster corner."[7] And Kolář: "The statues flirted with each other."[8] And Kainar: "Such frightening immobility/is merely proof/of a higher intoxication."[9]

There is an intense relationship between the writhings of Braun's statues and the anguish in the poetry of a Halas, Zahradníček or Holan. For the Baroque is the lifeblood of Czech poetry, and not only poetry. As

F. X. Šalda put it, "We still lack the vaguest notion of how the Czech national character fused with the Baroque and the crucial role it has assumed in the creative life of our people."[10] In its robust metaphors, its visual and theatrical bias, its use of paradox, hyperbole, verbal embellishment, symbolism, its accumulation of asyndeta, its sense of rapture and decay, its desire for a nothingness that transforms everything into dead ashes – in all this a good deal of modern Czech verse, following Mácha's example, harks back to the poetry and sculpture of Baroque Prague.[11] "You know the eternal yearning," we read in Holan. "It is the nothingness for which we have yearned. Because man truly has nothing at all. Not even Death."[12] And in the same collection: "Beauty, you are a cluster of roses with a skull betwixt your roots, immortal beauty!"[13] The grinning skull we find in Mácha – the singer of "eternal nothingness",[14] of the snares set by beings from the other world and of the inexorable transience of the things of this world[15] – takes its place alongside the emaciated heads of Baroque saints.

Like Arcimboldo's composite puppets, the Baroque statues of Prague form a harmonious group, a perennial conclave. On grey days their desire to soar, their transcendent quality, the graceful curves of their domes stand in sharp contrast to the tread of sullen inhabitants in gloomy coats, trudging along all-too-familiar routes and lugging large, unwieldy shopping bags in their hands. Many of them are close to me. I am fascinated by Saint Hubertus with the miraculous stag as sculpted by Brokof (1726) on the façade of The Golden Stag in Malá Strana. I shall never forget the *Father Time* created by Brokof (1716) for the tomb of Jan Václav Vratislav z Mitrovic in Saint James', a vigorous old man as brimming with life as Apollinaire's Wandering Jew, a sullen, unflinching curmudgeon, *ah quantum currit*. *Day* and *Night* by Brokof (1714), two busts that grace the façade of the Malá Strana Morzin Palace, constantly come to mind: *Day* a short, handsome, curly-headed beau with the sun – a practice target – on his chest and sunflowers on his cloak; *Night* a melancholy maid, fast asleep, with a sweet mouth, a star-studded mantle and a half-moon resting on the mantle like a skiff. Do you remember walking past them, inspired by their poetic nature to recite Nezval?

> Our lives are like night and day
> Good-bye stars birds women's lips
> Good-bye death beneath the blossoming hawthorn
> Good-bye farewell good-bye farewell
> Good-bye good night and good day
> good night
> sweet dreams.[16]

82

(Moldava stellis lustratur.)

We used to walk down from the Castle in the evening with Brokof's Moorish atlantes glaring at us sullenly from the façade of Morzin Palace. Light from the trams' windows flickered out over the Vltava. "Above Valdštejn Palace," Holan writes, "male stains shone on the sheet of the moon."[1] Do you remember the green tint of the lamps on the magic Charles Bridge? Even then rickety carriages with rosolio-yellow lamps rode along it past sandstone statues. Next to those saintly actors in regal poses stood bit-part drunks, clinging fast to the parapet and delivering their lines to the river or the stars reflected therein.

Five stars, five small stars as blue as punch sparkled on the waters when Jan Nepomucký was hurled from the bridge and disappeared. The legend goes further: *ignes et flammae, innumera et miri candoris lumina, flammae pulcherrimae, luminaria caelestia* (fire and flames, innumerable lights of wondrous radiance, beautiful flames, heavenly bodies). It was 16 May 1383. The entire Vltava shone with a "greenish glitter".[2] "You would have seen countless bright lights, as if fire and water had made peace and were flowing together."[3]

Every year on 16 May swarms of devout women and masses of pilgrims gathered from villages in Bohemia and Moravia to render homage at the place on the bridge from which the canon of the Prague Cathedral Chapter and Deacon of All Saints John of Pomuk (or Nepomuk) was flung into the water by the thugs of wicked King Wenceslas IV because, or so the legend goes, he refused to reveal what the Queen had told him in the confessional.[4] I will not enter into the disquisitions surrounding the controversial hagiographical issue of whether Nepomuk actually existed or was in fact a doctor of ecclesiastical law and vicar of the archbishop of Prague by the same name who was drowned ten years later because he had confirmed the abbot of Kladruby Monastery against the will of Wenceslas IV (whom all chronicles brand as a Herod and a Nero).[5]

The symbology of Nepomuk's stars has inspired many Czech works of art. The pentagonal plan of the delightful church at Zelená Hora near Žd'ár, as compact and pointed as a crystal druse, derived from the quintet of stars that surged out of the water where he went under. The motif reappears, albeit in jest, in Hašek's novel when Švejk must drag home the tipsy chaplain Otto Katz: "He exhibited yearnings for martyrdom, asking him to cut off his head and throw him in a sack into the Vltava: 'Some stars round my head would suit me very well,' he said with enthusiasm, 'I should need ten.'"[6]

The Jesuits encouraged the cult of the contentious canon with prayers, tridua, celebrations and homilies. Nepomuk the Martyr arose from five rays: heavenly manna, a tall cedar planted in Lebanon, *thesaurus sine defectione*, a new Elisha, a solid, indestructible fortress in suffering. The pity aroused for the violence he suffered helped to expunge the memory of the heretic Jan Hus. He therefore served as a clear-cut image, free of abstruse claims and complex dogmatic arguments, in their disputations against Hus's "falsehoods". Nor did they rest until they had placed him in heaven among the host of saints.

On 15 April 1719 Nepomuk's purported tomb in Saint Vitus' Cathedral was opened before a group of doddering academics, jurists, patricians and prelates. An assembly of surgeons presided over by František Löw z Erlsfeldu, a sage smothered under a huge curly wig, identified the skeleton. The physicians pronounced the skeleton intact – though the bones were broken in several places, as the victim had struck a pier while falling from the bridge – and carefully scraped tufts of mold and clumps of clay from the cranium until, lo and behold, there appeared in the earth-filled mouth cavity a tongue still red and fresh and full of life.[7]

This miracle increased the martyr's fame and accelerated his ascension to the ranks of the blessed. On the day of his beatification (4 July 1721) the tongueless skeleton, laid out in canon's robes complete with tricorn and rochet, was placed in a glass coffin; the skull was propped on an embroidered silk cushion; the right hand held a cross and a silver ear of corn, the left a palm branch fashioned of precious metals. A procession accompanied by trumpet fanfares transported the coffin to the large square in front of the Castle. Behind the transparent coffin the ancient archbishop, carefully raising and lowering his tiny red slippers, walked with the Holy Tongue, now separated from the Skeleton forever, in a cylindrical silver reliquary. That night all Prague was illuminated by an arabesque of lights. Huge torches burned on either side of the triumphal arch erected in front of Schwarzenberg Palace. Beer and wine flowed from the archbishop's fountains.[8]

Then the entire country dug in its heels and waited for the canon to be sanctified. Pilgrims streamed in from the provinces. Prayers, illuminations and water music below the bridge prepared the faithful for the solemn event. While certain nullifidians insinuated that the devil was using his wiles to hold up the *sanctificetur*, in point of fact the Congregation of Rites in Rome merely needed more information about the magic tongue. Which is why in 1725 Löw z Erlsfeldu bowed his bewigged head a second time – in the presence of the archbishop and assorted dignitaries. And behold, the tongue, which at first was dry and greyish, swelled and turned bright crimson in the surgeons' hands, as though engorged with blood.

The glowing ruby of your tongue
lifted from the bed of worms
flames unchanged from the vortex divine,
untouched by the primeval power of dust,

writes Jan Zahradníček in a hymn to Nepomuk.[9]

In Prague mythology the Grand Penitentiary's tongue joins the artificial nose of Tycho Brahe, the *Jezulátko*, the waxworks, Arcimboldo's figures and the stuffed horse in Valdštejn Palace, the horse on whose back the silent generalissimo galloped during the Battle of Lützen. "Was this animal as mute when the bugle sounded as its master was when glory befell him? There must be a reason why of all others this charger was granted immortality. Perhaps it never neighed."[10] Brave horses are stuffed, not fallen heroes, Liliencron remarked when he saw the Duke of Friedland's steed, by then a moth-eaten mannequin.[11]

Nepomuk's tongue, which had refused to betray its vow of secrecy, became the symbol of a stubborn silence paid for by eternal rest, a silence at odds with the equally Prague-like loquacity of the pub-crawlers. When the Tongue, shining like a gem in a cathedral chapel, meets other tongues soaked in beer, the latter ask the former mockingly, "How could you keep silent, you fool?" The streets of Prague are full of racy stories that take Silence, like death, quite lightly.

The canonization was finally announced. The celebration dragged on for the entire week of 9–16 October 1729. What rapture for the sanctimonious! In Saint Vitus' Cathedral alone there were 32 000 masses celebrated; 186 000 worshippers received communion.[12] Triumphal arches and lunettes and banners with the new saint's effigy, flaming pyramids, torches, allegorical structures and quintets of stars ornamented the city. At dawn on the first day a gala procession of gold brocade gonfalons and vexilla set out for the Castle amidst a haze of incense and lantern and candle smoke, amidst throngs of Capuchins, Jesuits, Knights of the Cross, Barnabites, Hibernicans, Dominicans, Trinitarians, Carmelites, Servites and Premonstratensians dotted with musicians and teeming with scapulars, habits, knotted cords and cowls: a study in white, grey and black. But there were splashes of colour too: six priests, surrounded by swarms of clerics, deacons and parish priests in red pluvials, conveying a garish statute of the saint; seminary teachers waving huge flags; officials of the three Prague municipalities – coadjutors, vicars, capitular canons – bearing crosses studded with gems and rock crystal on their chests; the archbishop carrying the reliquary with the Saint's crimson tongue; the "estates" sporting tricorns and plumes of every hue in the rainbow; and, last but not least, a great host of peasants in folk costumes chanting Ave Marias and paternosters between hymns.[13]

The cathedral was ostentatiously adorned with red drapery, with paintings depicting the saint's miracles and with festoons and damasks and standards and gleaming liturgical utensils and endless candles in silver candelabra. Such magnificence banished all thought of punishment or exile *in ignem aeternum* for at least a week. Under a canopy of purple, silver-embroidered velvet, its corners held by four celestial messengers, a silver statue of Nepomuk reigned on the main altar. On another altar, near the glass tomb that housed the Grand Penitentiary's skeleton, the reflection of countless lamps flickered across a priceless golden monstrance. The frontal was piled high with votive offerings: chalices, hearts, tongues, skulls, statuettes, lapis lazuli, jasper, medals and myriad jewelled trinkets. Sermons were introduced by festive artillery salutes and followed by masses both inside the cathedral and in the courtyard, which overflowed with worshippers. There was a brief cloudburst, whereupon the vault of th' heav'ns returned serene and everyone stayed on into the night to watch the magnificent fireworks.[14]

Before long the Nepomuk myth had become the emblem, the obsession of Baroque Bohemia and Moravia. Poems, churches, chapels, paintings, music, frescoes, statues and triumphal arches zealously produced variations on the theme of his martyrdom. Constant liturgical ceremonies, constant lavish processions exalted the Saint's memory *usque ad sidera* and kept it alive. His fame spread throughout the Catholic world, yea even to the ends of the earth.

The Charles Bridge originally contained a single crucifix and a Calvary, but for the celebration of the three hundredth anniversary of Nepomuk's death (1683) a statue was erected at the spot where the thugs had thrown him into the river. It was the bridge's first Baroque procession. Matyáš Rauchmüller's bronze Nepomuk wears a goatee, a rochet and the three-cornered biretta; he holds a palm branch and a cross in his long fingers. The five-star aureole circling his head has been lost. Since the Vltava played so central a role in his death, the rise of his cult and the creation of the statue gallery on the bridge, its centrality in these lines by Jan Zahradníček is not surprising.

> Intercede for us, Saint John,
> thrown to the fish in the river's mire!
> All the sewage it has set in motion,
> all the shipwrecks it has dragged down,
> all the slaughter-stained rags,
> all the sin-stained linen,
> all the rot it has wrung –
> finds in you its confessor.[15]

I picture all the unwholesome ghosts from Nezval's *Edison* – drunks, fallen women, suicides and gamblers – converging in the Vltava from the Legion Bridge to the Charles Bridge.

Rauchmüller's Nepomuk became the archetype for the innumerable statues of the holy canon placed by Baroque piety at crossroads, on bridges and beneath the shade of linden trees in small squares of Bohemian and Moravian villages.[16] As for the Charles Bridge, burghers, nobles, teachers, monks – they all wished to see their patron saints on the bridge (in sandstone, not bronze). Hence the extraordinary statue gallery there, unique in all the world, a majestic, multi-headed centaur.

83

Do you remember the first signs of spring, when the gulls returned to the Vltava from Lake Mácha and Mrs Hlochová took Brussels lace out of her bottom drawer, when winter retreated into the milk shops with their cold zinc counters, onto the roof tops crusted over with snow, into the narrow, shaded Malá Strana streets? A straw-coloured sun, still weak, flickered as through a vase, yet Petřín Hill would soon explode with forsythia, lilacs and jasmine in a feverish, frenetic exuberance that both brought on one's allergies and took one's breath away. In the light of that intense flurry of blossoms, so out of keeping with Prague's usual gloom, one ponders Kafka's words: "What misery, a granary in spring, a consumptive in spring."[1]

April. We walked down from the Castle one Sunday at dawn. There was a pottery market on Kampa Island at the time. Seifert writes:

> The potters stand close to their stalls,
> tapping the pots with a finger,
> their hands filled with flowers.[2]

A puff of wind sculpted tiny waves along the river. The ducks, after warming up in the jets gushing from the Caroline Baths, swam arrogantly towards the boards protecting the piers of the Charles Bridge and past the pipe-smoking fishermen, as impassive as Lada's water demons, their lines dangling in the river. A weak glitter of sun would have sufficed to cleanse the saints on the bridge of their winter soot. I return there to this day in my memory, running down from the Castle like a single "intrusive" (*neodbytná*) line by Kupka, twisting and turning along the narrow streets, eager for love.

Construction of the bridge linking Malá Strana to the Old Town was begun in July 1357, that is, during the reign of Charles IV.[3] The architect was the Swabian Peter Parler, who had come to Prague in 1353 to complete the work on Saint Vitus' Cathedral begun by Mathieu d'Arras. The previous bridge, built (possibly by Italian stonecutters) between 1157 and 1172 at the instigation of Queen Judith, wife of King Vladislav II, was swept away by a flood in 1342. The new bridge used durable Nehvizdy sandstone instead of the customary marl, and the tale is told that the burghers of Velvary sent baskets of hard-boiled eggs and the burghers of Unhošt' – cheeses, crates of curds and whey to mix with the mortar and make it strong.[4] For centuries travellers have admired the bridge's span (which takes a sharp turn when it gets to Malá Strana), its sixteen piers and the Gothic towers at either end – those great compact prisms with ogee-arched gates and spire roofs, with statues on corbels, with coats of arms and battlements and spires.

For centuries it was called Stone Bridge or Prague Bridge; it did not receive the name of its founder until 1870. Legend has it that one of its pillars contains the mythical Prince Bruncvík's miraculous sword, which Saint Wenceslas will brandish to defeat his enemies when Bohemia is in peril.[5] Pipe dreams, castles in the air. Besides, according to a cruel prophecy Czechs on the bridge will one day be rarer than stags with golden horns.

The ravages of time, bombs and floods have tested the bridge's solidity more than once. When in 1890 the Vltava swept away part of it and swallowed up several statues (they were later recovered), the Czech people grieved as much as it had nine years earlier when the Národní divadlo (National Theatre) was gutted by fire.

Natural disasters notwithstanding, however, the bridge was once a busy thoroughfare, a central artery of the city, which explains why the popular imagination used to say a busy place was "like the Prague Bridge". A popular song once claimed that "rosemary grows/on the Prague Bridge".[6] There was a toll levied on goods crossing the bridge, and Jews had to shell out a special duty or *meches*.

Swarms of idlers and paupers camped out there, especially during the Baroque period – beggars like the one holding his hand out to Saint Martin in the group sculpted by Konrád Max Süssner (1690) for the nearby Church of Saint Francis of the Knights of the Cross and scoundrels who pretended to have the scourge of Saint Lazarus or Saint Anthony's fire, flaunting fistulas and furuncles cunningly crafted of mistletoe, menstrual fluid and flour. The Jesuit Albrecht Chanovský was not beyond perching atop carts of mud and dung as if they were triumphal wagons and walking with outcasts and beggars "like a mendicant with a knapsack slung over his shoulder along the most crowded streets of the city and even across the Prague Bridge".[7] The foppish, debt-ridden drunkard painter Petr Jan Brandl (1668–1735) must often have stopped there. And following the Battle of White Mountain the poet Šimon Lomnický z Budče, a virtual symbol of the collapse and humiliation of the Czech nation and protagonist of Zeyer's tale "Inultus", is said to have begged there, a legend conceivably inspired by the fact that the poet, who was also a known turncoat, used the name Ptocheus or Beggar.[8]

84

By the beginning of the eighteenth century, therefore, the Charles Bridge was populated with statues symbolizing the victory of the Counter-Reformation, the Church Triumphant, in post-White Mountain Bohemia. The statuary grew over a period of eight years (1706–14) at regular intervals along the parapets like the names in the liturgy. If down below, on Kampa Island, the poet frets over the suffocating closeness of the walls with their "statue nourished by the Baroque,/the statue of death",[1] then on the bridge above, which is modelled after the Ponte Sant'Angelo in Rome, the saints *in cymbalis bene sonantibus*, a mixture of visionary fervour and thirst for transcendence, are surrounded by air, water, clouds, huge baldachins of sky and a teeming of gulls spiralling into the water. University faculties, monasteries, seminaries and both noble and burgher families commissioned sandstone figures from a number of sculptors, the most prominent being Matěj Václav Jäckel, Jan Oldřich Mayer, Ferdinand Maximilián Brokof and Matyáš Bernard Braun. Dusty pilgrimages bearing wildflowers came from all over Bohemia and Moravia to recite paternosters before this showcase of heavenly warriors.

But it is impossible to appreciate the magic of the bridge without the surrounding buildings, which, to quote Miloš Marten, express "the entire drama of the Latin spirit":[2] on the Old Town side the intimate square of the Knights of the Cross, a Baroque jewel box, a "smiling flower-bed"[3] bordered by the churches of the Holy Saviour and Saint Francis and by the Klementinum; on the Malá Strana side – the Church of Saint Nicholas, on which "an enchanting whim has placed the upside-down emerald goblet of an ambergris cupola like a beacon of triumphal light";[4] on the Old Town side the Church of Saint Francis of the Knights of the Cross, with the supple curve of its pure, light dome, corresponding to the bridge's tower spires and thus contracting a marriage between Gothic and Baroque; on the Malá Strana side a perfect balance between the Gothic tower and the "enormous green rose"[5] of the malachite-coloured cupola of Saint Nicholas', which in turn harmonizes beautifully with the dome of Saint Francis of the Knights of the Cross.

Many statues of evangelists, Jesuits, theologians, bishops and angels bearing the instruments of Christ's martyrdom nest on the porch and roof of the Holy Saviour and the niches and attic of Saint Francis of the Knights of the Cross. It is from here, from this nursery, this emporium of saints, that the sandstone cortège sets out, proceeding as solemnly as the pageants depicted in Czech Baroque canvases towards Saint Nicholas', whose green dome seems to inflate through the interplay of hemispheres and triangles as one approaches.

Seifert in his Charles Bridge poem discourses on the bees in spring swarming amidst the cassocks of the holy doctors and soldiers of Christ lined up along the parapets.[6] This sandstone parade, which looked to one foreign visitor like a double row of musketeers,[7] is also a prodigious display of vestments – dalmatics, infulas, birettas, staffs, planetas, pluvials, robes, cascades of pleats and cowls resembling raging waves – and religious paraphernalia – crosses, gospel books, chains, haloes attached to the back of the head with a rod of candied floss, the books and quill of Saint Thomas Aquinas, the vessels of Saint Anthony of Padua, Saint Ives's codex, the club of Saint Jude, the ointment jars of the physicians Cosmas and Damian.

The heavenly barons have their own menagerie as well, but they are richest in cherubim: one angel carrying a bread basket, another emptying the sea with a shell, a third holding a beehive and still others bearing coats of arms, scrolls and the attributes of various patron saints; some cling to the rocks, others whirl through the air like winged flowers. In the group surrounding Saint Cayetanus small angels' heads are attached by wisps of stone clouds to an obelisk crowned by a large heart.

And rich as the bridge's circus of saints is in local heroes, it also testifies to the Baroque's predilection for the exotic.[8] I am thinking of the Turk and the Jew on an inverted frustum at the base of the statues of Saint Vincent Ferrarius and Saint Procopius (the bearded Jew wrapped in a tallith with wrinkled hands seems a consul from the fabulous Rabbi Loew) or the Turk who guards Christian prisoners on the pedestal below Saint Felix de Valois and Saint Jean de Matha or the Indian prince and two pages kneeling before Saint Francis Xavier as he raises the cross or the Negro, the Tartar, the Japanese and the Indian sculpted from the dado of the same group or Asia clad in the opulent garb of a sorcerer on the plinth of Saint Ignatius.

Several sculptures of the Vltava conclave produce an unforgettable impression. The Saint Lutgard configuration is especially fascinating. The Baroque poet and organist Adam Michna z Otradovic writes to Christ:

> Faithful Saint Lutgard,
> Thy beloved virgin lover,
> found in Thy heart refection

and exquisite hydromel.[9]

Braun's ballad in stone wonderfully expresses the pangs of the Christ-intoxicated vision of the Flemish Cistercian nun. *Vivificum latus exugit cor mutuans corde.* The kneeling Lutgard, languishing from the heat of her senses like a summer rose, grasps the knees of Christ, and although his left arm is nailed to the cross he rests the right on the shoulder of his mystical concubine. This scene of almost sensual passion, this reverie of angelic putti and dainty cloud puffs, this tête-à-tête between heaven and earth whose dramatic power stems from its asymmetrical disposition, takes place on a mighty precipice as violently undulating as the ample, cascading sleeves of the nun's habit. All Braun's statues share its transcendental restlessness and ardour, yet an even more violent passion stirs the tight fabrics entwining the body of the fierce, venerable old Saint Jude, a statue not of this areopagus and made of linden wood rather than sandstone.

The most disturbing figure in the riverside statue gallery is the Turk in a group by Brokof known as the Bridge Turk, a Prague oddity on a par with the Golem and the bearded phantom Saint Starosta (Heilige Kümmernis) in the Loreta Church. The group represents Saint Felix de Valois and Saint Jean de Matha, the founders of the Trinitarian Order, who resolved to redeem Christianity from the yoke of the infidel, and – though heaven knows why he was placed in their company – the Slav Saint Ivan. The three saints stand atop a barred stone prison from whose depths three writhing Catholics beg for help. The pot-bellied janissary, a Caucasian beglerbeg with a long drooping moustache, a tunic rich in braid, a scimitar and a turban, guards the cavern in a dignified, impassive manner, nodding off, perhaps, as he leans against the rock, his fierce cur so close to the parapet that he seems to sniff the passers-by. The stag of Saint Jean de Matha leans from the crag as if hearkening to the lamentations of the three wretches. The overall arrangement recalls the figurines in Bohemian crèches and the mine scenes sculpted by craftsmen from Krušné Hory.[10]

Oskar Wiener relates that Liliencron laughed heartily at the Turk's sullen expression during his lovesick *flâneries* through the streets of Prague and that he stuck an orange – an orange! – into Cerberus's open maw.[11] The tracks of the infidel were still fresh in the Central European countryside in 1714 when Brokof modelled the figure. There are images of Turks – echoes of the incursions that brought them as far as Vienna in 1683 – throughout Bohemian Baroque art not only in paintings and sculpture but also in street ballads, crèches, popular comedies, and Christmas and Carnival pageants.[12] Yet the Mustapha on the Charles Bridge is not a caryatid, a prisoner or slave as elsewhere; he is a wraith, an awe-inspiring gaoler of Meyrink's infernal ilk.[13]

Egon Erwin Kisch tells the tale of one Zadriades Patkanian, a rich, middle-aged Armenian-Persian carpet dealer who, after moving to Prague, marries the young daughter of a destitute saddlemaker. Patkanian never removes the sabre with which he has killed Erzurum, his first wife, from his waist. The terrified Miluška, his new wife, identifies the menacing Armenian with the evil Bridge Turk, but while her greybeard spends his evenings in taverns, the lass goes gallivanting with a gallipot her own age, who initiates her into the joys of the flesh. Once, returning late from an assignation, Miluška tosses a stone against the Moslem's stone scimitar for good luck, and the blade breaks off and crumbles on the pavement. When her spouse, who has been waiting at home for hours, boiling with the jealousy of a paladin and the sneer of an executioner, tries to draw his sabre to behead her, he is amazed to find nothing in his hand but the hilt.[14]

Whether flaunting their pride and fixing their calcareous eyes on an empty sky or indulging in exalted ecstasy or working conversions and miracles, all the statues along the parapet exhibit a fine sense of theatricality in their pathos, gestures and fluttering cowls. They combine hauteur – and a certain braggadocio – with a longing to overcome the gravity binding them to earth. I have in mind the bravura of Saints Cosmas and Damian displaying their medicines like quacks, the bombast of Saint Ives, the patron saint of pettifoggers, the bravado of Saint Vincent Ferrarius, as he revives a dead man in a coffin, or Saint Procopius, the great demon tamer, as a Satan squirms beneath his feet.

None of these saints appears inert or self-satisfied, and unlike Prague none of them suffers from catatony. High on their pedestals these heavenly ranters perform their roles with great brio, yet maintain just enough balance to keep from slipping. Some involve the passers-by by having their extras protrude so far as to all but brush them – the Turk's dog, for example, or the angel of Saint Francesco Borgia, whose legs dangle freely over the edge of the plinth. Nor do they stop once night falls. The *vox populi* used to say that they held highly learned theological disputations at midnight, passing on their captious concerns to the drunks in neighbouring taverns.

85

No one who has failed to see these statues leaving their suicidal pedestals on certain nights not recorded in the calendar, mixing with passers-by and admiring the twelve bridges of Prague (they are not all visible from here) can ever understand my poetry.[1]

After reading these words of Nezval's, I had the idea of staging an extravagant spectacle on the bridge, on that most elegant ship piled high with statues. So I turn to you, Mr Krejča, director of the Theatre Behind the Gate (Za branou) and most fertile repository of stage invention, to direct the production, which along with the sandstone figures will feature the water in the Vltava, the green curtains of Petřín Hill, the pit of Kampa Island below, the flies of the clouds above, and the backdrops of Malá Strana and the Castle. Use your imagination, your entire arsenal of tricks and devices to create magical effects, a diabolical din, brilliant fireworks, mysterious revelations.

I shall begin with illuminations reproducing a mis-en-scène from the evening of 9 October 1729 in honour of Saint John of Nepomuk. Sunset. As in a painting by Petr Brandl,[2] the dim light of the setting sun hidden behind a cloud, the listless light of the dying day does battle with a warm, luminous fluid, a holy light that seems to emanate from a long lost dove, long-since plucked – the dove of the Holy Spirit. A triple salvo of more than twenty springals daunts both daredevil gulls and pealing bells. Acrobatic torches cast swarms of lights over the windows of the palaces, the silhouettes of the monasteries and the zigzag outline of the Castle. Church façades exuberate with emblems, banners and allegorical hangings. The steep narrow Malá Strana streets flare up like rows of stage wings in perspective.

The glitter of the multicoloured fireworks set off on the bridge towers fuses in the water with the flare of red ornamental stars and a flaming crucifix atop the cupola of Saint Francis' Church. Skiffs bedecked with pine cones and flickering lanterns dart like fireflies along the river.[3] The faithful, like subjects of the Underground Kingdom, crowd the small square of the Knights of the Cross on Kampa Island, searching the sky for *trompes-l'œil*, and all at once a swarm of cherubim plummets out of the clouds as in the apotheoses of Baroque painting.

Three hundred musicians with trumpets and timbals strike up a water music from two boats moored to the bridge where Nepomuk's statue stands. And lo! a shower of Bengal lights hails down from the firmament, the spirals and twirling suns forming short-lived allegories above the mute saint. Now the river turns green like the olive grove at Gethsemane, now brown like the broth in which Pontius Pilate dipped his hands, now yellow like wine mixed with bile, now black like the darkness over Calvary at the sixth hour, now scarlet like the blood of Our Lord, now pale like His body nailed to the cross, now violet like the burial clothes of the Passion, now ash-grey like the lamentations of Prague – Prague, lifeless, waiting for a sponge soaked in vinegar.

The illuminations cease at midnight. The crowd disperses. Yet idlers drunk from the fountains gushing wine in front of the Archbishop's

Palace still totter across the bridge, singing in tipsy voices and carrying long candles like those depicted by Brandl in *Smrt svatého Vintíře* (The Death of Saint Vintíř, 1718) in the Church of Saint Margaret in Prague-Břevnov. Three musicians in black – frock coats, bowler hats – stroll past, red eyes staring out of faces white with chalk and ceruse, oboes under their arms. Five robust angels – each holding a lily, palm branch, torch, crown and cross (Nepomuk's attributes) and dancing, leaping like David before the Tabernacle – wend their way to the Ursuline Convent near the Castle to bring back the fresco by Václav Vavřinec Reiner (1727) they borrowed for the celebration. Harlequin informers pass by – Caiaphases, Iscariots, arrogant Epishevs or *Reichsprotektor*s or Don Marradases, sword in hand, evil scribes, corruptible clowns – paid agents all, wetting their pants at every foreign order. And I'll get me to a monastery if those three trudging by just now yelling "Illalla, illala Maumeth, russoillalla" aren't the three Christian slaves the Turk keeps in prison.

Suddenly I hear a booming, a din so unbearable it seems a witches' sabbath. The statues start twitching wildly as if possessed, as if dangling from the fingers of hidden puppeteers. Some break off from their plinths; the Latin inscriptions on their pedestals jumble into alphabetic tangles like Jiří Kolář's "crazygrams". Seized by fear, the last gaunt passers-by make a run for it.

But it does not last. Before long the saints return to their places like headstone ornaments. "Out of nowhere," Mrštík writes "the statues appeared along the sides of the bridge like black corpses."[4] Now they look like ashen carcasses without so much as a grain of the spirit usually animating them – they are mere grinning idols, sacred scarecrows. Yet through the bombast and arrogance comes a mixture of *vanitas*, grief, intoxication with nothingness and the keen presentiment of death. They have been infiltrated by the mummies preserved in the large crypts of the nearby "Spanish" Church of Our Lady Victorious.[5] At the top of the Castle an actor (Radovan Lukavský, perhaps) picks up a huge megaphone and recites the poem "Co Bůh? Člověk?" (What is God? Man?, 1658) by the Jesuit Bedřich Bridel. Bridel contrasts our worm-eaten clay nothingness with the immense power and aseity of the Lord.

At this point a raging hurricane approaches, a wind more oceanic than fluvial, the kind that blows the waves to the stars and sent carracks, the great ships of the East India Company, to the bottom. During the storm, which imitates the tempests frequently described in Czech Baroque literature,[6] the statues make a *repulisti me domine* and the sandstone saints disappear, leaving the bridge deserted and as ghostly as a long-abandoned abbey.

Back on their plinths at dawn, the statues resume their recitations and sermons, their flights of acrobatics and transcendence, while the pedestrians crossing the Vltavian corridor – overladen, absent-minded, sullen – do not so much as glance at the lithological cabaret. A spectral sun peeps out from behind the clouds; gulls soar and dive; the sun, to quote Holan, "plummets between the teeth of the statues".[7] "Calm madmen", the fishermen in their fluvial shells drop their lines into the water.[8] "Down on the river," Kafka writes in his diary, "lay several boats, fishermen had cast their lines, it was a dreary day. Some youths, their legs crossed, were leaning against the railing of the dock."[9] The banks will be teeming with these *čumilové*, Prague gawpers, motionless pilgrims who only stand and wait. A strange fellow in an *altmodisch* top hat strolls up and down the avenue selling small books, crying, "Fine stories! Get your fine stories! The Bridge Turk! The ecstasy of Saint Lutgard!"

86

Magic Prague: repository of musty old castoffs, assemblage of debris and detritus, *tandlmark* of gewgaws and gimcracks. It is no accident that since the seventeenth century a *tandlmark* (or *tarmark*) teemed in the very heart of the Bohemian capital, the centre of the Old Town, just outside the Ghetto. Hucksters and cozeners outdid one another hawking worn-out shoes, gold and silver coins, clocks, hats, daggers, parrots, canary cages, household utensils, old Bibles, incunabula, books, furs and coats. Here, during the eighteenth century, the painter Norbert Grund vended his pictures for a ducat apiece.[1] Pedlars sold pancakes and pork and peas with lard from kettles on wheels. Crowds of the curious streamed along the narrow streets and small squares formed by wooden shacks while beggars, whores and pickpockets plied their trade.

Although little is left of the old *tandlmark*, its teeming magic lives on in the essence of present-day Prague. According to Hrabal, you can still see

> colourful ribbons flow from the noses of the ribbon sellers when they measure their wares with their elbow, every day a new umbrella sprouts from the pate of the greengrocers, the flower girls keep tulips of every hue in their kangaroo pockets, parakeets flitter in cages like poetic metaphors and little old women with faces furrowed by signs of the zodiac and two leopard-skin flaps for eyes sell green roses made of feathers, sell admirals' swords and harmonica keys and enlisted men's gym shorts and canvas pails and stuffed monkeys.

To this day "it has a smell of newborn babies, soggy straw mattresses, vinegar and hemp".[2]

The *tandlmark* flourished as late as the turn of the century, especially at Christmas. A small shanty town would pop up overnight in the Old Town Square, its flickering candles and small rape-oil lamps vying with the street lamps,[3] a fabled land for swindlers with little Carthusian [sic] devils, fortune-tellers with parrots who chose your fortune with their beaks and Dalmatian pedlars whose baskets overflowed with mirrors, razor blades and prophylactics. "Zmrzlina, zmrzlina! Ovocná zmrzlina!" cried the ice-cream vendors, but there were also more exotic calls such as: "Figs, American figs. Braces from fair Queen Manda"! As Paul Leppin wrote, "People squeezed their way between gingerbread knights, yellow toy trumpets and bright toy drums . . . Lamps fluttering over the sweets on display lent a flickering light to the red turbans of the men hawking Turkish delight".[4]

Lethargic women curled up like curs watched over shooting galleries. Kašpárek acted his farce in wobbly puppet theatres. Singers crooned tales of crime and love, illustrating the plot with a pointer on painted oilcloth. The muddle was made even more picturesque by mechanical theatres with scenes of work in the mines, panoramas, museums, waxworks with a talking head, a beheaded lady and a water nymph or, rather, a combination of stuffed monkey and scaly carp.[5]

The Bulgarian Duko Petkovich sold *suchuk* and Turkish delight hard as granite, *rahat-lokum* sprinkled with bitter almonds and an almond nougat he sliced from a block with a small axe, or, as Kisch recalls, a guillotine.[6] The booths of the Prague *tandlmark* contained heaps of every delicacy imaginable: *peprmint*, fruit cake, "sweet wood", "Saint John's bread", *pendrek* (from *Bärendreck*, "bear shit") or licorice, *cukrkandl* (candied sugar), *mejdlíčko* ("little soap", a prism-shaped, rainbow like sweet with a soap-like flavour), snow horns, multicoloured balls of zedoary seeds reputed to repel worms, pretzels, wafers, macaroons, candy-floss, *špalík* (a small sugar log decorated with a floral pattern), sugarplums and endless other confections, sweetmeats and blancmanges including figurines of black chimney-sweeps (made of dried, wrinkled prunes skewered on long wooden sticks and topped by white paper hats and miniature ladders) alternating with gilt walnuts in shop windows for St. Nicholas' Day.[7]

Tandlmark Prague might well be epitomized by a certain Marát, who for the last twenty years of the last century sat like the subject of a weekend painter at his wretched stand beneath an archway in front of U Šturmů, a café in the Coal Market, that is, in the thick of things.[8] After serving as a grenadier in four wars, he had returned to Prague, poor as a church-mouse, to set up shop – his merchandise rejects from refuse bins, his clientele beggars. Rain or shine, the junkman with the heavily-lined face sat motionless against a backdrop of grey, peeling walls beside a rickety stand and two moth-eaten baskets displaying oily rags, scratched pots, china lamps, filthy ties, pipe bowls without stems and pipe stems without bowls, used studs, shoes without heels or soles, brushes without bristles, chain links, umbrellas missing both fabric and handle, dirty detachable collars, broken razors, eyeglasses and knives, bent forks, bundles of dog-eared penny dreadfuls – in short, a jumble of the most worthless chaff scrounged in the most remote dumps and middens of Prague – sat majestically in a wooden chair beside his Babel of bits and pieces wearing a patched burnous and a greasy army cap.

Prague is not only Baroque magnificence and Gothic verticality; it is also this *Merz* of junk, of cast-offs that have ended up in the street or in old chests, of rotting remainders and decaying relics that grow like mustard seeds in the garden of the imagination.[9] The Jewish presence and Czech parsimony – the Czechs' love for objects, "silent companions",[10] and especially for repairing old things in the absence of new ones – bears out my concept of Prague as market. Until quite recently the chests of middle-class families were piled high with faded detachable collars and top hats that our Mr Hloch, as a Habsburg official, once wore in Vienna. With broken bric-à-brac, down-at-heel boots, fading picture postcards – things long since useless yet kept to the bitter end like the ancient clothing in the stuffed chests of the Herrenhof's landlady.[11]

The metaphysical *tandlmark* of the city on the Vltava also includes the bagatelles of nineteenth-century soirées, the melancholy trinkets of fancy dress balls on Žofín Island organized by associations with floral names such as Tuberosa, Gardenie and Petunie, and the cotillion programmes that girls hid in bottom drawers till their dying day, favours of cardboard, silk, velvet or leather, in the shape of four-leaf clovers, linden leaves, quivers with arrows, albums with gilt borders or muffs with revolving cylinders containing lists of balls, programmes printed in gold, cinnabar red or silver on *glazépapír* with tiny pencils to help the young lady keep track of her dancing partners.[12]

There was another *tandlmark*, however, one that moved from tavern to tavern, turning all Prague into a mobile fair. The bustle of junkmen in the famous pub U Fleků at the end of the nineteenth century is characterized as follows by Vilém Mrštík in his novel *Santa Lucia*:

A tousled urchin girl ran from table to table selling boxes of matches; hawkers from Kočevje with panniers hung round their necks, dust-covered sculptors with plaster-of-Paris figures, humble old women with neatly stacked pyramids of oranges and Meissen apples, artists selling paintings of naked nymphs, their legs seductively crossed, next to blood-stained heads of Christ, Wallachians selling nuts and nut cakes, fairbooth fortune-tellers.[13]

One might add the numerous pedlars of candied fruit, barometers, balloons, lottery tickets, rollmops, toy vehicles, roasted almonds and pickles swimming in a filthy liquid. An endless caravan of goods went from tavern to tavern. And let us not forget the "little locomotives of the chestnut sellers" who "stood red-eyed by the edge of the roadway",[14] and the night-time portable tea kettles, the self-propelled samovars, whose prototype was a tiny dog-drawn steam engine called "the hot drink ambulance" or "Café Candelabra" (because the pedlar usually leaned against a lamppost).[15]

This theatre of hucksters and hawkers lived on in the Prague Surrealists, who like their Parisian brothers revelled in dusty flea-market fetishes. Old *Automaten* with dancing figurines, glass balls, practice targets, pilgrimage souvenirs, fortune-tellers' charts showing the curve of human life, masks, dull mirrors, cracked statuettes, tiny, vulgarly appointed coffins, headstone putti – the musty *tandlmark* mix blends well with the Surrealist props in the photographs of the cycle *Na jehlách těchto dní* (On the Needles of These Days, 1935) by the painter Jindřich Štyrský.[16] An angel spreading its wings outside a pharmacy holds a scroll bearing the word "Materialista". In a hairdresser's window female figurines with flowing hair flirt between flacons and advertisements for Odol and Birkenwasser. Štyrský's broken dolls and celluloid torsos exude the morbid atmosphere of an orthopedist's surgery. By virtue of their love for broken dolls (*rozbité panenky*), bull's-eyes, waxworks, barbershop dummies, wooden carousel figures, fair-booth posters and chipped and broken artefacts of all kinds, the Prague Surrealists are the heirs of the *tandlmark*.[17]

87

Magic Prague: taverns and pubs galore, a plexus of smoke-filled drinking establishments, a world of awe-inspiring drunks presided over by the protector of heavy drinkers, the guardian angel of merry misery: *Lumpazivagabundus*. Who can forget the dives in Hašek's *Švejk*? Who can forget U Kalicha (The Chalice), the promised land of Švejk and Vodička, and the Kuklík, where they "play the violin and the accordion" and "tarts come in and various other members of good society who aren't allowed in at the Represent'ák".[1]

During the second half of the nineteenth century the Jewish Town teemed with haunts that emptied the purse and destroyed the liver.

One of the best known was the shady U Dejlů, haven and hide-out for all manner of riff-raff. Founded by the penniless Mamert Dejl, the ex-proprietor of a Malá Strana "yellow house" (that is, a brothel) and of the Stará Slavia Café, U Dejlů was a gambling casino, tavern and hide-out for the underworld all in one, and in its damp, foul-smelling basement (called "Žbluňk", a word meant to imitate the sound of a body falling into a swamp) swarms of the squalid – scoundrels, thieves and counterfeiters – set up camp on rotten sacks of straw. There, by the flickering light of smoky oil lamps, the "žbluňkaři", who were forbidden entrance to the tavern proper, performed on combs wrapped in tissue paper, gave readings and played cards unbeknownst to the elect above. Every so often rooster-plumed policemen would burst into the catacombs, but the innkeeper managed to keep his guests fairly well concealed. When in 1893 he hanged himself from a tree, the police closed both the upstairs tavern and the basement.[2]

88

On the same day a pub known as The Battalion (Batalión) also closed its doors, a fact mentioned by the puppet master Zwakh in his tale of the vicissitudes of Dr Hulbert in Meyrink's *Golem*. Hulbert's real name was Uher, František Uher. He was born in 1830 and achieved a certain fame as a jurist and deputy to the Bohemian Diet. According to Zwakh, "his face was full of warts, and his legs as crooked as a dachshund's" and he lived like a beggar in an attic.[1] The beautiful woman he married – she was twenty years his junior – betrayed him with his best friend, a certain Lieutenant Hojer, the two of them fleeing overseas after robbing him blind.[2] In Meyrink's version, the frivolous wife – who is of noble birth, but utterly dowryless – runs off with a poor student whom the childless Hulbert had been supporting without the slightest suspicion.

Now the melodrama begins. Upon learning of her infidelity (or, in Meyrink, upon finding them together) Uher falls over like *an uprooted oak*. The traitorous jade! The shameless hussy! He recovers from his fainting spell, then shows signs of madness; he tries to kill himself twice, then seeks solace in alcohol. Meyrink has the husband surprise the adulteress as he brings her a bouquet of roses for her birthday:

> They say that the blue gentian can lose its colour forever once it has felt the pale, sulphurous lightning streak that announces the approach of a hailstorm. It is certainly a fact that the old man's soul was numbed from the day that saw the destruction of his happiness.[3]

He leaves his warm home and is reduced to sleeping in stalls and basements and on rubbish heaps like a *tandlmark* reject. Dressed in rags, quivering with fever, a shadow of his former self, he begs his former colleagues in juridical Latin for alms, which he spends on drink with his new colleagues, the dregs of society.

The novelist Ignát Herrmann recalls running into the real Uher for the first time in 1869.

> His feet swam in elastic-sided boots so loose and worn that they turned his short, jerky steps into a kind of shuffle, which was reinforced by a constant shaking of the knees. His trouser legs were frayed and covered with a thick crust of mud, his long, tight, heavily faded reddish-brown coat buttoned to just below the chin. Clearly the man was wearing no shirt and perhaps no undergarments, for the trousers flapped loosely as if blown by the wind. A filthy handkerchief covered his swollen, almost bloated face around the chin and ears; its knot on the top of his head was hidden by a threadbare bowler.

When Herrmann's brother, a lawyer, gave Uher a silver coin, "he greedily grabbed at it with his grimy hands. He had swollen cheeks, heavy bags under dull, watery eyes, a dripping wet moustache and a beard as bristly as a convict's."[4]

89

On the day Meyrink's Hulbert surprises his wife with her lover, he has come home drunk from the Salon Loisitschek, the tavern that later becomes his haunt. In fact, Meyring has confused Loisitschek's with The Battalion. The detail of the tin spoons chained to the table (Zwakh beats time with one of them)[1] identifies Hulbert's bar as the latter. (In Šmíd's comedy *Batalión* the spoons are secured with iron wires and to the pans rather than to the tables).

But Meyrink's Loisitschek, packed with ghost-like prostitutes and other diabolical types, differs both from The Batalión and the actual Loisitschek, a smoke-filled, down-at-heel dive located between the Jewish Town Hall and the Old-New Synagogue, which survived longer than most Fifth Quarter beerhalls. The Salon Loisitschek sprang to life after midnight, an out-of-tune piano played by an old lodger nicknamed Signor Maestro competing with the raucous singing of the whores as they drummed up business among the toughs and drunks, later retiring to be bedded and partake of the joys of the flesh. The owner, Alois Florian –

alias Lojza or Lojzíček (Loisitschek) – a chubby little man with a large pine cone of a head nestling between sunken shoulders, ended by committing suicide like Dejl.[2]

These holes and dives and dens of iniquity were as alike as two peas in a pod. Meyrink transforms Loisitschek's into a combination of *secese* and the Hoffmannesque, a *Tingeltangel* both bawdy and dream-like, a cavern of magic masks, ambivalent spirits and bistro wags disfigured by the angel of perdition.

90

The Battalion, the unsavoury Jewish tavern at the corner of Platnéřská and U radnice and opposite The Green Frog (U zelené žáby), was a hang-out for the destitute and forlorn, a natural headquarters for Hulbert-Uher.[1] If the smoke-filled darkness of its low, narrow basement could have been penetrated by a beam of light, it would have illuminated a swarm of deathly pale faces beggaring all description, drunken swindlers intoning in a hoarse singsong, foul whores breaking out in uproarious laughter, cloudy-eyed tatterdemalions breathing their last, panderers, card-sharps and ruffians. The furnishings in this lair of crumbling bricks and encrusted walls consisted of a few benches and tables (the ones the rusty spoons were fastened to), a broken mirror mounted near the door, a small stove, a pile of casks containing rum and other spirits, like juniper and *persiko*, which the regulars drank with the garlic soup they bought at the eating house across the road, and a counter bursting with decanters, jugs and greasy glasses, that is, the bar, behind which the innkeeper, a stocky, hunchbacked ex-sutler, reigned supreme together with his wife, who had once been a prison guard and was therefore called "the screw".

It had been known as The Battalion since the winter's night when a drunk scribbled the word in chalk on its decrepit door. Hulbert assumes leadership of the "lions of revelry" there, a brotherhood of outcasts ready to go through thick and thin for one another. The Battalion, the chorus of this "rag ballad",[2] obey him unquestioningly. He directs their incursions, administers the money they beg or steal, keeps the "archives" and maintains the collective wardrobe, a repository for two types of "dress attire": gala the one, begged from big wigs for special occasions like police summonses and weddings, in which the tramps looked distracted and out-of-place, like asses in robes, and business the other, a set of leprous rags so indecent that the police felt compelled to nab anyone who wore them (which was precisely the point: in prison the Battalion member would receive a better set, which upon release he would sell to a rag-and-bone man, the money thus earned going into a common kitty).

Meyrink's jurist drinks like one possessed until he drops under the table and falls fast asleep, and when (more melodrama!) he awakes and tells his cronies of his past and unhappy love – his foundry of woe, his custom-house of anguish, his warehouse of troubles – the buzzing, yelling and laughter cease as if by magic. The tramps doff their caps and lower their heads, and a whore places a half-wilted flower in his hand.[3]

Much as his friends try to tear him away, he always returns to his Battalion, his *persiko* and – after a joyous welcome from his mates – his tatters. In the novel he is found frozen to death one morning on a bench on the banks of the Vltava; in fact, he was found beaten and abandoned on a pile of refuse in a tenement entrance hall and taken to the Hospital of the Brothers of Mercy, where he died on 11 September 1871.

It was a custom at the time for the funeral of every alumnus of Charles University to be attended by the deacon and beadle of his Faculty. Behind the hearse transporting the mortal remains of Hulbert-Uher to the mortuary at Olšany Cemetery, the representatives of the Faculty of Jurisprudence and the beadle holding a gold chain on a purple brocade cushion proceeded in a solemn gait and full regalia, followed by the monks of the Brothers of Mercy and the entire weeping Battalion, the entire mob of ragamuffins, one of whom, according to Meyrink, was clad in strips of newspaper bound with string.

Meyrink also writes that Hulbert bequeathed each Battalion member a daily bowl of soup at Loisitschek's, whereas in fact the Battalion broke up after Uher's death and his acolytes soon gave up the ghost, through drink or malnutrition. As for the tavern, it fell victim to the exterminating angel of urban renewal.

91

Hulbert-Uher has become a key figure in Prague mythology, legend having made his story infinitely more sorrowful than it was in fact. The principal popularizer of the myth, an actor and folksinger by the name of František Leopold Šmíd, played Doctor Ungr (Uher), "king of the vagabonds", in his own one-act fantasy *Batalión*.[1]

Šmíd (1848–1915) founded the first Prague café-chantant at U bílé labutě (The White Swan Inn), the model for a large number of Prague cabarets (of which the U Rozvařilů is still remembered because of its association with Apollinaire). He specialized in sketches of such old-Prague figures as good-natured idlers and *pepíci*, that is, young toughs with berets pulled over one ear and cigars in their mouths.

His light comedies teemed with petty thieves, concertina players, slum philosophers, tavern whores and tavern heroes, all closely related to Uher and his ups and downs.

Šmíd's *Batalión*, "a portrait of an alcoholic milieu", describes that "den of iniquity" with tearful pathos, his main premise being that life in the underground is more honourable than the life of the so called upright and just. Although his colleagues do what they can to pull him out of the mire, Ungr returns time after time to the world of the rabble, so disgusted is he by the multifarious hypocrisy of "honest folk".

Šmíd poured his own bitterness as a small-time actor into the disappointments of the fallen jurist. His play exploits all the lachrymose resources of the nineteenth century, including the obligatory scene in which a streetwalker meets her tubercular son. Perched on a beer barrel, staring into empty space, Ungr-Šmíd emitted the most painful "woe is me" imaginable and with a drunk's halting voice sang a plaint that brought tears to the eyes of many a desperate, shattered soul:

> Oh, my life is all in shambles,
> a hopeless babe I cry.
> I've fallen into brambles,
> but what's the use to sigh?
>
> My sweetest love has vanished,
> my sun has lost its glow.
> may God now have you banished,
> for you have left me so.[2]

In another mediocre one-acter, *Vůdce "Bataliónu"* (The Commander of "The Battalion") by Josef Hais-Týnecký (1885–1964), Uher lands in the Na Karlově poorhouse, where he plays this song on the organ between hymns. Hais-Týnecký's hero overcomes his yearning for the low life, resuming an orderly existence in the hope that the woman who betrayed him for an officer's epaulettes will one day return. When she snubs him once and for all, however, Uher tears off tie and collar, bursts into insane laughter and curses decent society for its "window-dress morality".[3]

Legend has handed down the names of the lost souls who belonged to Uher's band. The Noseless One (Beznoska, alias Steinfelder) was a beanpole with a nose as flat as a pancake, who sold scissors and "remade nature", that is, painted living birds to give more sheen to their feathers and sewed one animal into the skin of another, turning sparrows into canaries and mice into moles and palming them off as "marvels" at the *tandlmark*. Something of a forerunner of Hašek-Švejk, he also caught mutts in the street, invented pedigrees for them and sold them to the gullible.

Vondra, a broad-shouldered, heavy man with a red nose and soldier's whiskers waxed into a handlebar moustache, told tall tales about his heroic deeds as a mercenary in the Papal Army. He fought so bravely against "Pimont" as a sergeant major of the "Primo Bataliono Catchatory Estery" that he was awarded a silver "medallo" he later pawned to pay for *persiko*. Vojta Mušek posed as a misunderstood dramatic genius. Tossing his luxuriant locks, he would declaim Shakespeare and lament having to throw his pearls before swine. Mušek came to Uher's nest direct from a provincial theatre in a costume that The Battalion quickly sold at the *tandlmark*. Bohouš Novák, a one-time student and full-time consumptive who had passed through a number of reformatories and prisons, hawked sketches, sang lewd songs in elegant haunts and turned over all his earnings to the Battalion kitty. Švarc, a chemist, arrived at the gin mill dressed as a Turk. After being dismissed from a brewery for drunken behaviour, he had travelled throughout the Balkans in the company of Gipsies, grooms, wild boar hunters, bandits and itinerant actors. The student Švestka, who was crazy for the guitar, dissipated the family wealth on binges. And of course, The Battalion had its poet, its bard of anguish and despair: Václav Šolc (1838–71), author of *Prvosenky* (Primroses, 1868).

92

The Uher myth parallels the trajectories of many nineteenth century *débauchés* whose lives came to an end in the morass of the taverns. Ignát Herrmann attempted to expose Uher's pathetic story by removing the allure with which Šmíd had embellished it – an undertaking at least as pointless as ousting the alchemists from the Golden Lane.

After careful research Herrmann ascertained that František Uher was born on 23 January 1825 in Bystré (Waltersdorf, district of Lanškroun) and studied law in Olomouc and Prague, where he earned his degree in 1856. He was elected deputy to the Bohemian Diet in 1861, but lost his seat on 26 April 1864 as a result of repeated absence or drunkenness. In 1861 he married a country girl, the sixteen-year-old daughter of a well-to-do soap manufacturer. Not only was Anita twenty years his junior; she was in love with a young merchant. But Uher's title and position had dazzled her mother and Uher needed the dowry to settle his debts. After the wedding Uher neglected his wife, disappearing for weeks at a time, and before long he had run through her estate and was forced to sell most of the furniture. At this point someone – her mother or stepfather – went to Prague to fetch her and what was left of her goods and chattels. According to Herrmann, then, she neither made off with Uher's money nor fled overseas with his best friend; she simply returned to the town of her birth in eastern Bohemia. Once there, she flirted, went to dances and eventually created a great stir by having an affair with a miller, whom she married after Uher's death. But the miller took to the bottle, contracted a pile of debts and kicked the bucket, and Anita moved away to Vienna and in with a railwayman.[1]

Thus with the intent of creating an Uher-Hulbert unlike that of the myth, an Uher who was a heavy drinker before being betrayed, Herrmann fabricated a melodrama no less mawkish, though lacking the magic, nocturnal, infernal element.

Uher's legal credentials bear no resemblance to the magical sciences of E. T. A. Hoffmann's archivists and doctors of law. Anyone wishing to bring him to literary life would have to remove him from the tender hands of the *feuilletonistes* and magnify the grain of madness, rebellion and desolation the legend has bestowed upon him, make Uher's stinking ditch of a kingdom a mysterious, malevolent *Panoptikum* rather than a gout-ridden refuge for pitiful derelicts.

There is much in the The Battalion – with its drunks and fallen women, its consumptives and fakers, its actor reciting *Hamlet* and despising those who do not understand him – reminiscent of Gorky's *Lower Depths*, though it lacks a Satin to express hope in the destiny of man and a Luka to play the beggar apostle. A demonic alcoholism has brought them down once and for all, and there is no powder to cleanse the lice from their rags, no drink to quench the thirst of their souls, in short, no salvation. As Hamm and Clov maintain, everything is nothing. Vojta Mušek may well have ended The Battalion by hanging himself – as does the actor in Gorky's play.

93

The dives, cafés and streets of Prague have had more than their share of eccentrics, *podivíni*, jokers, *Lustigmacher*, wiseacres and *meshugoim*.[1]

Examples from the early part of the last century abound in the novels and plays of Josef Jiří Kolár. Take the Baron Bonjour, dance master extraordinary. His face painted with pink and white greasepaint, his eyebrows and hair smeared with lampblack, he roams through Prague in tails, a flowered waistcoat, a red cravat and white *Lederhosen*. His beloved but frivolous Sidonie has run off with a circus rider, and the melancholy Baron patters along with small minuet-like steps muttering "Sidonie! Sidonie!" into his cravat and clutching – in a hand sheathed in a dirty yellow glove, like the Officer in Strindberg's *Dream Play* – a bouquet of wilted flowers.[2]

Rosina-Rosalia, the Misses Pug (*slečny Mopslové*), was the name given to a pair of old maid twins with the same features, gestures and hoarse voices who lived with their pot-bellied cur in a rat-hole in Dead Man's Street (Umrlčí ulice) in Malá Strana.[3] Thin, wrinkled and frowning, with hooked noses and vicious grey eyes, they wore the same faded petticoats with the same worn-out trains, black veils and – demonic figures that they were – crumpled violet hats with a nibbled puff of pheasant feather swaying on top.[4]

At the end of the nineteenth century middle-class Prague families kept bulging albums of head-and-shoulder daguerreotypes in the drawers of the writing desk, on the shelves of the *veškostn*[5] or in the sitting-room on an oval table, from which they peeked out at plump armchairs upholstered in percale and at porcelain statuettes and silver trinkets in the glass-front sideboard. I found an interesting old photo album in the Hlochs' house in Karolina Světlá Street containing silver-plated copper period portraits of lottery soothsayers with greasy sneers and Egyptian almanacs,[6] weather prognosticators, pub orators, purveyors of valuable secrets, actresses who had seen better days – in a word, all manner of outlandish specimens from late in the last century and early in ours.

One of the most prominent Prague *Lustigmacher* of the time was Karlíček Bumm, a poor fellow who lost his mind because of a girl who left him in the lurch or, according to another version, a fire that left him penniless.[7] He would sit mournfully on the steps of the Hybernská Street station selling paper flags and surrounded by riffraff, who mocked him as the riff-raff in one of Neruda's "arabesques" mocks Jóna the Idiot,[8] his humility exploding into a torrent of abuse whenever they yelled "Kapsa hoří" (Your pocket's burning). He was celebrated in a Czech-German ditty worthy of the nonsense rhymes of Wilhelm Busch.

A decided contrast to Karlíček's sullen expression was the jolly face of the Doctor (pan Doktor), an idiot who wandered about Malá Strana wearing lenseless horn-rimmed glasses and showing off the little Latin he knew like a bogus priest. Another idiot, "Chaloupko, tancuj!" ("Dance, Chaloupka!"), imitated the clumsy, simpering ways and dances of a bear for a few coppers from drunks.[9] Then there was *der schlafende Honzíček* (Sleeping Honzíček) who would walk the byways of the Old Town in the dark with a pannier of pretzels on his shoulders to which loiterers would help themselves without awakening the supposed sleepwalker.[10] Jakob Weiß, also called Haschile, was king of the beggars, oracle of the mendicants. He was known for his large nose and for walking at a dizzying pace in the middle of the road. He never accepted less than ten kreutzers from his tavern patrons.[11]

A veritable bedlam of eccentrics. But no one could outdo the imagination of the tall, slim Tobacco Man (Tabákový muž), who sashayed up and down the streets of Prague during the 1870s in a brown suit, a calico shirt with a brown pattern, a flowing brown silk fichu, a brown hat, brown cloth shoes and brown gloves and balancing a Virginia cigar between his fingers like Kokoschka's portrait of Baron Victor van Dirsztay. His hair was brown, as was his watch chain. Only his spectacles were of clear glass, but he often wiped them with a brown silk handkerchief. Thus completely orchestrated in Havana brown – even his skin and whiskers were dark – he looked like an oversized cigar, the god of nicotine; it was only natural he should be called Virginius.

A tobacco fanatic like Manilov in *Dead Souls*, Virginius (that is, the Czech-German writer Eduard Maria Schranka) kept a collection of every imaginable smoking requisite: Meerschaum pipes with silver trim and mouthpieces of every size and shape, pipes of briar, amber, clay, terra-cotta, Turkish hookahs and *čibuky* encased in silk and brocade, decorated with purl and pearls, opium pipes, matches, old lighters, agate and glass saucers with pinches of rappee, scaglietta and snuff. Facing the gargantuan cabinet where he kept it all stood a smaller cupboard piled high with books from every period on the cultivation and uses of Nicotiana Tabacum (Solanaceae).

Virginius's museum-like digs boasted brown wallpaper with arabesques of green tobacco leaves and a number of genre pictures portraying people smoking. The floor, the partition, the rug and bed (from pillow cases to eiderdowns and covers) were also brown, brown the slippers beneath the bed. Virginius displayed pyramids of boxes with shiny chewing or cut tobacco, Maryland tobacco, bowl reamers, wooden candlesticks for lighting cigars with "Fidibus" brand cigarette papers and myriad other trifles for smokers. In addition to histories of gloves, beer and soup, he had, needless to say, written a *Braunbuch*, a cento of anecdotes about tobacco.[12]

94

In a novella by Bohumil Hrabal[1] a loquacious old man of the sort Hašek used in his sketches churns out an endless monologue, an entertaining, babbly chat, a web of memories from the time of the Dual Monarchy, bombastic phrases, wild references to pious parables and dream books, erotic anecdotes, tall tales and tittle-tattle – a stream of chatter constantly shifting between subtle deceit and simplemindedness on parade. With these Prague eccentrics one is hard put to tell where the former begins and the latter ends. Perhaps the best one can say is that they are as multilayered as an onion.

One master of just such ambiguity was the vagabond Weissenstein

Karel, who frequented the German-Jewish literary café called the Café Arco. He was a hydrocephalic, he wore outlandish suits, he spoke an idiosyncratic mixture of Czech, German and Yiddish and he was always referred to by his last name first and his first name last. Weissenstein Karel's biographers (Haas, Werfel and Urzidil) have stylized his life story into a virtual parody of a motif dear to the Expressionists: the revolt of the son against a tyrannical father.[2] The father owned a filthy village tavern in Moravia; the son, who began reading teetotalist pamphlets as a child, climbed up on a table in the drunk-filled establishment one Sunday night and threatened fire and brimstone to both tipplers and father, who sold a yellowish grape marc as Kümmel and a nondescript blackberry brew as wine; father threw son out on his ear.

The deeds of Weissenstein Karel were inspired by a Salvation Army-like morality, a caricature of the fraternal tolerance advocated by Werfel in *Der Weltfreund*. After being ejected by his family, he wandered from fair to fair with a pedlar who sold wonder-working contraptions, then worked as an apprentice in a butcher's shop. As the butcher was constantly drunk and beat his wife, he advised her to leave him, and when she spilled the beans to her husband poor Weissenstein Karel had to make a run for it. He ended up at the Café Arco, where he made friends with the regulars and proceeded to live off them, amusing them with his half-serious tirades against alcoholism, adultery and loose morals. Try as they did to find him work, he always returned as if nothing had happened, as if he hadn't the heart to leave them.

Prague eccentrics are driven by an uncontrollable gift of gab that can produce an overwhelming effect on their interlocutors. Hrabal calls them *pábitelé*, "palaverers" – part teller of tales, part blusterer.[3] As a rule they are small men overpowered by their surroundings, "faded lives" (Neruda)[4], "miniature pearls at the bottom" (Hrabal),[5] who find consolation in the extravagance and orotundity of their own voices, in the magnificent variety of logorrhoea practised by Švejk. I once met one of these misfits burning to regale you with their verbal abundance. His name was Topol, and he was a blondish, washed-out sponger, but very handy, who took every kind of job from coalman to prop man, a false innocent with beady blue eyes who yearned for beer the way orioles yearn for pears and plums and claimed that cabbage juice lessened the smell of hops. When you dropped in on him, he tap-danced up to you like a provincial Fred Astaire, bombarding you with witticisms and anecdotes of his exploits with third-rate actresses enormous both in front and behind.

There was not much difference in old Prague between such voluble oddballs and the bohemians who gravitated towards Jaroslav Hašek. A typical example is the painter-actor Emil Artur Pittermann Longen, whom Kafka mentions in his diaries for his "mimic jokes", for a "pretty jump of a clown over a chair in the emptiness of the wings".[6] Longen – an easygoing chap, a "human rarity" and "unholy blend of urbanite and redskin", as he defines himself in the incoherent novel *Herečka* (The Actress)[7] – also wrote a number of comedies and cabaret farces set in the Austro-Hungarian world in which dramatis personae and subject matter resemble those in Kisch and Hašek: military, malingering and anal-oriented.[8] More important here, however, are his quizzical nature and propensity for prattle and provocation. It is no accident that Kubišta complains to a fellow painter, Vincenc Beneš, in a letter dated 1910, "Pittermann's garrulity and his constant bickering are a downright terror."[9]

Don't forget me, signor Ripellino, I hear one of the drollest *Lustigmacher* call out. Ferda Mestek de Podskal was a booth owner, junkman, *Hanswurst*, flea trainer and *Hochstapler*. A tiny man with a huge pointed nose,[10] he epitomized the fairgrounds atmosphere of Prague during the final decades of the Monarchy, the Prague that exhibited Donna Hypolita with bosoms as big as melons, semi-spheres capable of supporting a beam with two men on top;[11] the Moravian giant Josef Drasal, who could maim a cow with a single blow and light his cigar, slapstick style, from a street lamp;[12] and the Marquise de Pompadour, a midget in Rococo dress accompanied by an ingratiating retinue of dwarfs.[13]

With the arrogance of the toughs from the district of Podskalí where he was born, Ferda Mestek tacked the title "de Podskal" to his surname. He was to be found at all major fairs in the countries of the Austro-Hungarian Monarchy cajoling reluctant crowds in front of small circuses and menageries. According to Bass, "he had gone on tour with the highest-ranking officer in the Bulgarian Army, a flea circus, five midgets, three giant Russian brothers, a wax museum, a two-headed calf, a snake lady, a disappearing lady, a tattooed lady, a bearded lady, Ilona the levitating lady and Princess Ygarta the spider lady".[14] Most often, however, he sold patent medicines: "cold lemonade as a remedy for cholera, cloves as a prophylactic against illegitimate children, a soap guaranteed to cure the gout and sweets that prevented hair loss".[15] (Baldness seems to have been a central issue in the Habsburg Empire, as evidenced by the disquisition on hair delivered by Švejk to Major-General von Schwarzenberg[16] and the advertisement featuring the once bald Anna Csillag, whose ankle-long, flowing tresses were restored by a miraculous balsam she herself concocted.[17])

In one of his stories[18] Jaroslav Hašek describes a trip to the Bohemian provinces with the "snake-charmer" Ferda Mestek and a certain Švestka – the owner of a roller-coaster, a carousel and a shooting-gallery – to exhibit a shark ("the terror of the Northern seas") they had bought in Prague from a fishmonger one morning after an all-night spree. The public crowds round out of curiosity "as when there are holy relics to kiss". But the prank takes a bad turn and the trio ends up in the cooler when the shark decomposes and, despite liberal sprinklings of scent, spectators faint at the stench.

Ferda was dogged by bad luck, unable to hold any profession for long. "If you were an undertaker," his wife told him, "people would stop dying. If you got an order to make a coffin, the deceased would bring it back the next day and say the whole thing was just a joke."[19] Ferda spent his worst days in the taverns, his nose, an enormous growth, "hanging sentimentally over an empty glass like a pickle with the end bitten off", though once he scented filthy lucre it "bounced up like a clown about to do his act".[20]

But in the annals of Prague anecdotes the name Mestek will always be most closely identified with the flea circus. Quite common in Central Europe at the time,[21] it consisted of a parade of fleas drawing other fleas in a tiny cart. Ferda's performances were especially spectacular; he was the Barnum of the flea circus. He owned a huge assortment of fleas, a veritable stable: acrobat fleas, high-wire fleas, flea ballerinas in satin-paper tutus, fleas that duelled with paper sabres, a flea orchestra.[22] In the slapdash memoirs he tossed off at Kisch's instigation, he boasts of having purchased only "human fleas from good families" and rejected all those preserved in bottles of alcoholic drinks (he would not tolerate moral turpitude in his fleas) or boxes of Seidlitz salts (they had chronic diarrhoea).[23] His picaresque existence, his braggadocio and the fecal flavour of the stories surrounding him make the "noble" Mestek de Podskal, whose coat of arms shows "three slaps in the face against a blue field",[24] very much like Josef Švejk or, rather, his friend and drinking companion, Švejk's creator, Jaroslav Hašek.

95

The biography of Jaroslav Hašek (born in Prague on 30 April 1883) can be told as a series of silent films: Hašek the apothecary, Hašek the editor of a zoological journal, Hašek the husband, Hašek the dog seller, Hašek the political leader, Hašek the Bolshevik Commissar, but most of all Hašek the tramp and beer-hall clown. It is a biography strewn with anecdotes, in which the truth is all but inseparable from the nonsense brewed in the rambling reminiscences of his fellow revellers – the painter Josef Lada, the authors Emil Artur Longen and František Langer, the thespian Václav Menger, the cabaret artist and novelist Eduard Bass, the vagabond writer Zdeněk Matěj Kuděj and Franta Sauer, insurance agent, saccharine smuggler, itinerant bookseller, ham actor and *Spaßmacher*[1] – in their turn, heroes of other pranks and other stories, which taken together form an archipelago of buffoonery, a saga of suds.

We first encounter Hašek – like Ensor, who is immersed in the trinkets of his father's Ostend gift shop,[2] and Charlie Chaplin, who is absorbed in dismantling an alarm clock in a pawn shop[3] – as an apprentice in The Three Golden Balls (U tří zlatých koulí), the pharmacy of stubborn, sanctimonious Ferdinand Kokoška, nicknamed Radix, on the corner of Na Perštýně and Martinská. Like all "materialist shops" (apothecaries) in old Prague its sign was a brightly-coloured angel with spread wings.[4] By the dim light of that damp, narrow hole in the ground, which was rather like an alchemist's laboratory and smelled of lacquer, cinnamon, camphor drops, rat poison, turpentine, shoe polish, rosin, bear's foot and lime-blossom tea, Hašek mixed miracle-working infusions and concoctions such as beer laced with laxative powder.

The silent comedy in Kokoška's pharmacy did not last for long. Radix flew into a rage when Hašek added a beard and pince-nez to a cow he had painted – he made a hobby of glass painting – thereby turning the Alpine ruminant into a fair likeness of the severe shopkeeper. Švejk has another Kokoška tale to tell: "I was," he says,

> apprenticed to an apothecary, to a Mr Kokoška's at Na Perštýně, in Prague. He was an awfully rum fellow, and once when by mistake I set fire to a barrel of petrol in the cellar and the house burnt down he kicked me out. After that the guild wouldn't ever accept me anywhere and so because of that stupid barrel of petrol I couldn't finish my apprenticeship.[5]

Hoping to marry the woman he loved by securing steady employment, Hašek became the editor of a popular magazine for animal breeders and nature lovers, *Svět zvířat* (The Animal World), in 1908.[6] For publicity he would take a mastiff from magazine's kennel on walks around Prague, much like Jérôme Savary and his "sad beasts". The queen of the kennel was a trained but rather unruly ape named Miss Julie that Hašek had obtained from the Hagenbeck Circus in Hamburg.[7]

Hašek left his mark on the journal, turning it into a kind of fanciful Brehm, a catalogue of nonexistent animals worthy of a Grand Magic Circus or, better still, of Dr Katzenberger's cabinet of monsters as invented by Jean Paul: the tyrannosaurus, the cacatu bat, the Asvail bear, the cerulean shark, the paleozoic flea (*Paleopsylla khuniana*), the sulphur-bellied whale.[8] The whale, "equipped with a bladder full of formic acid", and "Engineer Khun's flea", a parasite of prehistoric moles, reappear in *Švejk* in the mouth of Hašek's alter ego volunteer Marek when he tells how as editor of *Svět zvířat* he devised

> the Artful Prosperian, a mammal of the kangaroo family; the Edible Ox, the ancient prototype of the cow; the Sepica Infusorian . . . Did Brehm and all those who followed him know of my bat from Iceland, the Faraway Bat, or of my domestic cat from the peak of Mount Kilimanjaro, called the Irritable Bazouky Stag-Puss?[9]

These articles, which he often signed with the name of his friend Josef Lada, raised eyebrows in the scientific community, yet with the straightest of faces Hašek continued to discourse upon alcoholism in animals or their reactions to music and announce that muskrats bred at Dobříš Castle had invaded the Vltava or that werewolves would soon be sold as pets like dogs. Although volunteer Marek states in *Švejk* that his bizarre inventions had driven the owner of the magazine, a certain Václav Fuchs, to distraction and death, the real-life silent animal-world film ended with the dismissal of the phlegmatic mystifier.[10]

There is a knowing shrewdness behind these *tandlmark* "marvels". No wonder Švejk tells the story of a "chap called Mestek" who had a peep-show in Havlíček Street where he exhibited a "mermaid", that is, a common Žižkov whore, whose "legs were wrapped in green gauze, which was supposed to represent a tail. Her hair was painted green and she wore gloves with green cardboard fins attached, and on her spine she had a kind of rudder fixed with a cord".[11]

Mr Josef Mayer, a highly respected stucco decorator and owner of a three-storeyed house, could scarcely have been inclined to grant his daughter's hand to a pauper, anarchist and drunk like Hašek, and although Mayer's daughter really longed for solid bourgeois *Gemütlichkeit* she admired her Grýša (her pet name for Richard the Lionhearted) for his acts of bravado and admired him even more when he was locked up on 1 May 1907 for assaulting a policeman.[12]

Hašek's letters to Jarmila – for such was her name – abound in mawkish banality, tokens of marital devotion, kitsch and childlike frankness. He constantly formulates resolutions to turn over a new leaf, give up drinking, dress decently, put an end to dissipation. Like his feigned return to the bosom of the Church and renunciation of anarchy, the affected, flowery style of these missives is nothing more than a comic ploy, a marital game in which the bohemian puts on the mask of the bourgeois. Only thus could he obtain Mr Mayer's long-contested consent.

After the wedding, which was celebrated on 15 May 1910 at Saint

Ludmila's in Prague's Vinohrady district, Hašek took on the role of a wedding-cake figure, telling his chums that he had been promised a large sum of money provided he kept away from the bottle for a year. But vagabond habits won out in the end, and he soon disappeared for days at a time. Nor did the birth of his son Richard (Ríša) in April 1912 cure him of his ways. According to one account, Hašek left the baby behind in a tavern where he had intended to show it off to his cronies; another story has it that he won the money for its pram at cards, a third that he bolted on the excuse of buying beer for the Mayers who had dropped in on the new mother.[13] The truth of the matter is that Jarmila took shelter with the newborn baby under her parents' roof.

In Russia, during the Civil War, Hašek married an orphan by the name of Shura, that is, Alexandra Gavrilovna Lvova, whom he had met at Ufa while a political commissar in the Fifth Army.[14] Although the Russian girl docilely followed him back to Czechoslovakia, Hašek attempted to patch things up with Jarmila in Prague, writing her sweet letters that exuded remorse, wished her luck as a writer of women's stories, described the persecution he had suffered under the Bolsheviks and begged forgiveness for his past sins. Much as he swore that his marriage to Shura was a mistake, he was unable to put the broken pieces of his marriage to Jarmila together again. Nonetheless Jaroslav and Jarmila saw each other in secret from time to time, and Jarmila introduced him to their nine-year-old son as "a journalist". Jaroslav, who had worn a locket around his neck with his son's picture the whole time he was in Russia, ran his hand through the boy's hair and addressed him with the formal "you". Ríša was told his father was a Legionnaire who had been killed in Siberia.[15]

Late in 1911, Hašek opened a Cynological Institute (Kynologický ústav) or dog shop in the Košíře district of Prague. Together with his wily assistant Čížek he caught stray dogs and sold them as thoroughbreds with trumped-up pedigrees.[16]

Although this slapstick was over almost before it began – his customers quickly caught on to the fraud – Hašek passed his experience in the field on to Švejk, who (as we know) "lived by selling dogs – ugly, mongrel monstrosities whose pedigrees he forged".[17] The good soldier carries on with the police informer Bretschneider as an obliging dog fancier[18] and gives expert advice to Lieutenant Lukáš on dyeing dogs to make them look younger and inventing pedigrees.[19] Švejk makes use of his creator's skill as dog catcher when he causes a row by pinching the pinscher of the dim-witted Colonel Friedrich Kraus von Zillergut.[20]

The dogs in Hašek's bestiary are unfailingly repulsive. At one end

of the scale are the meek, dream-like creatures of Franz Marc, at the other
the "awful monsters" he palms off on Bretschneider:

> The Saint Bernard was a mixture of mongrel poodle and common
> street cur, the fox terrier had the ears of a dachshund and was
> the size of a butcher's dog, with bandy legs as though it had
> suffered from rickets. The head of the Leonberger recalled the
> hairy muzzle of a stable pinscher. It had a stubbed tail, was the
> height of a dachshund and had bare hindquarters like the famous
> naked American dogs.[21]

Both *tandlmark* monsters are worthy of Ferda Mestek's anacondas and
fleas.

In the spring of 1911, just in time for the elections to the Bohemian Diet,
Hašek and a group of disciples founded the "Strana mírného pokroku
v mezích zákona" (Party of Moderate Progress Within the Limits of the
Law).[22] The bogus party of beer-joint bohemians set up headquarters at U
Zvěřinů, also known as Kravín, and other local taverns, because "alcohol
is the milk of politics".[23] The bittersweet essence, the supposed guiding
principle of the party was that all radicalism is harmful and society must
develop gradually, smoothly. On one level at least its comical platform
of feigned obedience reflected Hašek's philosophy of taking life easy.

The meetings of the outlandish coterie soon became a rallying ground
for Prague artists and intellectuals. They would gather at eight, and after
the singing of a choral anthem written by the poet Josef Mach, Jaroslav
Hašek, "the greatest Czech writer",[24] would go on for hours and with
jocular dignity about the evils of alcohol, the rehabilitation of animals,
about saints, suffragettes, missionaries and tainted food – an endless
stream of blather, bogus quotations, wild exaggerations, outrageous
promises, orotund phrases and hilarious parodies of the slogans and
leaders of the other parties. Oblivious to catcalls and hisses from the
regulars and fortified with long draughts of beer, he hammered away
at the urgent need to abolish the charge for the use of public toilets and
the tip paid to janitors – a professional group that had his undying enmity
– for unlocking front doors at night.[25]

This single-reeler, a cabaret send-up of conservatism in general and
loyalty to the Habsburgs in particular, ended in a fiasco: the ludicrous
party received a total of twenty votes.

Hašek had a genius for improvisation, and like other protagonists of the
Prague bohème (Bass, Mach, Longen, Langer) he performed in satiric light
comedies, sketches and parodies at the Montmartre, the Kopmanka and –

with the "Maccabean Brothers" – at U Zvěřinů.[26] As an actor, however, he proved absolutely and utterly hopeless.

Yet after returning from the Soviet Union he joined the Červená Sedma (Seven of Hearts) Cabaret. Unkempt and tottering uncontrollably, he would stammer his way through the story "How I Met the Author of My Obituary", an invective against the poet Jaroslav Kolman-Cassius, who had given him up for dead in the confusion of the Revolution in a nasty 1919 article entitled "Zrádce" (The Traitor) that characterized him as a "rascal and play-actor".[27] In January 1921 Hašek delivered a rambling talk at the Červená Sedma on "Chinese and Mongolian Dress and Mores", in which (pretending to look for words in a dictionary that was actually a railway time-table) he stated with scholarly gravity that in Mongolian "cho" means horse, a pair of horses is "chocho" and "chochochochochocho" an entire herd.[28] It was pure dada. In September of the same year Kurt Schwitters and Raoul Hausmann gave a performance in Prague entitled "Merz und Antidada".[29]

When called to arms in 1915, Hašek half-seriously assumed the role of Habsburg patriot. Before leaving for České Budějovice, where the infantry regiment he was assigned to, the Ninety-First, was stationed, Hašek belted out military songs in the taverns, looking down his nose at civilians as a pack of malingerers.[30] But soon rumours about his troubles as a soldier started making the rounds. It was said that he had been arrested for desertion, that he had been thrown out of officers' training school, that he was feigning epilepsy.[31] Then the rumours grew more dire: a court martial had sentenced him to the noose for insubordination, he had drowned in the Dnestr or fallen in action in Galicia, he had been murdered by drunken sailors during a free-for-all in an Odessa dive, he had perished at the hands of Czech Legionnaires outraged at his betrayal.[32] Thus it was that "the Czech tendency to invent ballads", as František Langer writes, "ascribed the saddest fates to the greatest Prague humorist".[33] Or as Hašek himself later put it:

> During my five or six years in Russia I was murdered a number of times by various organizations and individuals. After returning home I discovered I had been hanged three times, executed twice by firing squads and drawn and quartered once by Kirghiz savages near the small lake of Kale-Yshel. Last but not least, I was said to have been done in during a wild brawl with drunken sailors in a tavern in Odessa. I find this last version the most probable.[34]

What actually happened was that after a long and arduous journey he reached the front at Sokal on the River Bug in Galicia, where his company suffered heavy casualties in July 1915. The panic in the Austrian lines was so great that when the unruffled Hašek returned with three hundred Russians prisoners, the Austrian commander, thinking them another enemy attack, fled with his troops.[35] Soon thereafter, during the battle of Khorupany (24 September), Hašek found the moment to go over to the enemy. The swaggering, garrulous nature of his companion in flight, a bricklayer from Hostivice by the name of František Strašlipka, proved a major influence on the character of the good soldier Švejk.[36]

In the prison camp at Totsk near Samara, where typhoid fever, dysentery and the Cossacks' *nagaika* raged, the Bohemian barfly became a fervent supporter of anti-Austrian resistance. When the Russians, who viewed the restive subjects of the Austrian Empire with mistrust, allowed Czech units to be formed in 1916, he joined up immediately and, in the Kiev periodical *Čechoslovan*, accused the recalcitrant of being Austrophiles and philistines while praising the Slavophile, pro-Tsarist Kievan group, which was at odds with the pro-Western Czechs in Petrograd. He also advocated the union of Bohemia with Romanov Russia, that is, the coronation of the Russian Tsar as King of Bohemia, with the same disconcertingly inane fervour with which he had advocated the cause of The Party of Moderate Progress Within the Limits of the Law. Though detained for writing a violent pamphlet against the members of the Petrograd section of the Czecho-Slovak National Council, he fought in the front lines when Masaryk's brigades defeated large Austrian and German units at Zborov (July 1917) in the futile Kerensky offensive.

When the October Revolution broke out, he initially opposed the Bolsheviks and dreamed of the Legions attacking Austria via the Caucasus, Persia and Romania. Yet the moment Masaryk incorporated them into the French armed forces and ordered them to be transferred to the West via Siberia, he espoused the Bolshevik cause and called upon Czech troops to join forces with the Red Army. There was no better way to be arrested by the Czecho-Slovak command. He escaped by pretending to be the "congenital idiot son of a German colonist in Turkestan" in Samara in 1918. New ambivalences and a new mask: a lost simpleton amidst the Tartars.

In September 1918 he was thrown in jail by the Reds, who mistook him for an enemy agent. Another *coup de théâtre*: at the end of the year he turned up in Bugulma in the general staff of the Twenty-Sixth Soviet Division. Sucked into the maelstrom of the Civil War, Yaroslav Romanych Gashek gave it his all, racing from Ufa to Omsk, from Novosibirsk to Krasnoyarsk. He edited periodicals and newspapers in Russian, Serb, Hungarian, German and even Buryatin-Mongol; he organized the foreign units of the Fifth Army and a secret counter-espionage section against the

Legion; he made a much-feared political commissar and, like Kubin's satrap Patera, ruled a region in Asia larger than Czechoslovakia.[37] But the most amazing yarn of all is that he never touched a bottle the whole time he was there.[38]

Hašek's many masks never hide his true nature, that of a wandering mountebank. From his early youth he loved to roam, to live out the myth of the vagabond (*tulák*) so dear to his generation.

No sooner had he taken a post as clerk at the Slavia Bank in 1902 than he fled the office for Slovakia and the Balkans, where an anti-Turkish revolt had just broken out.[39] A list of his peregrinations would fill many pages: Zdeněk Matěj Kuděj has documented the zigzag treks they took through central Bohemia during the summers of 1913 and 1914.[40] Restlessness also explains Hašek's support for the group of anarchist poets, of which he was the most unruly,[41] and his tendency to write a bit too effortlessly even in the din of the pubs, to whisk whatever he came up with to the editorial offices for a fee, which he immediately squandered on drink or shared with the poor.[42]

Hašek was as rooted in the hops of Prague taverns as ivy in the bark of an oak. He was a regular at over a hundred of them, the main signposts in the flood of alcohol being Tůmovka, Hlavovka, Montmartre, Deminka, U Fleků, U Kalicha (The Chalice) and U Zlatého litru (The Golden Litre).[43] Only at night, inflamed by drink, in dark, spittle-plastered dens and caves, beside scrawny, sullen drunks wearing clownish little hats like the ones drawn by Josef Čapek, in the pungent stench of beer mixed with latrine ammonia – only in Prague taverns did his imagination take flight. For him the tavern was not merely a garden of delights; it was a metaphorical model of the world, a world seen dimly through smoke-filled eyes and the dark glasses of intoxication.

Often he returned from his escapades with a contrite face and a promise to mend his ways, only to flee again the following day. All attempts to divert him from the taverns ended in failure. The explorer A. V. Frič, for example, put him up in his villa in Košíře (where he also kept a Cherokee Indian among his exotic collections), but Hašek made off every night. Frič had him shut up with provisions and a ream of stationery and still he escaped, leaving behind an empty larder and a flotilla of paper boats.[44]

Pimps, streetwalkers and every kind of eccentric and derelict the Prague slums had to offer – these were his friends. There was Jakl the circus director and Čimera the penniless itinerant actor and Esmeralda the tightrope walker and Karlas the wrestler and Cléo de Merodo [sic], former concubine of the King of the Belgians and current palmreader, but first and foremost, Ferda Mestek de Podskal (Hašek had played huckster for his flea circus) and the amiable thief Oldřich Zounek, alias Hanuška, whom he had met in prison.[45] Friendships with questionable types, the masks he assumed over the years, the inability to live a settled existence and the ease with which he wrote make Hašek similar to the Russian storyteller Kuprin – a merry companion of Gipsies and drunks, horse thieves and gamblers, artists of the Big Top (like the clown Zhakomino) and weightlifters (like the mustachioed Ivan Poddubny) – the Kuprin who refereed French wrestling championships in circus tents, worked as a fisherman and fireman and at many other jobs, the Kuprin who wrote off the cuff at tavern tables.[46]

Hašek constantly changed lodgings, though more often than not he slept in the corner of a tavern or with friends, whom he typically annoyed or disgusted with his ways. He made do with very little: a sofa, an overcoat as blanket and a rolled-up rug as pillow. All he could think of was, How can I get out of here? Where can I go?, as if lingering in one place would arouse the curiosity of Death. His least irregular address – though here too he was prone to dis- and re-appear like the prodigal son – was the house of the painter Josef Lada, and during the short periods he lived there he would hang a black plaque with a silver, death-notice-like border on the door saying: "Jaroslav Hašek Imperial-Royal Writer, Father of the Poor in Spirit and Certified Parisian Clairvoyant".[47]

Hašek had a tremendous relish for practical jokes; he might have stepped out of a novella by a Czech Sercambi or Sacchetti. Once the whim for jest took hold of his imagination, adieu restraint and moderation. The reminiscences of his drinking mates abound in his antics. I shall confine myself to two examples.

One night in February 1911 he climbed onto the parapet of the Charles Bridge near the statue of Saint John of Nepomuk and pretended he was about to jump into the Vltava. A hairdresser who happened to be walking by grabbed hold of him and called for help. Two policemen ran up. He started pulling the plumes off their caps. By the time they got to the police station, they were convinced he was a madman and had him put in an insane asylum, which – like Švejk several years later – he did not want to leave.[48] Accustomed as we are to Hašek the hoaxer, we cannot help wondering whether this was really a jest, a *Schabernack*, a grotesque ruse, a bit of drunk bravado? Or have we failed to notice the despair that pervades the innumerable tricks he played on himself and others?

When the Russian Army broke through the front in Galicia late in 1914 and word spread through Prague that "people in Náchod have started speaking Russian", Hašek took a room at the U Valšů Inn in Karolina Světlá Street, signing his name in the guest book as Ivan Fedorovich Kuznetsov (or, in other versions, Lev Nikolaevich Turgenev, or Ivan Ivanovich Ledrpalesík), a Kievan merchant born in Moscow. Purpose of trip: "Inspection of the Austrian High Command". The speechless porter, who thought he had caught a brazen spy, ran straight to the police. At the police station, where he was made to serve a five days' sentence, Hašek declared with the open face of a moron that he had simply wanted to make certain that police regulations regarding the registration of foreign citizens in wartime were being strictly enforced.[49]

A mixture of obstinacy, drunken malice and infantile temper keeps exploding in this "tipsy, wobbly, ecstatic Villon", this "medieval ghost from a painting by Brueghel or Schwaiger, all dirty yellow and pale red".[50] At heart a sly Slav peasant steeped in the smells of Prague's rich pot – his face as pasty as a loaf of bread, his eyes tiny but lively, his hair as tousled as a sparrow's nest – an "idiot of genius",[51] a rascal who changed guises as clowns change bowlers, he made himself into the most evocative mask in the city on the Vltava. Cocksure and quarrelsome, a "slovenly drunkard with a huge belly bulging over the belt of his trousers",[52] he incited brawls, confusion and apocalyptic malentendus, which he immediately dispelled with a childlike smile.[53] He lived a carnival-like, tavern existence because the tavern (like the insane asylum) enabled him to live on the brink, in violation, defiance, in Dadaist rejection of regulations and prohibitions.

On 19 December 1920 Jaroslav Hašek, alias Staidl, alighted from a train in a long, dark winter coat, grey felt boots and a Caucasian cap with Shura on his arm.[54] From the station he took a hackney cab to the Café Union, where he triumphantly introduced his second wife as Princess Lvova, niece of the head of the Provisional Government, whom he had snatched from the clutches of the Bolsheviks.

The recently-returned commissar was the talk of the beerhalls. His horrible cruelty was described in endless anecdotes. It was rumoured that he had massacred Shura's entire family and turned the orphaned girl into his slave, that he had sent thousands of Czechs and Slovaks to their death. The right-wing press led the way and the Legionnaires made threats, but the left was suspicious too.[55]

Tired of being serious for so long, Hašek parked Shura in a hotel room, tore off his *rubashka* and boots and plunged back into street life and the malty lake of the taverns. He took special pleasure in spreading the news of wild atrocities committed by the Bolsheviks, confirming to the sensation-hungry writer Olga Fastrová, for example, that the Bolsheviks ate the flesh of kidnapped Chinese.[56] Yet the sprees lacked their former pizzazz; the clowning was undermined by pangs of uncertainty and gloom.

Unable to pay the hotel bill, he moved Shura in with his boon companion Franta Sauer in the Žižkov district.[57] But in the end he needed Shura more than Jarmila: the patient and submissive Tartar orphan never held his binges against him, her only support in a foreign land, and made no attempts to better him.

Between beers Hašek began writing the novel *Osudy dobrého vojáka Švejka za světové války* (The Good Soldier Švejk and his Fortunes in the World War), which he and his publisher Franta Sauer originally intended to compete with the stories of Nat Pinkerton and Nick Carter that were being rediscovered at the time by the avant-garde group known as Devětsil. Black and yellow posters announced the publication of the book in weekly instalments, and Hašek and Sauer later hawked them from one Žižkov pub to the next.[58]

Inducing Hašek to carry on with the novel was no easy matter. Shura and the young poet Ivan Suk, secretary and bookkeeper of the publishing house, made regular rounds of his favourite haunts in search of him, and he would greet them with nasty looks and insults, after which he would order something to drink for the "Princess" to keep her quiet, and go on guzzling without so much as a glance in her direction. All Shura could do was smile meekly at his incoherent ramblings and wait until he decided to come home with her.

In August 1921 Hašek moved to the village of Lipnice on the Sázava (in southeastern Bohemia) on the advice of the painter Jaroslav Panuška, another member of his Beer and Practical Joke Society.[59] There he continued work on *Švejk* in a tavern called U Invalidů, dictating to a twenty-year-old clerk, the son of a local policeman, but constantly interrupting himself to chat or argue with the regular patrons. As soon as a chapter was complete, he sent it off to his new publisher (Synek, not Sauer), keeping only the last page of the dictated text for himself.[60]

That autumn a dramatization of the novel appeared on the stage of Longen's Revoluční scéna. Švejk was played by Karel Noll as a sturdy, pot-bellied folk figure.[61] Max Pallenberg's Švejk later eclipsed Noll's typically Prague Švejk, but Noll interpreted the character in several film versions.

Hašek was never to never see them. He continued to drink excessively, treating his new cronies to rounds of drinks, celebrating birthdays and anniversaries with libations and speeches, telling all-night anecdotes, making sailor's grog and sticking his nose into the kitchen in search of tasty dishes. With the first royalties from the book he bought a dilapidated little house in Lipnice with four entrances, one of which faced the poor district known as "Mizérie". Though asthmatic and bloated, he drank to the end.[62]

When he died, on 3 January 1923, no one took the obituary notice seriously – his passing had been announced too many times before.[63] The only people who came from the capital for the funeral were Kuděj, Panuška, his brother and his son Ríša, whom he had met only two or three times in his life.[64]

96

The night he was taken to the mental hospital after trying to jump off the Charles Bridge, Hašek claimed to be Ferdinand the Benign.[1] No survey of Prague eccentrics would be complete without this bald, slender sovereign (1793–1875), who abdicated the throne on 2 December 1848 in favour of his nephew Franz Joseph and retired to the Prague Castle. Ferdinand V was the last Austrian emperor to be crowned King of Bohemia (1836).[2]

The photos in my album show him as old and thin: he has small, doll-like hands; his gaunt, bland face is framed by a white beard; he is slouching in an armchair with his oversize ball of a pate sticking up over the head-rest. Ferdinand spent his days playing billiards with the house steward and cultivating plants that won prizes at flower shows. A music lover, he had played Viennese songs and dances at the keyboard as a youth and Bedřich Smetana went to the Castle twice a week, albeit reluctantly, to perform waltzes and marches for him.[3]

He dressed in mufti except on his birthday, when he took his antiquated general's uniform out of mothballs and reviewed the troops of the Prague garrison from his window as they paraded past the Castle. He felt more at home in Prague than in Vienna – he even claimed that the Prague climate had cured his epilepsy – and while the cruel host of Viennese aristocrats treated him with indifference, in Bohemia he was at least regarded as a novelty, a curiosity.

Regardless of the weather, he took a daily ride with his physician and a servant in a coach drawn by two white Lipizzaners. For all its gold-leaf ornamentation, it could not hold a candle to the extraordinary equipage of Frederick William I, a.k.a. Hessenkassel (1802–75). The former Elector of Hessen, who had sided with the Austrians in the War of 1866, lived in the Prague Windischgrätz Palace with royal pomp. Three pairs of horses sporting deep-yellow blankets drew his clattering carriage on its sturdy gilt-spoked wheels. A groom wearing a jockey outfit and wielding a white crop rode on one of the first pair.[4]

Ferdinand's carriage would proceed from the Castle down Ostruhová (Nerudova) Street, across the Charles Bridge and along the embankment. Pedestrians stopped and respectfully doffed their hats, while Ferdinand, huddling in a corner with drooping lower lip and thin dangling legs, returned the greeting, constantly removing the top hat swaying on his huge head. Weather permitting, he might stop and walk slowly down Ferdinandova and Na Příkopě to the Powder Tower, followed discreetly by a butler wearing a tricorn and livery and carrying a plaid travelling-rug over his arm.

The top hat was in constant motion; he lifted it like an automaton, like a clown. Yet Prague never forgot that the hydrocephalic head beneath had been the last to wear the crown of Saint Wenceslas. Besides, the mere fact that the Viennese had a low opinion of him was reason enough for Czechs to fancy him. Simpleton though he was, therefore, the perambulatory Ferdinand captured the Prague imagination in a way that Procházka – that is, Franz Joseph – who rode through the streets of Vienna in pomp and splendour, never did.

Not that Prague of the gallows humour did not make fun of the enfeebled sovereign behind his back, calling him Ferdáček (Ferdy) because of his infantile nature. The brothel pianist in Werfel's story "The House of Mourning" boasts that as an "Imperial-Royal child prodigy" he once played for Ferdinand, and describes his eccentricities (like the habit of slapping people, which forced his servant to hold his hands during carriage rides).[5]

Prague was happy to count the wisp of a feeble-minded king among its "marvels", and when failing health kept him from going out, the curious contrived to make their way inside the Castle as gardeners to catch a glimpse of him sitting amidst the greenery in his wheelchair. A Gipsy woman had predicted he would live to a ripe old age, and the following dialogue between Ferdinand and his majordomo was repeated daily:

> *Ferdinand*: How many years have I left to live?
> *Majordomo*: Your Majesty might well live to ninety or a hundred.
> *Ferdinand*: A hundred? A hundred? And then?
> *Majordomo*: Who can tell: a hundred and twenty.
> *Ferdinand*: A hundred and twenty. And then?
> *Majordomo*: Then Your Majesty will have the grace to die.
> *Ferdinand*: Die. And then?
> *Majordomo*: Then there will be a magnificent funeral and everyone will make boom boom.
> *Ferdinand*: Boom boom? They'll make boom boom?

Thus do Ferdáček and Karlíček Bumm come together in the museum of Prague eccentrics.

97

Two gentlemen dressed in black, two pallid, plump third-rate actors in frock coats and top hats accompany Josef K. by moonlight across the Charles Bridge to Strahov and his execution. And in the morning, two limping soldiers – one lanky, the other short and tubby – escort Josef Švejk, his ill-fitting uniform inflated like a balloon, in the opposite direction: from the Castle guardhouse down Nerudova and across the Charles Bridge to Chaplain Katz in Karlín.[1] Early in 1921 a loud black and yellow poster was plastered all over walls and tavern windows of the working-class district of Žižkov boisterously announcing the publication of the novel *The Good Soldier Švejk and his Fortunes in the World War*.[2]

The novel is above all an apology for the *pucflek* or *burš*, that is, the batman. In an ardent harangue the narrator complains that no one has as yet written the history of orderlies. Superiors claim that the orderly is "only an object, a punch bag slave, a factotum"[3] or the officer's alter ego, whose vices and abuse he imitates.[4] In fact, however, he is a malevolent alter ego, an ambiguous slave, a sly object – in short, he is descended from the race of clever servants who make use of every device and trick to dupe their masters.

From sganarelle-*pucflek* to clown is merely a hop, skip and jump. And Švejk is a Prague clown: a loud-mouthed, beer-guzzling oaf. He wears clown's clothes, too. In the garrison jail he is given

> an old military uniform which had belonged to some pot-bellied fellow who was taller than him by a head. As for the trousers, three more Švejks could have got into them. An endless succession of baggy folds from his feet up to where his trousers reached over his chest involuntarily evoked the admiration of the spectators. A vast tunic with patches on the elbows, covered with grease and dirt, dangled around Švejk like a circus clown's costume. The military cap, which they had also changed in the garrison jail, came down over his ears.[5]

Thus garbed, thus bloated, a Grock or Zavatta in a flapping Austro-Hungarian uniform, Švejk walks down from the Castle while Josef K. is walking up, dressed in Chaplinesque black like the dapper figures in the bowlers and carefully pressed overcoats that later appear in Magritte's paintings. When called to arms, Hašek is said to have reported to the České Budějovice barracks in a wobbly top hat.[6]

Švejk's clown-like exterior tallies well with the idiocy he feigns with such brilliant consistency. For the servant-clown who knows how to play tricks on his masters, stupidity is a Brueghelesque Land of Cockaigne and expedient of capital importance. Švejk's main concern is to convince others of his simple-mindedness. He is proud that his superiors call him an ass, and if anyone has any doubts on the subject, he himself, beaming, boasts that a medical board has declared him a certified imbecile. "I'm an official idiot[7] . . . I'm a genuine idiot."[8] The word *blb*, idiot, assumes exaggerated proportions; it swells like a Boschian bubble. Švejk never ceases demonstrating his perfect stupidity, which is all the more ludicrous for being simulated,[9] a kind of blustering narcissism of stupidity. Lieutenant Lukáš insults him to no avail:

> Do look at yourself in the mirror. Doesn't it make you sick to see your own drivelling expression? You're the most idiotic freak of nature that I've ever seen[10] . . . Think carefully whether you aren't the bloodiest fool and bastard in the whole world . . . [11] I'm quite sick of calling you a bloody half-wit, but there are really no words to describe your idiocy. When I call you a half-wit I'm really paying you a compliment.[12]

Švejk feels no shame at this torrent of abuse; on the contrary, it fills him with bliss.

Hašek makes much of his character's gentle, lamb-like gaze.[13] The vapidity Švejk's pudding face registers throughout the muddles and predicaments he causes exudes perfect innocence, "complete assurance and ignorance of any offence".[14] Švejk counters Lukáš's outbursts of rage at his idiotic exploits – "Jesus Mary, Himmelherrgott, I'll have you shot, you bastard, you cattle, you oaf, you pig. Are you really such a half-wit"?[15] – with the pristine smile of his eyes, always glowing with tenderness and "complete composure",[16] as though nothing had happened, a smile that defuses rage and averts tempests.

But Hašek sees to it that the reader remains undecided until the last whether his character is in fact a sly fox or a gross idiot, "a cunning blackguard or a camel and fat-headed moron".[17] It is his infantile shenanigans and chatter, his bogus emotional outbursts and, most of all, his boundless imperturbability that enable him to sail through the most unpleasant situations unscathed. The refusal to bat an eyelid of that inscrutable mug provokes incongruously beneficial turmoil, sending his superiors up the wall – or down the other way.

98

To escape the cogs of the military machine, the *pucflek*, idiot, moron, clown resorts to the dogged hoax of total obedience, of perfect docility. Švejk's motto is to serve the Emperor "to my last drop of blood" ("do roztrhání těla", literally: "till my body is torn to bits", that is, "till I drop").[1] Though rejected by the authorities for both cretinism and rheumatism, he insists on facing every peril *ad majoram gloriam Austriae.*

Švejk's compliance with orders is so excessive, so deferential, that he proves an embarrassment to the lawyers, priests, doctors and the entire slow-witted military chain of command he comes into contact with. At police headquarters he cheerfully accepts the charges read to him by a monster whose features are worthy of Lombroso's *Criminal Types*:

> "I admit everything. You've got to be strict. Without strictness no one would ever get anywhere"[2] . . . "If you want me to confess, your worship, I shall. It can't do any harm. But if you say: 'Švejk, don't confess to anything', I'll wriggle and wriggle out of it until there isn't a breath left in my body."[3]

He returns to his cell happy after signing the confession, and declares to his cellmates, "I've just admitted that I might have murdered the Archduke Ferdinand."[4] And when asked by the magistrate at the regional criminal court whether the police used pressure on him, Švejk replies,

> "Why, of course not, Your Worship. I asked them myself if I had to sign, and when they told me to do so I obeyed. After all, I wouldn't want to quarrel with them just because of my signature, would I? It certainly wouldn't be in my interest to do that. There must be law and order."[5]

The theme of false, inscrutable guilt tied to the nature of Prague relates Hašek to Josef K, though Švejk neutralizes and minimizes guilt by the device of sham submissiveness. Švejk is the only one to be thrilled by the declaration of war and to sing the Emperor's praises, the only one to believe in victory, the only one to jump for joy at being called up. From the start he is singled out in the newspapers as a "shining example of loyalty and devotion to the throne of the aged monarch",[6] when he has himself wheeled to the barracks wearing the military cap and flowers of a recruit, waving his crutches and shouting, "To Belgrade, to Belgrade!" in the bathchair the local confectioner used "to push his lame and wicked old grandfather about in the fresh air".[7]

When entrusted with a task, he carries it out so punctiliously that he creates gross misunderstandings and minor catastrophes, which he then dispels with a half-witted smile on his big blank face. Playing the champion of discipline, he goes on about how a soldier is not supposed to think because his superiors do it for him. He even provides a foretaste of the joy of dying in battle:

> "I think that it's splendid to get oneself run through with a bayonet," said Švejk, "and also that it's not bad to get a bullet in the stomach. It's even grander when you're torn to pieces by a shell and you see that your legs and belly are somehow remote from you. It's very funny and you die before anyone can explain it to you."[8]

And when Lieutenant Lukáš announces their departure for the front with a march battalion:

> "Humbly report, sir, I'm awfully happy," replied the good soldier Švejk. "It'll be really marvellous when we both fall dead together for His Imperial Majesty and the Royal Family."[9]

Even in the latrine Švejk distinguishes himself for devotion to duty, presence of mind and, if I may say so, esprit de *corps*. Just as the soldiers have begun defecating into an open ditch, a half-wit Polish major general enters in full regalia. He has come on an inspection mission. Švejk, grasping the gravity of the moment, jumps up, wipes himself with a scrap of paper torn from a tear-jerker of a woman's novel by Růžena Jesenská, snaps to attention and salutes. "Two sections with their trousers down and their belts around their necks rose over the latrines. The major general smiled affably and said: 'Ruht, weiter machen.'"[10] The scene, a malicious mixture of fecality and military imbecility worthy of *Simplicissimus*, adorns one of the most comical and puppet-like sections in the novel.

Although Švejk impedes the action with his fulsome respect for superiors and idiotic observance of regulations, the novel has an even more effective means of retardation: anecdotes. Anecdotes constantly break up the flow of the narration, the development of the plot. Incongruity after incongruity, the riotous, obtrusive anecdotes constitute a level of narrative all their own, a long digressive zigzag, a beery, wild, sinister, meandering novel within the novel.

Švejk strings together whole series of stories reflecting an atavistic irony fed by centuries of bondage and born of the opaque, smoke-filled atmosphere of the legendary Prague beerhalls, *Grenzschenken*, border dives where the shades of police agents and agents provocateurs – the Bretschneiders of this world – are permanently listening in. Here the artful quietism of the Homo Bohemicus vents itself in prodigious bluster, picaresque deeds and castles in the sky. Švejk's tap-room tales pour forth a constant stream of rancor, the rancor of an oppressed people;

beneath the farcical garb of gallows humour the desires and frustrations of the subjugated run riot. These vulgar ballads, these drunken belches, these derisive flare-ups of chatter tally perfectly with the goal Švejk has set for himself: that of hollowing out the rotten pomposity of the system and, like the pilgrim in the Comenian labyrinth, casting a harsh light on the confusion of the world.

Much of the anecdotal material strewn throughout the novel involves judicial errors, death sentences delivered by mistake as it were. At a divisional court martial Švejk consoles a soldier who is languishing in jail for having written a poem on the "bastard Austrian he-louse" in the following terms:

"You're in a jam, but you mustn't lose hope. It can still change for the better as the Gipsy Janeček said in Pilsen when in 1879 they put the cord round his neck for double robbery with murder. He was right in his guess, because at the very last moment they took him away from the gallows, as they couldn't hang him, owing to its being the birthday of His Imperial Majesty which fell on the very same day when he ought to be hanged. And so they hanged him the following day after the birthday had passed. But just imagine the luck that bastard had, because on the third day he got a pardon and his case had to be taken up again, as everything pointed to the fact that another Janeček had committed the crime. So they had to dig him out of the convicts' cemetery and rehabilitate him in the Catholic cemetery in Pilsen. But afterwards it turned out that he had been Evangelical and so they transferred him to the Evangelical cemetery. And after that . . . "[11]

The motif of unmotivated guilt nags at Švejk and turns up transposed into the burlesque mode in a large number of anecdotes. For example:

"I remember once a woman was sentenced for strangling her newly-born twins. Although she swore an oath that she couldn't have strangled twins, when she'd given birth to only one girl, which she had succeeded in strangling quite painlessly, she was sentenced for double murder all the same."[12]

Švejk's arsenal of jokes, anecdotes and yarns reflects the condition of the Czech in the street. Excluded from an active role in history, he lets off steam in stories whose very preposterousness conceals venomous sarcasm. The tangled wild prattle of logorrhoea goes hand-in-hand with feigned obedience and the dim-wit mask.

99

Oh, the magic spell of the word *blb*, "idiot", that cluster of labials holding up a poor liquid like two third-rate actors, that "blbouquet" of clustered consonants, that plosive classification that enables Švejk to emerge from the hell of war unscathed. Amidst so much confusion the most sensible thing to do is lose one's mind: pretend to be an idiot and let things take their course, browbeat the powerful and save your skin under the guise of submission. Human flesh and bones is worth more than inhuman rules and regulations. Švejk, a jumble of outlandish clothes and anecdotes, outsmarts the enormous Austro-Hungarian war machine.

The Good Soldier Švejk is usually considered a comic novel, a series of tall stories and uproarious vignettes. And indeed it abounds in tom-foolery, clowning and jokes. The mass celebrated by the drunken wildly gesturing Chaplain Katz in an inside-out chasuble amidst sonorous snores is worthy of the medieval farce *Mastičkář* (The Quack).[1] More farcical still is the scene in which Katz, so drunk this time that he nearly falls off the pulpit, delivers a bombastically incoherent sermon to the soldiers in the garrison gaol. Švejk stands out in the group of angels in filthy white trousers as the only repentant sinner by breaking into uncontrollable sobs.[2]

The wealth of gestures in these pages recalls the Chaplin film in which Charlie, playing a runaway galley slave in the days of the Puritans, dons a minister's robes by way of disguise and instead of preaching a sermon performs a wild pantomime based on the story of David and Goliath.[3]

A number of references indicate that Hašek visualized Katz's pranks in terms of the stage. As the staff warder tells Švejk: "Tomorrow we're going to have a show. They'll take us to the chapel to hear a sermon. We shall all of us be standing in our pants right under the pulpit. There'll be some fun!"[4] The drunken chaplain scolds the soldiers with the words: "You don't know how to pray, and you think that going to chapel is some kind of entertainment like being at a theatre or cinema",[5] and when he celebrates the mass the soldiers have "the feeling [they] have in the theatre when [they] do not know what the play is about, when the plot develops and [they] breathlessly wait to see how it is going to end".[6] The sequence in which Švejk brings the drunken chaplain home in a carriage is a hilarious skit,[7] the scene in which Katz performs a drumhead mass – a veritable "Red Indian dance around a sacrificial stone", hopping from one side of the altar to the other – a magnificent circus act.[8]

Many of Katz's antics recall the routines of clowns with their accou-trements or again Charlie Chaplin, this time with his alarm clock. Unable to find a telephone, the staggering curate talks into a lampshade;[9] the tipsy chaplain and his *pucflek* lose the tabernacle of their folding altar in the tram on their way home from the open-air mass.[10] The entire concluding section of Part Two revolves around Švejk's high jinks with the telephone, that mad contraption serving to unmask the chaos of the military and the gross contradictions inherent in its orders.

All the jokes, pranks and ludicrous situations notwithstanding, however, the book is <u>no burlesque</u>. Lada's idyllic illustrations have accustomed us to seeing Švejk as an easy-going country uncle, a witty offspring of Bertoldino, a chubby little hobgoblin trudging along in a wrinkled uniform, all button nose and stubble.[11] Yet it becomes increasingly clear that Švejk's stupid face (which George Grosz catches perfectly) often twists into a malicious grimace, a grotesque mask. Thus the novel's high-spirited humour has another, chilling side that has much in common with *The Trial*, where mystery occasionally turns into sinister clowning.

With the relentlessness of a customs officer taking stock of the mummified monarchy, a world by then creaking like a badly-fitted ship with slack sails, Hašek exposes the stupidity of the regulations, the disastrous inhumanity of self-proclaimed high and mighty endeavours, the fragility of official institutions. Most of all, however, he attacks the macabre blood-thirsty witches' sabbath of war as it turns into a parade of crutches and ghosts. His descriptions of the struggle are suffused with an eerie, apocalyptic glow that brings him close to German Expressionist writers and painters.

In the third-class restaurant at the Tábor railway station Švejk meets

> soldiers of various regiments and formations and the most diverse nationalities whom the whirlwinds of war had swept into the hospitals of Tábor. They are now going back to the front to receive new wounds, mutilation and pains, and to earn the reward of a simple wooden cross over their graves. Years after on the mournful plains of East Galicia a faded Austrian soldier's cap with a rusty Imperial badge [*frantík*][12] would flutter over it in wind and rain. From time to time a miserable old carrion crow would perch on it, recalling fat feasts of bygone days when there used to be spread for him an unending table of human corpses and horse carcasses, when just under the cap on which he perched there lay the daintiest morsels of all – human eyes.[13]

Hašek the beerhall clown is suddenly a bard of mourning and affliction, reducing "the joys of war" with cold precision to rows of crosses with empty caps atop them and to banquets for the ravens:

The train went slowly over the freshly-built embankments so that the whole battalion could take in and thoroughly savour the delights of war. At the sight of the army cemeteries with their white crosses gleaming on the plains and on the slopes of the devastated hills all could prepare themselves slowly but surely for the field of glory which ended with a mud-bespattered Austrian cap fluttering on a white cross.[14]

Swarms of black ravens, a white mass of crosses, faded scarecrow caps and piles of chalky bones:

"They'll be a very good harvest here after the war," said Švejk after a while. "They won't have to buy bone flour. It's a great advantage for the farmers when their fields are covered with the dust of a whole regiment; in other words, it's a very good means of livelihood. The only thing which worries me is that the farmers shouldn't let themselves be cheated and sell these soldiers' bones unnecessarily for bone charcoal in the sugar refineries."[15]

In these passages Hašek's sarcasm takes on the harsh, twisted quality of a Dix, Grosz or Beckmann. The only work in Czech literature approaching this visionary power is Vančura's novel *Pole orná a válečná* (Fields and Battlefields, 1925) in which a Biblical language and constant *menetekel* evoke the horrors of the fight on the burnt Galician plains, the "cisterns of blood" and "caverns of thunder".[16] That Vančura knew Hašek's work is evident from a passage that describes the munitions wagons as being "driven by a good Švejk".[17]

When it is not twisting and turning in its anecdotes, when it openly confronts the hell of the military, Hašek's Švejkiad turns grim, grows claws. To quote Holan, Hašek can, when so inclined, "stick the thermometer up the rectum of war".[18] He brands the senseless slaughter, the collusion between Church and Army, the near-sighted stupidity of the commands, the sham of patriotic anthologies, of singing the joys of dying for the Emperor, of the holy pictures given to the soldiers by old maids. A lugubrious sense of tragedy emerges. As Holan says: "Irony does not die for the love of tragedy."[19]

Taking the ambiguity at the heart of his protagonist to the extreme, Hašek peppers the basically scurrilous text with stentorian references to world history and the Bible and hence with an ambivalent Le Douanier-like dignity. At police headquarters

mounting the staircase to the 3rd Department for questioning, Švejk carried his cross up on the hill of Golgotha, sublimely unconscious of his martyrdom.[20]

At the courthouse

> the glorious times of Roman rule over Jerusalem were coming back. The prisoners were led out and brought before the Pontius Pilate of 1914 down on the ground floor. And the examining magistrates, the Pilates of our times, instead of honourably washing their hands, sent to Teissig's for goulash and Pilsen beer.[21]

At the police station

> Police Inspector Braun set the scene for his meeting with Švejk with all the cruelty of Roman lictors in the time of the charming Emperor Nero.[22]

And in the barracks of the malingerers

> not even Socrates drank his hemlock bowl with such composure as did Švejk his quinine, when Dr Grünstein was trying out on him all his various degrees of torture.[23]

Leaving Tábor on foot at night on his "Budějovice anabasis", Švejk

> trudged through the snow along the road in the frost wrapped up in his military greatcoat, like the last of Napoleon's old guard returning from the Moscow campaign . . . Xenophon, that warrior of ancient times, travelled through the whole of Asia Minor and got to God knows where without any maps at all. And the Goths of old too made their expeditions without any knowledge of topography. Marching forward all the time is what is called an anabasis.[24]

One could quote dozens of analogous examples in which the ever fickle burlesque clads itself in solemnity.

At this point I should say something about Hašek's far from systematic reading habits. He preferred popular digests of history, palmistry, the occult, the Bible, *Otto's Encyclopedia* (whose entries often furnished the background for his anecdotes and humoresques), *A Treatise on the Odd and Eccentric* by the Czech neurologist Antonín Heveroch, recipes, the catechism, primers, the moralizing feminist novels of Olga Fastrová (Yvonna) and Pavla Moudrá, trade journals for shoemakers, brewers and tanners, Brehm's *Tierleben* (The Life of Animals), the *Kronenzeitung's* coverage of the House of Habsburg and, especially, the advertisements and letters to the editor in the daily *Národní politika*.[25] He puts his naive smattering of scientific knowledge to use in the theosophic rigmarole of the occultist cook Jurajda and the semi-serious discourse on cynology by Švejk himself (who is as much a connoisseur of dogs as Nozdryov in *Dead Souls*).

Anti-religious, foul-mouthed and myth-deflating as the novel is, it maintains its own cockeyed metaphysics, its own absurd vision of the supernatural. I am referring to the comical afterlife painted by Katz and to Cadet Biegler's dream outside of Budapest. For the drunkard chaplain hell consists of a pantry of huge pots, cauldrons and electric grills in which the sinners are fried in margarine, while paradise is an idyllic land where atomizers without number spray eau de Cologne, the Philharmonic plays so much Brahms you would rather be in hell and angels preserve their wings by installing propellers in their backsides.[26] In his dream the zealous Cadet Biegler reviews the troops in a general's uniform and inspects the front lines untouched by artillery fire until an explosion sends his car flying to the Milky Way, which is "as thick as cream". At the pearly gates he finds a crowd of invalids with a knapsack full of their limbs. Once he utters the password "Für Gott und Kaiser", General Biegler's car enters a barracks paradise, where angel recruits learn to shout "Hallelujah". God's headquarters is also a barracks: two angels wearing MP uniforms grab him by the collar and push him into a room filled with portraits of Habsburg princes and Imperial commanders. God is none other than Captain Ságner of the Eleventh Marschkumpanie, and he is so furious with Biegler for having unjustly abrogated the rank of general that he has two angels fling him into a stinking latrine.[27] This nightmare mixture of practical joke and metaphysics has something in common with the dreams in Chaplin's films and with the most madcap and cruel of slapstick comedies.

100

And while we're on the subject of ravens: there is a ballad in the play *Die letzten Tage der Menschheit* (1915–19) by Karl Kraus in which *Raben*, ravens, boast of not having to go hungry thanks to the war dead.[1]

Švejk belongs to Habsburg literature. For all its acrimony and rancor it still expresses the death struggle of an empire, the *finis Austriae*, the end of Cacania, which Robert Musil called "that misunderstood State that has since vanished, which was in so many things a model, though all unacknowledged".[2]

To be sure, *Švejk* is diametrically opposed to Joseph Roth's *Radetzky-marsch*. Unlike Roth and many other Austrian writers, Hašek feels not the slightest nostalgia for that vanished world; on the contrary, he pounces savagely on Austria and the Monarchy and like a Czech Simplicissimus reduces it to a fecal mess.

The *Latrinengeneral*, whose rule is "Um halb neun Alarm, Latrinen-scheißen, dann schlafen gehen", considers latrines so important that he claims, "Austria's victory crawled out of her latrines."[3] In the sick bay where the bowels of malingerers are flooded with enemas of soapy water and glycerine, Švejk urges the myrmidon responsible for drowning the poor wretches' guts: "Even if it was your father or your own brother who was lying here, give him an enema without batting an eyelid. Try hard to think that Austria rests on these enemas and victory is ours."[4]

Kafka notes in his *Diaries* (1911) that Kubin recommends Regulin – "a powdered seaweed which swells up in the bowels, shakes them up" – as a laxative.[5] Hašek's characters need no purgatives because they are loose as geese by nature. The conceited cadet Biegler is emblematic: after gobbling too many cream rolls he has such a violent attack of diarrhoea that he is taken to a Budapest hospital as a dysentery case and thus deprived of all his dreams of glory. "His shitted trousers got lost in the vortex of the world war."[6] "Stink awer d' Kerl wie a' Stockfisch" (The bastard stinks like a codfish), Captain Ságner's orderly says. "Muß d' Hosen voll ha'n" . . . "Stink wie a' Haizlputza, wie a' bescheißena Haizlputza" (He must have done something . . . He stinks like a shitted-up lat cleaner).[7]

As if to symbolize what Vančura calls "the painful, filthy death in the latrines",[8] the novel ends with a turbulent defecation contest between Biegler, who has turned into a beanpole running from one latrine to the next, and Dub, who also happens to be plagued by the trots.[9] Clearly for Hašek war is all physical, all bodily function and filth. Hence the spine-chilling pages about the mixture of excrement and blood that soils the trenches during the battle.[10] Immersed as he was in the obscenity of war, Švejk's creator saw the Habsburg Empire as a *Dreckkatafalk*, one large latrine, a fetid land of enteroclysms, shit-filled trousers and suppositories – in short, a Cacania-Arsinia.

Fecality also clings to the portrait of Franz Joseph. While the Viennese propagated the myth of the good-hearted autocrat, the guarantor of ancient splendour, their Prague cousins called the ageing sovereign Procházka, that is Mr Walker, a name that Max Brod said had "a bourgeois, philistine flavour to it reminiscent of an invalid or an easy-does-it caretaker".[11] And if in the works of two Galician Jews, Bruno Schulz and Joseph Roth, the Emperor's portraits, symbols of a lost world, are surrounded by a sad mythical halo,[12] for Jaroslav Hašek, citizen of Prague, the Emperor is simply a half-wit, a figure begging to be mocked. There is not the slightest trace of his severity in *Švejk*, nothing of his icy aura, the devotion to duty darkened by personal tragedy. Only once, at the beginning of the novel, in a feigned outburst of sympathy for the misfortunes of the Imperial family, does Švejk seem to allude to the emperor's *Lebensmotto*: "Mir bleibt doch nichts erspart" (I am spared nothing),[13] which Kraus has him sing in his mammoth, end-of-the-world cabaret of a play.[14]

Like Léon Bloy, who bestowed such charming epithets on Franz Joseph as "vieil imbécile" and "malodorant cacogénaire",[15] Švejk calls him a "notorious bigmouthed idiot"[16] and depicts him as a dotard plagued by the runs.

> "His Imperial Majesty must be completely off his rocker by this time," declared Švejk. "He was never very bright, but this war'll certainly finish him." "Of course he's off his rocker," the soldier from the barracks asserted with conviction. "He's so gaga he probably doesn't know there's a war on. Perhaps they're ashamed of telling him. If his signature's on the manifesto to his peoples, then it's a fraud. They must have had it printed without his knowledge, because he's not capable of thinking about anything at all." "He's finished," added Švejk knowingly. "He wets himself and they have to feed him like a little baby. Recently a chap at the pub told us that His Imperial Majesty has two wet nurses and is breast-fed three times a day."[17]

Even a guardian of the law like Police Sergeant Flanderka stammers, drunk, to the maid Pejzlerka, "Remember, old woman, that every emperor and king thinks only of his own pocket, and that's why they wage war, even if it's only an old dotard like Procházka, whom they can't let out of the rears in case he should shit up the whole of Schönbrunn."[18] In Hašek's book the Danube Monarchy is so detested that all Švejk has to do during a medical inspection is shout "Long live our emperor, Franz Joseph I, gentlemen!" and he is declared a "congenital idiot".[19] Where Schulz nostalgically cherishes the image of the Emperor with the white sidewhiskers reproduced "on every stamp, every coin and every customs stamp",[20] Hašek repeats with abject insistence that the old monarch's portrait is spotted with fly shit.[21]

Rooted in Prague soil, Hašek is immune to the effervescent opulence of Vienna, the Vienna of sybarite junior officers and merry widows, the spectacle of parades, the sugar-sweet opulence of waltzes and operettas, the hedonism, the oblivion, the blissful frivolity of *Austria felix*. There was a time when the most elegant soldiers of the Austrian Army, the grandiose dragoons of the Prince Eugene Regiment, were stationed in Prague, a constant parade of scarlet collars, black tricorns, cockades, long greatcoats lined in red, double rows of gold buttons, high boots with spurs and all manner of rifles, swords and pistols.[22] A far cry from the foul underdrawers in cell 16 or Švejk's drooping breeches.

As the satire of a sclerotic, mummified empire, Hašek's novel reflects the animosity of a people forced to put up a front for centuries. It is no accident that Dr Bautze states, "Das ganze tschechische Volk ist eine Simulantenbande" (The Czech people is nothing but a pack of malingerers).[23] Hašek does not miss a chance to point up the decay beneath the sedate bureaucracy, the reverse side of its pedantic punctilio, to expose the discord tearing apart the Monarchy's conglomeration of nations or, as Urzidil calls it, "hinternational" mosaic.[24] *Mitteleuropäisch* to the core, Hašek couches his characters' capers in a scurrilous macaronic mishmash the better to exemplify the babel of the Imperial-Royal regime, the dissolution of Habsburg culture. An absence of sentiment for the "world of yesterday", a total rejection of the Monarchy's values and a characteristically Bohemian relentlessness enable Hašek to bare the corruption of the system, its vast yet rusty apparatus of spies and hirelings, the inefficiency of the war machine, the stupidity and cruelty of the commanders – in short, to take leave of Austria without regrets. No frivolous operetta *Traumland*, Hašek's Austria, but a putrescent plexus of police headquarters, prisons, plodding troop trains, brothels, barracks, field hospitals and latrines. He thus portrays the remnants of Austro-Hungarian power (officers, policemen, major generals, commissioners, police employees, chaplains, charity ladies and sanctimonious spinsters) as silly masks and ominous wax-museum figures. Erwin Piscator rightly used a puppet metaphor[25] in his stage version of Hašek's "greedy zebras with yellow and black stripes".[26]

Because the rogue's gallery is so vast, we shall list only a few of the most comical. Let us begin with the highest in rank: a worthy old gentleman with a bald pate, the fearful Major-General von Schwarzenberg, who provokes Švejk's endless discourse on baldness during the train ride from Prague to České Budějovice;[27] then the dim-witted Polish general, "a ghost from the fourth dimension", who sends soldiers to the station latrines in the evening to keep them from soiling the tracks at night;[28] and "old death-watch" (*general chcípáček*), a classical case of second childhood, who inspects the troops at the Budapest station: "Austria had masses of generals like that."[29]

Going down the chain of command, we run into Colonel Kraus von Zillergut – "a most venerable idiot", "so colossally stupid that the officers avoided him from afar", puffed up with "corporal conceit"[30] and a fanatic of the military salute – and foolish Lieutenant Dub, the very model of thick-witted loyalty, a dogged advocate of discipline on whom Hašek foists the nickname "poloprd'och" (semi-fart)[31] and whom his orderly calls a "stinking fart".[32] Švejk eventually takes his revenge on Dub, who wears him out with upbraidings and dressings-down: after Dub forces him to guzzle a bottle of cognac in a single draught, he gives Dub a bottle of drinking water spiked with horse urine and manure,[33] and when Dub fulminates against brothels, threatening to court martial all soldiers who patronize them, Švejk catches him drunk, in his underwear, "in a paradise full of bugs", in flagrante, in the arms of Miss Ella.[34]

The chaplains, all of whom love wine and women in equal measure, constitute an amusing little group: from "Holy Father" Otto Katz – a Jew by birth and a gambler and regular patron of houses of ill repute by inclination[35] – to Father Lacina of the black bowler – an insatiable glutton and sot who sobers up after binges in long hibernations punctuated by burps and farts,[36] by way of Senior Chaplain Ibl, who rattles off stultifying homilies on patriotic sacrifice to troops leaving for the front,[37] and nitwit Father Martinec, who visits Švejk in his lice-ridden prison cell drunk, "floating into the gathering like a phantom in a fairy story".[38]

There is something repulsive about these numskull puppets, these morbid caricatures so like the gnomes and trolls and ambivalent faces in Kubin's drawings. Nor does Hašek spare the underdogs even as they suffer their superiors' contumely. He takes great relish, for example, in deflating the *pucflek* Baloun, a miller from the region of Český Krumlov, "a fat infantryman with bushy whiskers like Krakonoš"[39] – pot licker, *knedlík* downer, bottomless pit. Baloun is perpetually hungry. He steals food from others and dreams only of liver sausage, blood pudding, pork chops and the days when the pig is slaughtered in his village.[40] His bloated belly is matched only by a positively primordial fecality.[41] Thus the troops are allied with their officers by fatuity and vacuity and gastronomical and intestinal vagaries.

101

There is little talk of love in Hašek: love is confined to fleeting adventures with mismatched wives or to drunken brothel orgies. Nor does Kafka abound in deep love. As Bataille writes, "Eroticism in *The Trial* or *The Castle* is an eroticism without love, without desire and without energy, desert-like."[1] Instead, there are mountains of bureaucracy ruled from the summit by cagey Klamm-like characters with hordes of secretaries and herds of "striped predators" (resembling Klee's wily whiskered holy cat on its mountain).[2]

Hašek clears the rotten underbrush of the state apparatus with the scythe of satire. In *Švejk* the Danube Monarchy sprawls over an intricate maze of paragraphs and commas, secret directives, confused files and forms, contradictory sentences and "top secret" papers.[3] In the penal court

> all logic mostly disappeared and the § triumphed. The § strangled, went mad, fumed, laughed, threatened, murdered and gave no quarter. The magistrates were jugglers with the law, high priests of its letter, devourers of the accused, tigers of the Austrian jungle, who measured their spring on the accused by the number of clauses.[4]

Police headquarters "presented the finest collection of bureaucratic beasts of prey, to whom jails and gallows were the only means of defending the existence of the twisted clauses of the law".[5] Police Sergeant Flanderka is so upset by the chaos of figures in official memoranda that he dreams one night he is hanged for having jumbled them.[6]

Kafka too comes down hard on the elusive bureaucracy that buries the defenceless beneath piles of files and law codes, entangles them in procedural hairsplitting and pronounces arbitrary sentences. The examining magistrate Bernis

> kept losing the documents for the indictment and was compelled to invent new ones. He mixed up names, lost the threads of the indictments and spun new ones just as they happened to come into his head. He tried deserters for theft and thieves for desertion. He brought in political cases he had fabricated himself. He invented all manner of hocus-pocus to convict men of crimes they had never even dreamt of. He invented insults to the monarch and always attributed fabricated, incriminating statements to anyone, if the indictment and the informers' reports had got lost in the unending chaos of documents and official correspondence.[7]

Kafka's works, too, bristle with examples of administrative chaos, and none so much as *The Castle*. One need think only of the bundles of documents that clutter the mayor's house,[8] the mounds of papers the servants wheel from door to door in carts for the Herrenhof secretaries.[9] In Kubin's *Die andere Seite* the squalid Municipal Archives are packed to the ceiling with files and run by a mysterious Excellency dripping with medals and gold braid.[10] Kafka's cold, lethargic paper-pushers and Hašek's predatory pompous asses have much in common: they humiliate the individual with such wiles as shifting responsibility, hiding behind smokescreens and inventing ad hoc interdictions. But while Kafka's bureaucrats have interchangeable faces that flash past in the mist, Hašek's officers seem to have stepped out of a garish cabaret.

Certain passages in *Švejk* bring together the notion of the abuse of power with the notion of the sacrifice of the innocent and defenceless.

> From the Hradčany garrison the road led through Břevnov to the drill-ground at Motol. Along it a procession would pass, headed by a man under military escort with his hands manacled and followed by a cart with a coffin on it. On the drill-ground was heard the curt order: "An! Feuer!" And then in all the regiments and battalions they read out the regimental order that one more man had been shot for mutiny during call-up, when his wife, not bearing to be parted from him, had been slashed by the captain's sabre.[11]

When the supposed dimwit fails to return to his cell in the garrison jail because Katz has chosen him as his orderly, "a freckled soldier belonging to the Landwehr who had a very lurid imagination spread the news that Švejk had shot his captain and would be led away the same day to the drill-ground at Motol for execution".[12] Two soldiers with fixed bayonets, one thin and one tall, the other short and fat, escort him to Otto Katz.

> In Charles Street the small tubby one spoke to Švejk again: "Do you know why we're taking you to the chaplain?" "For confession," said Švejk nonchalantly. "Tomorrow they're going to hang me. This is what they always do on these occasions and they call it spiritual consolation." "And why are they going to . . . ?" the lanky one asked cautiously, while the tubby one looked pityingly at Švejk. Each was a small tradesman from the country, a paterfamilias. "I don't know," replied Švejk, with his good-natured smile. "I haven't the faintest idea. It must be fate."[13]

For all its gallows humour and self-defensive jesting, the mood in this passage is one with the desolate conclusion of Kafka's *Trial*. The Motol drill-ground is not far from Strahov. The coffin, the object representing the power of the state hierarchy, moves on a wagon, while the condemned man follows on foot.[14] Many innocents hang from the spreading tree of the paragraph sign. *L'esprit comique*, as Magritte shows in one of his paintings, is reft with chinks, cracks and crevices.

102

Švejk moves through the meanders of the Habsburg administrative stream, through the bottlenecks of its decrepit arteries as in a labyrinth. Forever humble and eager to please, he has nothing of the abulia of the pampered Kafka character, who often plays his part lying in bed. Add a pinch of allegory and one can equate the Austro-Hungarian labyrinth, in which Švejk the pilgrim wanders phlegmatically in the armour of indifference, with the Comenian "labyrinth of the world", a showcase of hyperbolized blemishes. In the course of a digressive journey that brings the *pucflek* to the fore, the labyrinth turns into a *via crucis*, a calvary.

This labyrinthine structure gives the work a strong kinetic impulse. Piscator correctly noted that despite the protagonist's passivity "everything is in constant motion", and his stage adaptation uses a conveyor belt, a *tapis roulant*, to reproduce the "restless succession of events".[1] Strictly speaking, there are three labyrinths: the jumble of police headquarters, barracks, wards, insane asylums, hospitals and prisons Švejk is plunged into at the beginning; the zigzag journey, the inextricable tangle of circuitous routes he deliberately takes during his Budějovice "anabasis"; and the confused maze of Cacania through which the indolent troop train, that carrack of fools on wheels, plods with its endless starts, stops, delays and detours.

In this bewildering journey the insane asylum proves a heavenly abode, a garden of bliss where man can rediscover his lost freedom in lunacy.

> I really don't know why those loonies get angry when they're kept there. You can crawl naked on the floor, howl like a jackal, rage and bite. If anyone did this anywhere on the promenade people would be astonished, but there it's the most common of garden variety thing to do . . . As I say, it was very pleasant there and those few days which I spent in the lunatic asylum are among the loveliest hours of my life: Everyone there could say exactly what he pleased and what was on the tip of his tongue, just as if he was in parliament.[2]

One madman Švejk meets there recalls one of Arcimboldo's composite figures, *The Librarian*:

> The wildest of them all was a gentleman who pretended to be the sixteenth volume of *Otto's Encyclopedia* and asked everybody to open him and to find the entry: "Cardboard box stapling machine", otherwise he would be done for. He only quietened down when they put him in a straightjacket. Then he was happy, because he thought he had got into a bookbinder's press and begged to be given a modern trim.[3]

So it is in folk ballads and fables: X thinks he is a hot coal and begs those around him to blow on him to keep him glowing; Z thinks he is a mustard seed and jumps into a vat of mustard at the market because without him it will have no flavour.

103

Let us assume that Švejk is Prague itself, its people constantly forced to submit. Let us assume that the *pucflek* mirrors the secret stubborn resistance of the Czech people, a people grown so accomplished in the practices of clever submissiveness that it knows no equal. What are the consequences of such an – all-too-true – identification? Clearly the theorem of false obedience has a demoralizing corollary: a propensity for accommodation, servility, a renunciation of imagination, élan.

But perhaps we have gone too far. Let us simply have Švejk – whose sham-idiot mug is as much a part of modern mythology as the frozen wax features of a Buster Keaton or the round Klee face with the bleary Senecio eyes – muddle through the oppressive system in wrinkled tunic and floppy trousers. He is no hero, and what good are grand gestures anyway? All he cares about is survival. There is a Czech word for this little man with the crafty look in his eyes; the word is *člobrda* and it denotes someone who likes his beer, knows how to keep his nose clean and jabbers a mile a minute.

Kafka is wrong when he states that "the great days of the court jesters are probably gone never to return".[1] So long as there are tyrants there will be fools. Like ravens attuned to the clangour of their bell-tower nests, the Švejks of this world prick up their ears at the sound of the first "thou shalt not", and if they dare to formulate otherwise intolerable truths it is because fools have a certain leeway.[2] They can point out that flies shit on sacred portraits or that the banners displayed in the streets of Prague to celebrate the victories of others fade into what Max Brod calls "sad soaked ghosts" and "shrouds".[3]

According to legend, the Golem will return to help the Jews in time of need. One cannot help thinking by analogy that in these seemingly endless dark days a Golem-Švejk, a monster of ersatz docility, of artificial, sheep-like humility, will inspire the inhabitants of Prague in their passive resistance to abuses of power on the part of their foreign overlords. Curiously enough, when Švejk dons a Russian uniform and falls in with a group of Russian prisoners of war, an Austrian NCO takes him for a Jew.

> "You don't need to deny it," the sergeant-major interpreter continued assertively. "Every single one of you prisoners who has known German has been a Jew and that's that. What's your name?

Schweich? Now look, why do you deny it, when you've got such a Jewish name?"

Not only that, the sergeant-major mistakes the anecdote the good soldier tells him for a Chassidic tale.[4]

The novel is suffused with Prague humour and Švejk's memories of his native Prague. In some of the roughest, most scurrilous passages an intense nostalgia for the city – and especially its taverns – shines through. What could be more melancholy than the farewell of Švejk and Vodička as they prepare to return to their units after being released from prison in Királyhíd?

"When the war's over come and see me. You'll find me every night from six o'clock onwards in The Chalice at Na Bojišti."

"Of course I will," answered Vodička. "Will there be any fun there?"

"Every day it goes with a bang there," Švejk promised, "and if it should turn out to be too quiet, we'll fix something."

They parted, and when they were already several paces away from each other, old Sapper Vodička called after Švejk: "Very well then, but see that you fix some fun when I come to see you!"

Upon which Švejk called back: "But be sure you come as soon as the war's over!"

After that they went further away from each other and some time later Vodička's voice could be heard from round the corner of the other row of huts:

"Švejk, what kind of beer do they have at The Chalice?"

And Švejk's answer came like an echo: "Velkopopovický."

"I thought they had Smíchovský!" Sapper Vodička called from the distance.

"They've got girls there too!" shouted Švejk.

"Very well, then, at six o'clock in the evening when the war's over!" shouted Vodička from below.

"Better if you come at half-past six, in case I should be held up somewhere," answered Švejk.

And then Vodička's voice could be heard again this time from a great distance:

"Can't you come at six?"

"Very well then, I'll come at six," Vodička heard his retreating friend reply.[5]

This two-part canon gradually fading into the distance movingly captures the agony of forced separation, the anguish at the inscrutable workings of fate.

Yet the war does end. Baloun returns to his village to devour his liver sausages. Švejk returns to the The Chalice to wait for Vodička. Instead of the sapper, however, who should turn up but the police informant Bretschneider. Haven't the seven horrible bastard mutts he bought from Švejk torn him to shreds by now?[6] Must Švejk then start from scratch with all his tricks and razzle-dazzle, wear his shrewd-fool mask ad nauseam? "Never give up hope, like the Gipsy Janeček said in Plzeň."[7]

104

"En mars 1902, je fus à Prague. J'arrivais de Dresde." Thus Apollinaire begins his story "Le passant de Prague".[1] This Czech episode, which the French poet placed in his "tour d'Allemagne", was of profound significance to Czech culture. (Interestingly enough, Rodin also visited Prague in 1902. He made the journey with a friend, the Czech painter Alfons Mucha, to take part in the Rodin exhibition in the Bohemian capital.)[2]

Let us dwell a bit on Apollinaire's tale, which flies through the topography of the city on the Vltava with fantastical invention and captures something of the vein of demonic Prague cultivated by Arbes, Meyrink and Karásek. The enchanted traveller asks several passers-by in German to recommend a hotel, but elicits no response until one finally explains to him somewhat bitterly that the Czechs hate everything German, and points to "a hotel located in a street whose name is spelt in such a manner as to be pronounced '*Porzhits*'".

Apollinaire found lodgings, therefore, in Na Poříčí, a street in the New Town far from lacking in brothels, pubs, *Tanztavernen* and *café-chantants*: The Green Ox, The Golden Pheasant, The Black Rooster, The White Swan.[3]

> The ground floor of the hotel that had been pointed out to me was occupied by a *café-chantant*. On the second floor I found an old woman who, after we had agreed on the price, brought me up to a narrow room with two beds. I explained that I intended to live there by myself. The woman smiled and told me to do as I pleased; in any case I should have no trouble finding a female companion in the ground-floor establishment.

There have been a number of conjectures as to the identity of the place. Nezval, like all the poets of his generation, was convinced that

Apollinaire had put up at the dilapidated Hotel Bavaria, which housed the U Rozvařilů Cabaret:

> I love the Karlín viaduct; I love the mysterious, crumbling Hotel Bavaria which to me is one of the most poetic buildings in the district and which I visit once a year as if I had an appointment with my destiny at its entrance. It has taken on the appearance of an arcane being, an illustration that fascinates me yet that I cannot recall, or an imaginary bawd who has resolved to make me vanish from the world. I shuffle certain bewitching buildings the way I shuffle playing cards and homonyms.[4]

And here comes Wilhelm de Kostrowitzky out of the dubious hotel to take his walk through Prague. He meets Isaac Laquedem – the Wandering Jew, *l'éternel juif*, Ahasuerus – who is reincarnated at various times and places and crops up in a medieval *complainte* by Tristan Corbière.[5]

With his long brown coat and otter collar, his tight black woolen trousers, the silk ribbon across his forehead and black felt hat on his head – "the kind German professors wear" – Isaac Laquedem satisfies all the requirements for inclusion in the museum of Prague phantoms:

> His face almost disappeared behind his heavy beard, his whiskers and extremely long hair were, however, neatly combed, white as ermine. All the same you could see his thick violet lips. He had a prominent, hairy hooked nose.

A vision in black and white with a dash of purple, Laquedem tells the poet of his various reincarnations over the centuries, of his

> endless, restless life . . . which has been and will be a walking, a perennial walking until the Final Judgment . . . Jesus ordered me to walk until he returns . . . yet I am not travelling a Way of the Cross: my roads are happy.

Apollinaire's Wandering Jew does not resemble Hanuš Schwaiger's, who is a ragged, decrepit vagabond, a transparent carcass, a virtual wisp of fog and member of the disquieting race of mice catchers, scarecrows and kobolds this late-nineteenth-century artist was fond of painting.[6] Despite the burden of his years, Laquedem is still fresh; his venerable age does not keep him from raising Cain in the taverns and in bed.

From afternoon until the wee hours of the night Laquedem keeps the poet company as he ambles through Prague. Yvan Goll later remarked that wherever Apollinaire-Kostrowitzky walked "the shadow of the Wandering Jew crossed his path".[7] As in a diorama, the Old Town Square, the Týn Church with the tomb of Tycho Brahe, the horologe of Mistr Hanuš with its moving figures, the Fifth Quarter with the Old-New Synagogue and the clock of the Jewish Town Hall, "whose hands move backward", the Charles Bridge decorated with the statues of saints from which "one enjoys the magnificent spectacle of the Vltava" – the entire city passes before our eyes. As Laquedem discourses on the fate of the Jewish people, he and his poet walk up to the Hradčany to visit Saint Vitus' Cathedral, "where the royal tombs and the silver reliquary of Saint Nepomuk are to be found". And there, in the chapel "where the kings of Bohemia are crowned and where the holy King Wenceslas suffered martyrdom", a chapel whose walls are encrusted with agates, jaspers, chrysopases, cornelians and the like, Laquedem points out to the poet, who believed in pentacles, talismans and every form of gramarye,[8] an amethyst whose nervations depict "a face with flaming, mad eyes": the mask of Napoleon.

> "It is my face," I cried, "with my dark, jealous eyes!" And it is true. It is there, my sorrowful portrait, near the bronze door with the ring Saint Wenceslas had in his hand when he was murdered. We had to go outside. I was pale and distraught at having seen myself insane, I who am so afraid of losing my mind.[9]

Nezval would later write,

> I did not fail to ask one of those who are close to my idea of poetry, Tristan Tzara, whether he had seen the agates on the walls of the chapel of Saint Wenceslas in Saint Vitus', the agates assured a second immortality, a new kind of immortality, by two passages in the works of Guillaume Apollinaire.[10]

During his stay in Prague in 1928, Jules Romains expressed a desire to visit the chapel and "find the image of Apollinaire in one of its semi-precious stones".[11]

The theme of agates with human features also appears in the Prague drama *Král Rudolf* by Jiří Karásek. Arthur Dee, returning from a journey, brings the Emperor a gamahe, one of those stones covered with hieroglyphics that later so fascinated Breton.[12] "It is the most mysterious talisman known to magic," he says. "In rare instants nature herself presses arcane pictures into the stones, metals and minerals." This gamahe, found in Venice among the refuse of an Oriental witch who died at the age of three hundred, is supposed to have the ability to prolong life. To Rudolf's horror, however, it shows him a symbol of death, a skeleton.[13] Apollinaire himself mentions ghostly imprints in another story, "La serviette des poètes" (1907), a tale of four poets who infect one another with consumption by wiping their mouths on the same napkin; after their deaths four faces emerge from the filthy clots like a quadruple Veronica.[14]

But let us resume Apollinaire's Prague itinerary with Laquedem and cross the river again at night "on a more modern bridge". Once they have eaten and danced in an *auberge* to the diabolical din of a three-man band, they return to the Jewish Town. After a few bottles of Hungarian wine in one of its tavern-brothels the sprightly Laquedem unsheaths his long staff, his "knotty trunk", his arborescent phallus of an alchemical symbol and dallies with a "large-breasted, large-buttoxed Hungarian". As the Wandering Jew wanders off in the chilly night, the poet follows his dancing shadow and the glimmering reflections that enhance it. Suddenly, with the scream of a wounded animal, Laquedem sinks to the ground. His time has come. He will spring to life again in other places, other shapes.

105

Ancient manuscripts represent alchemical operations as a series of jars teeming with symbols and simulacra. If I were to represent the magical transmutations of the essence of Prague in luted crucibles, I would most certainly include the image of Isaac Laquedem, a pilgrim and illusionist who is no less typical of Prague than Rabbi Loew or Hašek and whose cyclical reappearance recalls Meyrink's Golem. Moreover, with his uncomplicated longevity he seems to have drunk Kelley's or Sendivogius's elixir of life, and deserves a place alongside Emilia Marty-Makropoulos in Karel Čapek's play: "Every ninety or a hundred years I am struck by a terrible illness. But I recover and once more find the energy to live through another century."

Apollinaire intuitively grasped several fundamental elements of Prague's magical nature. (His Slav origins may have helped him here.) He perceived the sinister magic of the Fifth Quarter – its melancholy, its bordello bouquet, its mixture of the Talmudic and the not strictly kosher; he penetrated the curse on faces staring from semi-precious stones. The agates of Saint Vitus', in which he was terrified to see his own image, the taverns in which he listened to Czech songs, the hands of the Jewish Town Hall clock – they all reappear in the famous lines of "Zone" (1912), in which he also mentions a mysterious tavern in the outlying districts of the city:

Tu es dans le jardin d'une auberge aux environs de Prague
tu te sens tout heureux une rose est sur la table
et tu observes au lieu d'écrire ton conte en prose
la cétoine qui dort dans le cœur de la rose

Épouvanté tu te vois dessiné dans les agates de Saint-Vit
tu étais triste à mourir le jour où tu t'y vis
tu ressembles au Lazare affolé par le jour
les aiguilles de l'horloge du quartier juif vont à rebours
et tu recules aussi dans ta vie lentement
en montant au Hradchin et le soir en écoutant
dans les tavernes chanter des chansons tchèques

[You are in the garden of an inn on the outskirts of Prague
you feel quite happy a rose is on the table
and instead of writing your story in prose you watch
the chafer sleeping in the heart of the rose

To your horror you see your face drawn in the agates of Saint
    Vitus'
you were mortally sad the day you saw yourself there
you look like Lazarus crazed by daylight
the hands of the Jewish Quarter clock run backwards
and you too slowly step back through your life
as you climb to the Hradčany and listen
in the evening to Czech songs in the taverns]

As for the "*jardin* question", the poet Karel Toman surmises that
Apollinaire was alluding to the old Šipkapas Inn, a gathering place
for German students with a terrace overlooking Šárka Valley. Another
poet, Konstantin Biebl, was convinced it was the roof terrace of the Zlatá
studně (The Golden Well), a picturesque Malá Strana tavern nestled in
the greenery at the end of steep steps and affording a splendid view of
the verdigris dome of Saint Nicholas' and the whole panorama of Prague.
The fact that Malá Strana is not an outlying district has little bearing on
the matter.[1]

The publisher and writer Otakar Štorch-Marien once tried to locate
the *jardin* with Karel Čapek in the Hradčany district.

I remember very clearly the summer afternoon when we came to the
small square called U Daliborky, from which it is a short walk to the
Golden Lane. Opposite the barracks of the Castle Guard there was
a tavern, but I don't remember its name and there isn't a trace of
the name left. A number of years ago they gave the place a postcard

façade, and there is a window now where the main entrance used to be. It was patronized mainly by soldiers, who often sang there. That day as well there was a sad, languid chorus coming from within. We stopped to listen. "Apollinaire must have listened like this," Karel said after a moment, leaning on his walking stick. "Because of 'Zone' Prague taverns will be remembered forever," he added with a boyish smile, and lit a cigarette. "But which one 'on the edge of Prague' could be the one he referred to in 'Zone'?" I asked, peering into his blue, seemingly omniscient eyes. "Hard to tell," he answered, "though it shouldn't be taken too literally. It certainly wasn't on the outskirts of Prague. Maybe it was just a few steps from here, at the Zlatá studně."[2]

Štorch-Marien also recalls how Giraudoux praised "the intimacy of the Prague garden taverns" Apollinaire had discovered in his by then mythical journey.[3]

The passage described by the author of *Alcools* and *Calligrammes* tallies with the one undertaken by the German poet Detlev von Liliencron in May 1898. Liliencron had been in the Bohemian capital briefly, in 1866, during the Austro-Prussian War, but it was his later stay that made him fall in love with the city, and he returned a number of times with the vain desire of taking up residence there. "Once I am gone," he said to the Prague poet Oskar Wiener, who accompanied him, "write something about our scouting trips around Prague. Describe it all. I want everyone to know how happy I felt here."[4]

Liliencron gambolled through the streets like a deer, repeating, "Prag ist schöner als meine Lieblingsstadt Palermo!" ("Prague is more beautiful than my favourite city Palermo!"), though he had never been to Palermo. He ran after girls crying "tschippi tschappi", then smuggly bragged, "Wie schnell habe ich böhmisch erlernt" ("How quickly I've learned Czech").[5] They walked from Na Příkopě to Wenceslas Square, which Liliencron called "the proudest street in the world", to the Old Town Square, where he inspected Master Hanuš's horologe, the spot where the ignominious scaffold for the execution of twenty-seven Czech dignitaries was erected on 21 June 1621 and Tycho Brahe's red marble tombstone in the Týn Church. From there they went to the Fifth Quarter, where, amidst the remnants of hovels torn down during the *asanace,* he admired the Old-New Synagogue, the Town Hall clock with its backwards motion and Loew ben Bezalel's tomb in the Jewish Cemetery. They crossed the Charles Bridge and climbed Petřín Hill to watch the sparkling Vltava at sunset. Curiously enough, Liliencron's first day in Prague ended, like Apollinaire's, in a Jewish-Czech *Singspielhalle,* the Jewish element playing as prominent a role for him as for the French poet: "After we had walked all over the Jewish Cemetery, with its overpowering elder scent, we stood before the grave of the great Rabbi Loew and Liliencron said, 'You must tell me more about this people who cannot live and cannot die.'"[6]

This walk and, even more, the ones that immediately followed, the ones six years later and the last one, shortly before Liliencron's death, gave Wiener an excuse to extol the beauties of Prague, to interweave a Baedeker of pubs, churches, palaces, chapels and gardens with the appropriate legends. Yet the itinerary, at least in the beginning, is so similar to Apollinaire's as to arouse the suspicion that Wiener was inspired as much by Apollinaire's 1902 *vagabondages* as by the *Streifzüge* of his friend, the enchanted wanderer Liliencron.

106

"Prague is more beautiful than my favourite city Palermo," Liliencron declared, comparing them in a way that weighs upon my soul with a two-fold melancholy. In his tracking shot along the city on the Vltava "Světlem oděná" (Arrayed in Light, 1940) Jaroslav Seifert exclaims, "Prague was more beautiful than Rome!" These two claims trace the fluctuating triangle of my life.

The discovery of Apollinaire in Bohemia dates from 9 February 1919, when Karel Čapek published his translation of "Zone" in the journal *Červen* (June) with woodcuts by his brother Josef. The next year he included it in his splendid anthology of modern French poets, which Nezval called a "miracle in the art of translating poetry",[1] a measure of the fascination they held for their young Czech counterparts immediately after the Great War. The turbulent, proletarian-oriented members of the Devětsil (Butterbur) group,[2] founded in Prague on 5 October 1920, proclaimed Apollinaire "harlequin of Parnasse and Montparnasse[3] . . . without whom the poetry of the twentieth century could not exist".[4] He was their idol and patron, the chief gamekeeper in the wood of Apollo; he would revive Czech letters; he was their fountain of youth.

The image of the poet with a white bandage wrapped round his head was constantly before their eyes. Jiří Wolker, Zdeněk Kalista, Konstantin Biebl, Jaroslav Seifert, Vítězslav Nezval and countless others were so enthusiastic about his work that they would have said along with Blaise Cendrars:

> Apollinaire n'est pas mort
> vous avez suivi un corbillard vide
> Apollinaire est un mage.[5]

[Apollinaire is not dead
you followed an empty hearse
Apollinaire is a magus.]

Karel Teige, the much respected theorist of the Czech school of Poetism, called Apollinaire

> the symbol of the "new spirit" for whose victory we still struggle in his shadow. For us Apollinaire is the axis of all modern poetry, his work the milestone from which we date the new era of modern creation . . . In Paris and Prague, cities that live in his poetry and sparkle in a common free and creative springtime of art, we meet his face and his smile at every turn.[6]

The Poetists often recalled and portrayed the author of *Calligrammes* in their verses. "Paris is the mirror of Europe./In it I see your smile", Seifert wrote in his ode "Guillaume Apollinaire", comparing the figure of the "dead wizard" to the "Æolian harp" Eiffel Tower.[7] In his poem "Generation" Biebl imagines Apollinaire at the Zlatá studně with a group of Poetists, "young poets and old boors", at the next table imitating him, drinking French wine and smoking pipes: "We too try/to puff new clouds."[8] Later, Nezval begs for "someone to recite to me all the *fleurs du mal* like karel teige/or the *calligrammes* of guillame apollinaire whose name still moves me to tears".[9]

I love to follow Biebl's Apollinaire calmly smoking his pipe and gazing out from the terrace of the Zlatá studně across the glittering orography of Malá Strana roofs – that bizarre collection of towers, turrets, garrets, chimney pots – and the cupola of Saint Nicholas', "the purest emerald in the world".[10] The Poetists strolled briskly through their city at night, savouring its fascination through the verses of "Zone", listening for the steps and voice of the French poet along the squares, bridges and embankment, unable to imagine its emporium of wonders without his garrulous presence.

"The Wandering Jew in Apollinaire's story," Zdeněk Kalista writes,

> has become what amounts to a symbol of our wanderings among the gas lanterns and remote corners of the city. We could not pass the Old Town Hall in the dark of night without seeing the horologe scene we knew from "Le passant de Prague". Nezval could not walk along the walls of the Old Jewish Cemetery in the dark without the silence of the place merging with his picture of the Jewish Town at the beginning of the century, a world that no longer existed: the tavern at the corner of Josefská Street in Prague V of the time

would turn into the dive Laquedem visits with the poet, and a girl we met in the street would become "a matron mumbling the call to nocturnal love". We had to go to Vinohrady where one saw "fourteen- to fifteen-year-old girls even pederasts found to their liking"; we had to go to the boring cabaret U Rozvařilů because it was close to the Hotel Bavaria which, according to Nezval's interpretation of "Le passant de Prague", was where Apollinaire had stayed.[11]

"I cannot overemphasize the fact," says Nezval, "that it was he and he alone, his chimerically veiled eyes, who taught me to look differently at everything that till then had merely been the subject of Old Prague tales."[12] The Poetists regularly took foreign friends, especially the French, along the route of their idol Apollinaire. Nezval recounts a visit to the Jewish Museum with Paul Éluard in April 1935. Their escort, a "young Jew with the physiognomy of a puppet", whom they had thought a deaf-mute after he waited in silence as they observed the "miraculous rubbish", suddenly reproached them in a falsetto voice for being "surrealists". They later decided he was a reincarnation of Isaac Laquedem.[13]

To do justice to Apollinaire's influence on Czech literature would take a much longer account. Not a single poet during the period following the Great War failed to collect conches and pebbles from his sea. Seifert translated the "drame surréaliste" *Les mamelles de Tirésias*, which was first performed at the Osvobozené divadlo (Liberated Theatre) on 23 October 1926. The journal *ReD* (Revue Devětsil) devoted an issue to Apollinaire on the tenth anniversary of his death (9 November 1918). What they picked up from the French poet was a sense of the miraculous, of the instability of memory, of continuous metamorphosis, of the charm of frivolity and caprice plus a certain bad taste and superficiality. Traces of his *calligrammes* make themselves felt in the typographical structure of their books and in their "optical poems". Jiří Kolář has recently attempted to revive this approach in his pictographic "evident poetry", notably in the collection *L'Enseigne de Gersaint* (1966).

The poem "Zone" – which for Nezval "has no equal in the twentieth century"[14] and for Teige is "both deafening and sentimental, the rhapsody of a globe-trotter"[15] – became their holy writ, an omnium gatherum of archetypes. *Pásmo*, a cultural review edited by Bedřich Václavek, took its name from it, *pásmo* being the Czech for "zone". The young Czech lyric poets of the immediate postwar period were so under the spell of this "galloping drunken film"[16] that one could say along with Blaise Cendrars "ils parlent tous la langue d'Apollinaire".[17] His conception of poetry as an unrestrained flow of lyrical lava, his confrontation of dissimilar themes, his abolition of punctuation, his preference for incongruous analogy over logic proved instrumental in inspiring a series of seminal Czech poems of the period. I am referring to "Svatý Kopeček" (1921) by Jiří Wolker, "Panychida" (Requiem, 1927) by Vilém Závada, "Nový Ikarus" (The New Icarus) by Konstantin Biebl and *Edison* (1928) by Vítězslav Nezval.[18]

The latter bore especially strong traces of the Cubist poet, whom Teige called the "planet that created the fates in the horoscope of modern poetry".[19] Nezval's "Podivuhodný kouzelník" (The Wondrous Wizard, 1922) reworks motifs from "L'Enchanteur pourrissant". The prose-poem "Pražský chodec" (The Prague Pedestrian, 1938) is much indebted to Apollinaire's story of the same name. The comedy *Depeše na kolečkách* (The Dispatch on Wheels, 1924) is influenced by the concept of theatre expounded by the *directeur de la troupe* in the Prologue to *Les mamelles de Tirésias*. Bits and pieces of Apollinaire crop up throughout the whole of Nezval's vast production. Yet the Poetists did not merely raid his poetry; they adopted his love for Rousseau-Le Douanier, his belief in charms and his passion for pipes, of which he had a large collection.[20] Because they shared the Expressionists' view of the recent war as an apocalyptic catastrophe, however, they did not subscribe to his enthusiasm for the military, his tendency to turn war into a fairy tale, all bright and awesome.

The most striking play of reflection and refraction is the extraordinary similarity in character and physical appearance between Nezval and Apollinaire. Nezval had the same whimsical, bon-vivant, *dolce far niente* nature, the same embonpoint as the French poet.[21] Hoffmeister satirizes his rag-doll-cardinal corpulence in a cycle of collages entitled *Nezvaliáda*.[22] They show the leader of the Poetist school being hatched from a huge egg or in a fluttering theatrical overcoat like a rotund Romantic bard sailing towards an unknown continent of poetry or as a thickset D'Artagnan with a plumed hat or clinging to a garland of laurel leaves on a classical statue like a Fatty Arbuckle clutching a streetcar strap.

107

Viviane, the cruel and very art-nouveau Dame du Lac, puts Merlin the magician, who has fallen in love with her, to sleep and, content at having enchanted the enchanter, buries him in a coffin deep in the wood. Yet as night falls, creatures come from near and far to mourn the hypnotized magician and engage his voice from the grave. They include druids, snakes, toads, lizards, bats, frogs, a raven, a herd of sphinxes, an owl, Morgan le Fay, elves in glass shoes, Lilith, Angelica, Delilah, serpents, Magi imposters, Simon Stylites and innumerable other figures from bestiaries and ancient tales. I am referring to "L'enchanteur pourrissant",[1] in which Apollinaire reveals his love for the romances of the Round Table and medieval chivalric literature.[2] Among the wise old men who visit the tomb guarded by the Dame du Lac is the Wandering Jew, or Isaac Laqudem, the very figure who under the name of Laquedem wanders the streets of Prague.

Apollinaire's Merlin became the prototype for many sorcerers in modern Czech literature, most prominently the "wondrous wizard" (*podivuhodný kouzelník*) in Nezval's poem of the same name. Nezval explained that his mountebank, his quick-change artist was born of the magic released by the words "enchanteur pourrissant" and according to the axiom that beauty must be as "pure and cold as glaciers".[3] He imbued the poem with a taste for Apollinaire's "fantaisie magique" ("fantaisie de Noël funéraire") and with his wizard, to whom he adds features of a Nietzschean tightrope walker and the above-mentioned Lady of the Lake.

Nezval's "Wizard" revels in the joy of mutability and *žonglérství*, "juggling", the quest for the miraculous that provides the basic impulse for all his writing. Its frenetic series of metamorphoses fuses the demonism of the wizard with the dynamism of film. The visionary hero reappears in a number of reincarnations against a number of backdrops. Nezval replaces the parade of figurines before a static Merlin with a wizard more agile than a Fairbanks: Nezval's hero darts in multifarious disguises from the glaciers of Greenland to the rapids of the Amazon, from India to leper colonies, from a secret geyser to a cavern full of stalactites, from a coal mine to Moscow, where he turns revolutionary.[4] In short, the Poetist wizard's tale features the same rapid change of scenery as "Zone". Of course, Nezval's necromancer takes wing from a base of night-time Prague with its riverside "dark and phosphorescent as a mirage", its "milky rosary of arc lamps which, seen at a distance, create a gridiron of the city"; in other words, he is a Prague personality, one of the family of charlatans of which Prague was so rich.

The illusionist, then, the *kouzelník*, the *kejklíř*, the trickster, plays a crucial part in the Poetist aesthetic. The *kouzelník* Arnoštek throws the sleepy little town of Krokovy Vary into a turmoil with his diabolical tricks in Vladislav Vančura's tale "Rozmarné léto" (A Capricious Summer, 1926). The tightrope walker-miracle worker in Nezval's poem "Akrobat" (1927), dedicated to Vančura, is eagerly awaited by crowds of the sick and malcontent, who implore him to make them well and happy. Nezval's acrobat is thus the hypostasis of the poet. One Sunday he sets off to cross the continent on a tightrope and plant the red rose of Europe in the taiga of Siberia, but he falls (a reference to Nietzsche) and thereby symbolizes the impotence of poetry. Childhood, personified by a seven-year-old

legless boy in a sailor suit, leads him to a town of acrobats, dreamers
and madmen, a dream town with the lights and nocturnal filigree of
Prague. The poet has returned home "with his doubles in innumerable
shapes".[5]

The Grand Wizard of the Devětsil generation, however, was clearly
Edison, the maker of electrical miracles, and his name crops up time
and time again in the verse of Seifert, Nezval and Biebl. In Nezval's
passionate *Edison* motifs from the life of the Menlo Park champion of
speed and vitalism alternate contrapuntally with a damp, sad view of
Prague by night – an infirmary of shadows, a patchwork of drunken
lights spilling out over the embankments and bridges along the black
mirror of the Vltava, our Lethe, repository of tears, source of the malady
of melancholy. Here too, in the fourth canto, the memory of Apollinaire,
"the Wandering Jew in search of a country", finds its way into the text.

108

During the twenties, according to Yvan Goll, cafés were the "Geistzentrale
der Welt".[1] The history of the Czech avant-garde is closely linked to a
number of Prague *kavárny* such as the Unionka, Deminka, Tůmovka,
Hlavovka, Belvederka and above all the Národní (National) and Slavia.[2]
Battered Thonet chairs, wobbly sofas with black oil-cloth upholstery,
cracked plaster tables with marble tops like orthoceratite shells, wooden
newspaper racks on the wall – these were the mythological furnishings
of endless meetings and impassioned discussions. Spring 1923: in cafés,
taverns and smoke-filled nightclubs Devětsil poets, painters, actors and
directors invent a "poetry for all the senses": Poetism. As Nezval later
wrote, "Such an atmosphere of miracles can be experienced only once in
a lifetime."[3] The first Poetist manifesto, the article "Poetismus" by Karel
Teige, came out in 1924. In the same year Nezval published *Pantomima*,
a miscellany representing various genres – cycles of short lyric poems,
the "Podivuhodný kouzelník", a short pantomime libretto, a ballet, a
"photogenic poem", an essay on the profession of poetry, calligrams and
clusters of plays on words – and constituting a kind of trade fair of the
movement.[4]

Professors of carnival, master tightrope walkers, pyrotechnicians
extraordinary, the Poetists championed a joyful, frothy art – an art
inextricable from buffonery and eccentricity and reflecting the rhythm,
the tempo, the "nervous health" of the twentieth century with soaring
analogies and metamorphoses.[5] Every Poetist poet behaved like a pupil
of Chaplin and the Fratellinis: they were gag makers, image manipulators,
verbal agitators all. Lavish tropes leap from the folds of Nezval's writing

like frogs or the props from the pockets and secret pouches in the presti-digitator's costume Harold Lloyd puts on by accident in *Movie Crazy*.[6] And if a fondness for cartwheels, garish face powder and pastry-shop windows can turn the improvisations of a Seifert, a Nezval or a Biebl into the poetic equivalent of the Chinese lantern, no matter: their purpose is to dismantle holy cows, smash tradition and the hauteur of old art with a carefree counter-art, kitsch and all.

Karel Teige, the indefatigable Barnum of Devětsil and managing director of their fireworks, speaks in his fanfare of a manifesto of "lyrical and visual excitement at the spectacle of the modern world, . . . the passion of modernity, modernolatry, . . . a multiplicitous optimistic faith in the beauty of life".[7] The trend he proposed is called Poetism because it places poetry above all arts, including in its purview such sub-genres as film, flying, radio, sport, the music hall, the circus and the dance. "Sailing boats are also modern poems," he writes, "instruments of joy."[8]

109

Poetism is not confined to art; it was intended to act upon human exist-ence, become a "modus vivendi", "turn life into one big amusement park, an eccentric carnival, a harlequinade of emotions and ideas, a drunken film, a miraculous kaleidoscope".[1] As Teige states in his "instructions",[2] Poetism is "modernized epicureanism, . . . a source of common happi-ness and good cheer; it is unpretentiously pacifistic, a stimulator of life" that "dispels depression, cares and low spirits".[3] Poetry assumes a therapeutic, consolatory function, fanning flames of joy to the world with its robust bellows of metaphors and puns. "Juggler" poetry and a full and happy life are one. Evreinov seems to have had the same thing in mind when he ascribed therapeutic value to actors and the theatre. Because it set out to rediscover "all the beauties of the world",[4] because it favoured the light and airy over the ponderous severity of the bulk of Prague literature, Poetism may be considered a kind of non-mystical Chassidic interloper into Czech letters.

Poetism's programmatic cheer also makes itself felt in the ebullience and lust for life of a generation that had grown up during an age of terrible slaughter, an age begun by Mrs Müller telling Švejk "So they've killed our Ferdinand" and ending with an epidemic of the Spanish influenza. Having left behind the ruins of Cacania, Poetism, a Czech outgrowth of Dada, unleashed a revolution of joy against enemies like Dignity, Authority, Moderation. Yet at the same time, following in the footsteps of the Soviet Constructivists, Poetists tried to build a new life, set the tone of post-war society, provide not only a truly modern art but a totally new organization of the world. Here is where Communism, the Grand Illusion that was their credo, enters the picture, though – what happy times those were – they did not impoverish their works with compulsory themes and slogans. Constructivist ideas may have been appropriate for the architect Teige, who gave his book the title *Stavba a báseň* (Building and Poetry, 1927), but they did not agree with poetry as practised by Nezval, Seifert and Biebl, with its gushing stream of garish juggler metaphors and the unbridled associations they evoked. Nothing could have been more inimical to the Prague Poetists than the carefully prescribed, highly calculated coldness of the Moscow Productivists. How could one reconcile ascetic Constructivism with Nezval's opulent inventiveness, his "fantastical cabaret"?[5]

Poetist lyricism raised the expression of life's butterfly-like ephemerality to a creative principle, a source of energy and spiritual health. The Poetists dreamed of a laughing world and strove to create it by banishing gloom with nonsense, with outlandish analogies, in a word, with humour. This yearning for untrammeled gaiety comes out clearly in their nonsense rhymes, farcical plots, "optical poetry" (Teige's typographical compositions, in which letters of the alphabet and geometrical figures look for all the world like circus props) and – the prime example – the Dada-inspired musical comedies of the clowns Voskovec and Werich.

In the Logos of Prague, "a miraculous city created for poetry",[6] Poetism represents the triumph of horseplay and buffoonery over Golemic horrors, the triumph of the anti-Meyrink, anti-Kafka line; it represents an escape from the *Grübelei* and lugubrious hypochondria that are the *basso continuo* of Prague literature, a flight from the saturnine, petrified microcosm of Rudolf II, from the sinister melancholy that ulcerated the souls of the alchemists during the long "white nights" they spent in front of the athanora, a melancholy they symbolized with the colour black for putrefaction and with an arsenal of emblematic ravens, skulls, skeletons and coffins. To the hermetic katabasis into infernal regions, apocalyptic pallor, spectral blood, mental unbalance and malfunctioning metabolism of the literature of the unsmiling, Cimmerian city of Prague, the Poetists opposed the tonic quality of laughter and joyous alchemy of verbal association, "an alchemy speedier than the radio".[7]

Yet, as Banville says, "le poète n'est pas toujours/en train de réjouir les ours", poetry is more than entertainment. Like Švejk, who, for all his buffoonery, has moments of the deepest despair, so Poetism too can take on a thoroughly Prague-like tinge of grief. I am thinking not so much of the dark verses of Halas or Závada or the languor of Seifert's "embarquements pour Cythère" as of Nezval himself, the Grand Vizier of Poetism, whose *Edison* is drenched in a Prague mist as heavy as asphalt, in Prague's unique fluvial humours, the Nezval whose farewell gestures, wretched soot-stained spectres and nocturnal vistas owe so much to Mácha's desperate art.

110

Do you remember the poster for the Letná Circus? An Indian in a turban between two crocodiles. We climbed the Old Castle Steps, where Mould and Shadow hold sway, talking about the clowns and acrobats who perform in Poetist verse. Along the steep slopes the Hradčany street-lamps take on a ghostly air. Their whitish light topped with points black as sloe reminded us first of sad Nordic shrubs, then of severed heads on trays. How alien, how impossible the Poetists' gaiety seemed in such melancholy settings, especially when a hard rain turned the city into a maze of foggy corridors.

Nezval, however, leader of the Devětsil, writes at the end of his comedy *Depeše na kolečkách* (The Dispatch on Wheels): "Art runs across the stage on its hands dressed like a circus clown." In other words, art is a cartwheel, a top, a flashing of multicoloured patches, a garish harlequin quite different from the infernal buffoons and mercenaries of Satan who squint at us from the paintings of František Tichý. Poetry generates joy by changing into a joyful spectacle, a balancing act.[1] "Rather than philosophers and pedagogues," writes Teige, "it is clowns, ballerinas, acrobats and tourists who are the real modern poets."[2] "Our art," Nezval wrote in retrospect, "was closer to the acts of jugglers, circus riders and trapeze artists than to the magic of religious rites."[3]

Jugglers' balls replaced gripe's eggs. The Poetists transformed Prague into a three-ring circus (with starlight shining through), an arena for itinerant *artistes*. Seifert introduces Pom the clown, John the "famous fire eater", Chloe the tiny ballerina and a dreamy trapeze artist called Miss Gada-Nigi; Štyrský paints the Cirkus Simoneta, Toyen the Cirque Conrado. The clown in *Depeše* performs on a trapeze; in fact, Nezval teems with actors and jugglers. There is an entire "family of harlequins", including a "cyclist Pierrot" and a circus manager whose wagon is drawn by swans. In the poem "Abeceda" (Alphabet), where the letters suggest the mimetic figurations and vignettes of a Poetist primer, Nezval compares H to a clown leaping from the flying trapeze and I to the "agile body of a dancer". Seifert's delicate, filigreed writing abounds in doll-like ballerinas. Early Halas, a fervent Poetist for a time, daydreams about an "electric ballet of the Monde Circus" and a clown who loses his face beneath the hundredth mask.[4]

"The new freedom in art was born in the circus, the *variétés*, the music hall," writes Teige. "That is where genuine modern poetry lives, a poetry unconstrained and electric, alien to naturalism."[5] The passion for balancing acts, *amuseurs du tapis*, trapeze artists, horseback riders, tightrope walkers – in short, for all the attractions of the big top – was not confined to the Poetists. Yvan Goll's Welt-Varieté features an Orpheus act, a Yankee Girl and a snake man.[6] Cocteau lauded the Fratellini Brothers, the *foire*, the *bastringue*, the *bal musette*, Mistinguett, the Medrano Circus and "les orchestres américains de nègres".[7] Schlemmer noted in his diary: "Dadaismus, Zirkus, Varieté, Jazzband, Tempo, Kino, Amerika, Flugzeug, Auto."[8]

Like the rest of the European avant-garde the Poetists were fascinated by the cinema, "the Bethlehem whence the salvation of modern art shall come".[9] Pearl White, Harry Langdon, Buster Keaton, Ben Turpin, Mary Pickford, Alla Nazimova and Harold Lloyd captured their imaginations. The two great clowns of their generation, Voskovec and Werich, made extensive use of slapstick comedy and the whole bag of tricks of the silent screen. Charlie Chaplin, the hero of Yvan Goll's *Die Chaplinade* (1920) and Mayakovsky's poem "Kinopovetrie" (Movie Epidemic, 1923), was as indispensable as Douglas Fairbanks in Nezval's "Wondrous Wizard":

> Fairbanks lassos
> whatever enters his path
> Apollinaire Picasso
> my bewitching phantasts
>
> Chaplin brings his lady fair
> a gift in his sidecar
> mirror caviar star
> all the good things there are.

The Poetists were no less attracted to Dixieland jazz, which ousted reeling polkas and tavern ditties. Jazz was a source of joy:

> And the poets no longer ask
> for a pitiful prebend
> they have fun like the Blacks
> in the blare of the jazz band.

Here too melancholy can gain the upper hand: the Prague humus is most susceptible to the *cafard* aspect or *Weltschmerz* side of the blues, as in Nezval's collection *Skleněný havelok* (The Glass Havelock, 1932) or "Tmavomodrý svět" (A Dark-Blue World, 1929) by Voskovec and Werich and set to music by Jaroslav Ježek, which is imbued with the anguish of hopeless plights, not the least of which was Ježek's impending blindness. For the most part, however, the Poetists were keen on the "wonders" of progress. They listened attentively to the utopian bravado of Ilya Ehrenburg's book *A vse-taki ona vertitsia* (Eppur si muove, 1922) and glorified machines, transatlantic steamers, the Goliath plane and skyscrapers. A novelist among them, Karel Schulz, proclaimed that "the aerial of a radio-telegraphic transmitter is more beautiful than the Discus Thrower or the Apollo Belvedere or the Venus de Milo",[10] and Seifert called one of his books *Na vlnách T.S.F.* (On the Waves of the Wireless, 1925). In Nezval's *Depeše* a "radiotelegraphic poem" exhorts humanity to joy and laughter.

But the most striking thing about the Poetists' impulsive minds was their emphasis on themes from all over the globe, the purpose of which was clearly to free them from the unrelenting circle of "Pragueness" choking them like the alchemists' uroboros serpent, to release them from the inordinate gloom and tyranny of the city on the Vltava.

111

All the avant-gardes of the twenties were fuelled by exotic visions, but none dallied so enthusiastically with the exotic as the Czechs. The Poetists loved to flee Prague and the "Bohemian ponds green as a chorale of frogs"[1] for radiant picture-postcard lands. The longing for the sea and wide open spaces always present in Czech culture and in the very nature of the Homo Bohemicus grew into a mania among the Poetists, who fairly devoured the novels of Karl May and James Fennimore Cooper, the serialized stories of Buffalo Bill and Nick Carter, the travels of Rimbaud to Java and Abyssinia – the caravans, the jungle, the swaying of palm trees, the Indians, the natives, the Negroes, the prairies – and would run to see any film with a tropical or wild-west setting.

The Poetists cultivated a passion for travel; indeed, they claim to have raised tourism to a branch of poetry. In the collection *Na vlnách T.S.F.*, renamed *Svatební cesta* (Honeymoon) in 1938, Seifert glorifies *wagons-lits* as "marital carriages", calls the railway time-table a "poetic book",[2] bemoans the melancholy of ship departures:

> The girls wept I wept with them
> I too wanted to wave a handkerchief
> they waved blood-stained handkerchiefs
> of make-up red.[3]

Nezval entitled a volume of musical, Parisian-like lyric poems *Sbohem a šáteček* (A Farewell and a Handkerchief, 1934).

The flight to distant shores is one of the principal motifs of Poetist poetics. Nezval writes, "When it no longer makes sense to stay at home/slip away to Australia"[4] or "I'll flee the crowds go to Africa/my wooden hobby horse will take me there".[5] And Biebl: "With the ship that brings coffee and tea/I'll go to far-off Java one day."[6] Exotic plants and figures also make their way to Bohemia and Moravia. In "Abeceda" Nezval invites palms to move to the Vltava; in "Panoptikum" he conjectures that itinerant actors from Texas have arrived in his native Třebíč.[7] At times Bohemia itself becomes a colourful new landscape, the picture on the postcard, the slide in the stereoscope. During a stay in Java Biebl writes,

> At the far end of the earth is Bohemia
> a fair and exotic dominion
> full of deep and mysterious rivers.[8]

The imagination of the Devětsil jugglers would not have balked at a showboat plying its way among the gulls and ducklings of the Vltava.

We could go on and on listing exoticisms in Poetist verse, but the following will perhaps suffice: In the alphabet poem "Abeceda" Nezval likens I to the song "Indianola"; V is "the reflection of a pyramid on the burning sands"; C, "the moon on the water", inspires: "The romances of the gondoliers are dead and gone/so captain, off to America"; D, "a bow drawn from the West", brings to mind an Indian following tracks; R, "the Devětsil performers/set up their tents along the divine Nile"; S, "in the plains of deepest India/there lived a snake charmer named John". In Seifert's "abacus of love" the breasts of the persona's beloved are "two Australian apples";[9] the cranes in the harbour are "grotesque giraffes" and "palms of an unknown continent".[10] Biebl crams his verse full of exotic words (magistan, gamelan, rambutan),[11] and even the young Halas squanders coconuts, gondolas, atolls, palms, burnouses, nargilehs and every manner of outlandish bric-à-brac, going so far as to imagine a "carnival in the blue Sahara".[12]

All this *magasin pittoresque* goes back to the glowing metaphors of Rimbaud's "Le bateau ivre", of course, and at times it is a bit gratuitous. When Biebl writes "Today the poet gives his heart for a banana/a yellow banana, a tropical doll"[13] or "China is a poor, sad country/inhabited by canaries",[14] when Seifert writes "Beneath an artificial palm a Negro smiles/with a pink mask of light on his face"[15] or "The Chinaman straightens out his eyes and kisses a European woman/in the folds of his suit a dragon chews on chocolate",[16] when Nezval writes "A Moor plays billiards/with Sahara coconuts"[17] or "Fragrant Asia waved like a yellow banner/with woven ornaments of lotus gardens",[18] burlesque comes dangerously close to operetta kitsch, Poetist postcards to cheap backdrops. But if certain Poetist outpourings sink to the level of the pseudo-Oriental, hit-parade lyrics of the time, we must keep in mind that the Poetists consciously aimed to make a "cosmetics factory of poetry" and serve as "commercial travellers dealing in perfumes/lyrical powders/magical liqueurs".[19]

Poetist papier-mâché exoticism was thus meant as an antidote to Prague's insalubrious humours. But the antidote can be worse than the poison. What is the point of superimposing a "black Eden of palms"[20] on the palaces of Malá Strana? Nezval replaces the ambivalent, almost metaphysically downcast animals of Prague with the parrot, a living, talking emerald and symbol of Poetism's glittery verse. For the Poetists, poetry itself is a "miraculous bird, a parrot on a motorcycle", "a set of images, of parrots with magic names".[21] The parrot of poetry runs riot in the hands of the wizard-poet Celionati, from whom it demands "the elegance of a charlatan".[22] Nezval's *papoušek* (parrot) follows on the spurs of Cocteau's *coq*. *Le coq est parisien*, and in the end the Poetist parrot, despite its exotic plumage, is one with Prague, a city of whims with Mannerist tendencies and a laboratory of endless Arcimboldos.

112

There is a self-portrait in the Prague National Gallery that could serve as an emblem of Poetist inventiveness. It shows the "customs officer" Henri Rousseau – dressed in black, sporting a black beard and black painter's cap and holding a brush and palette – in his imperturbable, straight-backed dignity. Behind the huge figure we glimpse the Seine, a bridge, a sailing ship with bunting representing countries from all over the world, the Eiffel Tower, the roofs of Paris, two tiny Parisians out for a stroll and a hot-air balloon up in the clouds.[1]

Poetist primitivism revelled in details like the multinational bunting and especially in the dreamlike jungles and tropical scenes, the "peintures mexicaines", the artful amateur naïveté of the "myths" of Le Douanier. We may be a bit more tolerant of their contrived landscapes and Sunday-supplement garishness if we recall that the "petit père" did not hesitate to derive inspiration from the shrubs of the Jardins des Plantes for his fantastical vegetation and the *Bêtes sauvages* album of the Galleries-Lafayette for his animals.[2] A large number of poems by Nezval, Seifert and Biebl and a large number of paintings by Devětsil artists (Mrkvička, Muzika, Šíma, Hoffmeister, Piskač) imitate the lush scenery of his imaginary Mexico. The Poetists dearly loved Le Douanier's work, a preference perhaps influenced by Apollinaire. Hoffmeister, the sophisticate, sets himself up –

with Dadaist self-irony, to be sure – as a new Rousseau, imitating not only his subject matter but even his signature,[3] and Teige considers Zrzavý – whose paintings he calls "enchanted dreams in mysterious glass"[4] (especially the lunar background with pyramids and slender palms) – a Czech Rousseau.

The exotic, gay figures that appear regularly in the pictures and poetry of the Poetists derive partly from Rousseau and partly from posters for the circus and for the ballet *Parade* (Cocteau/Satie/Picasso, 1917), which Apollinaire loved so well. The cast of the ballet (a clown, a Negro, a sailor, a fishmonger, merchants: *exotové*) bears a clear resemblance to that of Nezval's comedy *Depeše na kolečkách*, which features analogous "masks" – acrobats, a music-hall Chinaman, an American girl and efficiency experts.[5] Nezval's *exotové* – "six boxes with only a head and legs sticking out" – clearly ape the latter, a group of *"hommes-décor"* in cumbersome Cubist structures. Together with the objects of this Montmartre Cubist folklore (Gambier pipes, guitars, bottles, fans, playing cards, tobacco pouches) the characters represent the passions of the Poetist generation (the Negro its love for jazz, the clown its love for the circus, the sailor its love for faraway lands); they constitute a kind of naive heraldry, a basic alphabet, the Devětsil *orbis pictus*.

The mainstay in the *magasin d'accessoires* of the entire European avant-garde – and hence the favourite hieroglyph, the hobby-horse of the Prague wizards during those zany years – was the Eiffel Tower. In a poem dedicated to the monument Yvan Goll imagines Monsieur Eiffel, a "Magier in Sportmütze" (sorcerer in a sports cap), inviting all the poets of Europe to dinner on the first platform of his tower, "a flute singing in the wind".[6] The Poetists often repeated the famous "Zone" verse: "Bergère ô tour Eiffel le troupeau des ponts bêle ce matin" (Shepherdess O Eiffel Tower the flock of the bridges bleats this morning). The Eiffel Tower as muse – "feu d'artifice géant de l'Exposition Universelle", (the World Fair's giant fireworks) and "sonde céleste" (heavenly probe) according to Cendrars,[7] "Æolian harp", according to Seifert[8] – crops up frequently in their poetry. Devětsil's enthusiastic Eiffelology is of a piece with its enthusiasm for Delauney's *fenêtres*, for *Paris qui dort*, for Rousseau and Chagall. In "Abeceda" Nezval urges the letter Z (for *zubatá dráha*, "rack-railway") up the Eiffelka and invokes the Eiffelka itself in *Depeše* as "tower of joy and love, tower of poor lovers, tower of first kisses", putting the sweet words in the mouth of the radio-telegraph operator in harmony with Cocteau's formulation, namely, that the tower "était reine des machines" and "maintenant elle est demoiselle du télégraphe" (was the queen of machines and is now the telegraph lady).[9]

The Eiffel Tower is Paris, and Paris is the Poetists' Mecca: Paris, "mirror of Europe"[10] (or, for Yvan Goll, the diamond on Europe's neck,

"Diamant am Halse Europas"[11]), of the Europe that still glittered – even
if the Great War had reduced it, as Seifert says, to a "harlequin's cloak"
and "smashed chess board"[12] – of the Europe that had not yet abandoned
Prague to the Nazis. When France signed the Munich Agreement, however, Holan exclaimed:

> Enough, Paris! Not another step in your maddening parks
> where I once waited for night to bring me suffering.
> Good-bye forever, you too, you sonorous
> Boboli Gardens!

and

> Meanwhile implacable hours
> Strike on Spasskaya Tower.[13]

Although many Poetists were as partial to vodka as they were to
wine, they never quite endowed the Kremlin's Spasskaya Tower with
the magic nimbus of the Eiffelka. It is nonetheless sad to think that
both great passions of the Czech avant-garde, Apollinaire's Paris and
"invisible Moscow",[14] betrayed its trust and that in Prague, overrun by
waves of foreigners and periodically written off by the indifferent, eyes
can only weep.

113

Still, bring on the tightrope walkers, clowns, lion tamers, horseback riders,
ventriloquists, snake-charmers, trapeze artists, acrobats, sword-swallowers, Esmeraldas and sleight-of-hand artists overrunning the canvasses
and sketches of František Tichý (1896–1961). Tichý's art, growing as it
does out of the "sandy humus of the circus manège",[1] shares a love
of spectacle and the exotic with the works of the Prague Poetists, so it
is no accident that Nezval published a cycle of poems in 1944 entitled
Kůň a tanečnice (Horse and Dancer), which transposes the visual images
of Tichý's paintings into verbal ones.[2] Tichý has kindled the imagination
of many Czech poets, from Holan and Seifert to Halas and Kolář.[3]

Of course, Tichý does more than simply paint circus performers; he
makes his own their hazardous virtuosity, their hard work and technical
perfection. Eager to "free heavy things of their weight",[4] he himself
becomes a juggler and tightrope walker. The "simple lines, at times as
thin as a fishing-line",[5] reflect darting, precarious movements that permit
no slips, the speed with which the attractions follow one another. In the

blinding glare of the floodlights, "under the artificial gleam of electric moons",[6] the artists stand frozen at the climax of their act when the director, "raises his arms to stop the orchestra before the death-defying leap"[7] and the act seems to extend into space.

Tichý's imagination was so drawn to life under the big top that he was said to have worked for the Pinder Circus in Marseille.[8] Tichý himself promoted such rumours by claiming that his mother had been an *artiste* in a Hungarian circus until she was crippled by a fall, and that he had run off with a troupe of itinerant actors at the age of sixteen.[9] After all, had not Alfons Mucha passed himself off as a "jeune peintre hongrois" descended from the Tartars when Sarah Bernhardt found him in the puszta?[10] In any case, Tichý befriended many circus and music-hall artists, including Alberto Fratellini, whose portrait he painted in 1937 with enormous shoes and a pale red wig. He admired the Medrano jugglers in the same way Mucha had admired the muscle men and wrestlers with twirled whiskers and striped bathing suits at the Place de l'Observatoire.[11] He kept close track of every circus that came to Prague and went on with great enthusiasm about Bosco, Grock, Houdini and Clement de Lyon, an amazing Medrano juggler who seemed transformed into a supernatural being during his act.[12]

Like the Poetists, Tichý dreamed of faraway places. He was especially partial to Marseille, a city "daubed with fish scales",[13] where his imagination found stimulation in the Pinder Circus, the port, the bull ring and the colourful swarms of sailors and fishmongers.[14] During his years of hunger and privation in Paris (1930–5) he derived strength from the Guimet, Galliéra and Carnavalet Museums and from the Marché aux Puces.[15]

But the clowns and tightrope walkers of Tichý's *Nachtstücke* lack the carefree brio and verve of Nezval's wizard. They are gloomy and gaunt, thin as grasshoppers, with so little flesh on their bones that if one held them up to the light it would shine through them. Even the horses are emaciated. Tichý's realm is a realm of marrowless bones, fleshless wraiths who seem to go back to Valentin le Désossé. The scrawny sword-swallowers, the scraggy bareback riders make one's flesh creep. As Kafka writes,

> If some frail, consumptive equestrienne in the circus were to be urged around on an undulating horse for months on end without respite by a ruthless, whip-flourishing ringmaster, before an insatiable public . . . [16]

The performers of these *capricci* have deformed faces, mushroom faces, elongated, bruised, nightmare faces, faces that melt into wicked sneers. They have rubbery, pliable heads that can be shaped like putty, squashed pumpkin pates, occasionally elongated by a cap that looks like a flabby growth. Or they have mortar masks, rough geological concretions – in Halas's words, "the caked make-up of old eccentrics".[17] Bleary eyes flash, false noses stick out of layers of grease paint that is closer to an ashen-white Chinese mourning mask than to the festive rice powder of the Poetist clowns Voskovec and Werich. Tichý's "white Negroes" or "negative Negroes" are taken from the Negro statuettes he bought at the Paris flea market,[18] off-white waxen faces with purplish lips and eyes, modelled perhaps on the Africans wandering through Paris without hope, "modestly dressed in shroud-like shirts", in a poem by Holan.[19] A repulsive wrinkled face of hardened plaster with narrow slits for eyes, a long neck and a hat with a bat-wing brim (the clown Bodlák, or Thistle) chomps the stem of a thistle in his teeth like Georg Pepusch in E. T. A. Hoffmann's *Master Flea*, the human shape of the melancholy thistle Zeherit.

I fear his pug-nosed mugs with their diabolic grins; I fear his thistles, his chthonic figures, his music-hall, *haute école* top hats teetering on the heads of stunt riders and ventriloquists. The world of magic has its diabolical side, a crazy quilt of ghosts. My dreams are constantly haunted by the Serpent Man (*Hadí muž*) so typical of Tichý's astrologies. Stare at this arabesque made flesh, this phantom "in the costume of a rolled-up anaconda" and you will swear "that the knot of limbs begins to come undone".[20]

The gestural hyperboles of Tichý's figures reflect his mimetic talent, and in fact he spent time as a cabaret actor.[21] Yet it is clear that the contortions by which Tichý, with the unerring precision of a Daumier, turns every clown into a Kateřinky lunatic, a phantom in a madhouse dance, an unholy mixture of scurrility and Lenten pallor reflect first and foremost the arcane, warped nature of Prague. The woman-faced horse with the horse-faced rider, the master conjurer with a halo of playing cards spinning above his bowler hat, the harlequins with tar-black masks and elephant-like snouts, the ventriloquists with floppy hats and noses of rubber or bread, the twins in top hats eyeing each other with cross-eyed sneers – they are all ghosts and witches incited by the despond of the city on the Vltava, messengers of death on the Prague-Hades line.

And what about Tichý's Paganini, a wiry *Höllenfürst*, a viscous heap of black locks, stick legs and overly long tapered hands ending in fingers as twisted as convolvulus? If we believe Chamisso when he writes that the devil is as thin as the end of a thread escaped from a tailor's needle,[22] then this Prague painter's Paganini is a portrait of Satan. Jiří Karásek invoked the Romantic Paganini-Satan analogy when he portrayed the violinist torturing his instrument with a red gleam in his eye.[23] Virtuosity

and deviltry join forces again in Tichý's *Nacht-Musicus*, whose phosphorescent sparks come from a primordial darkness within. If I did not know
that the two executioners in frock coats and top hats who execute Josef
K. and the pair of assistants who cause another K. so much trouble were
related to the *badchanim* of Yiddish popular theatre and the austere Jewish
undertakers dressed in long black robes and cake-shaped hats depicted
on Moravian votive pitchers from the late eighteenth century,[24] I might
imagine them – minions of an occult power, metaphysical spies – as
coming from the world of Tichý's ghostly clowns.

There can be no doubt of the connection between Tichý's demons
and Meyrink's nightmares. Tichý's acrobats resemble their counterpart
Monsieur Muscarius in the Amanita Cabaret, a lemur born of a hallucino-
genic mushroom with a neck as wrinkled as a turkey's, a flesh-coloured
sweater hanging loosely on a gaunt frame and a phalloid mushroom of a
hat; Tichý's trapeze artist from 1941, a repulsive vamp in black tights, her
teeth gnashing and her arms as knotty as roots, recalls Albine Veratrine,
a shady-looking whore in Meyrink's night spot, all chains and no body.[25]
Tichý also illustrated a number of Jakub Arbes's terrifying *romaneta*.[26]

In the end tomfoolery merges with Grand-Guignol and lowering
Prague becomes a satanic circus in which clowns flaunting bugbear mugs
turn every act into a lugubrious rite, send us to the devil, to eternal fire,
in ignem aeternum. But enough.

114

At this point "the visitor to the gallery lays his face on the balustrade
and, sinking into the closing march as into a heavy dream, weeps without
knowing why".[1]

115

Thank God, I have come to the end of this long and gruelling journey.
Like the Baroque painter Petr Brandl anxiously counting on his fingers
in his self-portrait, I had begun counting the days. I ought to be happy
to have found my way out of the maze; I ought to turn to Prague and
say, I've had it. And instead I tell her, I'm still yours, my *Schicksal*, my
folly. I don't mind being laughed at for being Prague-crazy. So I repeat
Nezval's words:

> time flies and I still have so much to say about you
> time flies and I have as yet said so little about you
> time flies and lights the old stars over Prague[1]

As in Kafka's story "Erstes Leid" (First Sorrow), the acrobat refuses to come down from the trapeze.

It is strange, sister city: the more they try to Russify you, the more you smell of Habsburg mould. At noon in Karmelitská Street the reek of cabbage, *knedlíky* and beer streams from every front door; the restaurant musicians go on playing Fučík polkas and waltzes. Once again people adapt; they mock the catechist, that is, pretend, postpone or, as they used to say during the Monarchy, simply *fortwursteln* (muddle through).[2] Jiří Orten hides from the Nazis only to find his end beneath a German ambulance on the Prague embankment. Paul Adler leaves Hellerau to find shelter in his native Prague only to spend the last seven years of his life confined to bed with the stroke he suffered in his Zbraslav hiding place.[3] Paul Kornfeld flees to Prague when the Nazis come to power, but he too falls into their clutches and dies in a concentration camp in Łódz.[4] One walks in a circle, ending where one began. There is no escape from Prague. "No Escape" – "Není uníkat" – is the title of this poem by Holan:

> Staggering at night over the Charles Bridge
> you knelt before each statue,
> on your way to Malá Strana.
> Yet at the Bridge Tower you crossed to the other side
> knelt before each statue on the way back to the Crusaders
> and ended up in the tavern
> you had left an hour before.
>
> You'd have done the same in another time as well.[5]

My friends have been pressing me to finish this pot-pourri, hoping it will rekindle the memory of a betrayed country without hope. "Ce que j'attends avec impatience c'est ton livre sur Prague" (I can't wait to see your book on Prague), Irina writes from Amsterdam, and Věra from Paris: "Těším se na Vaši magickou Prahu" (I'm looking forward to your magic Prague). The horse I have been riding all these years has yellowish glass eyes; it is stuffed and worm-eaten like Wallenstein's charger. And all my fury at the intricate lies and injustices blighting the country so dear to me is as futile as a bar-room brawl.

I refused to get off at Braník or Chuchle; I wanted to go to the heart, the essence of the city. I refused to settle for the *lógr*, the dregs in the coffee of the *automaty*, the grounds of overroasted chicory: I am no garrulous journalist. I have chafed my skin on the glowing hemp and singed sackcloth of the Czech language. But I am tired. I really do look like Brandl's self-portrait – hollow-cheeked, deep bags under dim eyes –

though I take the harbingers of age with a bitter smile. Has everything I have written about really happened or is Bohemia merely a figment of my imagination, a castle in the air accessible only by flights of fancy? My immediate melancholy response is Blok's cantilena:

> It happened in the dark Carpathians,
> it happened in distant Bohemia.[6]

No, the host of friends who have died of a broken heart during these years provides me with the absolute certainty that Prague exists. Now that ideological arrogance, police brutality and tautological tedium hold sway there yet again, I shall not be able to return. In "Eine Prager Ballade" Franz Werfel recounts a dream he had on a train from Missouri to Texas during the war. A cabby by the name of Vávra is taking him to Prague in a hackney cab, but the frightened poet stops him and says, "You can't go there. The Nazis have invaded." So the cabby takes him across the Atlantic by way of Zbraslav and Jílové.[7] "Do you intend to settle in Tel Aviv?" Werfel, already fatally ill, asked in his last letter to Max Brod. "Or do you sometimes think it will be possible to return to Prague?"[8] "Manchmal hab ich Sehnsucht nach Prag," Else Lasker-Schüler wrote to Paul Leppin. Sometimes I have a longing for Prague.[9]

Now that Moscow is quartering her troops there, Moscow the whore with whom all kings of this earth have committed fornication (Revelations 17:1–2), now that overzealous lackeys are glutting themselves while Christ fasts and waits, I cannot return. Now that Prague is again, as Marina Tsvetaeva once lamented, "more desolate than Pompei",[10] they will keep me at a distance. In the meantime, everything is a jumble in my grey memory: alchemy and defenestration, sausages and the White Mountain, Pilsner beer and the Prague Spring. Karl Kraus called Austria a country of "solitary confinement in which you are allowed to scream".[11] Ah yes, Tristium Vindobona.[12] But today one hears not so much as a whisper: there are too many microphones, too many cocked ears.

Today more cellulose is turned into denunciations, Acta Pilati[13] and anonymous letters than into books, and the much hated Čehona, archetype of the conservative Czech loyal to the Monarchy,[14] has returned to tend Moscow's stables. Today ambitious judges slap together ideological trials against anyone who dares to think, and Josef K., having committed yet another non-crime by signing the "Manifesto of Two Thousand Words", tries in vain to convince the pettifoggers of his innocence; today the house in Hrabal's stories dealing with the absurdities and pitfalls of the Stalinist period, *Advertisement for a House I No Longer Wish To Live In*, is as it was then: narrow, stuffy, full of snares; today Titorelli repeats that cases in which the accused are acquitted exist only in legends. Who is in the limelight today? Turnkeys, evil clowns, robots of decay, pharisees, necromancers: Satan's tribunal.

116

> People, you will not be wiped out!
> God will protect you!
> He gave you garnet for a heart,
> he gave you granite for a chest.
>
> Marina Tsvetaeva[1]

I should have liked to spend my *Lebensabend* there, but my dream has faded much like Przybyszewski's and Liliencron's. I have lost touch with the place, I who had sunk my roots into it like a tree. From time to time I receive a furtive greeting from a friend, but no woman writes to me, as Else Lasker-Schüler wrote to Max Brod, "Lieber Prinz von Prag".[2] I wait in vain for letters. Like Holan, "I have spent a third of my life waiting for the postman".[3] What difference does it make? I console myself by leafing through the Vienna phone book, overflowing as it is with Czech surnames: Vávra, Zajíc, Petříček, Fiala, Zakopal . . .

Yet I am unable to tear my thoughts away from your continued sterility, your wounds, your failings. I happened to be in Munich on 10 June 1972, the evening the Prague theatre Za branou (Behind the Gate) gave its last performance. The blockheads, scavengers and renegades ruling Prague, in their ruthless campaign to wipe out Czech culture, were closing Otomar Krejča's magnificent theatre, which was cherished by afficionados the world over. As I walked sadly through the Bavarian capital gazing at the gaudy shop windows, where amidst the piles of trinkets and stereotyped goods dazzling dummies beckoned, I thought of the theatre's farewell performance, Chekhov's *Seagull*, the play with which the Moscow Art Theatre had initiated a new age in theatre history. Stanislavsky's actors had wept for joy; Krejča's actors wept out of desperation and anger. Their strangled gull screamed a requiem for Prague and all European culture. For almost an hour the theatre shook with applause. The audience, itself in tears, threw flowers and shouted "Na shledanou!" Good-bye! But Good-bye is a hypocrite, a ham, a clown, a master of deception.

As I look back over these pages, I see I have written a gloomy book, a *Totenrede*, adding the *menetekel* of recent decline to the city's constant melancholy, its White Mountain legacy. Yet with the possible exception of the grim clowning of ghosts and the Poetists' black-bordered ruffles hardly any of the material gives cause for cheer. The true Prague Mozart is not the carefree prankster sequestered in a room in the Villa Bertramka to compose the overture to *Don Giovanni* while merry ladies pass him food and drink through the window;[4] he is a dark Holanesque figure who

> toppled the Alps like a drunk
> and placed the empty bottle
> on the creaky step of the fear of death.[5]

For the last few years I have been haunted by Nezval's image of Prague as a "dark ship" bombarded by pirates from "all parts of Europe".[6] For the last few years I have come to see Prague's buildings in terms of Kolář's collages, cracked by tremors and the unevenness of the terrain, ready to fall; I seem to see ravens circling above the Hradčany and the "caravan of bridges"[7] on the point of buckling and sinking into the river. Nezval voiced similar presentiments of ruin in the face of the Nazi threat. The fear that invasion and war might destroy the city's wonders induced him to pause "before Prague as before a violin", and "gently brush its strings as if tuning it".[8]

For the last few years I have seen the magic city from a distance in a white, blinding, cataclysmic light as in the Baroque prophecies of catastrophe after White Mountain, and I recall the prognostications of the Sibyls, who, according to Czech legend, prophesy that Prague will be transformed into a morass of mud and rubble crawling with vermin and foul devils.[9]

But this is all raving, the muddle of a diseased mind, nihilistic rubbish. For as Karel Toman says,

> The only law is germination and growth,
> growth in storms and squalls,
> in spite of it all.[10]

So the devil with soothsayers and whorish Sibyls! The fascination of Prague, the life of Prague has no end. Its gravediggers will vanish into the abyss. And perhaps I shall return. Of course I shall. I shall uncork a bottle of Mělník wine in a Malá Strana tavern – shades of my youth – then move on to the Viola to read my verse. I shall take along my grandchildren, my children, the women I have loved, my parents resurrected, all my dead. We will not admit defeat, Prague. Stiff upper lip. Resist. All we can do is walk together the endless Chaplinesque road of hope.

1973

Notes

PART ONE

1

1. Vítězslav Nezval, *Z mého života*, Prague 1959, 177–9; Jiří Svoboda, *Přítel Vítězslav Nezval*, Prague 1966, 203.
2. Miloš Marten, *Nad městem* (1917). Now in *Dílo*, I, Prague 1924, 24.
3. Josef Čapek, "Diktátorské boty" (1937) in *Dějiny zblízka. Soubor satirických kreseb*, ed. Otakar Mrkvička, Prague 1949. Cf. Jaromír Pečírka, *Josef Čapek*, Prague 1961, 82.

2

1. Cf. Oskar Wiener, *Alt-Prager Guckkasten (Wanderungen durch das romantische Prag)*, Prague, Vienna and Leipzig 1922, 87.
2. Cf. Gregorio Comanini, "Il Figino ovvero Del fine della pittura" in *Trattati d'arte del Cinquecento*, III, ed. Paola Barocchi, Bari 1962, 257.
3. Cf. Alfred Métraux, *The Incas*, London 1965.
4. Cf. Ignát Herrmann, *Před padesáti lety*, Prague 1926, I, 86.
5. Cf. *ibid.*, III, 44–5.
6. Franz Kafka, *The Trial* in *The Complete Novels of Franz Kafka*, London 1988, 125.
7. *Ibid.*, 150–68. Pavel Eisner writes in his commentary to the Czech translation of *The Trial* that Kafka developed something of an "Italian complex" at the time he began to work for the Prague branch of Assicurazioni Generali ("'Proces' Franze Kafky" in Franz Kafka, *Proces*, Prague 1958, 222). Kafka wrote to Hedwig W. in November 1907: "I am learning Italian, for I shall probably be sent to Trieste first" (*Letters to Friends, Family, and Editors*, New York 1977, 37). The names Sordini and Sortini in *The Castle* also bear witness to this "complex".
8. Kafka, *The Trial*, 113.
9. Jiří Kolář, "Svědek" in *Ódy a variace*, Prague 1946, 31.
10. Vladimír Holan, *První testament* (1939–40), Prague 1940, 11.

3

1. Franz Kafka, *Letters to Friends, Family, and Editors*, 5–7 (to Oskar Pollak, 20 December 1902).
2. Cf. Vítězslav Nezval, "Město kniha" (1936) in *Básně všedního dne*. Now in *Dílo*, XII, Prague 1962, 148–9.
3. Josef Hora, "Praha ve snu" in *Proud*, Prague 1946, 61.
4. André Breton, "Introduction à l'œuvre de Toyen" in André Breton, Jindřich Heisler and Benjamin Péret, *Toyen*, Paris 1953, 11.
5. Arnošt Procházka, "Kouzlo Prahy" (1913). Now in *Rozhovory s knihami, obrazy i lidmi*, Prague 1916, 96.
6. Gustav Meyrink, "Der Mann aus der Flasche".
7. Nezval, "Večerka" in *Praha s prsty deště*. Now in *Dílo*, VI, Prague 1953,

123.

8. Wiener, *Deutsche Dichter aus Prag*, Vienna and Leipzig, 1919, 5. "Prague, the city of eccentrics and dreamers, this restless heart of Central Europe."
9. Breton, *Nadja*, Turin 1972, 15–16.
10. Kafka, *The Trial*, 168–9.
11. Cf. Nezval, "Mluvící panna" in *Zpáteční lístek*, Prague 1933, 171–6.
12. Kafka, *op. cit.*, 86.
13. Cf. Eduard Herold, "Lví dvůr", in *Podivuhodné příběhy ze staré Prahy*, ed. Karel Krejčí, Prague 1971, 142–4.
14. Mikhail Bulgakov, *The Master and Margarita*, trans. Michael Glenny, London 1967, 260–74.
15. Robert Musil, *The Man Without Qualities*, London 1979, 32.
16. Guillaume Apollinaire, "L'Otmika" (1903) in *L'Hérésiarque et Cie* (1910). Now in *Œuvres complètes*, I, ed. Michel Décaudin, Paris 1965, 156.
17. Karel Toman, "Tuláci" in *Sluneční hodiny* (1913). Now in *Dílo*, ed. A. M. Píša, Prague 1956, 100.
18. Friedrich Nietzsche, *Basic Writings of Nietzsche*, New York 1968, 708.
19. Nezval, *Pražský chodec*. Now in *Dílo*, XXXI, Prague 1958, 280–1.
20. Marten, *op. cit.*, 20.

4

1. Oskar Wiener, *Deutsche Dichter aus Prag*, 5.
2. Miloš Marten, *Nad městem*, 21.
3. Miloš Jiránek, "O krásné Praze" in *Dojmy a potulky* (1908). Now in *Dojmy a potulky a jiné práce*, Prague 1959, 43.
4. Vilém Mrštík, *Santa Lucia*, Prague 1948, 137, 139.
5. Cf. Jiří Karásek ze Lvovic, "Vilém a Alois Mrštíkové" in *Impresionisté a ironikové*, Prague 1903, 76–7.
6. F. X. Šalda, "Vilém Mrštík" in *Duše a dílo* (1913), Prague 1947, 115.
7. Arne Novák, "Praha a slovesná kultura" in *Kniha o Praze*, III, ed. Artuš Rektorys, Prague 1932, 17; cf. Vladimír Justl, *Bratři Mrštíkové*, Prague 1963, 12–14.
8. Vilém Mrštík, *Santa Lucia*, 231.
9. Franz Werfel, "The House of Mourning" in *Twilight of a World. A Collection of Novels and Stories*, trans. H. T. Lowe-Porter, London 1937.
10. Cf. Antonín Matějček, *Max Švabinský*, Prague 1947, 20–2; Jan Loris, *Max Švabinský*, Prague 1949, 100–4.

5

1. E. T. A. Hoffmann, "The Golden Pot" in *Selected Writings*, 2 vols., Chicago 1969.
2. Cf. Jaromír Neumann, *Český barok*, Prague 1969, 65–6.
3. Cf. Eugen Dostál, *Václav Hollar*, Prague 1924, 20, 134; Johannes Urzidil, *Hollar: A Czech Emigré in England*, London 1942, 22–3, 29.
4. Cf. Daniela Hodrová, "Umění projekce", *Orientace*, 3 (1968).
5. Cf. *Joseph Sima*, catalogue of the exhibition at the Musée National d'Art Moderne, Paris, 7 November–23 December 1968, with essays by Jean Leymarie, František Šmejkal, Roger Gilbert-Lecomte, Roger Caillois, etc.
6. Cf. Else Lasker-Schüler, *Die Wolkenbrücke. Briefe*, Munich 1972.
7. Vladimír Holan, "Vezmi můj dík" from the cycle *Víno* in *Trialog* (1964). Now in *Lamento*, Prague 1970, 72.

8. Richard Weiner, *Lazebník*, Prague 1929, 12.
9. Cf. E. T. A. Hoffmann, *Prinzessin Brambilla*.
10. Věra Linhartová, *Meziprůzkum nejblíž uplynulého*, České Budějovice 1964, 11.

6

1. Cf. Zdeněk Wirth, František Kop and Václav Ryneš, *Metropolitní chrám Svatého Víta*, Prague 1945; Vojtěch Birnbaum, *Listy z dějin umění*, Prague 1947, 91–112, 113–19, 120–45; A. Kutal, D. Líbal and A. Matějček, *České umění gotické: Stavitelství a sochařství*, I, Prague 1949, 24–6; Jan Wenig, *Chrám chrámů*, Prague 1955; Jakub Pavel, *Chrám Svatého Víta v Praze*, Prague 1968; Viktor Kotrba, "Architektura" in *České umění gotické: 1350–1420*, ed. Jaroslav Pěšina, Prague 1970, 58–62.
2. Vítězslav Nezval, *Pražský chodec*, 374.
3. Jaroslav Seifert, *Světlem oděná* (1940), Prague 1946, 24.
4. Cf. Ladislav Sitenský and Jaroslav Herout, *Praha stověžatá*, Prague 1971.
5. From the comedy *Strakonický dudák* (The Bagpiper of Strakonice, 1847) by Josef Kajetán Tyl (1808–56).
6. Franz Kafka, "Description of a Struggle" (1904–05) in *The Complete Stories*, New York 1971, 10.
7. Cf. Jaroslav Patera, *Bertramka v Praze*, Prague 1948, 92–8.
8. Vladimír Holan, *Noc s Hamletem*, Prague 1964, 55. English translation in Clayton Eshleman, *Conductors of the Pit: Major Works by Rimbaud, Vallejo, Césaire, Artaud and Holan*, New York 1988, 201–30.
9. Cf. Jan Herain, *Stará Praha*, Prague 1906, 130.
10. František Kupka titled several of his paintings "Vanoucí modře" (Rippling Shades of Blue). Cf. Ludmila Vachtová, *František Kupka*, Prague 1968.
11. Cf. Jindřich Štyrský, *Sny*, ed. František Šmejkal, Prague 1970, 69–70.
12. Cf. Vojtěch Volavka, *Pout' Prahou*, Prague 1967, 288.
13. Jiří Kolář, "Litanie" in *Ódy a variace*, Prague 1946, 16.
14. Miloš Jiránek, *Josef Mánes*, Prague 1917, 28.
15. Cf. Jan Dolenský, *Praha ve své slávě a utrpení*, Prague 1903, 298–300, 307–315; Joseph Wechsberg, *Prague: The Mystical City*, New York 1971, 67–8.
16. Cf. Herain, *op. cit.*, 245–55.
17. Gustav Janouch, *Conversations with Kafka*, London 1985, 79.
18. Cf. Volavka, *op. cit.*, 98; Eduard Bass, "Labutí píseň Na poříčí" in *Kukátko*, Prague 1970, 211–12.
19. Kolář, "Svědek" in *op. cit.*, 33.
20. Cf. Dolenský, *op. cit.*, 172–5.
21. Cf. N. Melniková-Papoušková, "Domovní znaky a vývěsní štíty pražské" in *Kniha o Praze*, III, ed. Artuš Rektorys, Prague 1932, 128–45.
22. Cf. Volavka, *op. cit.*, 159–60.
23. Cf. Egon Erwin Kisch, *Die Abenteuer in Prag*, Vienna, Prague and Leipzig 1920, 68–77; Volavka, *op. cit.*, 74–5.
24. Cf. Volavka, *op. cit.*, 33.

7

1. Vladimír Holan, *Lemuria* (1934–38), Prague 1940, 70.
2. Cf. Miroslav Lamač and Dietrich Mahlow, *Kolář*, Cologne 1968; Miroslav Lamač, *Jiří Kolář*, Prague 1970; Arturo Schwarz et al., *Jiří Kolář. L'Arte come*

Forma della libertà, Milan 1972; A. M. Ripellino, "Il suo messaggio esce da un cesto di coriandoli", *L'Espresso*, 23 April 1972.
3. Paul Adler, "Nämlich" (1915) in *Das leere Haus. Prosa jüdischer Dichter*, ed. Karl Otten, Stuttgart 1959, 180.

8

1. Cf. Max Brod, *Streitbares Leben*, Munich 1960, 208.
2. *Ibid.*, 292, 295–6; Kurt Krolop and Barbara Spitzová, "Gustav Meyrink," introduction to Gustav Meyrink, *Černá koule*, Prague 1967, 7–8, 12; Joseph Wechsberg, *Prague*, 40–3.
3. Franz Werfel, "Ein Versuch über das Kaisertum Österreich" in *Zwischen oben und unten*, Munich and Vienna 1975, 503.
4. Cf. Klaus Wagenbach, *Franz Kafka. Eine Biographie seiner Jugend*, Bern 1958, 71, 205 (n. 241); Eduard Goldstücker, "Předtucha zániku. K profilu pražské poezie před půlstoletím", *Plamen* 9 (1960); Hans Tramer, "Die Dreivölkerstadt Prag" in *Robert Weltsch zum 70. Geburtstag von seinen Freunden*, ed. Hans Tramer and Kurt Loewenstein, Tel Aviv 1961, 138.
5. Cf. Egon Erwin Kisch, "Deutsche und Tschechen" in *Marktplatz der Sensationen* (1942), Berlin 1953, 93–4; Emanuel Frynta and Jan Lukas, *Franz Kafka lebte in Prag*, Prague 1960, 44.
6. Cf. Kisch, *op. cit.*, 94–5.
7. Cf. Dušan Hamšík and Alexej Kusák, *O zuřivém reportéru E. E. Kischovi*, Prague 1962, 11.
8. Kisch, *op. cit.*, 93.
9. Quoted in Karel Teige, *Svět, který voní*, Prague 1930, 96. Cf. Roman Jakobson, "O dnešním brusičství českém" in *Spisovná čeština a jazyková kultura*, ed. Bohumil Havránek and Miloš Weingart, Prague 1932, 94.
10. Oskar Wiener, *Deutsche Dichter aus Prag*, 6.
11. Kisch, *Die Abenteuer in Prag*, 276–85.
12. Cf. Wagenbach, *op. cit.*, 86.
13. Cf. Emil Filla, "Eduard Munch a naše generace" (1938) in *O výtvarném umění*, Prague 1948, 66–76; Jiří Kotalík, "Moderní československé malířství" in *Československo* 3 (1947).
14. Cf. Jindřich Vodák, *Tři herecké podobizny*, Prague 1953, 102; František Černý, *Hana Kvapilová*, Prague 1960, 268–9, 271, 277.
15. Cf. Tramer, *op. cit.*, 146; see also Karel Hugo Hilar, "Příklad Maxe Reinhardta, tvůrce scenického prostředí" in *Divadelní promenády* (1906–14), Prague 1915, 99–106.
16. Kisch, *Marktplatz der Sensationen*, 73; see also Tramer, *op. cit.*, 145–6.
17. Cf. Pavel Eisner, "Franz Kafka a Praha", *Kritický měsíčník*, 3–4 (1948); and "Franz Kafka", *Světová literatura* 3 (1957).
18. Cf. Willy Haas, *Die literarische Welt*, Munich 1960, 10, 17; Tramer, *op. cit.*, 153, 157.
19. Kafka, *Letters* (10 April 1920); see also Gustav Janouch, *Conversations with Kafka*, 17: "He spoke both Czech and German, but more German. And his German had a hard accent, like that of the German spoken by the Czechs."
20. Richard Weiner, "Prázdná židle" in *Prázdná židle a jiné prózy*, with an introduction by Jaroslav Mrnka, Prague 1964, 118. Cf. Jindřich Chalupecký, *Richard Weiner*, Prague 1947, 26–7.

21. *Korespondence Leoše Janáčka s Maxem Brodem*, ed. Jan Racek and Artuš Rektorys, Prague 1953, 17 (6 December 1916).
22. Haas, *op. cit.*, 10–11.
23. Cf. Eisner, "Franz Kafka".
24. Werfel, *Barbara, oder Die Frömmigkeit* (1929). Cf. Haas, *op. cit.*, 18–19.
25. Werfel, "Der dicke Mann im Spiegel" in *Der Weltfreund* (1911).
26. Paul Leppin, *Severins Gang in die Finsternis*, Munich 1914, 125.
27. Cf. Hamšík and Kusák, *op. cit.*, 18–19.
28. Haas, *op. cit.*, 38.
29. Eisner, *Milenky*, Prague 1930.
30. Cf. Eisner, "Franz Kafka".
31. Cf. Kotalík, *loc. cit.*; see also Libuše Halasová, *Antonín Procházka*, Prague 1949, 20; Jiří Kotalík, *Václav Špála*, Prague 1972, 22–3.
32. Cf. Luboš Hlaváček, *Životní drama Bohumila Kubišty*, Prague 1968, 59.
33. Cf. Peter Demetz, *René Rilkes Prager Jahre*, Düsseldorf 1953, 106; Haas, *op. cit.*, 37–8.
34. "Über die Schönheit häßlicher Bilder" (1913); "Adolf Schreiber, ein Musikerschicksal" (1921); "Sternenhimmel" (1923).
35. Brod, *Leoš Janáček. Život a dílo*, Czech translation by Alfred Fuchs, Prague 1924 (*Leoš Janáček. Leben und Werk*, Vienna 1925). See also *Leoš Janáček – Obraz života a díla*, ed. Jan Racek, Brno 1948; *Korespondence Leoše Janáčka s Maxem Brodem*, 8–11; Brod, *Streitbares Leben*, 419–36.
36. Cf. Brod, *Franz Kafka. A Biography*, New York 1960.
37. Cf. Erwin Piscator, *Das politische Theater*, Berlin 1929, 187–203.
38. Cf. Bohumír Štědroň, *Janáček ve vzpomínkách a dopisech*, Prague 1946, 131–7; Robert Smetana, *Vyprávění o Leoši Janáčkovi*, Olomouc 1948, 63–4.
39. Cf. Hana Žantovská, "Básník jako majordomus mundi" in Franz Werfel, *Přítel světa*, Prague 1965, 137.
40. Jiří Wolker, "Věci" in *Host do domu* (1921).
41. Werfel, "Ich habe eine gute Tat getan" in *Der Weltfreund*.
42. Kisch, *op. cit.*, 319–24.
43. Cf. Edmond Konrád, *František Langer*, Prague 1949.
44. Jiří Langer, *Nine Gates to the Chassidic Mystics*, trans. Stephen Jolly, New York 1961.
45. Brod, *Streitbares Leben*, 66–84.
46. Cf. *ibid.*, 32–5.
47. Cf. Goldstücker, "Předtucha zániku".

9

1. Cf. F. X. Šalda, "Problémy lidu a lidovosti v nové tvorbě básnické" in *Šaldův zápisník*, IV, Prague 1931–32, 181–2.
2. Willy Haas, *Die literarische Welt*, 22.
3. Otto Pick, "Erinnerungen an den Winter 1911–12" in *Die Aktion* 1916, 605, cited in *Expressionismus: Literatur und Kunst (1910–1923)*, exhibition catalogue of the Schiller-Nationalmuseum in Marbach (8 May–31 October 1960). Cf. Kurt Pinthus, "Souvenirs des débuts de l'Expressionnisme" in *L'Expressionnisme dans le théâtre européen*, ed. Denis Bablet and Jean Jacquot, Paris 1971, 36.
4. Cf. Haas, *op. cit.*, 29.
5. Hans Tramer, *Die Dreivölkerstadt*, 143–5.
6. Max Brod, *Streitbares Leben*, 297–301.

7. Cf. Karel Krejčí, *Jakub Arbes. Život a dílo*, Prague 1946, 332–3.
8. Paul Leppin, *Severins Gang in die Finsternis*, 41–2.
9. Jan Herain, *Stará Praha*, 124–5; Géza Včelička, "Auf den Spuren Kischs in Prag" in *Kisch-Kalendar*, ed. F. C. Weiskopf, Berlin 1955, 255–6.
10. Karel Konrád, "Rodák ze Starého Města" in *Nevzpomínky*, Prague 1963, 94.
11. Včelička, *op. cit.*, 257–8.
12. Cf. A. M. Ripellino, *Il trucco e l'anima*, Turin 1965, 196–202.
13. Cf. Zenon, *Jama Michalika: Lokal "Zielonego Balonika"*, Cracow 1930; Tadeusz Boy-Żeleński, *Znaszli ten kraj? . . . i inne wspomnienia*, Warsaw 1956.
14. Cf. *Kavárna Union (Sborník vzpomínek pamětníků)*, ed. Adolf Hoffmeister, Prague 1958.
15. Cf. Egon Erwin Kisch, "Zitate vom Montmartre" in *Die Abenteuer in Prag* in *op. cit.*, 399–404; Zdeněk Matěj Kuděj, *Ve dvou se to lépe táhne* (1923–27), Prague 1971, 288–95; Emil Artur Longen, *Jaroslav Hašek* (1928), Prague 1947, 37; Václav Menger, *Jaroslav Hašek doma*, Prague 1935, 247–9; Včelička, *op. cit.*, 259; Jiří Červený, *Červená sedma*, Prague 1959, 53; Hamšík and Kusák, *op. cit.*, 27–31; František Langer, "Vzpomínání na Jaroslava Haška" in *Byli a bylo*, Prague 1963, 30, 52–3; Ján L. Kalina, *Svět kabaretu*, Bratislava 1966, 369; Radko Pytlík, *Toulavé house. Zpráva o Jaroslavu Haškovi*, Prague 1971, 219–21.
16. Karl Kraus in *Die Fackel*, MCLVI–MCXL, 68.
17. Cf. Rober Bauer, "La querelle Kraus-Werfel" in *L'Expresionnisme dans le théâtre européen*, 141–51.
18. Kraus, *ibid.*, CCCXCVIII, 19.
19. Brod, *op. cit.*, 36.
20. Cf. *Deutsche Dichter aus Prag*, 5.
21. Cf. Karl Otten, Afterword to *Das leere Haus*, 610–12; Michel Zéraffa, "Le roman et sa problématique de 1909 à 1915" in *L'Année 1913*, I, ed. L. Brion-Guerry, Paris 1971, 649–53.
22. Brod, *ibid.*, 212; see also Tramer, *op. cit.*, 189–91.
23. Else Lasker-Schüler, *Die gesammelten Gedichte*, Munich 1920, 114–6.
24. Cf. Brod, *op. cit.*, 212, 215; Joseph Wechsberg, *Prague*, 43–5.
25. Haas, *op. cit.*, 12–3.
26. Franz Blei, *Das große Bestiarium* (1922), Munich 1963, 42.
27. Leppin, *op. cit.*, 42.
28. Cf. Brod, *op. cit.*, 300.
29. Ripellino, "Fuksiana". Introduction to Ladislav Fuks, *Il bruciacadaveri*, Turin 1972.
30. Czech expressions, mostly from German or Yiddish (e.g., *pajzl* from *bayis*, "house"), denoting dives, beerhalls, hotels renting rooms by the hour and houses of ill-fame.
31. Cf. Kisch, "Konsignation über verbotene Lokale" in *Die Abenteuer in Prag*, 301–17; Hamšík and Kusák, *op. cit.*, 30–1.
32. *Aus Prager Gassen und Nächten* (1908), *Prager Kinder* (1911), *Die Abenteuer in Prag* (1920), *Prager Pitaval* (1931) and *Marktplatz der Sensationen* (1942).
33. Konrád, *op. cit.*, 94.
34. Cf. Kisch, "Die Himmelfahrt der Galgentoni" in *Marktplatz der Sensationen*, 239–66.
35. Cf. Hamšík and Kusák, *op. cit.*, 32–7.
36. Werfel, *Zwischen oben und unten*, 504.

37. Goldstücker, "Předtucha zániku".
38. Brod, *op. cit.*, 301.
39. Lasker-Schüler, *op. cit.*, 154.

10

1. Bohumil Hrabal, "Kafkárna" in *Inzerát na dům, ve kterém už nechci bydlet*, Prague 1965, 17.
2. Franz Kafka, *America* in *The Collected Novels of Franz Kafka*, London 1988, 527.
3. Cf. Kafka, Diaries, London 1972.
4. Theodor W. Adorno, "Aufzeichnungen zu Kafka" in *Prismen*, Berlin 1955, 340.
5. *Ibid.*, 333.
6. Willy Haas, *Die literarische Welt*, 32.
7. Max Brod, *Streitbares Leben*, 272.
8. Franz Blei, *Das große Bestiarium*, 25. The reference to "bitter herbs" recalls the fact that Kafka was a vegetarian for a time. Cf. Brod, *Franz Kafka. A Biography*, 74.
9. Cf. Peter Demetz, "Franz Kafka a český národ" in *Franz Kafka a Praha*, Prague 1947, 46–8 and *René Rilkes Prager Jahre*, 113–35.
10. In a letter to Oskar Pollak dated 9 November 1903 (Kafka, *Letters*, 11).
11. Cf. Demetz, *René Rilkes Prager Jahre*, 11–29, 138–40, 146–50.
12. Cf. Brod, *op. cit.*, 11–15; Emanuel Frynta and Jan Lukas, *Franz Kafka lebte in Prag*, 70–4; Klaus Wagenbach, *Franz Kafka in Selbstzeugnissen und Bilddokumenten*, Reinbek bei Hamburg 1964, 11–17.
13. Cf. Wagenbach, *Franz Kafka, Eine Biographie seiner Jugend*, 74; František Kautman, "Kafka et la Bohême", *Europe*, November–December 1971.
14. Cf. Wagenbach, *Franz Kafka in Selbstzeugnissen*, 69.
15. Cf. Wagenbach, *Franz Kafka: Eine Biographie seiner Jugend*, 162–4; Frynta and Lukas, *op. cit.*, 12.
16. Cf. Hugo Siebenschein, "Prostředí a čas" in *Franz Kafka a Praha*, 22.
17. Egon Erwin Kisch, "Deutsche und Tschechen" in *Marketplatz der Sensationen*, 95.
18. Cf. Kautman, "Franz Kafka a česká literatura", in *Franz Kafka*, Prague 1963, 47. German edition: *Kafka aus Prager Sicht*, Prague 1966, 51.
19. Cf. Brod, *op. cit.*, 98–102; idem, *Streitbares Leben*, 66–7; Wagenbach, *Franz Kafka. Eine Biographie seiner Jugend*, 179–81.
20. Kafka, *Diaries*, 222 (1 July 1913).
21. *Ibid.*, 78–9 (16 October 1911).
22. In the story "The Cares of a Family Man" (1917). According to Max Brod (*Franz Kafka. A Biography*, 135), "say 'Odradek' and a whole range of Slav words is set ringing, which all mean renegade, renegade from one's race, 'rod', renegade from the council, 'rada', the divine decision of the creation, 'rat'".
23. Cf. Gustav Janouch, *Conversations with Kafka*, 138; Kautman, *op. cit.*, 46–7.
24. Cf. *Diaries*, 398 (23 December 1921).
25. Kafka, *Letters to Milena*, New York 1990, 8.
26. Max Beckmann, *Tagebücher 1940–1950*, Munich 1955.
27. Kafka, *Letters to Milena*, 14.
28. Cf. Brod, *op. cit.*, 189–209; Haas, *op. cit.*, 38–41; Wagenbach, *Franz Kafka in Selbstzeugnissen*, 122–6.

29. Cf. Jana Černá, *Adresát Milena Jesenská*, Prague 1969.
30. Kafka, *Letters*, 145.
31. *Ibid.*, 154.
32. Kafka, *Diaries*, 148–51.
33. Kafka, *Letters*, 151.
34. *Ibid.*, 198.
35. *Ibid.*, 308.
36. *Ibid.*, 145.
37. Kafka, *Letters to Milena*, 31.
38. Brod, *op. cit.*, 221.
39. Cf. František Kovárna, *František Bílek*, Prague 1941.
40. Kafka, *Letters*, 348–50; Brod, *op. cit.*, 134 [German edition].
41. Cf. *Dopisy Otokara Březiny Františku Bílkovi*, ed. Vilém Nečas, Prague 1932; *Básník a sochař. Dopisy Julia Zeyera a Františka Bílka z let 1896–1901*, ed. J. R. Marek, Prague 1948.
42. Cf. Wagenbach, *Franz Kafka in Selbstzeugnissen*, 20–1; Wagenbach, *Franz Kafka. Eine Biographie seiner Jugend*, 66–8; Frynta and Lukas, *op. cit.*, 74–81.
43. Rio Preiser, *Kapiláry*, Brno, 1968, 9, 13.
44. Kafka, "Description of a Struggle", 15.
45. Frynta and Lukas, *op. cit.*, 121.
46. Cf. Demetz, "Franz Kafka a český národ", 51–2.
47. Cf. Adorno, *op. cit.*, 327, 331: "A number of critical passages in Kafka read as though they retraced Expressionist paintings which had not yet been painted."
48. Cf. Pavel Eisner, "'Proces' Franze Kafky", 217.
49. Cf. Siebenschein, *op. cit.*, 16–17.
50. Cf. Adorno, *op. cit.*, 318.
51. Cf. Haas, *op. cit.*, 31.
52. Cf. Brod, *op. cit.*, 154.
53. Cf. Aleksandr Blok, *Zapisnye knizhki*, ed. N. Orlov, Moscow 1965.
54. Kafka, *Diaries*, 138.
55. Kafka, *Letters to Milena*, 41.
56. Kafka, *Letters*, 32.
57. *Ibid.*, 82–3.
58. *Ibid.*, 151.
59. *Ibid.*, 35.
60. Brod, *op. cit.*, 15.
61. Kafka, *Diaries*.
62. *Ibid.*
63. *Ibid.*
64. Walter Benjamin, "Franz Kafka" in *Gesammelte Schriften* II.2, Frankfurt am Main 1977, 431–2.
65. Cf. Kafka, *Diaries*, 321, 355, 368, 556–7, etc.
66. Vladimír Holan, "Kolury" (1932) in *Babyloniaca, Sebrané spisy*, Prague 1968, IX, 80.

11

1. Mikuláš Dačický z Heslova, *Paměti*, I, ed. Antonín Rezek, Prague 1878, 268.
2. Jan Amos Komenský, *Labyrint světa a ráj srdce*, Prague 1940, 15. (English

version, John Amos Comenius, *The Labyrinth of the World and the Paradise of the Heart*, trans. Matthew Spinka, Ann Arbor 1972, 4–5. Page numbers in parantheses below refer to this edition.)
3. *Ibid.*
4. Cf. F. X. Salda, "České zrcátko", *Šaldův zápisník*, VIII, Prague 1935–36, 78–81.
5. Komenský, *op. cit.*, 95 (84).
6. *Ibid.*, 113 (102).

12
1. Jan Amos Komenský, *Labyrint světa*, 20 (9).
2. *Ibid.*, 95 (84).
3. *Ibid.*, 97 (86).

13
1. Josef Čapek, *Kulhavý poutník*, Prague 1936, 14.
2. *Ibid.*, 36.
3. Věra Linhartová, *Meziprůzkum nejblíž uplynulého*, 70.
4. Josef Čapek, *op. cit.*, 29.
5. *Ibid.*, 169.
6. *Ibid.*, 65.
7. *Ibid.*, 107.
8. *Psáno do mraků*, Prague 1947.

14
1. Karel and Josef Čapek, *Ze života hmyzu*, Prague 1947, 16.
2. *Ibid.*, 81, 84.
3. *Ibid.*, 90–1.
4. *Ibid.*, 101.
5. Věra Linhartová, *Meziprůzkum nejblíž uplynulého uplynulého*, 10.

15
1. Karel Hynek Mácha, "Poutník" in *Dílo*, III, Prague 1948, 103.
2. *Máj* in *Dílo*, I, 49.
3. "Umírající" in *Dílo*, I, 127.
4. Cf. Albert Pražák, *Karel Hynek Mácha*, Prague 1936, 131–3.
5. "Pout' krkonošská" in *Dílo*, II, 157.
6. *Ibid.*, 159.
7. "Sen" in *Dílo*, III, 82–6.
8. "Pout' krkonošská" in *Dílo*, II, 166.
9. "Poutník" in *Dílo*, III, 144.
10. Cf. Bohumil Novák, "Četba a zážitek jako prameny básníkovy tvorby" in *Věčný Mácha*, Prague 1940, 131–4.
11. "Cikáni" in *Dílo*, II, 293, 303.
12. "Karlův Tejn" in *Dílo*, II, 93.
13. "Pout' krkonošská" in *Dílo*, II, 159–60.
14. *Ibid.*, 165.
15. "Dobrou noc!" in *Dílo*, I, 124–5.
16. "Umírající" in *Dílo*, I, 127.
17. "Zastaveníčko" in *Dílo*, I, 78.

18. See also "Literární zápisníky" in *Dílo*, III, 68.

16

1. Franz Kafka, *The Castle*, 220.
2. *Ibid.*, 268.
3. *Ibid.*, 362.
4. Kafka, *The Trial*, 172.
5. Marthe Robert, *Kafka*, Paris 1960, 88.
6. Kafka, *The Trial*, 85.
7. *Ibid.*, 40.
8. Robert, *op. cit.*, 145: "small closed circles, with him [the protagonist] the only possible link between them".

17

1. Franz Kafka, *The Castle*, 429.
2. Jiří Orten, *Deníky*, ed. Jan Grossman, Prague 1958, 89.
3. "Cvičení o sněhu" in *Deníky*, 158.
4. *Deníky*, 204.
5. *Deníky*, 190.
6. "Sněžná pout'" in *Deníky*, 333.
7. "Mlčení" in *Deníky*, 347.
8. "Bílý obraz" in *Deníky*, 159.
9. "Devátá elegie" in *Deníky*, 402.
10. "Sníh nebo réva" in *Deníky*, 449.
11. Paul Leppin, *Severins Gang in die Finsternis*, 49.
12. Hugo Salus, "Wintertag auf dem Hradschin" in Oskar Wiener, *Deutsche Dichter aus Prag*, 306.
13. Orten, *Deníky*, 231.
14. František Halas, *Magická moc poesie*, Prague 1958, 111.
15. Cf. Antonín Brousek, "Hrst kamínků na nepřítomný hrob Jiřího Ortena" in Orten, *Čemu se báseň říká*, Prague 1967, 14–15.
16. Orten, *Deníky*, 267.
17. Halas, *op. cit.*, 110.
18. Orten, "Sedmá elegie" in *Deníky*, 393.
19. Cf. Ota Ornest, "O bratrovi" in Orten, *Deníky*, 465.
20. Orten, *Deníky*, 155.
21. *Ibid.*, 89.
22. *Ibid.*, 165–6.
23. Cf. Jan Grossman, "Deníky Jiřího Ortena" in Orten, *Deníky*, 7–32.
24. Orten, "Zákazy" in *Deníky*, 303–4.
25. Vladimír Holan, *Lemuria*, 18.
26. Orten, *Deníky*, 318.
27. Orten, "Věčně" in *Dílo*, Prague 1947, 398.
28. "Co jsem odpověděl kanárkovi" in *Deníky*, 282.
29. "Poslední báseň" in *Deníky*, 289.
30. Cf. Václav Černý, "Za Jiřím Ortenem" (1947), *Host do domu*, 9, 1966; Josef Kocián, *Jiří Orten*, Prague 1966, 56–7.
31. Orten, "První elegie" in *Deníky*, 367.
32. "Scestí" in *Deníky*, 408.
33. Halas, *op. cit.*, 110.
34. Orten, "Po hudbě" in *Deníky*, 300.

35. "Epitaf" in *Deníky*, 326.
36. "Báseň kamene" in *Deníky*, 119.

18

1. A Czech translation by Karel Vratislav (*Pražská čarodějka*) appeared in 1912.

19

1. Jaroslav Vrchlický, "Slavík v městě", "U Seminářské zahrady", "Motiv z Hradčan" in *Mythy. Selské balady. Má vlast*, Prague 1955, 413–14, 424, 426.
2. Guillaume Apollinaire, *Œuvres complètes*, I, ed. Michel Décaudin, Paris 1965, 106, 110.
3. Vítězslav Nezval, *Pražský chodec*, 241.
4. *Ibid.*
5. *Ibid.*, 235.
6. *Ibid.*, 252–3, 259.

20

1. Jaroslav Seifert, *Světlem oděná*, 11.
2. Cf. *Město vidím veliké . . .*, ed. Vincy Schwarz, Prague 1940, 476.
3. Jaroslav Vrchlický, "Praha v květu" in *Mythy. Selské balady. Má vlast*, 383.
4. Seifert, *op. cit.*, 39.
5. Vrchlický, *op. cit.*, 425.

21

1. Vladimír Holan, *První testament*, 9–10.
2. Cf. Jiří Kotalík, "Několik poznámek o Skupině 1942" in *Život*, 4–5 (1946) and "Moderní československé malířství" in *Československo*, 3 (1947).
3. Cf. Kotalík, *František Gross*, Prague 1963; and František Gross, *František Gross*, Prague 1969.
4. Cf. Eva Petrová, *František Hudeček*, Prague 1969.
5. Franz Kafka, *America*, 483.
6. Cf. Jan Grossman, "Horečná bdělost Jiřího Koláře" in Jiří Kolář, *Náhodný svědek*, Prague 1964, 186.
7. Kolář, "Ráno" in *Ódy a variace*, Prague 1946, 47.
8. "Litanie", 15.
9. "Ráno", 47.
10. "Litanie", 16.
11. "Svědek", 31.
12. Ivan Blatný, "Tabulky", *Kytice*, 6 (1947); "Den" *Blok*, 1 (1947); "Hra", *Kritický měsíčník*, 1947, 385–90.

22

1. Jiří Kolář, "Ráno", *Ódy a variace*, 47.
2. "Druhá ranní", 52.
3. Ivan Blatný, "Podzimní den" in *Tento večer*, Prague 1945, 28.
4. "Krajina", 36.
5. Cf. Ludvík Souček, *Jiří Sever*, Prague, 1968.
6. Jiří Wolker, "Návrat" in *Básně*, Prague 1950, 61.
7. Franz Kafka, "Description of a Struggle" in *The Complete Stories*, 14.

8. Paul Leppin, *Severins Gang in die Finsternis*, 73, 144, 12–13.
9. *Ibid.*, 109.
10. *Ibid.*, 145, 77.
11. Max Brod, *Streitbares Leben*, 212, 214.
12. Karel Hynek Mácha, *Zápisník* (1833) in *Dílo*, III, 131.

23
1. Jan Amos Komenský, *Labyrint světa*, 51 (39).
2. Mikuláš Dačický z Heslova, *Paměti*, I, 152 (1577), 189 (1596), 208 (1605), 250 (1619).
3. *Ibid.*, 208 (1605).
4. Jiří Karásek ze Lvovic, *Král Rudolf*, Prague 1916, 37.

24
1. Jaroslav Seifert, "Praha" in *Poštovní holub* (1929).
2. Vítězslav Nezval, "Podivuhodný kouzelník" (1921), zpěv sedmý.
3. Jiří Karásek ze Lvovic, *Král Rudolf*, 24–5.
4. Mikuláš Dačický z Heslova, *Paměti*, I, 195 (1599).
5. *Ibid.*, 190 (1596).

25
1. Jiří Karásek ze Lvovic, *Román Manfred Macmillena*, Prague 1907, 105.
2. Josef Svátek, *Astrolog* (1890–91), Prague 1924–28, 31.
3. *Ibid.*, 103, 116.
4. Vítězslav Hálek, *Král Rudolf*, Prague, 1862, IV.iii.
5. Voskovec and Werich, *Hry Osvobozeného divadla*, II, Prague 1955, 104.
6. Věra Linhartová, *Meziprůzkum nejblíž uplynulého*, 80.

26
1. Cf. Karel Pejml, *Dějiny české alchymie*, Prague 1933, 48–9; Karel Krejčí, *Praha legend a skutečnosti*, Prague 1967, 157.
2. *Město vidím veliké* . . . , 373.
3. Max Brod, *Tycho Brahes Weg zu Gott*, Leipzig 1916, 37.
4. Cf. "Neu vermehrter Curieuser Antiquarius" (1746) in *Město vidím veliké* . . . , 93.
5. Galileo Galilei, *Dialogo sopra i due massimi sistemi del mondo tolemaico e copernicano*, Turin 1970, 65.
6. Cf. F. J. Studnička, *Prager Tychoniana*, Prague 1901, 63–6; Ingvald Undset (1810) in *Město vidím veliké* . . . , 175; Jan Dolenský, *Praha ve své slávě i utrpení*, Prague 1903, 327–30.
7. Guillame Apollinaire, "Le passant de Prague" in *Œuvres complètes*, I, 109.
8. Karásek ze Lvovic, *Román Manfreda Macmillena*, 38.
9. F. Marion Crawford, *The Witch of Prague*, New York and London 1891, 7, 28–9.
10. Brod, *op. cit.*, 63–4, 109–10, 311.

27
1. Jiří Karásek ze Lvovic, *Ganymedes*, Prague 1925, Ch. 14, 49.
2. Cf. Jan Dolenský, *Praha ve své slávě a utrpení*, 99–100.
3. Cf. Karel Pejml, *Dějiny české alchymie*, 49.
4. Cf. *Město vidím veliké* . . . , 430.

5.   Cf. *Dějiny českého divadla*, ed. František Černý, I, Prague 1968, 194–6.
6.   Cf. Dolenský, *op. cit.*, 221–2.

28

1.   Voskovec and Werich, *Golem* in *Hry Osvobozeného divadla*, II, 94.
2.   Cf. Jan Bedřich Novák, *Rudolf II. a jeho pád*, Prague 1935, 3; Kamil Krofta, *Dějiny československé*, Prague 1946, 364–89; Krejčí, *Praha legend a skutečnosti*, 145; Philippe Erlanger, *Rudolphe II de Habsbourg*, Paris 1971.
3.   Cf. Novák, *op. cit.*, 5, 9.
4.   Cf. Josef Polišenský, *Doba Rudolfa II.*, Prague 1941, 15.
5.   Cf. *ibid.*, 20.
6.   Cf. *ibid.*, 20, 22.

29

1.   Cf. Jan Bedřich Novák, *Rudolf II. a jeho pád*, 19–20.
2.   Max Brod, *Tycho Brahes Weg zu Gott*, 375–8; Josef Jiří Kolár, *Magelóna* (1852), I.ii.; Vítězslav Hálek, *Král Rudolf* (1862); Jiří Karásek ze Lvovic, *Král Rudolf*, 15.
3.   Karásek ze Lvovic, *op. cit.*, 59.
4.   Karel Pejml, *Dějiny české alchymie*, 43.
5.   Cf. Kolár, *Pekla zplozenci*, Prague 1862, 16; Josef Svátek, *Astrolog*, 66–70; Jan Dolenský, *Praha ve své slávě a utrpení*, 87–8; Brod, *op. cit.*, 375–8; F. X. Harlas, *Rudolf II., milovník umění a sběratel*, Prague 1916, 27; Augustin Vojtěch, *Praha kamenný sen*, Prague 1941, 144; Karel Krejčí, *Praha legend a skutečnosti*, 152.
6.   Cf. Novák, *op. cit.*, 21.
7.   Cf. Kolár, *Magelóna*, II.ii.; Karásek ze Lvovic, *Král Rudolf*, 15.
8.   Cf. Novák, *op. cit.*, 25.
9.   Cf. *ibid.*, 22–3.
10.   Karásek ze Lvovic, *Král Rudolf*, 10–11.
11.   Cf. Novák, *op. cit.*, 21.
12.   Cf. *ibid.*, 24.
13.   Cf. Anton Gindely, *Rudolf II. und seine Zeit*, II, Prague 1865, 337.
14.   Cf. *ibid.*, 338–43.
15.   Kolár, *op. cit.*, II.ii.

30

1.   Cf. Jan Bedřich Novák, *Rudolf II. a jeho pád*, 25.
2.   Cf. *ibid.*, 25–6.
3.   Cf. Karel Pejml, *Dějiny české alchymie*, 49.
4.   Karásek ze Lvovic, *Král Rudolf*, 10–11.
5.   *Ibid.*, 39, 66.
6.   Vítězslav Hálek, *Král Rudolf*, V.ii.
7.   Josef Jiří Kolár, *Magelóna*, II.ii.

31

1.   Cf. Karl Chytil, *Kunst und Künstler am Hofe Rudolfs II.*, Prague 1913; Jaromír Neumann, *Obrazárna Pražského hradu*, Prague 1966.
2.   Josef Svátek, *Astrolog*, 72, 74.
3.   Cf. Jan Morávek, "Dvůr Rudolfův: sbírky na Pražském hradě" in *Co daly naše země Evropě a lidstvu*, ed. Vilém Mathesius, Prague 1940, 143–5.

4. Cf. Neumann, *op. cit.*, 32.
5. Cf. Svátek, "Poslední dnové Rudolfových sbírek v Praze" in *Obrazy z kulturních dějin českých*, Prague 1891, I, 50; F. X. Harlas, *Rudolf II.*
6. Svátek, *Astrolog*, 49, 71.

32

1. Max Brod, *Tycho Brahes Weg zu Gott*, 397.
2. Cf. Jaromír Neumann, *Obrazárna Pražského hradu*, 18.
3. Cf. F. X. Harlas, *Rudolf II.*, 49, 58, 60, 66, 67, 68.
4. Cf. Neumann, *op. cit.*, 156–8.
5. Cf. Karel Chytil, *La Couronne de Rudolphe II*, Prague 1921.

33

1. Cf. F. X. Harlas, *Rudolf II.*, 60.
2. Cf. *ibid.*, 60–8.
3. Alfred Kubin, *The Other Side: A Fantastic Novel*. New York 1967, 150.
4. Cf. Harlas, *op. cit.*, 64.

34

1. Max Brod, *Tycho Brahes Weg zu Gott*, 395.
2. Jiří Karásek ze Lvovic, *Král Rudolf*, 16.

35

1. Jaroslav Seifert, "Praha" in *Poštovní holub* (1929).
2. Cf. F. X. Harlas, *Rudolf II.*, 23.
3. Mikuláš Dačický z Heslova, *Paměti*, I, 261 (1619); cf. Pejml, *Dějiny české alchymie*, 49–50.
4. Cf. Josef Svátek, "Poslední dnové Rudolfových sbírek v Praze" in *Obrazy z kulturních dějin českých*, 47–67.
5. Cf. Jaromír Neumann, *Obrazárna Pražského hradu*, 21.
6. Cf. *ibid.*, 24–7.
7. Cf. *ibid.*, 16, 33.
8. Cf. *ibid.*, 33.
9. Cf. *ibid.*, 38.
10. Cf. *ibid.*, 42.
11. Cf. *ibid.*, 43.
12. Cf. Svátek, *op. cit.*, 62.
13. Cf. Neumann, *op. cit.*, 11.
14. Seifert, "Praha" in *Poštovní holub* (1929).
15. Cf. Neumann, *op. cit.*, 50–1.
16. Cf. *ibid.*, 53–4.
17. Seifert, *Pražský hrad*, Prague 1969.

36

1. Jaroslav Hašek, *Osudy dobrého vojáka Švejka za světové války*, Prague 1968, I–II, 193. (English edition: *The Good Soldier Svejk and His Fortunes in the World War*, trans. Sir Cecil Parrott, London 1974, 211. Page numbers in parentheses refer to this edition.)
2. Daniello Bartoli, "La ricreazione del savio" in *Trattatisti e narratori del Seicento*, ed. Ezio Raimondi, Milan and Naples 1960, 555.
3. Gregorio Comanini, *Il Figino*, 257. Cf. Benno Geiger, *I dipinti ghiribizzosi di*

Giuseppe Arcimboldi, Florence 1954. German edition: *Die skurrilen Gemälde des Giuseppe Arcimboldi*, Wiesbaden 1960.
4. Jaroslav Vrchlický, *Rabínská moudrost* (1886), Prague 1902, 31–2.

37

1. Cf. Gustav René Hocke, *Die Welt als Labyrinth*, Hamburg 1957, 45–6, 144–9.
2. Gregorio Comanini, *Il Figino*, 266.
3. Jan Amos Komenský, *Labyrint světa*, 40 (28–9).
4. Jaroslav Hašek, *Švejk*, 38.
5. Komenský, *op. cit.*, 98 (87).
6. Comanini, *op. cit.*, 266–7 .

38

1. Cf. Oskar Kokoschka, *Schriften 1907–55*, Munich 1956, 593.
2. Gregorio Comanini, *Il Figino*, 269–70.
3. Cf. Pavel Preiss, *Giuseppe Arcimboldo*, Prague 1967, 17.
4. Cf. Lucy Lippard, *Pop Art*, London 1966, 110.
5. Cf. Marcel Mauss, *Manuel d'ethnographie*, Paris 1967, 60, 95, 97.

39

1. Gregorio Comanini, *Il Figino*, 269.

40

1. Cf. Marcel Mauss, *Manuel d'ethnographie*, 249.
2. Cf. Čeněk Zíbrt, *Veselé chvíle v životě lidu českého* (1909–11), Prague 1950; Petr Bogatyrev, *Lidové divadlo české a slovenské*, Prague 1940; *Dějiny českého divadla*, I, 285–7.
3. Cf. Jan Port, "Divadelní výtvarníci staré Prahy" in *Kniha o Praze*, ed. Artuš Rektorys, Prague 1932, III, 75–8; Pavel Preiss, *op. cit.*, 10; *Dějiny českého divadla*, I, 140.
4. Cf. Ivo Pondělíček, *Fantaskní umění*, Prague 1964, 99–102.
5. Gregorio Comanini, *Il Figino*, 258–64

41

1. Vítězslav Nezval, *Řetěz štěstí*, Prague 1936, 35, 42.
2. *Absolutní hrobař*, Prague 1937, 9–20. Cf. Jan Mukařovský, "Semantický rozbor básnického díla: Nezvalův "Absolutní hrobař" (1938) in *Kapitoly z české poetiky*, Prague 1948, II, 269–89.
3. El Lissitzký, *Sieg über die Sonne* (1923), Cologne 1958.
4. František Halas, "U hrobu" and "Ticho" in *Sepie* (1927).
5. Cf. *Kreslíř Adolf Hoffmeister*, Prague 1948; Miroslav Lamač, *Výtvarné dílo Adolfa Hoffmeistera*, Prague 1966.

42

1. In *Poštovní holub*, 1929.
2. Cf. Josef Svátek, "Alchymie v Čechách za doby Rudolfa II." in *Obrazy z kulturních dějin českých*, II, 43; Karel Pejml, "Alchymie v Čechách před Bílou Horou" in *Co daly naše země Evropě a lidstvu*, 149–53; V. H. Matula, "Alchymie v českých zemích" in *Hledání kamene mudrců*, Prague 1948,

69–97; Alois Míka, "Alchymisté a šarlatáni v rudolfinské Praze" in *Kniha o Praze*, ed. Josef Janáček, Prague 1965, 282–96.

3. Cf. Svátek, "Alchymie," 59; Pejml, *Dějiny české alchymie*, 44, 50.
4. Cf. J. van Lennep, *Art et alchimie*, Brussels 1966, 201–2
5. Cf. Svátek, *Alchymie*, 60–1; Pejml, 65.
6. Cf. Pejml, *op. cit.*, 43.
7. Cf. Zdeněk Kobza, *Alchymie*, Prague 1916, 28; Pejml, *op. cit.*, 19, 43.

43

1. Max Brod, *Streitbares Leben*, 304.
2. Gustav Meyrink, *The Golem*, New York 1976. Chapter "Woman". See also Johannes Urzidil, *Prager Triptychon*, Munich 1960, 11–12.
3. Oskar Wiener, *Alt-Prager Guckkasten*, 67.
4. Cf. *ibid.*, 67–8.
5. Cf. J. van Lennep, *Art et alchimie*, 86–7.
6. Meyrink, *Der Engel vom westlichen Fenster*, Bremen 1927, 249.
7. Cf. Emanuel Poche, *Zlatá ulička na Pražském hradě*, Prague 1969.
8. Cf. Svátek, "K dějinám katů a poprav v Čechách" in *Obrazy kulturních dějin českých*, II, 160; Alois Jirásek, *Staré pověsti české* (1894), Prague 1949, 190–6; Jan Dolenský, *Praha ve své slávě a utrpení*, 100; Wiener, *op. cit.*, 66; Adolf Wenig, *Staré pověsti pražské*, Prague 1931, 289–91.
9. Cf. Brod, *Franz Kafka*, 156; Emanuel Frynta and Jan Lukas, *Franz Kafka lebte in Prag*, 108; Wagenbach, *Franz Kafka in Selbstzeugnissen*, 103–4; Poche, *op. cit.*, 40.
10. Franz Kafka, *The Castle*, 188.
11. Vítězslav Nezval, "U alchymistů" in *Zpáteční lístek*, 25.
12. Eric Bentley, ed., *The Genius of Italian Theater*, New York 1964, 223.
13. Jan Amos Komenský, *Labyrint světa*, Chapter 12.
14. Jaroslav Seifert, *Světlem oděná*, 22.
15. Jiří Karásek ze Lvovic, *Král Rudolf*, I.xi.
16. Cf. Stanisław Helsztyński, *Przybyszewski*, Cracow 1958, 167–76, 449; Otakar Štorch-Marien, *Sladko je žít*, Prague 1966, 178–82; Poche, *op. cit.*, 40.
17. Cf. Otakar Štorch-Marien, *op. cit.*, 130–1; Poche, *op. cit.*, 48–9.

44

1. Cf. Alexandr Kraushar, *Czary na dworze Batorego. Karta z dziejów mistycyzmu w XVI. wieku, jako przyczynek do charakterystyki króla Stefana*, Cracow 1888, 129–30; The portrait I have created of John Dee is based on legends and reflects the Bohemian point of view. For an objective depiction of this Prospero of an alchemist see the excellent essay by Furio Jesi, "John Dee e il suo sapere" in *Comunità*, 166 (1972), 272–303.
2. Josef Svátek, "Anglický alchymista Kelley v Čechách" in *Obrazy z kulturních dějin českých*, I, 136; cf. C. A. Burland, *The Arts of the Alchemists*, London 1967, 91–3.
3. Cf. Svátek, *op. cit.*, 136–7; Karel Pejml, *Dějiny české alchymie*, 54.
4. Meyrink, *Der Engel vom westlichen Fenster*, 206.
5. Cf. Kraushar, *op. cit.*, 132–3; Svátek, *op. cit.*, 137–8.
6. Giordano Bruno, *La Cena delle Ceneri* (Dialogue Four).
7. Kraushar, *op. cit.*, 136; Svátek, *op. cit.*, 138–9.
8. Cf. *ibid*, 159.
9. Cf. *ibid.*, 182–3, 200.

10. Cf. *ibid.*, 165–6, 167–8; Pejml, *op. cit.*, 52.
11. Cf. Svátek, *op. cit.*, 64–5; Pejml, *op. cit.*, 38–40.
12. Cf. J. van Lennap, *Art et alchimie*, 236–41.
13. Cf. Kraushar, *op. cit.*, 215, 217; Pejml, *op. cit.*, 53.
14. Cf. van Lennap, *op. cit.*, 69.

45
1. Cf. Josef Svátek, "Anglický alchymista Kelley v Čechách", 142–3; Karel Pejml, *Dějiny české alchymie*, 55.
2. Cf. Svátek, *op. cit.*, 144.
3. Cf. *ibid.*, 143.
4. Cf. *ibid.*, 145–6; Pejml, *op. cit.*, 55–6.
5. Cf. *ibid.*, 146–7.
6. Cf. Karel Krejčí, *Praha legend a skutečnosti*, 170–2.
7. Cf. *ibid.*, 154.
8. Cf. Carl August Schimmer (1845) in *Město vidím veliké . . .* , 365; Krejčí, *op. cit.*, 172–3.
9. The plural of *pimprle*, "puppet, marionette" (from the German *Pumpernickel*).
10. Cf. Richard Andree (1872) in *Město vidím veliké . . .* , 414–15.
11. Cf. Svátek, *op. cit.*, 147–8
12. Cf. *ibid.*, 149–50.
13. Cf. *ibid.*, 150–1; Pejml, *op. cit.*, 57.
14. Cf. *ibid.*, 152–3.

46
1. Also given as Michał Sędziwój, Sendivoy, Sendživoj ze Skorsky na Lukavici a Lygotě. Cf. Josef Svátek, *op. cit.*, 54; Karel Pejml, *op. cit.*, 59.
2. Cf. Josef Svátek, "Anglický alchymista Kelley v Čechách", 146.
3. Eric Bentley, ed., *The Genius of Italian Theater*, New York 1964, 226.
4. Cf. Zikmund Winter, "Kámen filosofický" (1893) in *Panečnice a jiné pražské obrázky*, Prague 1949, 83–111.
5. Cf. Svátek, *op. cit.*, 59; Pejml, *Dějiny české alchymie*, 60.
6. Cf. Winter, *op. cit.*, 104.
7. Cf. Svátek, "Alchymie v Čechách za doby Rudolfa II.", 37–75; Pejml, *op. cit.*, 64–5.
8. Cf. Meyrink, "Die Abenteuer des Polen Sendivogius" in *Goldmachergeschichten*, Berlin 1925, 197–261.
9. *Ibid.*, 256.
10. Cf. Svátek, *op. cit.*, 51–2; Pejml, *op. cit.*, 61–3.

47
1. Cf. Josef Svátek, "Alchymie v Čechách za doby Rudolfa II.", 48–9; Karel Pejml, *Dějiny české alchymie*, 64.
2. Cf. Svátek, *op. cit.*, 49–51; Pejml, *op. cit.*, 63–4.
3. Mikuláš Dačický z Heslova, *Paměti*, 175.
4. *Ibid.*, 198. See also Josef Polišenský, *Jan Jesenský-Jessenius*, Prague 1965, 29, 97–122.
5. Voskovec and Werich, *Golem* in *Hry Osvobozeného divadla*, 91–184.
6. Cf. Dačický z Heslova, *op. cit.*, 195 (1599), 201 (1601); Svátek, *K dějinám katů a poprav v Čechách*, II, 195–6.

7.   Jan Erazim Vocel, *Labyrint slávy*, Prague 1846, 13–14, 49, 55.

48

1.   It opened on 21 November 1922 at the Vinohradské divadlo, where Čapek served as dramatic adviser between 1921 and 1923. He directed the production himself.
2.   Karel Čapek created the role of Emilia Marty for the actress Leopolda Dostalová. Cf. Otakar Štorch-Marien, *Sladko je žít*, 177.
3.   Cf. Jaroslav Šeda, *Leoš Janáček*, Prague 1961, 322–3. See also Jaroslav Vogel, *Leoš Janáček dramatik*, Prague 1948, 87–92.
4.   Cf. Bohumír Štědroň, *Janáček ve vzpomínkách a dopisech*, Prague 1946, 233.
5.   Cf. Šeda, *op. cit.*, 309.

49

1.   Guillaume Apollinaire, "Zone" (1913) in *Œuvres poétiques*, Paris 1956, 43.
2.   Blaise Cendrars, "Prose du Transsibérien et de la petite Jeanne de France" (1913) in *Du monde entiers au coeur du monde*, Paris 1957, 48.
3.   Vítězslav Nezval, *Pražský chodec*, 324.
4.   Cf. Hana Volavková, *Zmizelé pražské ghetto*, Prague 1961, 4.
5.   Cf. Alois Jirásek, "Syn ohnivcův" (second part of the novel *Mezi proudy*, 1888).
6.   Cf. Volavková, *Zmizelá Praha: Židovské město pražské*, Prague 1947, 32.
7.   Cf. *ibid.*, 15.
8.   Cf. *ibid.*, 34, 37.
9.   Cf. *ibid.*, 42.
10. Cf. *ibid.*, 18–19.
11. Cf. *ibid.*, 31.
12. Cf. Volavková, *Židovské město pražské*, Prague 1959, 3.
13. Cf. *ibid.*
14. Cf. Volavková, *Zmizelá Praha*, 61.
15. Cf. *ibid.*, 59–60.
16. Gustav Janouch, *Conversations with Kafka*, 80.
17. Cf. Herbert Jhering, "Der Schauspieler im Film" (1920) in *Von Reinhardt bis Brecht*, Berlin 1958, I, 380–2; Lotte H. Eisner, *L'Écran démoniaque*, Paris 1965, 48–9.
18. Cf. Eisner, *op. cit.*, 24–5; Ado Kyrou, *Le Surréalisme au cinéma*, Paris 1953, 80.
19. Cf. Volavková, *Zmizelá Praha*, 28–30; Volavková, *Židovské město pražské*, 24–5; Volavková, *Zmizelé pražské ghetto*, 30–4; Jiří Weil, "Současníci o Mordechajovi Mayzlovi" in *Židovská ročenka* (5718), Prague 1957–58, 77–85; cf. Jirásek, "Ze Židovského města" in *Staré pověsti české*, 200–6.
20. Cf. Zikmund Winter, "Část kulturně-historická" in *Pražské ghetto*, ed. Ignát Herrmann, Josef Teige, Zikmund Winter, Prague 1902, 12.
21. Cf. *ibid.*, 70.
22. Cf. *ibid.*, 68.

50

1.   Cf. Hana Volavková, *Zmizelá Praha*, 23; *Židovské město pražské*, 15–16; *Zmizelé pražské ghetto*, 10–14; Vojtěch Volavka, *Pout' Prahou: Dějiny a umění*, Prague 1967, 59.
2.   Jiří Karásek ze Lvovic, *Gotická duše* (1905), Prague 1921, Chapter 21, 91.

3. Hans Christian Andersen, "Nádherné seskupení" in *Město vidím veliké* . . . , 411.
4. Cf. Alois Jirásek, "Ze Židovského města," *op. cit.*, 199–200; Karel Krejčí, *Praha legend a skutečnosti*, 177.
5. Lasker-Schüler, "Der alte Tempel in Prag" (1920) in *Dichtungen und Dokumente*, Munich 1951, 38.
6. Cf. Henri Sérouya, *La Kabbale*, Paris 1947, 98.
7. Cf. Adolf Wenig, "O Staronové synagoze" in *Staré pověsti pražské*, 309–14; Karel Hádek, "Pověsti o Staronové škole" in *Čtení o staré Praze*, Prague 1948, 27–31.

51

1. Cf. Hana Volavková, Walter Sojka, Jiří Weil, *Průvodce po Státním židovském museu v Praze*, Prague 1956, II, 15–16; Hana Volavková, *Příběh židovského musea v Praze*, Prague 1966.
2. Cf. Hana Volavková, *Židovské město pražské*, 19–20, *Zmizelé pražské ghetto*, 22–4 and *Starý židovský hřbitov v Praze*, Prague 1958, 7.
3. Cf. Hana Volavková, "Okolo starého židovského hřbitova v Praze" in *Židovská ročenka* (5717), Prague 1956–57, 75–84.
4. Cf. *Starý židovský hřbitov v Praze*, 8.
5. Cf. *ibid.*, 19; Karel Krejčí, *Starý židovský hřbitov pražský v pověsti a legendě* in *Staletá Praha*, Prague 1967, III, 41.
6. Cf. Krejčí, *Praha legend a skutečnosti*, 192–3.
7. Vladimír Holan, "Modlitba kamene" in *Na postupu* (1943–48), Prague 1964, 12.
8. Cf. Otto Muneles and Milada Vilímková, *Starý židovský hřbitov v Praze*, Prague 1955, 55.
9. Holan, *Lemuria*, 147.
10. Cf. Muneles and Vilímková, *Starý židovský hřbitov v Praze*, 10; Volavková, *Židovské město pražské*, 20 and *Zmizelé pražské ghetto*, 23, 28.

52

1. Cf. Otto Muneles and Milada Vilímková, *Starý židovský hřbitov v Praze*, 10–11; Hana Volavková, *Zmizelé pražské ghetto*, 28.
2. Cf. Karel Krejčí, "Starý židovský hřbitov pražský v pověsti a legendě" in *Staletá Praha*, Prague 1967, III, 44–5.
3. Cf. Muneles and Vilímková, *Starý židovský hřbitov v Praze*, 61–93.
4. Cf. Miroslav Lamač, *Výtvarné dílo Adolfa Hoffmeistera*.
5. Kafka, "A Dream" (1914–15) in *The Complete Stories*, New York 1971, 399–401.
6. Jiří Karásek ze Lvovic, *Ganymedes*, 42–3.
7. Cf. Krejčí, "Starý židovský hřbitov pražský", 45–6.
8. Jaroslav Seifert, *Světlem oděná*, 30.
9. Cf. Krejčí, "Starý židovský hřbitov pražský"; Munueles and Vilímková, *Starý židovský hřbitov v Praze*, 17–18.

53

1. Cf. *Město vidím veliké* . . . , 412, 460–1.
2. Cf. Stanisław Helsztyński, *Przybyszewski*, 451.
3. Cf. Otakar Štorch-Marien, *Sladko je žít*, 104–6, 212.
4. Jiří Karásek ze Lvovic, *Ganymedes*, 44.
5. Cf. Egon Erwin Kisch, "Aus Glaubenshaß" in *Prager Pitaval* (1931), Berlin

1953, 85–98 (in Czech as "Ex odio fidei" . . . in *Pražský Pitaval*, Prague 1968, 103–11).

6. Cf. Zikmund Winter, "Část kulturně-historická" in *Pražské ghetto*, 52; Karel Krejčí, *Praha legend a skutečnosti*, 178.

54

1. Hana Volavková, *Zmizelá Praha*, 50 and *Židovské město pražské*, 29, 32; Karel Krejčí, *Praha legend a skutečnosti*, 381.
2. Cf. Pavel Eisner, "Franz Kafka a Praha" in *Kritický měsíčník*, 3–4 (1948).
3. Cf. Ignát Herrmann, *Před padesáti lety*, Prague 1926, I, 207–8.
4. Herrmann, *Před padesáti lety*, Prague 1938, IV, 120–1.
5. Jiří Karásek ze Lvovic, *Ganymedes*, 42.
6. Cf. Herrmann, *op. cit.*, IV, 122–3.
7. Jaroslav Vrchlický, "Z ghetta" from the cycle *Pražské obrázky* in *Má vlast* (1903).
8. Guillaume Apollinaire, *op. cit.*, I, 109.

55

1. Derived from the German *handeln*, "to bargain".
2. Cf. Karel Hádek, *Čtení o staré Praze*, 265–6.
3. "Have you anything to sell?"
4. *čachrn* from the German *Schachern*, "small-scale bargaining". The Czech verb *čachrovati* is pejorative.
5. Cf. Ignát Herrmann, *Před padesáti lety*, I, 202–9.
6. Cf. *Ibid.*, IV, 123–4.
7. *kudlmudl* from the German *Kuddelmuddel*, "muddle, hotchpotch". See Otakar Štorch-Marien, *Sladko je žít*, 107.
8. Meyrink, *The Golem*, 11.
9. Corruption of the German *Bestandteil*, "component part".
10. Cf. Zikmund Winter, "Čast kulturně-historická" in *Pražské ghetto*, 61.

56

1. Guillaume Apollinaire, "Le passant de Prague" in *Œuvres complètes*, 111–12.
2. Cf. Jan Neruda, *Obrázky policejní* (1868), II.
3. Cf. Karel Hádek, *Čtení o staré Praze*, 262–3.
4. Cf. Barry Ulanov, *A History of Jazz in America*, New York 1952, 38.
5. Kafka liked the word *bludička* (will-of-the-wisp): "How wretched, abandoned, frozen men must be if they wish to warm themselves on these marsh gases!" (Janouch, *Conversations with Kafka*, 180).
6. Cf. Paul Leppin, "Das Gespenst der Judenstadt" in *Deutsche Dichter aus Prag*, ed. Oskar Wiener, Vienna and Leipzig 1919, 197–8.
7. Cf. Ignát Herrmann, *Před padesáti lety*, IV, 131–2.
8. Apollinaire, *op. cit.*, 111–12.
9. Cf. *Písně lidu pražského*, ed. Václav Pletka and Vladimír Karbusický, Prague 1966, 93.
10. Cf. Herrmann, *op. cit.*, IV, 137.
11. Cf. *ibid.*, 135.
12. Cf. *ibid.*, 133.
13. Oskar Wiener, *Alt-Prager Guckkasten*, 115–16.
14. Cf. Herrmann, *op. cit.*, IV, 129–31.

57

1. Cf. Hana Volaková, *Zmizelá Praha*, 66–79.
2. Cf. Karel L. Kukla, "Žbluňk. Obrázek života v noční krčme" in *Ze všech koutů Prahy*, Prague 1894, 165.
3. Cf. Karel Krejčí, *Praha legend a skutečnosti*, 274.
4. Vilém Mrštík, *Bestia triumphans*, Prague 1897, 12.
5. *Ibid.*, 14.
6. Miloš Jiránek, "O krásné Praze" in *Dojmy a potulky a jiné práce*, 45.
7. Jaroslav Vrchlický, "Stará Praha" from the cycle *Pražské obrázky* in *Má vlast* (1903).
8. Paul Leppin, "Das Gespenst der Judenstadt" in *Deutsche Dichter aus Prag*, 197–202.
9. Vrchlický, "Staré synagogy" from the cycle *Nové hebrejské melodie* in *Západy* (1907).
10. Gustav Janouch, *Conversations with Kafka*, 80.
11. Vítězslav Nezval, *Pražský chodec*, 324.
12. Nezval, *Řetěz štěstí*, 118.

58

1. King James Version.
2. Cf. Beate Rosenfeld, *Die Golemsage und ihre Verwertung in der deutschen Literatur*, Breslau 1934, 1–2.
3. Cf. *ibid.*, 2.
4. Cf. *ibid.*, 3–4.
5. Cf. Chajim Bloch, *Der Prager Golem. Von seiner "Geburt" bis zu seinem "Tod"*, mit einem Geleitwort von Hans Ludwig Held, Berlin 1920, 177; French translation: *Le Golem. Légendes du Ghetto de Prague*, ed. François Ritter, Strasbourg 1928, 167; see also Henri Sérouya, *Le Kabbale*, 355–60.
6. Cf. Rosenfeld, *op. cit.*, 10.
7. Cf. *ibid.*, 11.
8. Cf. *ibid.*
9. Cf. Bloch, *op. cit.*, 196; and Bloch, *Le Golem*, 8–9; Rosenfeld, *op. cit.*, 20–1.

59

1. Cf. Chajim Bloch, *Le Golem*, 213–14; Beate Rosenfeld, *Die Golemsage*, 26.
2. Maharal (MHRL): abbreviation for "morenu harab Rabbi Loew". See Rosenfeld, *op. cit.*, 22.
3. Cf. *ibid.*, 26.
4. Rudolf Lothar, *Der Golem. Phantasien und Historien*, Munich and Leipzig 1904, 4–5.
5. Cf. Rosenfeld, *op. cit.*, 25.

60

1. Cf. Beate Rosenfeld, *Die Golemsage*, 27.
2. Jaroslav Vrchlický, *Rabínská moudrost*, 18.
3. Cf. Alois Jirásek, *Staré pověsti české*, 207–8; Adolf Wenig, *Staré pověsti pražské*, 318; Eduard Petiška, *Golem a jiné židovské pověsti a pohádky ze staré Prahy*, 1968, 44–5; German translation: *Der Golem. Jüdische Märchen und Legenden aus dem alten Prag*, Wiesbaden 1972, 52–3.
4. Cf. Jirásek, *op. cit.*, 208–9; Wenig, *op. cit.*, 319–20; Rosenfeld, *op. cit.*, 28; Petiška, *op. cit.*, 58–60.

5.   Jiří Karásek ze Lvovic, *Ganymedes*, 43.
6.   Cf. Georges Sadoul, *Histoire générale du cinéma: L'Invention du cinéma*, Paris 1946, 99–100.
7.   Goethe's Faust summons Paris and Helen to the Emperor and his court from the smoke of a tripode (II.i.). In the Czech puppet play *Jan doktor Faust*, based on Marlowe's drama and performed by the *Englische Komödianten* in Bohemia, Faust brings tiny David and huge Goliath up from Hades at the request of the King of "Portukal" (or the Shah of Persia). Cf. *Loutkářské hry českého obrození*, ed. Jaroslav Bartoš, Prague 1952, 26–7 and *Komedie a hry českých lidových loutkářů*, Prague 1959, 54–5.
8.   Cf. Henri Sérouya, *Le Kabbale*, 416–17.
9.   Cf. Jirásek, *op. cit.*, 209–10; Chajim Bloch, *Le Golem*, 182–6; Wenig, *op. cit.*, 319; Petiška, *op. cit.*, 51–3.
10. Cf. Rosenfeld, *op. cit.*, 28–9.
11. Vrchlický, *op. cit.*, 108, 31, 102.
12. *Ibid.*, 105, 108–9.
13. Cf. Bloch, *op. cit.*, 195–9; Karásek ze Lvovic, *op. cit.*, Chapter 12, 43; Rosenfeld, *op. cit.*, 29; Wenig, *op. cit.*, 326–7; Petiška, *op. cit.*, 89–91.
14. Vítězslav Nezval, "Rabi Löw" in *Praha s prsty deště* (1936). The lion and grapes are the attributes (emblems) of Jehuda Loew.

61

1.   Cf. Chajim Bloch, *Der Prager Golem*, 47–52; Eduard Petiška, *Golem*, 61–4; Pavel Grym, *Té noci povstal Golem*, Prague 1971, 11–63.
2.   Cf. Bloch, *Le Golem*, 40–2; Jiří Karásek ze Lvovic, *Ganymedes*, 57–8.
3.   Cf. Rosenfeld, *Die Golemsage*, 148; Lotte H. Eisner, *L'Écran démoniaque*, 47–8.
4.   Jaroslav Vrchlický, *Rabínská moudrost*, 32.
5.   Cf. Alois Jirásek, *Staré pověsti české*, 210–11; Karásek ze Lvovic, *op. cit.*, 60; Rosenfeld, *op. cit.*, 31–2; Adolf Wenig, *Staré pověsti pražské*, 320–3; Karel Hádek, *Čtení o staré Praze*, 30–1; Petiška, *op. cit.*, 84–8.
6.   Cf. Rosenfeld, *op. cit.*, 146.
7.   Cf. Bloch, *op. cit.*, 160–2; Karásek ze Lvovic, *op. cit.*, Ch. 16, 61.
8.   Cf. Bloch, *op. cit.*, 208–10; Rosenfeld, *op. cit.*, 32–3.
9.   Cf. Krejčí, *Praha legend a skutečnosti*, 186–7.
10. Cf. Bloch, *op. cit.*, 163–5; Karásek ze Lvovic, *op. cit.*, 93–4.

62

1.   Cf. Chajim Bloch, *Le Golem*, 50–3.
2.   Cf. Henri Sérouya, *Le Kabbale*, 176–7.
3.   Cf. Bloch, *Der Prager Golem*, 177.
4.   Cf. Beate Rosenfeld, *Die Golemsage*, 34.
5.   Cf. Bloch, *Le Golem*, 109–10.
6.   Cf. *ibid.*, 43–4.
7.   Cf. *ibid.*, 108.
8.   Cf. *ibid.*, 65–75.
9.   Cf. Rosenfeld, *op. cit.*, 22–4; Karel Krejčí, "Starý židovský hřbitov" 36, and *Praha legend a skutečnosti*, 179–80.

63

1.   Jaroslav Vrchlický, *Já nechal svět jít kolem* (1901–02), Prague 1902, 151–4.

2. Detlev von Liliencron, "Bunte Beute" in *Sämtliche Werke*, Berlin and Leipzig, n.d., X, 25–7.
3. Voskovec and Werich, *Hry Osvobozeného divadla*, II, 122–6.
4. Cf. Chajim Bloch, *Der Prager Golem*, 178.
5. Hugo Salus, "Vom hohen Rabbi Löw" in *Ernte*, Munich 1903, 91–2.
6. Arthur Holitscher, *Der Golem. Ghettolegende in drei Aufzügen*, Berlin 1908. See Beate Rosenfeld, *Die Golemsage*, 138–45.
7. Rudolf Lothar, *Der Golem.* See Rosenfeld, *op. cit.*, 135–8.
8. Lothar, *op. cit.*, 22.

64

1. Rudolf Lothar, *Der Golem*, 16.
2. Karásek ze Lvovic's trilogy *Romány tří Mágů* (Novels of the Three Magi) consists of *Román Manfreda Macmillena* (1924), *Scarabeus* (1925) and *Ganymedes* (1925).
3. Cf. Anton Sailer, *Franz von Stuck: Ein Lebensmärchen*, Munich 1969, 30.
4. Cf. Chajim Bloch, *Der Prager Golem*, 179–80.
5. Achim von Arnim, *Isabella von Ägypten, Kaiser Karls V. erste Jugendliebe* (1812); cf. André Breton's preface to Achim d'Arnim, *Contes bizarres*, Paris 1953.
6. Jiří Karásek ze Lvovic, *Ganymedes*, 68.
7. *Ibid.*, 64–5.
8. *Ibid.*, 82.

65

1. Cf. Beate Rosenfeld, *Die Golemsage*, 158–68.
2. Cf. *ibid.*, 146–7.
3. Gustav Meyrink, "Das Präparat".
4. *Die Pflanzen des Dr. Cinderella.*
5. Max Brod, *Streitbares Leben*, 292.
6. Cf. *Kavárna Union. Sborník vzpomínek pamětníků*, Prague 1958.
7. Cf. Rosenfeld, *op. cit.*, 162.
8. Cf. *ibid.*, 163–4.
9. Jiří Karásek ze Lvovic, *Ganymedes*, 51.
10. Cf. Hans Ludwig Held, Introduction to Chajim Bloch, *Der Prager Golem*, 11.

66

1. Josef Jiří Kolár, *Pekla zplozenci*, 77–8.
2. Cf. Beate Rosenfeld, *Die Golemsage*, 66–7.
3. Gustav Meyrink, "Das Präparat".
4. Cf. Ignát Herrmann, *Před padesáti lety*, I, 78–9, 91–8. See also Paul Leppin, *Severins Gang in die Finsternis*, 25; The word *šibřinky*, "masked ball", comes from the German *Schabernack*, "prank".
5. Cf. Karel Hádek, *Čtení o staré Praze*, 50–4; Karel Krejčí, *Praha legend a skutečnosti*, 220–1; Vojtěch Volavka, *Pout' Prahou*, 230.
6. Paul Adler, "Nämlich" (1915) in *Das leere Haus*, 193.

67

1. Cf. Rolf Strehl, *I robot sono tra noi*, Milan 1954, 106–8, 117–32.
2. The expression comes from Villiers de l'Isle-Adam, *L'Ève future*, Book Two, IV.

3. It opened at the Prague Národní divadlo (National Theatre) on 25 January 1921. Vojta Novák directed. Sets were by Bedřich Feuerstein, costumes by Josef Čapek.
4. *Robot* (feminine form *robotka*) recalls the Russian verb *rabotat'*, "to work", from which *rabotiaga*, "drudge" (*dříč* in Czech). More recently it has come to denote prisoners forced to perform the heaviest and dirtiest work in Soviet labour camps. Čapek originally wanted to call his automatons "laboři" after the Latin *labor*, "work", but he discarded it as too bookish. The term *robot* was suggested by his brother Josef (cf. Karel Čapek in *Lidové noviny* of 24 December 1933). The word and its derivations began to enter Western languages following the success of *R.U.R.* in London in 1923 (cf. Otakar Vočadlo, "Česká literatura na světovém foru. Oblast anglosaská" in *Co daly naše země Evropě a lidstvu*, 406).
5. Josef Čapek, "Umělý člověk" in *R.U.R.* (a collection of sources by Miroslav Halík), Prague 1966, 160.
6. Walter Mehring, *Die verlorene Bibliothek*, Icking and Munich 1964, 240.
7. Cf. Otakar Štorch-Marien, *Ohňostroj*, Prague 1969, 110–11.
8. Karel Čapek, *Válka s mloky*, Prague 1965, 209. (English edition: *The War with the Newts*, trans. Ewald Ösers, Highland Park 1990, 199. Page numbers in parentheses below refer to this edition.) See also Stanisław Lem, *Fantastyka i futurologia*, Cracow 1970, I, 90–2.
9. Cf. Lotte Eisner, *L'Écran démoniaque*, 153–8.
10. From a letter from Čapek to Olga Scheinpflugová in *R.U.R., op. cit.*, 106.
11. *Ibid.*
12. Mehring, *op. cit.*, 240.
13. Čapek, *Válka s mloky*, 247 (237).
14. Cf. Ivan Klíma, "Moderní mythy" in *R.U.R., op. cit.*, 193.
15. *Ibid.*, 196.
16. In "Krakonošova zahrada" (1918).
17. Cf. Curt Seckel, *Maßstäbe der Kunst im 20. Jahrhundert*, Düsseldorf and Vienna 1967, 39–48.
18. Ludovico Ariosto, *Orlando furioso*, (XI, 27), trans. Barbara Reynolds, London 1975, 351.

68

1. Cf. Ignát Herrmann, *Před padesáti lety*, II, 88–9, 94–5.
2. Vladimír Holan, *Lemuria* (1934–38). Now in *Babyloniaca*, Prague 1968, 269.

PART TWO

69

1. Cf. Mikuláš Dačický z Heslova, *Paměti*, I, 272–3; Josef Svátek, "K dějinám katů a poprav v Čechách" in *Obrazy z kulturních dějin českých*, 202–4.
2. Josef Svatopluk Machar, "Večer Jana Mydláře v pondělí 21. června 1621" in *Apostolové* (1911).
3. Svátek, *Paměti katovské rodiny Mydlářů v Praze* (1886–89), Prague 1924, II, 201–48.
4. Aleksandr Pushkin, "O zapiskakh Samsona" (1830) in *Polnoe sobranie sochinenii*, Moscow, Leningrad 1949, VII, 104–6.
5. Cf. Karel Krejčí, *Praha legend a skutečnosti*, 310–11 and "Symbol kata a

odsouzence v díle Karla Hynka Máchy" in *Realita slova Máchova*, ed. R. Grebeníčková and O. Králík, Prague 1967, 230–6.

6.   Cf. Svátek, "K dějinám katů a poprav v Čechách", 142.
7.   In *Pražský žid* as reworked by Vladislav Vančura (Prague 1959, with a note by František Götz). We have taken Aleš Podhorský's version (Prague 1947) into consideration as well. See also Ljuba Klosová, *Josef Jiří Kolár*, Prague 1962.
8.   Jaroslav Vrchlický, "Jessenius" in *Já nechal svět jít kolem*.
9.   Cf. Dačický z Heslova, *op. cit.*, I, 279.
10.   Cf. Josef Janáček, *Malé dějiny Prahy*, Prague 1968, 208–9.
11.   Cf. Adolf Wenig, *Staré pověsti pražské*, 15–16; Karel Krejčí, *Praha legend a skutečnosti*, 131–2.

70

1.   In addition to Kamil Krofta, *Bílá Hora* (1913) and Josef Pekař, *Bílá Hora, její příčiny a následky* (1921), see *Doba bělohorská a Albrecht z Valdštejna*, ed. Jaroslav Prokeš, Prague 1934; Josef Polišenský, *Tricetiletá válka a český národ*, Prague 1960; Kamil Krofta, *Dějiny československé*, Prague 1946, 389–407; Zdeněk Kalista, *Stručné dějiny československé*, Prague 1947, 141–8; Josef Janáček, *Malé dějiny Prahy*, 197–212.
2.   Jan Dolenský, *Praha ve své slávě a utrpení*, 559.
3.   Cf. Mikuláš Dačický z Heslova, *Paměti*, I, 267.
4.   The expression occurs in *Pražský žid* by Josef Jiří Kolár.
5.   Cf. Dačický z Heslova, *op. cit.*, I, 294 (1623).
6.   Cf. Jan Norbert Zatočil z Levenburku, *Kronika obléhání Prahy od Švédů* (1685), Prague 1914.

71

1.   Caroline de la Motte-Fouqué, *Reise-Erinnerungen von Friedrich de la Motte Fouqué und Caroline de la Motte Fouqué* quoted in *Město vidím veliké . . .*, 203–4.
2.   Cf. F. Gustav Kühne (1857) and William Ritter (1895) in *Město vidím veliké . . .*, 384, 454.
3.   Karel Hynek Mácha, "Návrat" in *Dílo*, II, 177, 181.
4.   Jiří Karásek ze Lvovic, *Román Manfreda Macmillena*, Prague 1907, 133. See also his sonnet "Bílá Hora" (1904) from the cycle *Pasiflora* in *Hovory se smrtí*, Prague 1922, 32.
5.   Gustav Janouch, *Conversations with Kafka*, 17.
6.   Jan Neruda, "Hastrman" (1876) in *Povídky malostranské* (1877).
7.   Franz Kafka, "Description of a Struggle" in *The Complete Stories*, 14.
8.   Gustav Meyrink, "Praha" in *Černá koule*, Prague 1967, 31.
9.   Cf. Gaston Bachelard, *Lautréamont* (1939), Paris 1965, 17–8: "La métamorphose de Kafka apparaît nettement comme un étrange ralentissement de la vie et des actions."
10.   Albert Camus, "La mort dans l'âme" (1937) in *L'envers et l'endroit*, Paris 1958, 86.
11.   André Gide, *Journal 1889–1939*: 5 August 1934, Paris 1951, 1214.

72

1.   Jiří Karásek ze Lvovic, *Gotická duše*, 48.
2.   *Román Manfred Macmillena*, 39–40.

3. *Ibid.*, 20–1.
4. *Ganymedes*, 50.
5. Cf. *ibid.*, 59.
6. *Román Manfred Macmillena*, 111.
7. *Král Rudolf*, Act Two, 39.
8. Francis Marion Crawford, *The Witch of Prague*, 34–5.
9. Karel Hynek Mácha, *Dílo*, I, 125, 160, 168, 185.
10. Rainer Maria Rilke, *Sämtliche Werke*, Frankfurt am Main 1961, IV, 107.
11. Karásek ze Lvovic, *Ganymedes*, 49.
12. Arnošt Procházka, "Kouzlo Prahy" (1913) in *Rozhovory s knihami, obrazy i lidmi*, Prague 1916, 97.
13. Oskar Wiener, *Alt-Prager Guckkasten*, 91–2.
14. Cf. N. Melniková-Papoušková, "Domovní znaky a vývešní štíty pražské" in *Kniha o Praze*, ed. Artuš Rektorys, Prague 1932, III, 128–45.
15. Alfred Kubin, *The Other Side*, 53.
16. Albert Camus, "La mort dans l'âme" (1937) in *L'envers et l'endroit*, Paris 1958, 89.

73
1. Francis Marion Crawford, *The Witch of Prague*, 34.
2. Leo Heller, "Prag" in *Deutsche Dichter aus Prag*, 137.
3. Gustav Meyrink, *The Golem*, Chapter "Prague".
4. "Die Pflanzen des Dr. Cinderella".
5. Kubin, *The Other Side*, 91.
6. *Ibid.*, 263.
7. Cf. Lotte Eisner, *L'Écran démoniaque*, 24–30.
8. Popelka Bilianová, "U Zlaté studně" (1904–05) in *Podivuhodné příběhy ze staré Prahy*, ed. Karel Krejčí, Prague 1971, 200–4.
9. Meyrink, "Das Präparat".
10. "Die Pflanzen des Dr. Cinderella".
11. Jakub Arbes, "Ethiopská lilie" (1886), Prague 1940, 132–5.
12. Cf. Jiří Karásek ze Lvovic, *Ganymedes*, 66–8.
13. Cf. *ibid.*, 21, 40.
14. Paul Leppin, *Severins Gang in die Finsternis*, 8–9.
15. Arbes, *Svatý Xaverius* (1878), Prague 1963, 25.
16. Karolina Světlá, *Zvonečková královna* (1872), Prague 1950, 7–8.
17. Kubin, *op. cit.*, 76.
18. *Ibid.*, 41.
19. *Ibid.*, 74.
20. *Ibid.*, 141.
21. *Ibid.*, 189.
22. Cf. Emanuel Frynta and Jan Lukas, *Franz Kafka lebte in Prag*, 80.
23. Cf. Radko Pytlík, *Toulavé house*, 55–6.
24. Meyrink, *The Golem*, Chapters "Free" and "End".
25. Adler, *op. cit.*, 174.
26. Kubin, *op. cit.*, 46.
27. Vladimír Holan, "Zed'" in *Na postupu*, 69.

74
1. Cf. Vojtěch Jirát, "Hlas Prahy v českém písemnictví", *Kritický měsíčník*, 2 (1941).

2. Vladimír Holan, "Mladost" in *Triumf smrti* (1930). Now in *Jeskyně slov, Sebrané spisy*, Prague 1965, I, 14.
3. Ingvald Undset (1810) in *Město vidím veliké* . . . , 175.
4. Cf. Arne Novák, *Praha barokní* (1915), Prague 1947, 33.
5. Cf. Karel Krejčí, *Praha legend a skutečnosti*, 300.
6. Jiří Karásek ze Lvovic, *Román Manfreda Macmillena*, 124.
7. *Ibid.*, 30.
8. Karásek ze Lvovic, *Gotická duše*, 13.
9. Krejčí, *op. cit.*, 205.
10. Karásek ze Lvovic, *Gotická duše*, 35.
11. *Ibid.*, 31.
12. Julius Zeyer, "Tereza Manfredi" (1884) in *Novely*, Prague 1947, 291.
13. Paul Leppin, *Severins Gang in die Finsternis*, 100.
14. Meyrink, *The Golem*, Chapter "Woman".
15. *Ibid.*, Chapter "Snow".
16. Jan Neruda, *Povídky malostranské*, 187.
17. Cf. Krejčí, "Franz Kafka a Jakub Arbes", *Plamen*, 2 (1965).
18. Franz Kafka, *The Trial*, 162.
19. Karásek ze Lvovic, *Román Manfreda Macmillena*, 125.
20. Karásek ze Lvovic, *Gotická duše*, 97, and 31, 35.
21. Cf. Karolina Světlá, *Zvonečková královna*, 25.
22. Cf. Jakub Arbes, "Sivooký démon" (1873) in *Romaneta*, Prague 1924, I, 7.
23. Julius Zeyer, "Inultus" in *Legendy*, Prague 1949, 294.
24. *Ibid.*, 299.

75

1. Cf. Karel Krejčí, *Praha legend a skutečnosti*, 313–4.
2. Cf. Josef Svátek, *Tajnosti pražské* (1868), Prague 1912, I, 76–7.
3. Cf. *ibid.*, 83–90.
4. Svatopluk Čech, *Nový epochální výlet pana Broučka tentokrát do patnáctého století* (1889).
5. Karel Chalupa, "Hrůznou cestou" in Krejčí, *Podivuhodné příběhy ze staré Prahy*, 227–31.
6. Vladimír Holan, *Sen* (1939).
7. Cf. Krejčí, *Praha legend a skutečnosti*, 154, 173–6. See also Friedrich Heinse (1834) in *Město vidím veliké* . . . , 259; Grym, *Té noci povstal Golem*, 109–71.
8. Jan Erazim Vocel, *Labyrint slávy*, I, 8, 45.
9. Josef Jiří Kolár, *Pekla zplozenci*, 8–9.
10. Cf. Adolf Wenig, *Staré pověsti pražské*, 165–73.
11. Charles Patin (1695) in *Město vidím veliké* . . . , 45.

76

1. Jan Neruda, "Doktor Kazisvět" (1876) in *Povídky malostranské*.
2. Jakub Arbes, "Zázračná madona" (1884).
3. Arbes, "Odumírající drahokam" (1889).
4. Arbes, "Ethiopská lilie" (1886).
5. Eduard Bass, "Pražské starosti duchovní" (1937) in *Pod kohoutkem svatovítským*, Brno 1942, 221.
6. Cf. Karel Krejčí, *Praha legend a skutečnosti*, 299–300 and *Podivuhodné příběhy ze staré Prahy*, 183–4.

7. Cf. N. Melniková-Papoušková, "Domovní znaky a vývešní štíty pražské" in *Kniha o Praze*, III, 140–1.
8. Cf. Bass, *op. cit.*, 217–18; Popelka Bilianová, "V bývalém klášteře u Sv. Máří Magdalény" in Karel Krejčí, *Podivuhodné příběhy*, 192–3.
9. Bass, *op. cit.*, 216; Bilianová, *op. cit.*, 194–8.
10. Cf. Adolf Wenig, *Staré pověsti pražské*, 90–3.
11. Cf. Bass, *op. cit.*, 211–12.
12. Cf. *ibid.*, 212–13:
13. Cf. Wenig, *op. cit.*, 232–3.
14. Cf. Krejčí, *op. cit.*, 299.
15. Cf. Bilianová, "Tlustá domácí" in Krejčí, *op. cit.*, 218–21.
16. Cf. Bilianová, "Tancující židovka" in Krejčí, *op. cit.*, 224–7.
17. Cf. Bass, *op. cit.*, 222.
18. Cf. Ignát Herrmann, *Před padesáti lety*, III, 26–7.
19. Cf. Bilianová, "U Zlaté studně" in Krejčí, *op. cit.*, 201–3; Bass, *op. cit.*, 222.
20. Cf. Karel Chalupa, "U Černého kocoura" in Krejčí, *op. cit.*, 190–2.
21. Cf. Bilianová, "Hrabě Deym v chudobinci" in Krejčí, *op. cit.*, 204–5.
22. Cf. Bass, *op. cit.*, 218–9.
23. Cf. Karel Chapula, "U Smrti" in Krejčí, *op. cit.*, 187–9.
24. Herrmann, *op. cit.*, II, 174–88.
25. Cf. *ibid.*, III, 10–11.
26. A "pitaval" is a story or article dealing with a police case. It comes from the French attorney François Gayot de Pitaval, author of a collection of *causes célèbres* (1745–51). Egon Erwin Kisch wrote a *Prager Pitaval* (1931).
27. Krejčí, *Praha legend a skutečnosti*, 319–21, 337.
28. Vítězslav Nezval, "Pražský chodec", 278.
29. Nezval, *Řetěz štěstí*, 76.
30. Eduard Herold, "Lichtensteinský palác" in Krejčí, *Podivuhodné příběhy*, 146–7. See also Wenig, *op. cit.*, 303–5.
31. Bass, *op. cit.*, 220–1.

77

1. Vítězslav Nezval, "Pražský chodec", 318.
2. Cf. Josef Svátek, "K dějinám katů a poprav v Čechách," 182.
3. Aloysius Bertrand, "Le cheval mort" in *Gaspard de la nuit* (1842).
4. Mikuláš Dačický z Heslova, *Paměti*, I, 292 (1623).
5. Bohumil Hrabal, Introduction to *Knihy smolné*, ed. Zdeněk Bičík, Hradec Králové 1969, 5. These *knihy*, "books", were called *smolné*, "pitch", because the condemned were scorched by the executioners with *smolnice*, "torches dipped in pitch". Cf. Josef Svátek, *op. cit.*, 192.
6. Cf. Dačický z Heslova, *op. cit.*, I, 209, 211 (1605); Svátek, *Paměti katovské rodiny Mydlářů*, II, 87–122 and "K dějinám katů", 198–9; Egon Erwin Kisch, "Zwei Edelleute" in *Prager Pitaval*, *op. cit.*, 37–53.
7. Cf. Svátek, *Paměti katovské rodiny Mylářů*, II, 132–54 and "K dějinám katů", 170–1.
8. Cf. Svátek, "Alchymie v Čechách za doby Rudolfa II." in *Obrazy z kulturních dějin českých*, II, 41.
9. Josef Jiří Kolár, *Pekla zplozenci*, 26.
10. Franz Kafka, *The Trial*, 168.
11. Jakub Arbes, *D'ábel na skřipci* (1865) in *Romaneta*, IV, Prague 1926, 34.
12. Karel Krejčí, "Franz Kafka a Jakub Arbes".

78

1. Franz Kafka, *The Trial*, 169.
2. Cf. Karel L. Kukla, "U kata před popravou. Z ovzduší popraviště" in *Ze všech koutů Prahy*, 167–186. See also Kisch, "Wohlschläger" in *Pražský pitaval*, 20–31.
3. Cf. Josef Svátek, *Paměti katovské rodiny Mydlářů*, II, 116–17.
4. Jaroslav Hašek, *Švejk*, I–II, 344 (381).
5. *Píseň o katu Pipergrovi* in *Písně lidu pražského*, ed. Václav Pletha and Vladimír Karbusický, 47–8.
6. Hašek, III–IV, 95 (546).

79

1. At the Prague D 36, 22 June 1936. See E. F. Burian, "Máchovo divadlo" in *Ani labut' ani lůna*, Prague 1936, 63–8.
2. Vítězslav Nezval, *Pražský chodec*, 318.
3. Cf. Karel Krejčí, "Symbol kata a odsouzence v díle Karla Hynka Máchy" in *Realita slova Máchova*, 236–7 and *Praha legend a skutečnosti*, 84–7.
4. Karel Hynek Mácha, "Křivoklád" in *Dílo*, II, 12.
5. Cf. F. V. Krejčí, *Karel Hynek Mácha*, Prague 1916, 28–9; Albert Pražák, *Karel Hynek Mácha*, Prague 1936, 113–14.
6. Cf. Karel Krejčí, "Symbol kata", 253.
7. Mácha, "Křivoklád", 50.
8. Cf. Bohumil Novák, "Četba a zážitek jako prameny básníkovy tvorby" in *Věčný Mácha. Památník českého básníka*, Prague 1940, 132–3.
9. Josef Svátek, *op. cit.*, 141–2, 183, 185–6.
10. Mikuláš Dačický z Heslova, *Paměti*, I, 163. See also Josef Svátek, "K dějinám katů a poprav v Čechách", 186–7.
11. Mácha, *op. cit.*, 51.
12. Jiří Kolář, "Rada slouhům", *Literární listy* 10 (1968).
13. Cf. Ivo Pondělíček, "Jak zabít lidskou osobnost", *Literarní listy* 20 (1968). See also Artur London, *L'Aveu*, Paris 1968.
14. Jiří Orten, *Zcestí* (22.4.1941) in *Dílo*, Prague 1947, 227.

80

1. Cf. Karel Mádl, *Sochy na Karlově mostě v Praze*, Prague 1921; Vilém Bitnar, *O českém baroku slovesném*, Prague 1932; Oldřich Stefan, "Pozadí pražského baroku" in *Kniha o Praze*, III, Prague 1932, 54–66; Bohdan Chudoba, "Počátky barokní myšlenky"; Zdeněk Kalista, *Úvod do politické ideologie českého baroka*; Josef Vašica, "O české barokní poesii"; Jan Racek, "Slohové a ideové prvky barokní hudby"; Albert Kutal, "Výtvarné umění baroka" in *Baroko. Pět statí*, Prague 1934; Oskar Schürer, *Die Stadt des Adels* in *Prag*, Munich and Brno 1935, 213–56; F. X. Šalda, "O literárním baroku cizím i domácím" in *Šaldův zápisník*, Prague 1935–36, 71–7, 105–26, 177–82, 232–46; Václav Černý, *Esej o básnickém baroku*, 1937; Josef Vašica, *České literární baroko*, Prague 1938; *Pražské baroko* (catalogue of an exhibition held at the Valdštejn Palace, Prague, May–September 1938, with essays by Zdeněk Kalista, O. Stefan, V. V. Štech and Emanuel Poche); *Zrození barokního básníka*, ed. Vilém Bitnar, Prague 1940; Antonín Matějček and Zdeněk Wirth, "Český barok výtvarný" in *Co daly naše země Evropě a lidstvu*, 200–6; Zdeněk Kalista, *České baroko*, Prague 1941; Oskar Kokoschka, "Böhmisches Barock" in *Stimmen aus Böhmen*, London 1944,

15–19; Antonín Novotný, *Praha "Temna"*, Prague 1946; Arne Novák, *Praha barokní* (1915), Prague 1947; Kamil Novotný, Emanuel Poche, *Karlův most*, Prague, 1947; Antonín Novotný, *Z Prahy doznívajícího baroka*, Prague 1947; Oldřich Blažíček, *Rokoko a konec baroku v Čechách*, Prague 1948; Václav Mencl, Emanuel Poche, *Vzpomínka na Prahu*, Prague 1949, 112–66; Oldřich Blažíček, *L'Italia e la scultura in Boemia nei secoli XVII e XVIII*, Prague 1949; Olga Strettiová, *Das Barockporträt in Böhmen*, Prague 1957; Jaromír Neumann and Josef Prošek, *Matyáš Braun-Kuks*, Prague 1959; *Barock in Böhmen*, ed. Karl Swoboda (including Erich Bachmann, "Die Architektur und Plastik"; Erich Hubala, "Die Malerei"; Hermann Fillitz and Erwin Neumann, "Die Kunstgewerbe"), Munich 1964; Emanuel Poche, *Matyáš Bernard Braun*, Prague 1965; *L'Arte del Barocco in Boemia* (catalogue of an exhibition in the Palazzo Reale, Milan, April–May 1966, with essays by Josef Polišenský, Oldřich Blažíček, Pavel Preiss, Dagmar Hejdová); Alois Kubíček, *Barokní Praha v rytinách B. B. Wernera*, Prague 1966; *Kéž hoří popel můj*, ed. Václav Černý, Prague 1967; Vojtěch Volavka, *Pout' Prahou*, Prague 1967; *Kapka rosy tekoucí*, ed. Milan Kopecký, Brno 1968; Christian Norberg-Schulz, *Kilian Ignaz Dientzenhofer e il Barocco boemo*, Rome 1968; *Smutní kavaleři o lásce. Z české milostné poezie 17. století*, ed. Zdeňka Tichá and Josef Hrabák, Prague 1968; Václav Mencl, "Ve stínu Bílé Hory" and "Smysl pražského baroka" in *Praha*, Prague 1969, 120–35, 136–71; Jaromír Neumann, *Český barok*, Praha, 1969; *Umění českého baroka* (catalogue of an exhibition at the Valdštejnská jízdárna, Prague, February–April 1970, with essays by Oldřich Blažíček, Dagmar Hejdová and Pavel Preiss); Pavel Preiss, *Václav Vavřinec Reiner*, Prague 1970; *Růže, kterouž smrt zavřela*, ed. Zdeňka Tichá, Prague 1970; Zdeněk Kalista, *Česká barokní gotika a její ž'dárské ohnisko*, Brno 1970; Oldřich Blažíček, *Umění baroku v Čechách*, Prague 1971.

2. Cf. Girolamo Brusoni, "Il carrozzino alla moda" in *Trattatisti e narratori del Seicento*, 878. See also Carl August Schimmer (1845) and Baroness Blaze de Bury (1850) in *Město vidím veliké . . .* , 356, 366. Hellmut Diwald, *Wallenstein*, Munich and Esslingen 1969; Golo Mann, *Wallenstein*, Frankfurt am Main 1971.

3. Cf. Gustav Janouch, *Conversations with Kafka*, 84.

4. Giordano Bruno, *Spaccio della bestia trionfante*, First Dialogue, in *Opere*, ed. Augusto Guzzo, Milan and Naples 1956, 474.

5. Vladimír Holan, "První testament", 89.

6. Miloš Marten, *Nad městem*, 24.

81

1. Oskar Kokoschka, "Böhmisches Barock" in *Stimmen aus Böhmen*, 16.

2. Vladimír Holan, *Kolury*, 31.

3. Cf. *Smutní kavaleři o lásce: Z české milostné poezie 17. století*, ed. Zdeňka Tichá and Josef Hrabák, Prague 1968.

4. Holan, *Lemuria*, 70.

5. František Halas, "Za Jiřím Ortenem" in *Ladění* (1942), Prague 1947, 102.

6. Jaroslav Seifert, *Světlem oděná*, 74.

7. Holan, "Toskána" (1956–63) in *Příběhy*, Prague 1963, 192.

8. Jiří Kolář, "Přespolní dělník" in *Křestní list*, Prague 1941, 13.

9. Josef Kainar, "Sochy" in *Osudy* (1940–43), Prague 1947, 28.

10. F. X. Šalda, "O literárním baroku cizím i domácím", *Šaldův zápisník*, VIII, 245.
11. Cf. Zdeněk Kalista, "Barokní prvek v naší nové poezii" *Arch*, 4 (1969); A. M. Ripellino, Introduction to Halas, *Imagena*.
12. Holan, *Kolury*, 40.
13. *Ibid.*, 9.
14. Karel Hynek Mácha, "Těžkomyslnost" in *Dílo*, I, 117.
15. Cf. Dmitrij Čiževskyj, "K Máchovu světovému názoru" in *Torso a tajemství Máchova díla*, ed. Jan Mukařovský, Prague 1938, 111–80.
16. Vítězslav Nezval, "Edison" (1927) in *Básně noci* (1930), Prague 1959, 116.

82

1. Vladimír Holan, "Toskána" in *Příběhy*, 196.
2. Jan Zahradníček, "Svatý Jan Nepomucký" in *Korouhve*, Prague 1940, 69.
3. Bohuslav Balbín, "Život svatého Jana Nepomuckého" in Zdeněk Kalista, *České baroko*, 157.
4. Cf. Johann Georg Keyssler (1732) and Ingvald Undset (1810) in *Město vidím veliké* . . . , 62–3, 175.
5. Cf. Karel Hádek, "Blahořečení Jana Nepomuckého" in *Čtení o staré Praze*, 194–201; Karel Krejčí, *Praha legend a skutečnosti*, 222–36.
6. Jaroslav Hašek, *Švejk*, 114.
7. Cf. Antonín Novotný, *Praha "Temna"*, 252–6.
8. Cf. *ibid.*, 260–1; Hádek, *op. cit.*, 196–8.
9. Zahradníček, *op. cit.*, 71.
10. Baroness de Bury (1850) in *Město vidím veliké* . . . , 366.
11. Cf. Oskar Wiener, *Alt-Prager Guckkasten*, 50.
12. Cf. Novotný, "Kolem 'Temna'" in *Staropražské sensace*, Prague 1937, 48.
13. Cf. *ibid.*, 40–1.
14. Cf. *ibid.*, 42–3.
15. Zahradníček, *op. cit.*, 73.
16. Cf. Rainer Maria Rilke, "Heilige" in *Larenopfer* (1895). Now in *Sämtliche Werke*, Wiesbaden 1955, I, 31–2.

83

1. Franz Kafka, *Oktavhefte, Zweites Heft*, 1916–1918.
2. Jaroslav Seifert, "Kamenný most" (1944) in *Kamenný most*, Brno 1947, 21.
3. Cf. Jan Dolenský, "Karlův most" in *Praha ve své slávě i utrpení*, 260–72; Kamil Novotný and Emanuel Poche, *Karlův most*; Karel Krejčí, "Nesrozumitelní svatí" in *Praha legend a skutečnosti*, 213–50.
4. Cf. Adolf Wenig, *Staré pověsti pražské*, 102.
5. *Ibid.*, 101–4.
6. "Na tom Pražským mostě/rozmarýnka roste." See Karel Jaromír Erben, *Prostonárodní české písně a říkadla* (1863), Prague 1939, 232 (nápěv 442).
7. Cf. Jan Tanner, "Pokora Pátera Albrechta Chanovského" (1680) in Zdeněk Kalista, *České baroko*, 159–61.
8. Cf. Wenig, *op. cit.*, 110; Krejčí, *op. cit.*, 132–4.

84

1. Vladimír Holan, "Zeď III" in *Asklépiovi kohouta*, Prague 1970, 164.
2. Miloš Marten, *Nad městem*, 24.
3. *Ibid.*

4. *Ibid.*, 25.
5. *Ibid.*, 24–5.
6. Jaroslav Seifert, "Kamenný most," 18.
7. D. Moores (1779) in *Město vidím veliké* . . . , 101.
8. Cf. Germain Bazin, *Destins du Baroque*, Paris 1968, 212–20.
9. Adam Michna z Otradovic, "Česká mariánská muzika" (1647) in *Růže, kterouž smrt zavřela*, ed. Zdeňka Tichá, Prague 1970, 91.
10. Cf. Jaromír Neumann, *Český barok*, 131.
11. Oskar Wiener, *Alt-Prager Guckkasten*, 42.
12. Cf. Jan Kopecký, "České barokní divadlo lidové" in *Dějiny českého divadla*, Prague 1968, I, 326.
13. Cf. Bazin, *op. cit.*, 212–17.
14. Kisch, "Wie der Türke auf der Karlsbrücke um seinen Säbel kam" in *Prager Pitaval*, 230–9.

85

1. Vítězslav Nezval, *Pražský chodec*, 347.
2. I am referring to the painting *Křest Kristův* (The Baptism of Christ, 1715–16) in the Church of Saint John the Baptist in Manětín.
3. Antonín Novotný, "Kolem 'Temna'" in *Staropražské sensace*, 43–4.
4. Vilém Mrštík, *Santa Lucia*, 67.
5. Vojtěch Volavka, *Pout' Prahou*, 230.
6. Cf. *Zrození barokového básníka*, ed. Vilém Bitnar, 110–11, 167–9, 203–4, 257–9, 331–4, 459–60.
7. Vladimír Holan, "První testament", 9.
8. Cf. Eduard Bass, "Rybáři na mostem" in *Kukátko*, Prague 1970, 191–5.
9. Franz Kafka, *Diaries* (20 July 1913), 224.

86

1. Cf. Karel Hádek, "O tandlmarku", *Čtení o staré Praze*, 21.
2. Bohumil Hrabal, "Kafkárna" in *Inzerát na dům, ve kterém už nechci bydlet*, 139.
3. Cf. Ignát Herrmann, *Před padesáti lety*, II, 74; Johannes Urzidil, *Prager Triptychon*, 15–17.
4. Paul Leppin, *Severins Gang in die Finsternis*, 50–1.
5. Herrmann, *op. cit.*, II, 72–4.
6. Cf. Egon Erwin Kisch, *Pražská dobrodružství*, Prague 1968, 52–4.
7. Herrmann, *op. cit.*, II, 70–1.
8. Cf. Karel K. Kukla, "Pan Marát od Šturmů. Obrázek z pražského podloubí" in *Ze všech koutů Prahy*, 102–3.
9. Cf. Bohumil Hrabal and Miroslav Peterka, *Toto město je ve společné péči obyvatel*, Prague 1967.
10. Jiří Wolker, "Věci" in *Básně*, Prague 1950, 75.
11. Franz Kafka, *The Castle*, 431–2.
12. Cf. Herrmann, *op. cit.*, I, 121–4.
13. Vilém Mrštík, *Santa Lucia*, 181–2.
14. Leppin, *op. cit.*, 25.
15. Cf. *ibid.*, 137, 139, 140. See also Kisch, "Café Kandelabr" in *Die Abenteuer in Prag*, 353–6.
16. Jindřich Štyrský, *Ne jehlách těchto dní* (1935), Prague, 1945.
17. In addition to Nezval, Biebl, Štyrský and Toyen I include among the

Surrealists the poets and painters of Skupina 42 (Group 42), the writers Holan, Hrabal and the photographers Miroslav Hák and Jiří Sever. Cf. Toyen, *Střelnice* (1939–40), Prague 1946; Miroslav Hák, *Očima svět kolem nás*, Prague 1947; Ludvík Souček, *Jiří Sever*, Prague 1968.

87

1. Jaroslav Hašek, *Švejk*, I–II, 97 (101).
2. Cf. Karel L. Kukla, "Žbluňk" in *Ze všech koutů Prahy*, 157–60.

88

1. Gustav Meyrink, *The Golem*, 38.
2. Cf. Max B. Stýblo, *Český národní zpěvák, vlastenec, humorista a spisovatel Fr. Leopold Šmíd: jeho život, dílo a kritická literární studie*, Praha 1923, 16–17.
3. Meyrink, *op. cit.*, 39.
4. Ignát Herrmann, *Před padesáti lety*, II, 195–6.

89

1. Gustav Meyrink, *The Golem*, 38.
2. Cf. Karel K. Kukla, "Pražský tah. Obrázek z loterního ředitelství" in *Ze všech koutů Prahy*, 191; Herrmann, "Pražské ghetto" (1902) in *Před padesáti lety*, IV, 137–8.

90

1. Cf. Karel Kukla, "Batalión (Obraz z ovzduší alkoholu)" in *Ze všech koutů Prahy*, 19–38.
2. *A Ballad of Rags* is the title of a comedy (1935) by Voskovec and Werich. Cf. *Balada z hadrů* in *Hry Osvobozeného divadla*, I, Prague 1954, 145–254.
3. Cf. Gustav Meyrink, *The Golem*, 38–9.

91

1. Cf. F. L. *Šmída výstupy, kuplety, dvojzpěvy, komické scény*, Prague 1904; Max Stýblo, *Český národní zpěvák*; Karel Hádek, "Zpěváčkové" in *Čtení o staré Praze*, 178–9.
2. Cf. Eduard Bass, *Pod kohoutkem svatovítským*, 29–30; Karel Krejčí, *Praha, legend a skutečnosti*, 360–1.
3. Josef Hais-Týnecký, *Vůdce "Bataliónu" (Obraz ze života doktora Fr. Ungra o jednom dějství)*, Prague 1922, 16.

92

1. Cf. Ignát Herrmann, *Před padesáti lety*, II, 200–29.

93

1. Cf. Hans Tramer, "Die Dreivölkerstadt Prag" in *Robert Weltsch zum 70. Geburtstag*, 187–8.
2. Josef Jiří Kolár, "Blázni" (1888) in Karel Krejčí, *Podivuhodné příběhy ze staré Prahy*, 246–9.
3. Now Břetislavova (formerly Truhlářská), so called for the coffinmakers with shops here.
4. Kolár, *op. cit.*, 257–8.

5. The word *veškostn*, "linen cupboard" (*prádelník* in standard Czech), comes from the German *Wäschekasten*.
6. The "lutristé". Cf. Karel Kukla, "Pražský tah" in *Ze všech koutů Prahy*, 190–4.
7. Cf. Oskar Wiener, *Alt-Prager Guckkasten*, 114–16. See also Egon Erwin Kisch, "Typen der Strasse" in *Die Abenteuer in Prag*, 341.
8. Jan Neruda, "Blbý Jóna" in *Arabesky* (1864–80).
9. Cf. Kisch, *Typen der Strasse*, 339–40.
10. Cf. *ibid.*, 343.
11. Cf. *ibid.*, 338–9.
12. Cf. Herrmann, *Před padesáti lety*, III, 218–19, 221–3, 224–36.

94

1. *Taneční hodiny pro starší a pokročilé*, Prague 1964.
2. Franz Werfel, "Weißenstein, der Weltverbesserer" in *Erzählungen aus zwei Welten*, Frankfurt am Main 1952, III, 59–66; Willy Haas, *Die literarische Welt*, Munich 1960, 58–65; Johannes Urzidil, *Prager Triptychon*, 65–178.
3. Cf. Přemysl Blažíček, "Hrabalovy konfrontace" in *Příběhy pod mikroskopem*, ed. Radko Pytlík, Prague 1966, 9–27; Pytlík, "Pábitelé jazyka" in *Struktura a smysl literárního díla*, ed. Milan Jankovič, Zdeněk Pešat and Felix Vodička, Prague 1966, 198–214; Jiří Opelík, "Rozkoš z povídání" in *Nenáviděné řemeslo*, Prague 1969, 125–6.
4. Jan Neruda, "Ošumělé existence" in *Obrázky ze života pražského*, Prague 1947, 247–55.
5. Bohumil Hrabal, *Perlička na dně*, Prague 1963.
6. Franz Kafka, *Diaries*, 57 (29 September 1911).
7. Emil Artur Longen, *Herečka*, Prague 1929, 22.
8. *C. a k. marodka* (Imperial-Royal Military Infirmery), *C. a k. polní maršálek* (Imperial-Royal Field Marshal), *Osud trůnu Habsburgského* (The Fate of the Habsburg Throne), etc.
9. Bohumil Kubišta, *Korespondence a úvahy*, Prague 1960, 125.
10. Cf. Eduard Bass, "Ferda Mestek de Podskal" in *Kukátko*, 188.
11. Cf. Ignát Herrmann, *Před padesáti lety*, II, 23.
12. Cf. *ibid.*, III, 28–9, 31.
13. Cf. *ibid.*, 25.
14. Bass, *op. cit.*, 189.
15. Egon Erwin Kisch, "Memoáry nebožtíka Ferdy Mestka de Podskal, ředitele a majitele blešího divadlo" in *Pražská dobrodružství*, Prague 1968, 226–7; "Dramaturgie des Flohtheaters and Typen der Straße" in *Die Abenteuer in Prag*, 318–36, 343.
16. Cf. Jaroslav Hašek, *Švejk*, I–II, 199–204 (220–1).
17. Cf. Karel Konrád, "Já, Anna Czilagová . . . " in *Robinsoniáda* (1926). Now in *Robinsoniáda, Rinaldino, Dinah*, Prague 1966, 49. See also Zdeněk Matěj Kuděj, *Dobrodružné cestování*, Prague 1959, 304; Andrzej Banach, *Podróże po szufladzie*, Cracow 1960, 125; Bruno Schulz, *Cinnamon Shops*, trans. Celina Wieniewska, London 1963 (= *The Street of Crocodiles*, New York 1977).
18. Cf. Hašek, "Tři muži se žralokem" (1921). Now in *Moje zpověd'*, Prague 1968, 76–81.
19. Kisch, *op. cit.*, 227–8.
20. Bass, *op. cit.*, 188.

21.   Cf. Herrmann, *op. cit.*, III, 6.
22.   Cf. Kisch, *op. cit.*, 233–4, 244.
23.   Cf. *ibid.*, 228–9.
24.   Cf. *ibid.*, 244.

95

1.   Cf. Gustav Janouch, *Prager Begegnungen*, Leipzig 1959, 243–4.
2.   Cf. Michel Ragon, *L'Expressionnisme*, Paris 1966, 63.
3.   *The Pawnshop* (1916). See Georgii Avenarius, *Charls Spenser Chaplin: Ocherk rannego perioda tvorchestva*, Moscow 1939, 121–2.
4.   Cf. Václav Menger, *op. cit.*, Prague 1935, 38–49; Zdena Ančík, *O životě Jaroslava Haška*, Prague 1953, 14; Radko Pytlík, *Toulavé house*, 61.
5.   Jaroslav Hašek, *Švejk*, I–II, 365 (408). Cf. also "Z drogerie" (1904) and "Ze staré drogerie" (1909–10) in *Zrádce národa v Chotěboři*, Prague 1962, 15–17, 116–45.
6.   Cf. Hašek, "Svět zvířat" in *Dějiny strany mírného pokroku v mezích zákona* (1912), Prague 1963, 44–6; Václav Menger, *Jaroslav Hašek doma*, 234–36; Josef Lada, *Kronika mého života*, Prague 1947, 312–14; Pytlík, *op. cit.*, 159–65.
7.   Cf. Hašek, "Má drahá přítelkyně Julča" in *Dekameron humoru a satiry*, Prague 1968, 195–211.
8.   *Malá zoologická zahrada*, Prague n.d., 166–75.
9.   *Švejk*, I–II, 291–2 (325).
10.   Cf. *ibid.*, 295 (328).
11.   *Ibid.*, 296 (329).
12.   Cf. Menger, *op. cit.*, 110–11, 120–7, 141–3, 151–88, 192–208, 227–30; Ančík, *op. cit.*, 25–61; Pytlík, *op. cit.*, 137–54.
13.   Cf. Menger, *op. cit.*, 234; Pytlík, *op. cit.*, 194–5.
14.   Cf. Nikolai Elanskii, *Iaroslav Gashek v revoliutsionnoi Rossii* (1915–20), Moscow 1960, 162; Stanislav Antonov, *Iaroslav Gashek v Bashkiri*, Ufa 1960, 28–30; Aleksandr Dunaevskii, *Idu za Gashekom*, Moscow 1963, 73–7; Pytlík, *op. cit.*, 220–1.
15.   Cf. Emil Artur Longen, *Jaroslav Hašek* (1928), Prague 1947, 172–3; Ančík, *op. cit.*, 87–9; Pytlík, *op. cit.*, 344–5.
16.   Cf. Hašek, "Můj obchod se psy" in *Malá zoologická zahrada*, 105–15.
17.   Hašek, *Švejk*, I–II, 11 (3).
18.   *Ibid.*, 49–50 (48–9).
19.   Cf. *ibid.*, 160–2 (173–5).
20.   Cf. *ibid.*, 176–83 (190–60).
21.   *Ibid.*, 53–4 (53).
22.   Cf. Longen, *op. cit.*, 10–31; Menger, *op. cit.*, 74–5, 244–7; Langer, "Vzpomínání na Jaroslava Haška" in *Byli a bylo*, Prague 1963, 34–44; Ančík, *op. cit.*, 64–5; Pytlík, *op. cit.*, 205–15.
23.   Hašek, *Dějiny strany mírného pokroku v mezích zákona*, 48.
24.   *Ibid.*, 136.
25.   Cf. Menger, *op. cit.*, 136–8. See also Hašek, "Boje s domovníky" (1908) in *Dědictví po panu Šafránkovi*, Prague 1961, 113–22.
26.   Cf. Langer, *op. cit.*, 44–50; Pytlík, *op. cit.*, 216–33.
27.   Hašek, "Jak jsem se setkal s autorem svého nekrologu" (1921) in *Moje zpověď*, Prague 1968, 14–17. See also "Dušička Jaroslava Haška vypravuje" (1920) in *ibid.*, 333–7.

28. Cf. Longen, *op. cit.*, 143–4; Jiří Červený, *Červená sedma*, Prague, 1959, 255–7; Pytlík, *op. cit.*, 341–4.
29. Cf. Raoul Hausmann, *Courrier Dada*, Paris 1958, 112–14; *Am Anfang war Dada*, ed. Karl Riha and Günter Kämpf, Steinbach-Giessen 1972, 64–6.
30. Cf. Longen, *op. cit.*, 130–1; Lada, *op. cit.*, 334–5.
31. Cf. Ančík, *op. cit.*, 74; Pytlík, *op. cit.*, 255.
32. Cf. Ivan Olbracht, "Osudy dobrého vojáka Švejka za světové valky" (1921) in *O umění a společnosti*, Prague 1958, 180; Longen, *op. cit.*, 42; Ančík, *op. cit.*, 82.
33. Langer, *op. cit.*, 64.
34. Hašek, "Jak jsem se setkal s autorem svého nekrologu", 14.
35. Cf. Pytlík, *op. cit.*, 262–3.
36. Cf. Ančík, *op. cit.*, 70.
37. Cf. Hašek, *Velitelem města Bugulmy* (1919–21), Prague 1966; Elanskii, Antonov, Dunaevskii, *op. cit.*; Langer, *op. cit.*, 42; Ančík, *op. cit.*, 82; Pytlík, *op. cit.*, 266–93, 300–35.
38. Cf. Olbracht, "Deset let od Haškovy smrti" (1933) in *op. cit.*, 182; Ančík, *op. cit.*, 81; Pytlík, *op. cit.*, 319.
39. Cf. Menger, *op. cit.*, 64–71; Pytlík, *op. cit.*, 75–82.
40. Cf. Zdeněk Matěj Kuděj, *Ve dvou se to lépe táhne* (1923–24), *Ve dvou se to lépe táhne, ve třech hůře* (1927); Pytlík, *op. cit.*, 234–5. For information on Kuděj, see Janouch, *Prager Begegnungen*, 5–32.
41. Cf. Menger, *op. cit.*, 114–19; Ančík, *op. cit.*, 21.
42. Cf. Menger, *op. cit.*, 148–9, 212–18; Lada, *op. cit.*, 318.
43. Cf. Langer, *op. cit.*, 63; Pytlík, *op. cit.*, 176–81.
44. Cf. Menger, *op. cit.*, 255–6, 261; Pytlík, *op. cit.*, 225–6.
45. Cf. Hašek, "Můj přítel Hanuška" in *Dekameron humoru a satiry*, 353–6; Kuděj, *op. cit.*, 95–128; Menger, *op. cit.*, 107, 242, 252–6; Pytlík, *op. cit.*, 237–47.
46. Cf. Kornei Chukovskii, "Kuprin" in *Sovremenniki*, Moscow 1962, 256–91.
47. Cf. Lada, *op. cit.*, 307–10, 315.
48. Cf. Hašek, "Psychiatrická záhrada" (1911); Longen, *op. cit.*, 32–6; Menger, *op. cit.*, 230–4; Ančík, *op. cit.*, 64; Pytlík, *op. cit.*, 186–90.
49. Cf. Longen, *op. cit.*, 38–42; Menger, *op. cit.*, 263–4; Červený, *op. cit.*, 86; Ančík, *op. cit.*, 66; Pytlík, *op. cit.*, 250.
50. Langer, *op. cit.*, 63.
51. Olbracht, "Osudy dobrého vojáka Švejka za světové valky", in *op. cit.*, 180.
52. Langer, *op. cit.*, 63.
53. Lada, *op. cit.*, 326.
54. Cf. Pytlík, *op. cit.*, 337–8.
55. Cf. Longen, *op. cit.*, 132–7; Janouch, *op. cit.*, 259–64; Pytlík, *op. cit.*, 338–9.
56. Cf. Hašek, "Za Olgou Fastrovou" (1922) in *Moje zpověď*, 260–2.
57. Cf. Longen, *op. cit.*, 145; Pytlík, *op. cit.*, 346.
58. Cf. Franta Sauer, *Franta Habán ze Žižkova*, Prague 1923; Longen, *op. cit.*, 146; Janouch, *op. cit.*, 246–9; Pytlík, *op. cit.*, 348–55.
59. Cf. Lada, *op. cit.*, 345–53.
60. Cf. Longen, *op. cit.*, 147, 171–2; Pytlík, *op. cit.*, 25–6, 362–5, 368–70.
61. Cf. Longen, *op. cit.*, 147–8, 214–15; Pytlík, *op. cit.*, 31–2.
62. Cf. Longen, *op. cit.*, 213–15; Pytlík, *op. cit.*, 38–9, 360–1.
63. Cf. Olbracht, *op. cit.*, 182.
64. Cf. Langer, *op. cit.*, 87–8; Pytlík, *op. cit.*, 18.

96

1. Cf. Václav Menger, *Jaroslav Hašek doma*, 233.
2. Cf. Ignát Herrmann, *Před padesáti lety*, I, 212–16; *Bilder aus Böhmen* (Leipzig 1876) in *Město vidím veliké* . . . , 420–2; Eduard Bass, *Křižovatka u Prašné brány*, Prague 1947, 199; Karel Krejčí, *Praha legend a skutečnosti*, 96–7.
3. Cf. Josef Teichman, *Bedřich Smetana*, Prague 1946, 84, 158; *Rok Bedřicha Smetany*, ed. Mirko Očadlík, Prague 1950, 127.
4. Cf. Herrmann, *op. cit.*, I, 217.
5. Cf. Franz Werfel, "The House of Mourning".

97

1. Franz Kafka, *The Trial*, 169–71; Jaroslav Hašek, *Švejk*, I–II, 95–102, (99–108). See also Karel Kosík, "Hašek a Kafka neboli groteskní svět" in *Plamen*, 6 (1963).
2. Cf. Emil Artur Longen, *Jaroslav Hašek*, 145–6; Radko Pytlík, *Toulavé house*, 349.
3. Hašek, I–II, 150 (163).
4. *Ibid.*, III–IV, 134–5 (590–1).
5. *Ibid.*, I–II, 95 (99).
6. Cf. Pytlík, *op. cit.*, 252.
7. Hašek, I–II, 24 (20) and 33 (26).
8. *Ibid.*, 37 (35).
9. *Ibid.*, 145 (153).
10. *Ibid.*, 193 (211).
11. *Ibid.*, 200 (220).
12. *Ibid.*, III–IV, 35 (475).
13. *Ibid.*, I–II, 18 (12).
14. *Ibid.*, 277 (308).
15. *Ibid.*, 191 (209).
16. *Ibid.*
17. *Ibid.*

98

1. Jaroslav Hašek, *Švejk*, I–II, 18, 59 (12, 61).
2. *Ibid.*, 25 (20).
3. *Ibid.*, 27 (22).
4. *Ibid.*
5. *Ibid.*, 29 (25).
6. *Ibid.*, 58 (59).
7. *Ibid.*, 57 (55).
8. *Ibid.*, 143 (153).
9. *Ibid.*, 195 (213).
10. *Ibid.*, III–IV, 90 (540).
11. *Ibid.*, I–II, 344 (381).
12. *Ibid.*, 22–3 (18).

99

1. Jaroslav Hašek, *Švejk*, I–II, 86–7 (89–90).
2. *Ibid.*, 81–4 (85–8).
3. *The Pilgrim* (1923).
4. Hašek, 78 (82).

5. *Ibid.*, 83 (87).
6. *Ibid.*, 86 (89).
7. *Ibid.*, 102–9 (110–15).
8. *Ibid.*, 122–4 (132–3).
9. *Ibid.*, 102 (110).
10. *Ibid.* 126, (135).
11. Cf. Josef Lada, *Můj přítel Švejk*, Prague 1968.
12. The word *frantík* (a diminuitive of František, the Czech equivalent of Franz) refers to the round metal button containing the initials FJI (Franz Joseph I) on the caps of soldiers in the Austro-Hungarian Army.
13. Hašek, 209 (230).
14. *Ibid.*, III–IV, 136 (592).
15. *Ibid.*, 202 (664).
16. Vladislav Vančura, *Pole orná a válečná* (1925), Prague 1947, 21.
17. *Ibid.*, 152.
18. Holan, *Noc s Hamletem*, Prague 1964. English translation in Clayton Eshleman, *Conductors of the Pit: Major Works by Rimbaud, Vallejo, Césaire, Artaud and Holan*, New York 1988, 201–30.
19. *Ibid.*
20. Hašek, *Švejk*, I–II, 28 (19).
21. *Ibid.*, 24.
22. *Ibid.*, 38 (37).
23. *Ibid.*, 68 (69).
24. *Ibid.*, 217 (241).
25. Cf. Pytlík, *op. cit.*, 228–9.
26. Hašek, 128–9 (495–6).
27. *Ibid.*, III–IV, 50–5 (499).

100
1. Karl Kraus, *Die letzten Tage der Menschheit*, Act Five, Scene Fifty-Four.
2. Robert Musil, *The Man Without Qualities*, London 1953, 31.
3. Jaroslav Hašek, *Švejk*, III–IV, 87–8 (535–8).
4. Hašek, I–II, 67 (69).
5. Franz Kafka, *Diaries*, 55, 57, 60.
6. Hašek, III–IV, 59 (504).
7. *Ibid.*, 55 (499).
8. Vladislav Vančura, *Pole orná a válečná*, 157.
9. Cf. Hašek, III–IV, 270–6 (743–8).
10. Cf. Hašek, I–II, 312–13 (346).
11. Max Brod, *Steitbares Leben*, 121.
12. Cf. Angelo Maria Ripellino, Introduction to the Italian edition of Bruno Schulz, *Le botteghe color cannella*, Turin 1970, xx–xxii. See also Claudio Magris, *Il mito absburgico nella letteratura austriaca moderna*, Turin 1963, 277–86 and *Lontano da dove? Joseph Roth e la tradizione ebraico-orientale*, Turin 1971.
13. Cf. Hašek, I–II, 17–18 (9–10).
14. Kraus, *op. cit.*, Act Four, Scene Thirty-One.
15. Léon Bloy, *Au seuil de l'Apocalypse*, Paris 1916, 69.
16. Hašek, 185 (207).
17. *Ibid.*, 189–90 (208).
18. *Ibid.*, 241 (270).

19. *Ibid.*, 32–3 (29–30).
20. Schulz, *Cinnamon Shops* (=*The Street of Crocodiles*).
21. Hašek, 14, 19, 24 (8, 14, 19).
22. Cf. Karel Hádek, "Život vojenský – život veselý" in *Čtení o staré Praze*, 164.
23. Hašek, 59 (61).
24. Johannes Urzidil, *Prager Triptychon*, 14.
25. Cf. Erwin Piscator, *Das politische Theater*, 198.
26. Hašek, 45 (44).
27. *Ibid.*, 199–204 (221–2).
28. *Ibid.*, 84–5 (534).
29. *Ibid.*, 74 (522).
30. *Ibid.*, I–II, 184–9 (201–6).
31. *Ibid.*, III–IV, 147–8 (603–4).
32. *Ibid.*, 134 (590).
33. *Ibid.*, 121–3 (579).
34. *Ibid.*, 161 (620).
35. *Ibid.*, I–II, 80–1 (83–4).
36. *Ibid.*, 281–2 (340–1.)
37. *Ibid.*, III–IV, 10–11 (447–8).
38. *Ibid.*, 233 (706).
39. *Ibid.*, I–II, 356 (396).
40. *Ibid.*, 382 (416).
41. *Ibid.*, III–IV, 180–1 (639–40).

101

1. Georges Bataille, "Kafka" in *La littérature et le mal*, Paris 1957, 186.
2. *Der Berg der heiligen Katze* (1923).
3. Jaroslav Hašek, *Švejk*, I–II, 231–3 (258–60).
4. *Ibid.*, 28 (24).
5. *Ibid.*, 45 (44).
6. *Ibid.*, 234–5 (262).
7. *Ibid.*, 87 (91).
8. Franz Kafka, *The Castle*, Chapter 5, 229.
9. *Ibid.*, Chapter 19, 397–401.
10. Alfred Kubin, *The Other Side*, 93.
11. Hašek, *op. cit.*, 76–7 (80).
12. *Ibid.*, 94 (98).
13. *Ibid.*, 96 (100).
14. Cf. Karel Kosík, "Hašek a Kafka neboli groteskní svět", *Plamen* 6 (1963).

102

1. Erwin Piscator, *Das politische Theater*, 189–90
2. Jaroslav Hašek, *Švejk*, I–II, 34–5 (31).
3. *Ibid.*, 34 (31–2).

103

1. Franz Kafka, *Diaries*, 374 (29 July 1917).
2. Cf. Jan Grossmann, "Kapitoly o Jaroslavu Haškovi", *Listy*, 1 (1948).
3. Max Brod, *Streitbares Leben*, 130.
4. Jaroslav Hašek, *Švejk*, III–IV, 211–12 (673–4).

5. *Ibid.*, I–II, 355–6 (394–5).
6. *Ibid.*, 54 (54).
7. *Ibid.*, 344 (381).

104

1. The story first appeared in *La Revue Blanche* of 1 June 1902. It later figured in the collection "L'Hérésiarque et Cⁱᵉ". Now in Guillaume Apollinaire, *Œuvres complètes*. See also Pierre-Marcel Adéma, *Guillaume Apollinaire*, Paris 1968, 74.
2. Cf. Jiří Mucha, *Kankán se svatozáří (Život a dílo Alfonse Muchy)*, Prague 1969, 209–12.
3. Cf. Bass, "Kukátko", 211–12
4. Vítězslav Nezval, *Pražský chodec*, 358, 361, 373. See also *Les Amours jaunes* in *Z mého života*, 168.
5. Cf. Charles Cros and Tristan Corbière, *Œuvres complètes*, Paris 1970, 749, 760.
6. Cf. Miroslav Lamač, *Hanuš Schwaiger*, Prague 1957, 27.
7. Yvan Goll, "Brief an den verstorbenen Dichter Apollinaire" (1918). Now in *Dichtungen (Lyrik-Prosa-Dramen)*, Darmstadt 1960, 43.
8. Cf. Pascal Pia, *Apollinaire par lui-même*, Paris 1958, 148–50.
9. Cf. Karel Krejčí, *Praha legend a skutečnosti*, 197–200.
10. Nezval, *op. cit.*, 373.
11. Cf. Otakar Štorch-Marien, *Ohňostroj*, 110.
12. Cf. André Breton, "Langues des pierres" (1957) in *Perspective cavalière*, Paris 1970, 149–51.
13. Jiří Karásek ze Lvovic, *Král Rudolf*, Act I, 26–7.
14. Guillame Apollinaire, "La serviette des poètes" in "L'Hérésiarque et Cⁱᵉ". Now in *Œuvres complètes*, I, 200–2.

105

1. Cf. Zdeněk Kalista, "Legenda o Apollinairovi", *Host do domu*, 4 (1968).
2. Otakar Štorch-Marien, *Sladko je žít*, 130.
3. Štorch-Marien, *Ohňostroj*, 69.
4. Oskar Wiener, *Alt-Prager Guckkasten*, 100.
5. *Ibid.*, 35, 37.
6. *Ibid.*, 40.

106

1. Vítězslav Nezval, *Z mého života*, 65.
2. The term *devětsil*, which the Čapek brothers suggested as a name for the group (see Adolf Hoffmeister, "Ach, mládí" in *Předobrazy*, Prague 1962, 34), is the botanical name for common butterbur (*petasites officinalis*), often confused with *tussilago farfara* (*podběl*, coltsfoot, *Pestwurz*). The separate parts of the term – "devět" (nine) and "sil" (strengths, forces) – probably represent an allusion to the nine Muses.
3. Karel Teige, "Guillaume Apollinaire a jeho doba" (1928) in *Svět stavby a básně*, Prague 1966, 373.
4. Vítězslav Nezval, "Guillaume Apollinaire" (1955) in *Moderní poezie*, Prague 1958, 25.
5. Blaise Cendrars, "Hommage à Guillaume Apollinaire" (1918) in *Du monde entier au cœur du monde*, 252.

6. Teige, *op. cit.*, 403.
7. Jaroslav Seifert, *Na vlnách T.S.F.* (1925).
8. Konstantin Biebl, "Generace" (1930) in *Dílo*, Prague 1954, V, 125.
9. Vítězslav Nezval, "Vyzvání přátelům" in *Skleněný havelok*, Prague 1932.
10. Miloš Jiránek, "O krásné Praze" in *Dojmy a potulky*, 43.
11. Zdeněk Kalista, "Legenda o Apollinairovi", *Host do domu*, 4 (1968); Nezval, *Z mého života*, 168.
12. Nezval, *Pražský chodec*, 373.
13. *Ibid.*, 325–6.
14. Nezval, *Z mého života*, 65; see also his *Moderní poezie*, 28. Yvan Goll, much admired by the Poetists, wrote in his "letter to the deceased poet Apollinaire": "Your poem "Zone" is the first revelation of our century and the source of powerful currents" (*Dichtungen*, 43).
15. Teige, *op. cit.*, 389.
16. *Ibid.*, 390.
17. Cendrars, *op. cit.*, 253.
18. Cf. Milan Kundera, "Veliká utopie moderního básnictví", Introduction to Guillaume Apollinaire, *Alkoholy života*, Prague 1965, 9.
19. Teige, *op. cit.*, 344.
20. Cf. Pierre-Marcel Adéma, *Guillaume Apollinaire*, 182.
21. Cf. Kundera, *op. cit.*, 9–10.
22. Cf. Adolf Hoffmeister, *Čas se nevrací*, Prague 1965; Miroslav Lamač, *Hanuš Schwaiger*.

107

1. Written in 1898, "L'enchanteur pourrissant" was published 1904 in the journal *Le Festin d'Esope*. It appeared in book form in 1909 (it was Apollinaire's first book) with illustrations by André Derain. See Pierre-Marcel Adéma, *Guillaume Apollinaire*, 161–2.
2. Cf. Adéma, 45.
3. Vítězslav Nezval, Introduction to *Most*, Prague 1937, 22–3.
4. Cf. Milan Blahynka, "Proměny Podivuhodného kouzelníka", *Nový život*, 1 (1959).
5. Cf. Antonín Jelínek, *Vítězslav Nezval*, Prague 1961, 47–9.

108

1. Yvan Goll, "Der Eiffelturm" (1924) in *Dichtungen*, 138.
2. Cf. Karel Honzík, "Kavárny Devětsilu" in *Ze života avantgardy*, Prague 1963, 54–63.
3. Vítězslav Nezval, "Vyzvání přátelům" in *Skleněný havelok*, 154.
4. Cf. Angelo Maria Ripellino, *Storia della poesia ceca contemporanea*, Rome 1950; *Poetismus*, ed. Květoslav Chvatík and Zdeněk Pešat, Prague 1967.
5. Nezval, "Papoušek na motocyklu" in *Pantomima* (1924).
6. Cf. Roland Lacourbe, *Harold Lloyd*, Paris 1970, 66.
7. Karel Teige, "Poetismus" (1924) in *Svět stavby a básně*, 123–4.
8. *Ibid.*, 126.

109

1. Karel Teige, "Poetismus" (1924) in *Svět stavby a básně*, 124.
2. *Ibid.*, 125.
3. *Ibid.*, 126.

4. Cf. Teige, "Umění dnes a zítra" (1922) in *Svět stavby a básně*, 23; Jaroslav Seifert, "Všechny krásy světa" in *Samá láska*, Prague 1923, 59.
5. Vítězslav Nezval, *Skleněný havelok*, 83.
6. "Vyzvání přátelům" in *Skleněný havelok*, 154.
7. "Papoušek na motocyklu" in *Pantomima*, 73.

110

1. Vítězslav Nezval, "Papoušek na motocyklu" in *Pantomima*, 7.
2. Karel Teige, "Poetismus" (1924) in *Svět stavby a básně*, 124.
3. Nezval, *Z mého života*, 97.
4. Cf. František Halas, "Básně rukopisné" in *Krásné neštěstí*, Prague 1968, 348, 340.
5. Teige, "Foto kino film" (1922) in *op. cit.*, 80.
6. Yvan Goll, "Der neue Orpheus" (1925) in *Dichtungen*, 191.
7. Jean Cocteau, "Le coq et l'arlequin" (1918).
8. Oskar Schlemmer, *Briefe und Tagebücher*, Munich 1958, 191.
9. Teige, "Umění dnes a zítra" in *op. cit.*, 10.
10. *Poetismus*, ed. Květoslav Chvatík and Zdeněk Pešat, 124.

111

1. Vítězslav Nezval, "Premier Plan" in *Menší růžová zahrada*.
2. Jaroslav Seifert, "Svatební cesta" in *Na vlnách T.S.F.*
3. Seifert, "Odjezd lodi" in *Na vlnách T.S.F.*
4. Nezval, "Poetika" in *Pantomima*.
5. Nezval, "Na cestu" in *Pantomina*.
6. Konstantin Biebl, *S lodí, jež dováží čaj a kávu*.
7. Nezval, "Panoptikum" in *Pantomima*.
8. Biebl, "Protinožci" in *S lodí, jež dováží čaj a kávu*.
9. Seifert, "Počitadlo" in *Na vlnách T.S.F.*
10. Seifert, "Přístav" in *Na vlnách T.S.F.*
11. Biebl, "Na hoře Merbabu", "Amín", "Toké" in *S lodí, jež dováží čaj a kávu*.
12. František Halas, *Krásné neštěstí*, 355–6.
13. Biebl, *Zlatými řetězy*.
14. Biebl, "Jaro" in *Zlatými řetězy*.
15. Seifert, "Večer v kavárně" in *Na vlnách T.S.F.*
16. Seifert, "Paraván" in *Slavík zpívá špatně*.
17. Nezval, "Slunce" in *Nápisy na hroby*.
18. "Premier plan" in *Menší růžová zahrada*.
19. Halas, *op. cit.*, 355–6.
20. Nezval, "Premier plan" in *Menší růžová zahrada*.
21. "Papoušek na motocyklu" in *Pantomima*.
22. "Poetika" in *Pantomima*.

112

1. Cf. Vratislav Effenberger, *Henri Rousseau*, Prague 1964, 38. See also Otto Bihalji-Merin, *Die naive Malerei*, Cologne 1959, 43–4.
2. Cf. René Passeron, *Histoire de la peinture surréaliste*, Paris 1968, 43.
3. Cf. Miroslav Lamač, *Výtvarné dílo Adolfa Hoffmeistera*.
4. Karel Teige, *Jan Zrzavý*, Prague 1923, 6. See also Vítězslav Nezval, *Z mého života*, 98.
5. Cf. Antonina Vallentin, *Storia di Picasso*, Turin 1961, 233–6; Ronald Penrose,

Picasso: His Life and Work, London 1958, 195–201. See also Jean Cocteau, *Entre Picasso et Radiguet*, ed. André Fermigier, Paris 1967, 63–76.

6. Yvan Goll, "Der Eiffelturm" in *Dichtungen*, 139.
7. Blaise Cendrars, *Dix-neuf poèmes élastiques* (1919) in *Du monde entier au cœur du monde*, 81–2.
8. Jaroslav Seifert, "Guillaume Apollinaire" in *Na vlnách T.S.F.*
9. Jean Cocteau, *Carte blanche* (1920).
10. Seifert, *op. cit.*
11. Goll, *op. cit.*
12. Seifert, "Staré bojiště" in *Slavík zpívá špatně*.
13. Vladimír Holan, "Odpověd' Francii" (1938).
14. Nezval entitled a 1935 article "Invisible Moscow".

113

1. František Halas, "Svět Františka Tichého" (1940) in *Obrazy*, Prague 1968, 104.
2. Vítězslav Nezval, *Kůň a tanečnice*, Prague 1962.
3. Cf. Jaroslav Seifert, "Před obrazy Františka Tichého" in *Ruka a plamen*, Prague 1948, 36–9; Jiří Kolář, "František Tichý" in *Dny v roce*, Prague 1948, 97, 98 and "Báseň na přání F. T." in *Ilustrace Františka Tichého*, ed. František Dvořák, Prague 1969, 3–4; Vladimír Holan, "Vzpomínka II (Františku Tichému)" in *Bolest*, Prague 1966, 83–4, now in *Lamento*, Prague 1970, 188–9.
4. Nezval, "Levitace" in *op. cit.*
5. Karel Konrád, "Na visuté hrazdě" (1944) in *Nevzpomínky*, Prague 1963, 212.
6. Halas, *op. cit.*, 105.
7. Franz Kafka, "Up in the Gallery" in *The Complete Stories*, 401.
8. Cf. Václav Nebeský, *L'Art moderne tchécoslovaque* (1905–33), Paris 1937, 157.
9. Cf. Miloš Šafránek, *Francouzská léta Františka Tichého*, Prague 1965, 30.
10. Cf. *La Plume*, numéro consacré à Alphonse Mucha, n. 197, Paris, 1 July 1897.
11. Cf. Jiří Mucha, *Kankán se svatozáří (Život a dílo Alfonse Muchy)*, 73.
12. Cf. František Dvořák, *Circus a varieté Františka Tichého*, Prague 1967, 25–6.
13. Seifert, *Světlem oděna*, 66.
14. Cf. Šafránek, *op. cit.*, 21.
15. Cf. *ibid.*, 74.
16. Kafka, *op. cit.*, 401–2.
17. Halas, "Klid" in *Sepie*, Prague 1957, 67.
18. Cf. Šafránek, *op. cit.*, 17, 68–9; Vojtěch Volavka, *František Tichý: Kresby*, Prague 1968, 9–10.
19. Holan, "Na bleším trhu v Paříži" in *Na postupu*, 29.
20. Halas, *op. cit.*, 105.
21. Cf. Dvořák, *op. cit.*, 11; Šafránek, *op. cit.*, 14; Volavka, *op. cit.*, 7.
22. Adalbert von Chamisso, *Peter Schlemihls wundersame Geschichte* (1814).
23. Jiří Karásek ze Lvovic, "Paganini" in *Endymion*, Prague 1922, 52–3.
24. Cf. Hana Volaková, *Příběh židovského muzea v Praze*, Prague 1966, 75, 106.
25. Gustav Meyrink, "Bal Macabre" in *Wachsfigurenkabinett*, Munich 1918, 139–53.
26. Cf. Dvořák, *Ilustrace Františka Tichého*.

114

1. Franz Kafka, "Up in the Gallery" in *The Complete Stories*, 402.

115

1. Vítězslav Nezval, "Praha s prsty deště" in *Praha s prsty deště* (1936). Now in *Dílo*, VI, Prague 1953, 214.
2. Cf. Franz Werfel, "Zwischen oben und unten", 510, 518.
3. "Das leere Haus", 625.
4. Cf. Karl Ludwig Schneider, "La théorie du drame expressioniste et sa mise en œuvre chez Paul Kornfeld" in *L'Expressionnisme dans le théâtre européen*, 113.
5. Vladimír Holan, "Není úniku" in *Trialog* (1964). Now in *Lamento*, 65.
6. Aleksandr Blok, "O chëm poët veter" (1913) in *Sobranie sochinenii*, III, Leningrad 1932, 213.
7. Franz Werfel, "Eine Prager Ballade" from *Kunde vom irdischen Leben* (1943) in *Das lyrische Werk*, Frankfurt am Main 1967, 489.
8. Brod, *Streitbares Leben*, 104–5.
9. Else Lasker-Schüler, *Die Wolkenbrücke. Ausgewählte Briefe*, ed. Margarethe Kupper, Munich 1972, 53 (12 April 1913).
10. Marina Tsvetaeva, *Stikhii k Chekhii* (1939) in *Izbrannye proizvedeniia*, Moscow and Leningrad 1965, 332.
11. Karl Kraus, "Sprüche und Widersprüche" in *Beim Wort genommen*, Munich 1955, 137.
12. The title of a collection of verse by Josef Svatopluk Machar (1893).
13. The expression comes from Holan's poem "Cesta mraku", Prague 1945, 52.
14. Čehona is the protagonist of the novel *Můj přítel Čehona* (1925) by Viktor Dyk. The name comes from altering a line in the Czech version of the Austrian national anthem "Čeho nabyl občan pilný" (What a diligent citizen has acquired) to "Čehona byl občan pilný" (Čehona was a diligent citizen).

116

1. Marina Tsvetaeva, *Stikhii k Chekhii* (1939) in *Izbrannye proizvedeniia*, 338.
2. Else Lasker-Schüler, *Die Wolkenbrücke*, 38.
3. Vladimír Holan, *Lemuria*, 148.
4. Cf. Jaroslav Patera, *Bertramka v Praze*, Prague 1948, 96–8.
5. Holan, *Mozartiana*, Prague 1963, 73.
6. Vítězslav Nezval, "Defenestrace" in *Hra v kostky* (1928). Now in *Dílo*, XII, Prague 1962, 54.
7. "Večerka" in *Dílo*, VI, 121.
8. *Pražský chodec*, 244.
9. Cf. Alois Jirásek, *Staré pověsti české*, 299–307; Karel Krejčí, *Praha legend a skutečnosti*, 140–1.
10. Karel Toman, "Duben" from the cycle *Měsíce* (1918). Now in *Dílo*, I, Prague 1956, 116.

Index